T0122790

Get the eBook FREE!

(PDF, ePub, Kindle, and liveBook all included)

We believe that once you buy a book from us, you should be able to read it in any format we have available. To get electronic versions of this book at no additional cost to you, purchase and then register this book at the Manning website.

Go to https://www.manning.com/freebook and follow the instructions to complete your pBook registration.

That's it!
Thanks from Manning!

Azure Infrastructure as Code

Azure Infrastructure as Code

WITH ARM TEMPLATES AND BICEP

HENRY BEEN
EDUARD KEILHOLZ
ERWIN STAAL
Foreword by SCOTT GUTHRIE and ALEX FRANKEL

MANNING
SHELTER ISLAND

For online information and ordering of this and other Manning books, please visit
www.manning.com. The publisher offers discounts on this book when ordered in quantity.
For more information, please contact

> Special Sales Department
> Manning Publications Co.
> 20 Baldwin Road
> PO Box 761
> Shelter Island, NY 11964
> Email: orders@manning.com

Manning Publications Co. 20 Baldwin Road PO Box 761 Shelter Island, NY 11964	Development editor: Doug Rudder Technical development editor: Alain Couniot Review editors: Mihaela Batinić Production editor: Deirdre S. Hiam Copy editor: Andy Carroll Proofreader: Jason Everett Technical proofreader: Aleksandar Nikolic Typesetter: Dennis Dalinnik Cover designer: Marija Tudor

ISBN: 9781617299421
Printed in the United States of America

contents

foreword   xii
preface   xiv
acknowledgments   xvi
about this book   xvii
about the authors   xxi
about the cover illustration   xxii

PART 1   INTRODUCTION 1

1   ***Infrastructure as Code   3***

1.1   Working with infrastructure   4

DevOps   5 ▪ Preventing configuration drift   7

1.2   The benefits of Infrastructure as Code   8

*IaC allows for automation   9 ▪ IaC allows for a declarative
approach   9 ▪ IaC provides a human-readable format   10*

1.3   The Azure Resource Manager   11

*Control plane and data plane   11 ▪ ARM templates   12
The Bicep language   13 ▪ Azure Service Management
(ASM is not ARM)   13*

1.4   Other tools   14

    AWS CloudFormation   14 ▪ Google Cloud Deployment Manager   14 ▪ Terraform   15 ▪ Pulumi   16 ▪ Choosing between cloud-specific and multi-cloud solutions   16

2 *Writing your first ARM template*   *18*

2.1   Working with JSON files   19

    Installing the ARM templates extension in VS Code   20

2.2   Writing ARM templates in VS Code   20

    Adding a resource   22 ▪ Leveraging IntelliSense in VS Code   24

2.3   Deploying an ARM template   25

2.4   Monitoring template deployments   27

2.5   Finding example templates   28

2.6   Visualizing templates   29

PART 2   TAKING IT UP A NOTCH 33

3 *Writing ARM templates*   *35*

3.1   Resources   36

    Child resources   38

3.2   Parameters   39

    Parameter types   40 ▪ Limiting and describing parameter values   45 ▪ Specifying parameter values   46

3.3   Variables   50

3.4   Outputs   52

3.5   Functions   54

    Expressions   54 ▪ Built-in functions   56 ▪ User-defined functions   64

4 *Deploying ARM templates*   *66*

4.1   An overview of the deployment process   67

4.2   Submitting a deployment   68

    Choosing a deployment scope   68 ▪ Submitting a template using different tools   70

4.3   The execution phase   75

    Role-based access control   76 ▪ Azure Policy   79 ▪ Resource locks   81 ▪ Resource provisioning   82

4.4   The clean-up phase   82

     Incremental deployment mode   *83* ▪ *Complete deployment*
     mode   *83* ▪ *Combining deployment modes*   *84*

4.5   Template validation and what-if deployments   85

     Validating an ARM template   *85* ▪ *What-if deployments*   *86*

4.6   Troubleshooting template deployments   87

5   Writing advanced ARM templates   89

5.1   Deploying to multiple scopes using nested templates   90

     Nested templates on a management group   *94* ▪ *Evaluation*
     scope   *96* ▪ *Outputs*   *99*

5.2   How to structure solutions   99

     Small to medium solutions   *99* ▪ *Large solutions*   *100*

5.3   Modularizing templates with linked templates   102

     Using a URI   *103* ▪ *Using a relative path*   *106*

5.4   Deploying resources in order   107

     Explicit deployment ordering   *107* ▪ *Implicit deployment*
     ordering   *109*

5.5   Conditionally deploying resources   109

     Applying conditions to output   *112*

5.6   Using loops to create multiple resources   112

     Using copy on variables   *114* ▪ *Using copy on properties*   *115*
     Using copy on output   *116* ▪ *Waiting for a loop to finish, using*
     dependsOn   *117*

5.7   Deployment scripts   118

5.8   Reverse engineering a template   125

     Exporting templates   *125* ▪ *Using Resource Explorer*   *126*
     Using the JSON view   *127* ▪ *For a new resource*   *127*

6   Simplifying ARM templates using the Bicep DSL   129

6.1   Bicep: A transpiler   130

     Deploying   *132* ▪ *Transpiling*   *132* ▪ *Decompiling*   *133*

6.2   Bicep syntax differences   134

     Parameters   *134* ▪ *Variables*   *135* ▪ *Outputs*   *135*
     Conditions   *135* ▪ *Loops*   *136* ▪ *Targeting different*
     scopes   *138* ▪ *Known limitations*   *138*

6.3   Other improvements with Bicep   138

Referencing resources, parameters, and variables   138 ▪ Using references in variables and outputs   139 ▪ Referencing existing resources   141 ▪ Dependency management   141 ▪ String interpolation   141 ▪ No mandatory grouping   142 Comments   143 ▪ Using the contents of other files   144

6.4   Modules   145

Deploying to another scope   146 ▪ Debugging Bicep deployments   146

6.5   A larger Bicep example   147

AppConfiguration.bicep   148 ▪ ApplicationInsights.bicep   149 Configuration.bicep   151

7   *Complex deployments using Azure DevOps   155*

7.1   Meet Toma Toe Pizzas   156

7.2   Crafting the Bicep files   157

Describing the App Service plan   157 ▪ Describing the App Service   159 ▪ Finalizing the template   160

7.3   Storing templates in source control   162

7.4   Automated build and release pipelines   163

Using triggers   164 ▪ Creating tasks   165 ▪ Grouping tasks in a job   166 ▪ Creating service connections   167 ▪ Configuring Azure DevOps to run your pipeline   171

7.5   Adding logical phases to your pipeline   173

Identifying the logical phases   173 ▪ Accessing artifacts from different jobs   175 ▪ Transpiling Bicep in a pipeline stage   175 Deploying a template from a pipeline artifact   176

7.6   Adding the Traffic Manager   178

Deploying the Traffic Manager   181

7.7   Creating a real-world example pipeline   182

Completing the pipeline   182

8   *Complex deployments using GitHub Actions   188*

8.1   Forking a repository   189

8.2   Getting to know GitHub Actions   190

Workflow events   190 ▪ Runners   191 ▪ Jobs   191 Steps   191 ▪ Actions   191

8.3 Building a GitHub Actions workflow   191

Adding a job to a GitHub Actions workflow   192

8.4 The deployment phase in GitHub Actions   193

Connecting to Azure from your GitHub workflow   194
Generating a service principal using the Azure CLI   194

8.5 Deploying ARM templates from GitHub Actions   195

Completing the deployment   198

9   **Testing ARM templates   201**

9.1 Static analysis and validation   203

Visual Studio Code extensions   204 ▪ *Validation using PowerShell
or Azure CLI   207* ▪ *ARM template test toolkit   208* ▪ *Custom
tests using Pester   212*

9.2 Unit tests   216
9.3 Integration tests   218
9.4 End-to-end tests   222
9.5 Pester in CI/CD   229

PART 3   ADVANCED TOPICS..235

10   **Template specs and Bicep registries: Building
a repository of templates   237**

10.1 Use case: A repository of compliant resources   238
10.2 Creating a template spec   239

Listing template specs   242 ▪ *Template spec versions   243*
Creating a template spec from multiple ARM templates   243
Deploying a template spec using IaC is impractical   246

10.3 Deploying a template spec   246

Deploying template specs from an ARM or Bicep template   248
Upgrading to a newer version of the template spec   253

10.4 An alternative: A Bicep registry   253
10.5 Sharing templates using a package manager   255

Publishing an ARM template as a package   256 ▪ *Deploying
an ARM template that is in a package   259* ▪ *Yet another
approach   260*

10.6   Design considerations   260

*Choosing an approach   261 ▪ Pros and cons of template
specs   261 ▪ Pros and cons of using a Bicep registry   261
Pros and cons of using a package manager   262*

11   Using deployment stacks for grouping resources   263

11.1   Grouping resources by their lifetime   264

*Complete deployment mode is not good enough   266 ▪ Deployment
stacks to the rescue!   267 ▪ Creating a deployment stack   268
Updating a deployment stack   269 ▪ Removing a deployment
stack   270*

11.2   Provisioning resources for others, but disallowing
updates   271

Azure Blueprints: A first solution   272

11.3   The future of deployment stacks   274

12   Governing your subscriptions using Azure Policy   275

12.1   Azure Policy   277

*Policy definitions   278 ▪ Initiatives or policy sets   280
Assignment   280*

12.2   Examining the built-in policies and initiatives   284

12.3   Using custom policies   287

Creating a custom policy   287 ▪ Testing a policy   290

12.4   Using the different effects   294

*Append effect   294 ▪ Audit effect   295 ▪ AuditIfNotExists
effect   297 ▪ DeployIfNotExists effect   298 ▪ Disabled
effect   301 ▪ Modify effect   301*

12.5   Creating your own initiative   304

12.6   Assigning a policy or initiative   305

12.7   Reviewing compliance status   308

*Remediating noncompliant resources   310 ▪ Creating an
exemption   311*

13   Case studies   316

13.1   Building an Azure foundation   317

*The management group layout   317 ▪ Assigning a policy
initiative   319 ▪ Creating a management subscription   321
Creating workload subscriptions   322*

13.2 Subscription level deployments 324

Configuring budgets 324 ▪ Configuring Microsoft Defender for Cloud 325 ▪ Creating resource groups and providing access 327

13.3 Creating a highly-available microservice architecture 327

Resources organized in resource groups 329 ▪ Networking with Bicep 332 ▪ Using the existing keyword to set access to a Key Vault 333

index 337

foreword

As an engineer, I know how important it can be to find a solid introduction to a new topic. Blogs, documentation, and Q&A platforms can be a great source of information, but they almost always assume basic knowledge of a topic. A good book is unique in the sense that it can provide you with that basic knowledge.

A good book is designed to take you on a well-thought-out journey along one subject after another to help you build a fundamental understanding of the topic. Once you have completed that journey, other sources can augment your knowledge and help you overcome specific problems. Without that fundamental understanding, other sources can help you overcome problems, but you might have difficulty connecting these smaller nuggets of knowledge to what you already know.

This book, *Azure Infrastructure as Code*, is such a book that takes you on a learning journey. First, you will learn the basics of IaC and how the Azure Resource Manager works. From there, it takes you on a journey past ARM template syntax, to an understanding of the deployment process, up to Azure Bicep or *BicepLang*, the latest IaC language for Azure.

Once you have the syntax down and are able to work with Bicep, the remainder of the book takes you past many other capabilities of the Azure Resource Manager that will help you to scale your use of IaC to multiple teams or even complete organizations.

I hope you will join Henry, Erwin, and Eduard on a journey to learn all about Azure Infrastructure as Code!

—Scott Guthrie, Executive Vice President at Microsoft

Henry, Erwin, and Eduard are all deeply involved in the Azure, ARM template, Bicep, and DevOps communities. As a result, all three are experts in this field, and it is no surprise that this book is an immensely valuable resource when it comes to learning about Infrastructure as Code (IaC) on Azure.

What I particularly like about this book is its focus on the fundamentals—first focusing on Infrastructure as Code as a general concept, then spending lots of time on ARM templates, all before teaching Bicep itself. This foundation is something we always try to teach Azure users, as it allows you to learn not just what Azure is today, but how to keep up with Azure as it evolves.

Finally, the last third of the book covers how you use IaC in practice by teaching you how to integrate your code with CI/CD tooling, Azure Policy, testing strategies, and deployment stacks. This next level of depth is what supercharges your already valuable infra code.

This book is exactly what you need to go from 0 to 100 with Azure Infra-as-code. Enjoy!

—Alex Frankel, Program Manager
on the Azure Resource Manager team at Microsoft

preface

Well over a year ago, the three of us set out to write a book to teach people how to manage Azure Infrastructure as Code (IaC) with native Azure tools. Since then, we have written a total of thirteen chapters that we believe will take you from "zero to hero!"

IaC is an important topic, as not a single line of code can run on its own. Everything has to run on top of something. An OS runs on top of the hardware, a program on top of the OS, and most modern applications on top of a runtime. As engineers, we consider most of these things our programs "run on top of" to be infrastructure.

The cloud has changed the way we look at infrastructure. It is no longer bought and nurtured for two to five years. Instead, it is created when we need it and disregarded when we no longer need it. To fully exploit this flexibility that cloud offerings like Microsoft Azure bring, we need a way to quickly and reliably create our infrastructure. And for engineers, is there a better way than through code?

There are many resources already available about these topics—many blogs written by experienced engineers, and a body of MS Learn and MS docs materials and write-ups about individual features. Yet, there was still one thing missing: a single body of knowledge that captures all you need to get you fully up to speed. A single comprehensive body of knowledge, organized so that you can read it front to back. We hope that is changed by this book.

In this book, we have chosen to take a bottom-up approach, where you will first learn about the basics that will directly help you in your job and also help you understand the topics that follow. A deep understanding of these basics will help you throughout your career, not only when you're working with the current technologies, but also with what the future will bring.

However, that doesn't mean that this book doesn't contain the latest and greatest. Quite the opposite. After the foundational part, you will find more advanced topics that you can use to take your IaC practices to the next level, such as Azure Policy and testing templates. We've also added sections about recently released features like template specs and the Bicep registry.

Whether you are just getting started with Azure IaC or are an experienced engineer who wants to keep learning, we believe that there is value in this book for everyone!

acknowledgments

Writing a book is a great undertaking, and it's not possible without the help of a great many people. We'd like to thank our wives and girlfriend Marjoleine, Gerja, and Marloes for their support when we were on yet another call in the evening, or when we needed another afternoon to write just one more section. We also want to thank the Azure Resource Manager product group, Alex Frankel and Brian Moore in particular, for their support and for reviewing parts of this book.

Also, no book sees the light without reviewers and a whole team of editors who help steer the direction of the book. Thanks to our reviewers: Aleksandar Nikolic, Alexey Vyskubov, Amado Gramajo, Amanda Debler, Aron Trauring, Bikalpa Timilsina, Casey Burnett, Chris Heneghan, Conor Redmond, Daniel Berecz, Danilo Tiago, Darrin Bishop, Edin Kapic, George Chang, Giuliano Latini, James Black, Kamesh Ganesan, Karthikeyarajan Rajendra, Lachman Dhalliwal, Lakshminarayanan A.S, Maciej Jurkowski, Michael Bright, Michael Langdon, Nasir Naeem, Quentin Fortier, Radhakrishna M.V., Renato Gentile, Richard Vaughan, Robin Coe, Ronald Cranston, Sebastian Rogers, Stephen Goodman, Steve Atchue, Steven Oxley, Sylvain Groulx, Vishal Singh, Vivek Dhami, and Vivek Lakhanpal, for your invaluable feedback and tips for improvement. And finally, to Doug Rudder, the development editor; Mihaela Batinić, the reviewing editor; Deirdre Hiam, the project manager; Andy Carroll, the copyeditor; and Jason Everett, the proofreader, thank you for reviewing, commenting, rewriting, redrawing, and crafting it into the work it is now.

about this book

Azure Infrastructure as Code teaches you to use Azure's native Infrastructure as Code (IaC) tools, like ARM templates and Bicep, to build, manage, and scale infrastructure with just a few lines of code. You'll discover ARM templates, deployment stacks, and the powerful new programming language Bicep. You'll see how easy they make it to create new test environments, safely make infrastructure changes, and prevent configuration drift. Loaded with in-depth coverage of syntax and lots of illustrative examples, this hands-on guide is a must-read for anyone looking to expand their knowledge of provisioning.

Who should read this book

This book is for anyone who has been provisioning or managing cloud infrastructure for three months or more. You could be any of the following:

- A software engineer who writes software for Azure and also contributes to managing the infrastructure your software runs on
- An IT professional who is responsible for operating any workload that runs in the Microsoft Azure cloud
- A cloud engineer who deploys and maintains applications in the cloud, be it on virtual machines or container platforms
- A network engineer who manages software-defined networks for Azure

To work with and test the examples in this book, you will need at least one Azure subscription.

How this book is organized: A roadmap

This book has three parts consisting of 13 chapters.

Part 1 explains Infrastructure as Code, talks about its benefits, introduces ARM templates, and walks you through writing and deploying a first template.

- Chapter 1 covers the basics of Infrastructure as Code and talks about its benefits. It also gives a preliminary introduction to ARM templates, Bicep, and the Azure Resource Manager. Lastly, it identifies a few other tools that you could use to manage infrastructure that are not created by Microsoft.
- Chapter 2 introduces ARM templates and walks you through creating a first one. It also explains how to deploy the template to Azure.

Part 2 goes deep into ARM templates and Bicep, explains the deployment process in detail, and talks about testing templates.

- Chapter 3 discusses ARM templates in more detail. It explains all the parts that make up an ARM template, like resources, parameters, variables, functions, and outputs.
- Chapter 4 describes the deployment of a template in detail. It talks about different deployment scopes, different tools for initiating a deployment, the different phases within the deployment, and the validation steps you can use during the deployment.
- Chapter 5 goes deep into ARM templates and touches on the more advanced topics like modularization, loops, deployment scripts, and nested templates.
- Chapter 6 introduces Bicep and explains how to use your knowledge of ARM templates to write Bicep templates.
- Chapter 7 gives a detailed overview into deploying your Infrastructure as Code using Azure DevOps. The different parts that make up a deployment pipeline are discussed and used to deploy your infrastructure into multiple environments and regions.
- Chapter 8 is also about deploying your infrastructure, but this time using GitHub Actions.
- Chapter 9 discusses how to analyze and test your templates and infrastructure using different tools and techniques.

Part 3 discusses a few advanced topics to help you take your infrastructure to a higher level.

- Chapter 10 explains how you can share your templates across your organization for optimal reuse and compliant-by-default infrastructure. It lists various methods and talks about their pros and cons.
- Chapter 11 talks about deployment stacks, which are used to deploy your resources into logical groups.

- Chapter 12 discusses Azure Policy, which allows you to govern your Azure resources. This chapter explains how to create and apply the policies across your environment using Bicep templates.
- Chapter 13 contains a few case studies that will show you larger examples of how to build infrastructure using the practices you've seen throughout the book.

In general, you should be sure to read the first six chapters. These cover the basics of both ARM templates and Bicep that you should know. The next two chapters, 7 and 8, discuss how to deploy Infrastructure as Code using either Azure DevOps or GitHub Actions. You can pick neither or read one or both depending on your situation or preference. The rest of the book contains chapters on topics like testing templates, sharing templates, or using policies, and these can be read out of order, based on your particular needs or interests.

About the code

This book contains many examples of source code both in numbered listings and inline with normal text. In both cases, source code is formatted in a `fixed-width font like this` to separate it from ordinary text. Sometimes code is also **in bold** to highlight code that has changed from previous steps in the chapter, such as when a new feature adds to an existing line of code.

In many cases, the original source code has been reformatted; we've added line breaks and reworked indentation to accommodate the available page space in the book. In rare cases, even this was not enough, and listings include line-continuation markers (➡). Additionally, comments in the source code have often been removed from the listings when the code is described in the text. Code annotations accompany many of the listings, highlighting important concepts.

You can get executable snippets of code from the liveBook (online) version of this book at https://livebook.manning.com/book/azure-infrastructure-as-code. The complete code for the examples in the book is available for download from the Manning website at https://www.manning.com/books/azure-infrastructure-as-code, and from GitHub at https://github.com/AzureIaCBook.

liveBook discussion forum

Purchase of *Azure Infrastructure as Code* includes free access to liveBook, Manning's online reading platform. Using liveBook's exclusive discussion features, you can attach comments to the book globally or to specific sections or paragraphs. It's a snap to make notes for yourself, ask and answer technical questions, and receive help from the authors and other users. To access the forum, go to https://livebook.manning.com/book/azure-infrastructure-as-code/discussion. You can also learn more about Manning's forums and the rules of conduct at https://livebook.manning.com/discussion.

Manning's commitment to our readers is to provide a venue where a meaningful dialogue between individual readers and between readers and the authors can take place. It is not a commitment to any specific amount of participation on the part of the authors, whose contribution to the forum remains voluntary (and unpaid). We suggest you try asking the authors some challenging questions lest their interest stray! The forum and the archives of previous discussions will be accessible from the publisher's website as long as the book is in print.

Other online resources

Need additional help?

- *ARM overview*—https://docs.microsoft.com/en-us/azure/azure-resource-manager
- *ARM template specs*—https://docs.microsoft.com/en-us/azure/templates
- *QuickStart templates*—https://github.com/Azure/azure-quickstart-templates

about the authors

HENRY BEEN is an independent DevOps & Azure Architect from the Netherlands. He has been active in software development for over 15 years, of which close to 10 years have involved working with Microsoft Azure. He enjoys working with and within DevOps teams to design, write, and deliver great software. He believes in cross-functional teams that own the full delivery process, from inception to delivery and operations, of the software they write. Next to his work, he is active in the community writing blogs, creating videos, hosting MeetUps, and speaking at international conferences. For his community activities, he has been awarded the Microsoft MVP Award since 2019.

EDUARD KEILHOLZ is an Azure Architect at 4DotNet (Meppel, the Netherlands). He likes to help customers with their journey to the cloud and build highly performant, scalable cloud solutions. He enjoys lifting team members to a higher level as software engineers and as team members. His focus is on the Microsoft development stack, mainly C# and the Microsoft Azure Cloud. He also has a strong affinity for Angular.

ERWIN STAAL is an Azure Architect and DevOps Consultant at Xpirit (Hilversum, the Netherlands). He has more than 10 years of experience with both small and large organizations. He likes to immerse himself in the latest technologies. Currently he is working a lot with ASP.NET Core, Docker, and Kubernetes. As a DevOps Consultant, he helps companies with the implementation of DevOps and Continuous Delivery.

about the cover illustration

The figure on the cover of *Azure Infrastructure as Code* is "Ingrienne," or "A Woman from the Ingria," taken from a collection by Jacques Grasset de Saint-Sauveur, published in 1797. Each illustration is finely drawn and colored by hand.

In those days, it was easy to identify where people lived and what their trade or station in life was just by their dress. Manning celebrates the inventiveness and initiative of the computer business with book covers based on the rich diversity of regional culture centuries ago, brought back to life by pictures from collections such as this one.

Part 1

Introduction

In this part of the book, we'll explain what Infrastructure as Code (IaC) is and why you will want to consider using it for your cloud environment. The anatomy of the Azure Resource Manager (ARM, the system responsible for provisioning cloud resources in Azure) is explained, and you will learn how deployments on the Microsoft Azure Cloud work. Finally, you will learn how to write a basic ARM template. These templates drive the Azure Resource Manager and are fundamental to working with Infrastructure as Code for Azure.

Infrastructure as Code

1

This chapter covers

- Working with infrastructure
- The benefits of Infrastructure as Code
- The difference between Azure Service Management and Azure Resource Manager
- Other Infrastructure as Code tools available for Azure

If you have worked with Microsoft Azure before, you may have managed infrastructure in one way or another. In Azure, just as in any cloud platform, infrastructure can be created and altered quickly and easily. Using one or more of the Azure portal, PowerShell cmdlets, RESTful HTTP calls, SDKs, or ARM templates, you can create servers or PaaS and SaaS services in minutes or even seconds. This is in contrast to how infrastructure was managed in the past, or often still is on-premises.

The unique proposition of the cloud has transformed the way we create and operate software in the last decade. In particular, the way we manage infrastructure that runs applications has changed. Creating cloud infrastructure on demand and discarding it hours or days later has become a common approach, especially for test environments.

Two characteristics of the cloud, in particular, have accelerated this change:

- Elasticity
- Self-service

Elasticity is a characteristic of cloud computing. In the context of the cloud, elasticity is the capability to quickly add or remove resources from your infrastructure. Unlike traditional server deployments, clouds allow you to pay for infrastructure by the hour, minute, or even second, which allows for flexibility and encourages different approaches to provisioning infrastructure.

Self-service is a second characteristic. All of the major cloud vendors provide their users with graphical user interfaces (GUIs), command-line interfaces (CLIs), and APIs that they can use to create, update, and remove instances of the services they make available. Nowadays, all cloud providers use an API-first strategy, and one outcome of this is that every operation is also available through their management APIs, not just through the user interface or other tools.

The combination of these characteristics causes us to treat cloud infrastructure differently than traditional on-premises infrastructure. Spinning up complete configurations spanning tens of services can now be done in a matter of minutes. You can do this either using the major cloud providers' portals or by using scripts in your deployment pipelines.

However, using portals or CLIs to do this does present downsides—it is challenging to manage your cloud infrastructure reliably over time. Examples include changes being incompletely tracked, developers needing to access production environments with personal accounts, and many more. For this reason, another approach to managing infrastructure has become the go-to option for most teams: Infrastructure as Code (IaC.)

In this chapter, you'll learn more about managing cloud infrastructure in general and about the benefits of using IaC over manual and scripted approaches. Then we'll look at the Azure Resource Manager (ARM), the service that you interact with to manage your infrastructure in Azure, and at a few other tools for managing Azure infrastructure.

1.1   *Working with infrastructure*

Infrastructure as Code (IaC) is a modern approach for managing infrastructure. Instead of creating and configuring infrastructure manually, using graphical interfaces, all infrastructure is described in configuration files that are then used to create the infrastructure automatically. For Azure, IaC is written in Azure Resource Manager (ARM) templates or Bicep files, which are submitted to ARM for processing.

When we talk about infrastructure in the context of Azure, we are referring to all Azure resources that you can use as part of your solution architecture. An obvious example would be a virtual machine or storage account, but infrastructure in the context of IaC also includes service bus messaging queues, dashboards, app services, and any other deployable Azure resource.

Before we dive into the background of ARM and the benefits of IaC, let's look at an example. Figure 1.1 shows a small snippet of an ARM template and how it can be used to create Azure resources, like an Azure storage account.

```
{
    "name": "myStorageAccount",
    "type": "Microsoft.Storage/storageAccount",
    "apiVersion": "2021-02-01",
    "location": "westeurope",                    Create deployment
    "kind": "storage",
    "sku": {
      "name": "Premium_LRS"
    }
}
```

Figure 1.1 From ARM template to Azure infrastructure

ARM templates (at the left of figure 1.1) are formal descriptions of what infrastructure needs to exist and how it is configured. These templates are then applied to an Azure environment, creating the infrastructure described (at the right of figure 1.1). If a resource with the specified name and type already exists, its configuration is updated instead.

As you have already seen, the characteristics of the public cloud encourage the use of IaC, but that's not the only reason for using IaC. Two other drivers are the DevOps culture and the desire to prevent configuration drift. The next sections discuss these two topics in detail.

1.1.1 DevOps

DevOps is a cultural movement that aims at breaking down the traditional barriers between development and operations teams. In a traditional organization with operations and development teams, the two types of teams have clear responsibilities.

- *Development* or *application teams* are mainly responsible for implementing new requirements. They are concerned with introducing as many changes as possible, as that is how they implement new user requirements.
- *Operations teams* are responsible for managing the infrastructure and often any applications deployed to it. The operations team is mainly concerned with keeping things running, which, in general, works best when there are as few changes as possible.

Figure 1.2 shows what this looks like. Here you see a dedicated operations team that manages infrastructure and other runtime components. A separate development team writes updates and hands them over to operations for deployment. If such an update requires a change in the infrastructure, this has to be requested beforehand, often well in advance. These infrastructure changes have to be coordinated between teams and are often slow to complete.

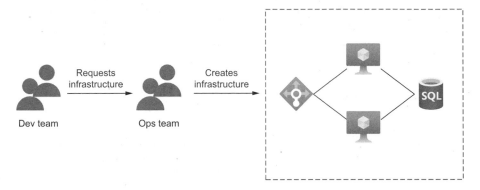

Figure 1.2   Development and operations teams coordinating on infrastructure changes

In many organizations, the opposing goals of these teams or even of complete departments lead to unhealthy situations, such as these:

- Operations teams can become resistant to change because changes introduce new risks into the environments they have to manage. The introduction of validation procedures, quality controls, approvals, or any other type of gatekeeping behavior limits the flow of change.
- Development teams push changes of insufficient quality because they receive praise for the amount of change they create. At the same time, operations teams are impacted by any downtime that results from bugs or issues in the software that is released.

Of course, this causes problems for the organization as a whole, which is served best by controlled, well-coordinated changes that implement new requirements while the existing infrastructure and applications keep running smoothly.

The DevOps movement advocates that developers and operators should work together in a single team toward this shared goal: the continuous delivery of high-quality software that creates business value. The subgoals of stability and change should be committed to by this single team that combines operations and development expertise. While doing this, a DevOps team often adopts development practices to perform operational duties.

In practice, this means that a new, now-combined, DevOps team is responsible for creating their own infrastructure (see figure 1.3). Often this also means that IT professionals start to apply development techniques to their day-to-day work. They transition from the user interface and manual application and the verification of changes to adopting advanced text editors, automated installation scripts, and IaC. IaC allows developers and operators to work together to describe and configure any infrastructure needed by their application deployment. Together they can promote the infrastructure changes and the application artifacts to a test environment, and after verification to a production environment.

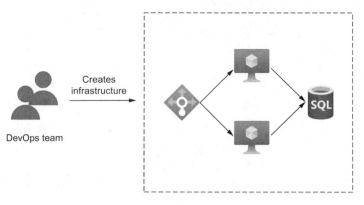

Figure 1.3   A DevOps team is aligned with the applications and infrastructure it is responsible for managing.

1.1.2 Preventing configuration drift

Next to self-service APIs and DevOps, another driver for the adoption of IaC is the prevention of a problem called *configuration drift.* Configuration drift is a phenomenon observed on infrastructure that is managed manually. It doesn't matter if it is managed through the command line or a graphical interface—configuration drift can happen in both cases.

Configuration drift refers to differences that develop over time on either of two dimensions:

- A difference between environments, such as between test and production
- A difference within an environment, such as between two virtual machines that should be configured exactly the same and host two instances of the same application

To see how this configuration drift can occur, imagine an infrastructure configuration of two identical virtual machines (VMs), with one being a test and the other a production environment. The two environments should be configured in precisely the same way, because the test environment is also used for load and stress testing.

Figure 1.4 illustrates two types of configuration drift. First, there is an unintended difference between the test and the production environment, as the production VMs

Figure 1.4   Two types of configuration drift: between environments and within an environment

have more memory allocated than the test VMs. Second, there is a drift within the production environment, as one of the VMs has four cores instead of the desired two.

Configuration drift is often the result of an unexpected, incomplete, or incorrectly executed change. When a change is required to the configuration of any infrastructure component, that change must be applied to each instance of the infrastructure, one by one. But other things can happen as well:

- A change is made to the development, test, acceptance, and production environments, after which an issue with the change is found at night: a bug. The change can easily be reverted, so it is reverted in the production environment. There is a lot of user feedback to deal with the next day, and reverting the change in the other environments is forgotten.
- During a major outage, all non-production environments go down and have to be restored manually. Accidentally, a more recent build of the operating system is used on the virtual machines, making them behave differently than the virtual machines in production.

Differences between environments like these can cause future problems. For example, test results from the test environment will no longer be representative of how a particular change will affect the production environment. Given enough time, configuration drift will affect any environment and result in unpredictable behavior. IaC can help remediate configuration drift by re-applying the infrastructure specification regularly. Because all settings are stored in source control and applied automatically, all changes are detected and corrected automatically.

We've mentioned three main drivers for using IaC—namely the cloud, DevOps, and the prevention of configuration drift—but there are still other benefits of IaC. Let's take some time to explore the benefits IaC offers over managing infrastructure manually or through scripts.

1.2 *The benefits of Infrastructure as Code*

Once a team moves to IaC, often because of one of the drivers we've already discussed, they will also start observing other benefits. As with many developments in our field, this change will not only help to overcome existing problems but will also inspire new ways of working.

These are three common benefits:

- IaC allows for automation, which saves time if you are often creating new environments.
- IaC allows for a declarative approach, which allows you to focus on the desired state and not on how to get there.
- IaC provides a human-readable format, which allows developers to reason about the state of the infrastructure.

The next three subsections discuss these benefits in turn.

1.2.1   IaC allows for automation

As you may have guessed by now, IaC is applied using tools, and tools imply automation. This delivers two additional benefits, besides saving time: guaranteed outcomes and environment reproducibility.

GUARANTEED OUTCOMES

Automatically creating and configuring environments not only saves time, it also provides guaranteed outcomes. When creating and configuring an Azure virtual machine manually, there are tens if not hundreds of configuration options that have to be checked. In practice, this is very error-prone work, and mistakes are very likely to happen. Asking five different people to create an Azure VM with 4 CPU cores, 8 GB of memory, and running Windows Datacenter 2019, will most likely result in five virtual machines all configured differently.

With IaC, this is not the case. After you write the desired infrastructure in a code file, the same file can be applied repeatedly, and the IaC tools guarantee that the outcome is the same every time. Verifying configuration or testing outcomes is no longer necessary when working with IaC. It not only saves a lot of time; it also improves quality.

ENVIRONMENT REPRODUCIBILITY

Once an IaC file is written, the cost of creating the described infrastructure is almost zero. It is just a matter of starting the tool, and the required infrastructure resources are created and available a few minutes later. This unlocks all kinds of new approaches to testing, deploying, and running infrastructure.

Just the ability to automatically remove development and test environments at 6 P.M. and re-create them automatically at 7 A.M. on working days can save organizations anywhere between 30% and 60% of their infrastructure costs, compared to keeping infrastructure running 24/7.

Also, if you have ever been responsible for test infrastructure, you'll know how hard it is to keep test infrastructure usable. Every test failure can pollute the infrastructure and trigger false test failures in the future, due to the inconsistent state of the previous run. Just imagine the possibility of creating new infrastructure, in a guaranteed state, before each test run starts. And all of this at no additional cost. The reduction in false test failures will save a lot of time, money, and negative energy spent by you and your team.

1.2.2   IaC allows for a declarative approach

IaC can be written in two different styles: declarative and imperative. With the declarative style, the source files describe the desired state of the infrastructure. The execution engine is then responsible for comparing the desired state with the actual state, determining the differences, and identifying and executing a series of commands to make the actual state correspond to the desired state.

This approach is similar to Structured Query Language (SQL). You can use SQL to describe which records should or should not be in your result, rather than having to specify the commands to execute. The database engine is then responsible for determining which commands should be executed to reach that desired result.

With the imperative style, you do not describe the intended end result but instead describe the series of commands, steps, or program code to execute.

> **NOTE**   The term *Infrastructure as Code* is also used for approaches where scripts are stored in source control. While this is a correct use of the term, most IaC approaches, including ARM templates, use a declarative approach.

The first benefit of a declarative approach is that it enhances both the ease of writing and the ease of reading. Writing in a declarative style is easier, because the writer does not have to worry about *how* the infrastructure is created. They just need to describe *what* is needed in the end, and the tool translates this into the *how*. This applies both to when infrastructure is created the first time and when infrastructure configuration is updated. In an imperative approach, this would result in a lot of if-then-else coding; in a declarative approach, if-then-else is not necessary. As an example, see these declarative statements:

```
There should be a car
The car should be green
The car should have four wheels
```

Compare that with these imperative statements:

```
If there is no car
       Create a car
If the car is not green
       Make the car green
While the car has more than four wheels
       Remove a wheel from the car
While the car has fewer than four wheels
       Add a wheel to the car
```

As this example shows, the declarative style improves the ease of writing and also enhances reading ease, as it focuses solely on the desired state.

The second benefit of a declarative approach is that the execution engine can be optimized without impacting the IaC declarations. In the similar case of SQL statements, SQL database engines have seen significant changes and optimizations over the last few decades, but most SQL statements written years ago still execute without any changes.

1.2.3   *IaC provides a human-readable format*

The third benefit of IaC is that it leverages human-readable formats. Some IaC tools use JSON or YAML, and others use a *custom domain-specific language* (DSL) or existing programming language. Azure Resource Manager templates use JSON, which stands for JavaScript Object Notation. This human-readable format provides us with a version-controllable, auditable, and reviewable definition of application infrastructure.

On top of ARM templates, an easier, more approachable, DSL has been introduced, called Bicep.

VERSION CONTROLLABLE

Human-readable, non-binary files can be stored in a source control system, just like source code for an application. Source control systems provide users with a centralized, single source for the latest version of a file, along with a full history of all changes. Gone are the days when you had to record all the infrastructure changes manually to go back and find out which changes were made when, by who, and why. With source control, you automatically have the complete change history readily available. Another consequence of this is that if there is ever the need to roll back a change, the previous configuration can quickly be restored.

AUDITABLE

IaC files are readable and all changes are recorded in source control, which makes them instantly auditable by security reviewers, external auditors, and any other party interested in the changes you are making. Source control provides a full audit log of all the changes made and by whom.

REVIEWABLE

Source control systems allow you to automatically enforce standards before any change is made final. This can include automated formatting checks, automated build checks, or even enforced peer reviews—this functionality is built into most source control systems.

Now that you know about the extra benefits you can get with IaC, let's turn to the Azure Resource Manager. Azure Resource Manager is Azure's service for working with IaC.

1.3 *The Azure Resource Manager*

We've discussed the drivers and benefits for IaC, so it's now time to dive a bit deeper into the IaC system for Azure. The first thing to understand here is that all Azure infrastructure management is done using the Azure Resource Manager (ARM). ARM is a RESTful HTTP API that you can call to list, create, update, and delete all resources in your Azure subscriptions. If you interact with Azure through the portal, the CLI, or Azure PowerShell, you are also using ARM under the hood.

ARM is the basis for the Azure IaC capabilities provided via ARM templates. ARM is the execution engine for IaC. But before we dive into ARM templates, it is important to know what the control plane and data plane are, how they differ, and what you can and can't do with ARM templates.

1.3.1 *Control plane and data plane*

Each interaction you have with Azure is either a *control plane* or a *data plane* operation. Simply put, you use the control plane to manage resources in your subscription, and you use the data plane to employ the capabilities exposed by your instances of specific resource types. In Azure, there is a single, unified control plane: the Azure Resource Manager.

To make the difference between the control plane and data plane clearer, here are a few examples:

- You create an Azure SQL database through the control plane. Once it's created, you use the data plane to connect to it and perform SQL queries.
- You create a Linux virtual machine through the control plane. Then you use the data plane to interact with it over the SSH protocol.

Requests sent to the control plane are all sent to the Azure Resource Manager URL; for the global cloud, that is https://management.azure.com. From this URL, it is possible to build complete URLs that identify any Azure resource. For example, the following pseudo URL points to a virtual machine:

```
GET https://management.azure.com/subscriptions/{subscriptionId}/resourceGroups/
    ➥ {resourceGroupName}/providers/Microsoft.Compute/virtualMachines/
    ➥ {virtualMachineName}?api-version=2021-04-01
```

Suppose you are logged into the Azure portal and you copy this URL into your browser with valid values for subscriptionId, resourceGroupName, and virtualMachineName. The response would be a JSON description of the virtual machine. If you study the response in detail and compare it to an ARM template for virtual machines, you'll quickly notice that they are the same (with only a few default properties omitted).

Interactions with a resource on the data plane always happen on an endpoint specific to that resource. This means that data plane operations are not limited to REST but could use HTTPS, FTP, or any other protocol. Interactions with the control plane happen through the ARM APIs or through ARM templates.

1.3.2   ARM templates

The ARM APIs can be used to manage infrastructure in an imperative style, using provisioning scripts. If you prefer a declarative style, ARM templates are available.

ARM templates are written in JSON or Bicep and are used for any of the following purposes:

- A *resource group template* is used to deploy one or more resources into an Azure resource group.
- *Subscription templates* are used to deploy resource groups, policies, and authorizations to an Azure subscription.
- *Management group templates* are used to deploy subscriptions, nested management groups, policies, and authorizations into a management group.
- *Tenant-level templates* are used to deploy nested management groups, policies, and authorizations into the Azure Active Directory.

If you already have a basic understanding of the Azure hierarchy, the preceding list will show that you can completely manage Azure using ARM templates. If you don't understand all the terms mentioned here, don't worry—all these concepts will be explained in more detail in chapter 3.

   While ARM templates are compelling and they allow you to manage all of Azure, an often-heard complaint is that they can be challenging to write and pretty verbose to read. To provide a solution to this, Microsoft recently launched project Bicep.

1.3.3   The Bicep language

ARM templates are written as JSON files, but one of the disadvantages of JSON is that it can become quite lengthy when expressing complex structures. This lengthiness can make files difficult to maintain or read. Another downside of JSON is that there is no out-of-the-box support for control structures like loops or conditions. While ARM provides workarounds for this, ARM templates do take a while to master.

   To provide a solution to these problems, Microsoft has introduced a new domain-specific language (DSL) as an alternative way to write ARM templates. This DSL is called Bicep, a play on the name ARM. Chapter 6 discusses Bicep in depth.

1.3.4   Azure Service Management (ASM is not ARM)

Before the existence of the Azure Resource Manager, another system was available for managing resources within Azure: Azure Service Management (ASM). ASM is no longer in use, but it is good to know of its existence and how it differs from ARM. Even if you only use that knowledge to detect and discard outdated online content, it is worth it.

   Microsoft introduced Azure Service Manager (ASM) as part of the Azure cloud (then still named Windows Azure) around 2009. ASM was the first HTTP interface provided for managing Azure resources. Before that, while Azure was still in preview, the management of resources was only possible using a web interface now called the *classic portal*. Looking back, ASM was the first iteration of an interface for managing Azure resources.

   ASM has no built-in support for IaC and is rarely ever used in production nowadays. Still, it is good to know what ASM is and to stay away from anything related to it. While the names Azure Resource Manager and Azure Service Management may look similar at first sight, they are nothing alike.

> ### Drawbacks of Azure Service Management
> The lack of support for IaC was not the only reason Microsoft replaced ASM. Other drawbacks include the lack of grouping options for resources, no options for managing authorizations at the individual resource level, the lack of a fine-grained permission set, and many more.

Azure Resource Manager and its ARM templates are the built-in approach for managing infrastructure within Azure. But there are also other tools available for IaC both on Azure or in other public clouds. The next section describes some of them to help you build a broader understanding of IaC.

1.4   *Other tools*

ARM templates are just one of many IaC approaches available. This section will explore a few other well-known tools to help you understand which tools are available and which one makes sense in which situations.

> **NOTE** Our focus here is on tools that can be used for IaC in cloud environments. There are other tools available for managing state within virtual machines, such as PowerShell DSC, Puppet, Chef, and Ansible. We won't be discussing those here.

When considering IaC tools for the cloud, one characteristic is the most important: is the tool single-cloud or multi-cloud? When you're working in only one cloud, you can consider using the IaC tool specifically intended for that cloud. For Azure, you can use ARM templates; for Amazon Web Services (AWS), you can use CloudFormation; and for Google Cloud Platform, there is the Google Deployment manager. Alternatively, there are multi-cloud options like Terraform or Pulumi. While these tools allow you to manage multiple environments or clouds from a single IaC script, it is also possible to use them when you're only working with Azure.

Multi-cloud or single-cloud

There is much debate around the topic of multi-cloud strategies. There are both pros and cons for working with only a single cloud provider or working with more than one vendor. This discussion is out of scope for this book, but when weighing your options and determining your strategy, you should consider your IaC options.

We'll look at all these tools in the next few sections.

1.4.1   *AWS CloudFormation*

CloudFormation is an AWS service for managing infrastructure. Each deployment of a group of resources is called a *stack*. A stack is a persistent grouping of resources that can span multiple AWS regions or accounts. When you redeploy a template to the same stack, all existing resources in the stack are updated. CloudFormation also deletes resources that are part of the stack but no longer part of the template. Overall, CloudFormation templates are very comparable to ARM templates when it comes to their layout and capabilities.

1.4.2   *Google Cloud Deployment Manager*

Google Deployment Manager is the built-in approach to IaC for the Google Cloud Platform (GCP). To deploy a simple set of resources, YAML is used in a very similar layout and style to CloudFormation or ARM templates. However, the Deployment

Manager's YAML configuration is more limited, as it does not allow for parameters, variables, and outputs, like CloudFormation and ARM templates do.

For more advanced features, Deployment Manager allows you to write reusable templates using Python (preferred) or Jinja2. When using Python, the Python language's full power can be used, including loops, conditionals, and external libraries, to build and return an array of resources. Note that doing so removes the declarative nature from templates. These templates are then imported into the YAML files and deployed from there.

1.4.3 *Terraform*

HashiCorp has developed an IaC tool called Terraform. Terraform is open source and is based upon a split between the DSL used for declaring resources and the so-called providers that specify which resources are available for use. The DSL used by Terraform is called HashiCorp Configuration Language (HCL), which defines its structure, syntax, and semantics.

Terraform providers are available for all major cloud providers and other target platforms and tools, including VMware, Azure DevOps, GitLab, Grafana, and many more. Another thing that differs between ARM templates and Terraform is that Terraform uses a state file.

> **A state file or cache**
>
> What ARM, CloudFormation, and Deployment Manager have in common is that they operate on the difference between the desired state (the template) and the actual state of the resources. The changes they make to the cloud environment are determined by comparing these two.
>
> Another group of IaC tools operates on the difference between the desired state and a state file. A state file is a file or cache that captures what the tool believes the cloud environment's state is after the previous deployments. The changes it makes to the cloud environment are determined by comparing these two.
>
> IaC tools use a state file to quickly decide which changes should be made without querying the complete actual state from the cloud environment. The risk of this approach is that there might be mismatches between the state file and the actual state, resulting in an incorrect execution. To counter this, tools that use a state file often allow for updating the state file from the actual state.

For Azure, there is a Terraform provider developed by Microsoft. This Terraform provider is almost as feature-complete as ARM templates, but it can sometimes still lag in functionality. The reason for this is straightforward: ARM templates use built-in functionality, while functionality needs to be explicitly added to the Terraform provider.

1.4.4   *Pulumi*

Pulumi differs from most other IaC tools in that it doesn't use YAML, JSON, or a DSL, but actual program code for managing IaC. Pulumi has language support for Node.js, Python, .NET Core, and Go. Cloud-wise, there is support for Azure, AWS, and GCP. Using one of the supported languages, a model is constructed that represents the desired infrastructure stack. The outcome of the program code, the declaration, is this model that starts the Pulumi engine's execution.

One of the significant advantages of using an existing programming language for defining infrastructure is that all of the tools and technologies surrounding that programming language are also available for your infrastructure definition. The most prominent example of this is the ability to run unit tests against the infrastructure definition.

Besides supporting all Azure resources, including Azure policies, Pulumi also has a built-in policy engine. This engine allows the use of a single policy engine for more than one cloud. The advantage of this is that you have a single entry point for all policy evaluations. The disadvantage is that the policies are only executed during deployment and not continuously in a deployed environment. Azure Policy, which is the topic of chapter 12, does allow for this continuous evaluation.

1.4.5   *Choosing between cloud-specific and multi-cloud solutions*

When you are consistently working across more than one cloud, you have to choose between using two or more cloud-specific solutions or a single multi-cloud IaC solution.

Cloud-specific solutions often have deeper integration with the underlying platform and provide unique benefits that multi-cloud solutions might not. The downside of using more than one solution is the increased number of tools. On the other hand, multi-cloud solutions can offer specific options that cloud-specific options do not. As an example, look at the policy engine that Pulumi offers. In the end, it is up to you to weigh both alternatives' pros and cons and make the best decision for your context.

Summary

- Almost everyone who works with Microsoft Azure has been managing cloud resources one way or another. Typical management of cloud resources includes creating, configuring, and removing resources in Azure. Examples of resources are virtual machines, App Service plans, and storage accounts.
- Manually managing cloud infrastructure at scale is tedious, repetitive work that can introduce errors. The elasticity and self-service characteristics of public clouds, the DevOps culture, and the prevention of configuration drift are three drivers toward IaC.
- The benefits of IaC for Azure are automation, its declarative approach, and its human-readable nature. These characteristics provide you with repeatable and

guaranteed outcomes, ease of understanding, and an auditable and reviewable history of infrastructure changes.

- Azure Resource Manager (ARM) is the API or application used for managing Azure resources since 2015. ARM templates are written in JSON, which can be lengthy to write and read. Bicep, a new DSL, has been introduced by Microsoft to overcome this.

Writing your first ARM template

This chapter covers

- Writing your first ARM template
- Using VS Code to write and validate templates
- Deploying a template using the Azure portal
- Creating a visual representation of your template

With the theory covered, it's time to write your first ARM template. While writing ARM templates may seem like a tough job at first, you'll get the hang of it soon enough. Experience shows that it takes most people one or two days of practice to get familiar with the syntax.

Getting started is easier when you use the right tools for the job. ARM templates are written as JSON documents, so a powerful text editor is recommended. For ARM templates specifically, Visual Studio Code (VS Code) is the best choice. VS Code is not only a powerful text editor, but there is an extension that supports writing ARM templates. This chapter will help you set up VS Code and the extension.

When writing ARM templates, you need to be at least somewhat familiar with the infrastructure you want to create. For example, in this chapter, you will deploy an Azure storage account. Storage accounts are, amongst other things, used for storing files, often referred to as binary large objects (BLOBs). In Azure, the storage account is called a *resource type*, of which you can create instances. When you create an instance of a storage account, that storage account is called a *resource*. A storage account is one of many resource types available in Microsoft Azure.

One reference you can use when writing ARM templates is the Microsoft Docs website. The Azure templates section contains a list of all resource types you can deploy using the Azure Resource Manager, and it's available at https://docs.microsoft.com/azure/templates. Besides listing all the resource types, you can find the allowed properties for each resource type, whether they are mandatory or not, and the type of each property. In this chapter, you'll learn how to use that reference for storage accounts.

To help you prepare for the remainder of this chapter, the next section explains JSON and how to configure your working environment by installing VS Code and the ARM Tools extension for VS Code.

2.1 *Working with JSON files*

As you learned in chapter 1, ARM templates are JSON files that describe the infrastructure you need in a formal format. JSON stands for *JavaScript Object Notation,* and it's a structured but lightweight text format for describing information. This section will briefly introduce JSON—if you already know JSON, you can skip ahead to section 2.1.1.

A valid JSON file or snippet has to evaluate to a value. The following example shows a valid JSON object that explains its own syntax.

```
{
    "string": "Text is started and ended using double quotes",
    "thisIsANumberProperty": 4,
    "thisIsABooleanProperty": true,
    "thisIsANotSetOrMissingProperty": null,
    "thisIsAnArray": [
        "Square brackets are used for arrays",
        "Curly braces are used for objects",
        "Property names are quoted, as they are also of type string"
    ]
}
```

A value can be of any of the following six types: string, number, Boolean, null, array, or object. Four of these six are primitive data types: `string` (text), `number` (integer or decimal), `boolean` (true or false), and `null` (nothing). Null is used for an empty or non-existing value and is not the same as the value zero. Besides these primitive types, JSON has support for arrays and objects. An *array* is an unordered list of elements, whereas an *object* is a collection of name/value pairs, and such a pair is often called a *property*.

This should be enough of an introduction to JSON for this book, which discusses ARM templates at length. If you want to dive deeper into JSON, you can look at the formal JSON specification at www.json.org. There you'll also find illustrations that describe the makeup of JSON in more detail, as well as links to libraries for working with JSON in many programming languages.

2.1.1   Installing the ARM templates extension in VS Code

When you start working with ARM templates or JSON files in general, you'll find that a good text editor is indispensable. For ARM templates, VS Code is highly recommended, not only because it has built-in support for editing JSON, but also because it has extensions that support writing ARM templates. You can download VS Code from https://code.visualstudio.com if you do not have it installed yet.

After installing and starting VS Code, the window in figure 2.1 should be displayed. Here you see VS Code's default editing window that is used throughout this chapter.

**Figure 2.1   VS Code; the arrow points out the
icon for managing extensions**

Before you get started, you should install the ARM template extension. To do this, follow these steps:

1 Click on the Extensions icon (marked with an arrow in figure 2.1) to navigate to the extensions view.
2 In the search box that appears, search for "Azure Resource Manager".
3 Select the extension named Azure Resource Manager (ARM) Tools, published by Microsoft. It may appear confusing that the version number is lower than 1 (0.15.5 at the time of writing), but this is perfectly fine.
4 In the window that opens on the right, click Install.

You should now have both VS Code and the ARM template extension installed. It is time to start writing your first ARM template from scratch.

2.2   Writing ARM templates in VS Code

Let's imagine you're employed by a small company that works with large amounts of data, such as images or video files. These files consume a lot of storage, and you are running out of on-premises storage. As your company is already using some Azure capabilities, you are responsible for creating an Azure storage account where you and your colleagues can store more files in the future. To prepare for future changes and leverage the benefits of IaC, you decide to complete this task using an ARM template.

To start writing that template, first open VS Code. A welcome screen will open. Press Ctrl-N to open a new file. To ensure that the ARM Tools extension starts, save the file under the name azuredeploy.json. You can use any filename with an extension of .json, and the ARM Tools extension should start.

Fixing extension problems

Sometimes the ARM Tools extension does not start properly when it has just been installed in VS Code. To solve this problem, save your file, close and reopen your ARM template JSON file, and the extension will initialize properly.

Start writing your first ARM template by typing `arm!` at the beginning of the file. This notation is a shortcut that triggers the ARM Tools extension in VS Code. When you press Enter, the extension will insert a predefined piece of code called a *snippet*. In this case, you should see a snippet like this:

```
{
    "$schema": "https://schema.management.azure.com/schemas/
        ➥ 2019-04-01/deploymentTemplate.json#",
    "contentVersion": "1.0.0.0",
    "parameters": {},
    "functions": [],
    "variables": {},
    "resources": [],
    "outputs": {}
}
```

Every ARM template must be a valid JSON object. This snippet contains all the top-level properties that are available for you to use.

The first property of this object, called `$schema`, is always a reference to the JSON Schema for ARM templates. JSON Schema is a formal notation for describing the structure of the content in this file. The specified URL is valid, and you can copy it into your browser to read the specification, but JSON Schemas are difficult to read. They are only used by tools to validate JSON files against the specified schema. Specifying the JSON Schema is mandatory in ARM templates, but you don't need to understand its details. The date you see as part of the URL serves as the version number, which may change as newer versions of the schema become available.

The second property specifies what is called the `contentVersion`. Here you can use a four-part version number for the template. This version is not used by ARM in any way, and if you choose to version your templates, you can follow any system you like. The `contentVersion` property is optional.

After these two properties, the five properties that make up the main template follow. For now, we will not use the `parameters`, `functions`, `variables`, and `outputs` properties, so you can remove these four lines to keep your first template simple and easy to understand. This leaves you with an empty shell to which you can add your first Azure resource.

2.2.1   *Adding a resource*

In most ARM templates, the `resources` property makes up the majority of the template. The `resources` property is an array, which allows you to specify any number of resources within a single template. Each resource is declared as a JSON object.

To declare a resource, navigate your cursor between the two square brackets that make up the still-empty `resources` array, and press Enter to create some whitespace. ARM templates are not whitespace-sensitive, and this includes line breaks. Whitespace can be anywhere that it is convenient for readability.

> **NOTE**   When typing in VS Code, you can at all times press the Ctrl-. (Ctrl and a period) key combination to invoke VS Code autocomplete and see context-based suggestions.

Next, type `arm-storage` and watch how the ARM Tools extension pops up with a list of snippet suggestions. While you type, the list will continue to filter, showing only snippets that match what you have typed so far. When "arm-storage" is at the top, press the Tab key to accept the snippet and insert the ARM template snippet for creating a storage account. This snippet contains all the mandatory properties for creating an Azure storage account.

Observe how the extension automatically highlights all the properties for which a value is required. First, it selects the value for the new resource's `name` property in all locations where it appears. Give your resource a more meaningful name and press Tab again. The cursor will move to the next property.

In this case, updating the other properties is unnecessary, so keep pressing Tab until the cursor stops moving through them. With all the properties filled in, let's explore them in turn.

- `name`—Every Azure resource has a mandatory name. The naming rules are different for every type of resource, and most names must be globally unique.
- `type`—This property specifies the type of resource you want to create. The resource type consists of multiple parts separated by slashes. In chapter 3, you'll learn more about the makeup of resource types.
- `apiVersion`—This property specifies which version of the resource type you want to use.

The combination of the resource type and API version determines which other properties are available to describe the resource. You can find these in the documentation at https://docs.microsoft.com/azure/templates (see figure 2.2). Look up Storage > Storage Accounts in the tree on the left. Next, in the drop-down list at the top, select the correct version of the resource or leave it at the default of Latest. The remainder of the page shows an example resource declaration followed by documentation for every property. If you have followed along with this example, your ARM template should now look like listing 2.1.

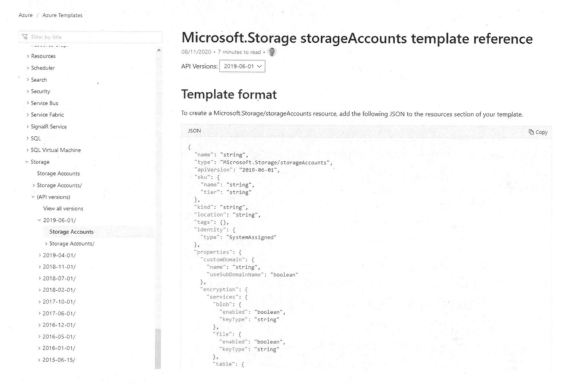

Figure 2.2   Finding resource properties using the ARM template reference

```
Listing 2.1   Your first ARM template
```

```
{
    "$schema": "https://schema.management.azure.com/schemas/2019-04-
        ➥ 01/deploymentTemplate.json#",
    "contentVersion": "1.0.0.0",
    "resources": [
        {
            "name": "storage20201227",
            "type": "Microsoft.Storage/storageAccounts",
            "apiVersion": "2021-04-01",
            "tags": {
                "displayName": "storage20201227"
            },
            "location": "[resourceGroup().location]",
            "kind": "StorageV2",
            "sku": {
                "name": "Premium_LRS",
                "tier": "Premium"
            }
        }

    ]
}
```

Congratulations! That's it. You have just successfully created your first ARM template, ready for deployment. But before you deploy it, let's first explore VS Code and see how it can help you write templates a bit more.

2.2.2 *Leveraging IntelliSense in VS Code*

So far you have used code snippets in VS Code to write a template quickly and have most of it generated automatically. But these code snippets only generate the required properties. When you need to configure optional properties, you have to add them manually. When you're adding these properties, the ARM Tools extension helps by popping up suggestions.

For storage accounts, it is possible to enforce HTTPS while connecting to the storage account. Using HTTPS is a general recommendation in our field, so let's enable this on our resource by setting the supportsHttpsTrafficOnly property to true. This property has to be nested in another object, called properties.

> **NOTE** Many Azure resources have most or all of their extra properties grouped within another object. This object is then used as the value for a property called properties.

To make this change, scroll down to the bottom of your template and add a new property at the end of the resource: add a comma, and start typing properties. As soon as you have typed the p, the suggestion for properties should already pop up. Just pressing Tab will complete the entry. Continue by typing a colon and then "This is a mistake". Once you have done this, hover over properties with your mouse, and your editor will show something like figure 2.3.

```
1  {
2      "$schema": "https://schema.management.azure.com/schemas/2019-04-01/deploymentTemplate.json#",
3      "contentVersion": "1.0.0.0",
4      "resources": [
5          {
6              "name": "storage-account-name",
7              "type": "Microsoft.Storage/storageAccounts",
8              "apiVersion": "2021-04-01",
9              "tags": {
10                 "displayName": "storage-account-name"
11             },
12             "location": "[resourceGroup().location]",
13             "kind": "StorageV2",
14             
                properties The parameters used to create the storage account.

                Value must be one of the following types: object arm-template (schema)

                View Problem   No quick fixes available
18             "properties": "This is a mistake"
19         }
20     ]
21  }
```

Figure 2.3 A validation error in VS Code

In figure 2.3, you can see that the editor not only automatically completes the entries you are making, but it also continuously validates the template and provides you with feedback when there are any errors. In this case, the error is that the `properties` property should not be of type `string`, but of type `object`. Replacing the text and the enclosing quotes with curly brackets, {}, removes the error.

Within the curly brackets, press Enter and start typing `supportsHttpsTrafficOnly` to invoke autocomplete again, and add the property. The value of this property should be `true`.

After making these changes, your template should look like the following listing.

Listing 2.2   Complete ARM template

```
{
    "$schema": "https://schema.management.azure.com/schemas/2019-04-
        ➡ 01/deploymentTemplate.json#",
    "contentVersion": "1.0.0.0",
    "resources": [
        {
            "name": "storage20201227",
            "type": "Microsoft.Storage/storageAccounts",
            "apiVersion": "2019-06-01",
            "tags": {
                "displayName": "storage20201227"
            },
            "location": "[resourceGroup().location]",
            "kind": "StorageV2",
            "sku": {
                "name": "Premium_LRS",
                "tier": "Premium"
            },
            "properties": {
                "supportsHttpsTrafficOnly": true
            }
        }

    ]
}
```

You've now completed an ARM template for deploying a storage account in Azure. But writing templates doesn't deliver value unless you deploy them. So let's go and deploy this template!

2.3   *Deploying an ARM template*

There are quite a few ways of deploying an ARM template, and chapter 4 will discuss their pros and cons in detail. For now, you can deploy your template manually from the Azure portal.

First, navigate to the Azure portal (https://portal.azure.com) and log in. As soon as you have logged in, click the Create a Resource button. This will open a new view with a search bar at the top. Here, search for "Template Deployment (deploy using custom templates)" and select it. This type of resource allows you to deploy the ARM template you created in the previous section. Once it's selected, click the Create button to proceed—this should open a new view very similar to figure 2.4.

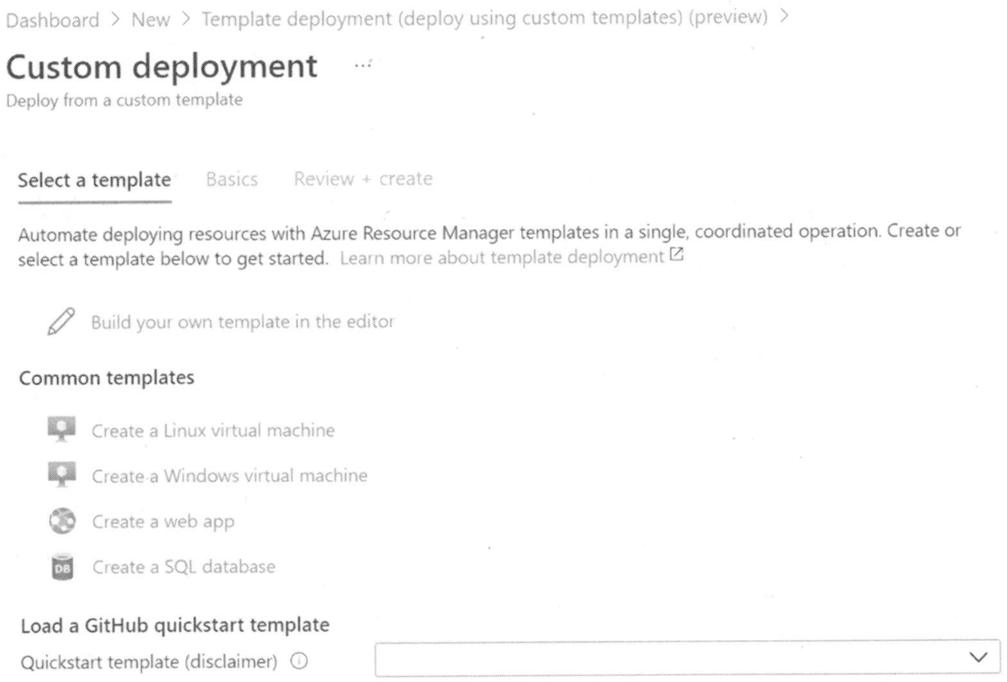

Dashboard > New > Template deployment (deploy using custom templates) (preview) >

Custom deployment
Deploy from a custom template

Select a template   Basics   Review + create

Automate deploying resources with Azure Resource Manager templates in a single, coordinated operation. Create or select a template below to get started. Learn more about template deployment ↗

   ✎   Build your own template in the editor

Common templates

   🖥   Create a Linux virtual machine

   🖥   Create a Windows virtual machine

   ⚙   Create a web app

   🗄   Create a SQL database

Load a GitHub quickstart template

Quickstart template (disclaimer) ⓘ   [⌄]

Figure 2.4   Creating a custom deployment in the Azure portal

In this view, you can open an online editor by clicking Build Your Own Template in the Editor. Once the editor is open, copy your template into the online editor and click Save. Saving closes the editor, and you'll see a new view where you can select or create the resource group to which you want to deploy the template. Create a new resource group with a name that's easy to remember.

> **NOTE**   In Azure, every resource is part of a *resource group,* which is a logical grouping of resources. You can decide what a logical grouping of resources is, based on the requirements of your work. Chapter 4 will discuss resource groups and other ways of grouping your resources into a hierarchy.

To start the deployment of your template, click the Review + Create button. The Azure Resource Manager will first validate your template. Validation is performed on the structure, syntax, validity of names and properties, and much more. Once the validation is complete, click the button again, now titled Create.

Within a few seconds of starting the deployment, the portal will navigate to a new *blade* (a new *view* in the Azure portal) where you can see your template's deployment status. Storage accounts provision quite quickly, and within a minute you should see a message telling you that your deployment is complete. You can now click Go to Resource and work with the storage account in Azure.

> **Managing costs in Azure**
>
> You may want to try and test ARM templates or snippets published in this book. Please note that creating ARM deployments does create actual resources in the Azure cloud for which you may be charged. It's a good idea to remove resources from Azure that you are not actually using, to reduce costs.

You have now successfully deployed your first ARM template into Azure. It may not feel like much of an improvement over manual deployments yet, but that's because you have just deployed one resource so far. If you wanted, you could deploy tens or even hundreds of resources using the same steps, taking no extra time. In the remainder of this book, you'll learn how to reuse your ARM templates to improve the speed of deployments.

Another benefit of deploying resources using ARM templates is that ARM allows you to view a list of all your recent deployments and how they went. The next section discusses monitoring deployments that way.

2.4   *Monitoring template deployments*

In the previous section, you used the Azure portal for deploying an ARM template, which provides good visibility into how your deployment is going. When you deploy using other means, progress reports might be missing or unclear, or might not provide enough information for troubleshooting. For this reason, monitoring the progress of deployments is one reason you might keep returning to the Azure portal, even when practicing IaC.

You can use the list of deployments in the Azure portal to monitor the status of your running or previously run deployments. You can find this list by navigating to any resource group in the portal and selecting the Deployments blade on the left (see figure 2.5).

The Deployment blade shows your most recent 800 deployments. Clicking the name of any deployment allows you to drill down to a list of all resources created, updated, or deleted. And if your deployment failed, this overview also displays any errors encountered, grouped by the resources involved.

Now that you have written and deployed a template once, it is time to pick up the pace a bit and play with deploying pre-existing templates. In the next section, you'll learn how to find example templates on the Microsoft Docs website and deploy them directly to your Azure environment.

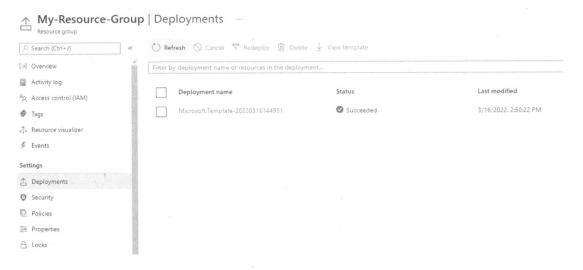

Figure 2.5 **For each resource group, recent deployments are listed in the Deployments blade.**

2.5   *Finding example templates*

If you're working with VS Code and the ARM Tools extension, writing ARM templates from scratch will becomes easier over time. Still, it might be helpful to start out by editing examples to fit your own needs, instead of writing templates from scratch.

The Microsoft Docs website (https://docs.microsoft.com/azure/templates) contains full documentation of all the resources you can describe using IaC. This is a good source of documentation and examples. Another source of many examples is the Azure Quickstart Templates GitHub repository at https://github.com/Azure/azure-quickstart-templates. Microsoft owns this repository and continuously updates it with new and updated examples. The repository contains hundreds of folders, each detailing a single example, as shown in figure 2.6.

Every example is in a separate folder with a descriptive name, and each folder contains a file called azuredeploy.json that contains the ARM template itself. Each example also contains a description and provides a button to deploy it directly to Azure. Clicking this button sets up a new Template Deployment, as you did when working along with section 2.3.

Each example also features a Visualize button, which opens a visualization of the template to show the Azure resources that are in the template.

The next section explores an extra benefit of IaC: other tools that can also parse and work with ARM templates.

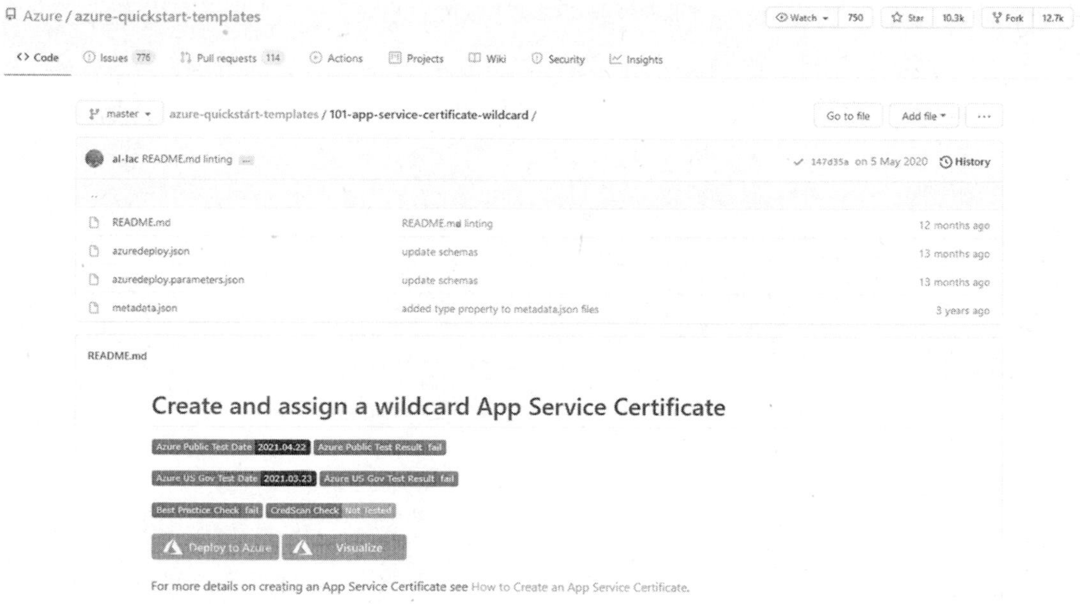

Figure 2.6 Quickstart ARM templates on GitHub

2.6 *Visualizing templates*

You have created and deployed your first ARM template, and while you have only deployed a single resource yourself, you have probably already speculated that ARM templates can rapidly increase in size. And yes, ARM templates for real-world Azure environments can be hundreds or even thousands of lines of JSON long. Visualizing your ARM template can help you get a better overview of its content and can remove the need to draw these images manually as part of your documentation efforts.

The Azure portal provides an easy way to visualize the content of a resource group. Navigate to the resource group and click Resource Visualizer to get an overview of the contents of your resource group (see figure 2.7). This doesn't, however, visualize your template. If you want to visualize an ARM template, you can use the ARMVIZ website.

ARMVIZ is an easy-to-use online tool for visualizing ARM templates. It is also the tool used by Microsoft itself for its examples on GitHub. To use ARMVIZ to visualize your own ARM templates, navigate to http://armviz.io to start the tool. By default, a graphic model of a random template is generated, as shown in figure 2.8. Here you see each resource's name, an icon representing the resource's type, and lines representing the dependencies between resources.

If you click the view-source button (marked with an arrow in figure 2.8), you can see the ARM template that is the diagram's source. The template is opened in an online editor where you can edit the template in place or paste in any template of

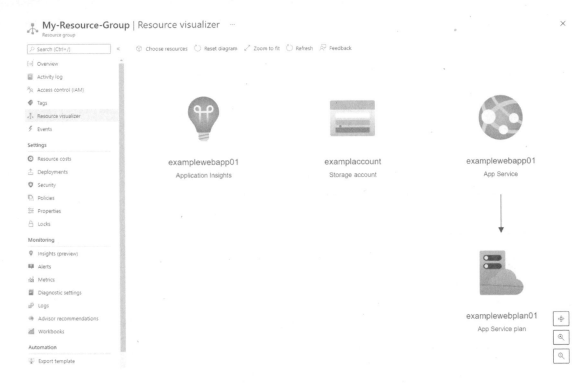

Figure 2.7   Visualizing the content of a resource group

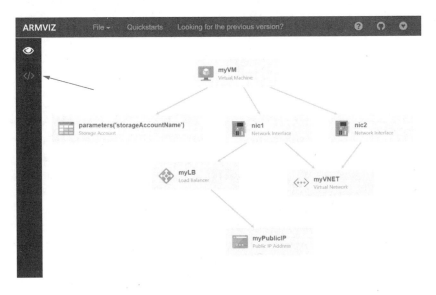

Figure 2.8   A visual representation of an ARM template

your own. Using the other button on the left (the eye button), you can switch back to the visual representation.

The ARM Template Viewer, a VS Code extension written by Ben Coleman, does the same thing within your VS Code environment. Once it's installed, the extension appears as an eye icon in the upper-right corner of VS Code when you open an ARM template file. When you click the eye icon, the screen changes into a split view, and any change you make to the ARM template is immediately reflected in the visual representation.

Summary

- ARM templates are written as JSON documents.
- VS Code is a text editor, and an extension is available that supports writing ARM templates.
- ARM templates may be composed largely of the `resources` property, which is an array that specifies any number of resources within a single template.
- Templates can be deployed manually by using the Azure portal.
- During deployment, the Azure Resource Manager validates the template, including structure, syntax, names, properties, and more.
- Azure portal allows you to monitor the progress of your deployments.
- It can be helpful to edit existing ARM templates when you're starting to learn to write them. The Azure Quickstart Templates GitHub repository is a good source of quality examples.
- Azure portal provides a resource visualizer that provides a visual representation of your resource group, so you can see a visual representation of the resources described in a resource group.

Part 2

Taking it up a notch

In this part of the book, we'll explain more advanced scenarios and possibilities when working with ARM templates. The Bicep domain-specific language is introduced, which makes writing IaC from scratch and maintaining existing templates a lot easier. We'll introduce some practices, like deploying IaC using continuous delivery pipelines, and you'll build your confidence on deployments with testing templates.

Writing ARM templates

This chapter covers

- The structure of an ARM template
- Declaring resources and child resources
- Working with parameters and variables
- Returning outputs
- Using and writing functions

In chapter 2 you were introduced to a simple ARM template, and you saw how to deploy it. This chapter goes into much more depth on ARM templates, exploring various techniques and features. While chapter 2 showed how to create your first template and briefly introduced an ARM template layout, this chapter covers declaring resources, parameters, variables, functions, and output sections in depth.

To help illustrate these topics, you'll create an ARM template over the course of the chapter. This infrastructure hosts an API, which is the backend for a web shop. It can accept, process, and store orders. The API saves all orders in a SQL database and generates a PDF file, which is sent to the customer via email. These PDF files are also stored in an Azure storage account for later use. The API itself runs on an Azure App Service and uses Key Vault as a secret store. Finally, we'll throw Application Insights into the mix, which allows for monitoring the API. Figure 3.1 provides a visualization of this infrastructure.

35

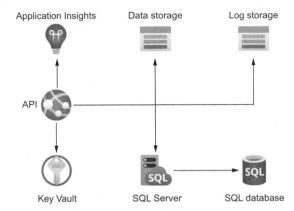

Figure 3.1   A simple application architecture

While reading this chapter, you'll create a template with these components one by one. As ARM templates can become quite lengthy, the ever-growing template will not be repeated throughout the chapter, and some examples will not be shown in their full length.

For your reference, the complete template and templates for each section are available on GitHub at https://github.com/AzureIaCBook/book-templates/tree/main/Chapter_03. The discussion of each code listing will identify the name of the file in source control, so you can easily find it. Not all code snippets in this chapter will be in the complete template. Sometimes we'll discuss more than one way to complete a particular task, and only one of those options will be used in the final template. The complete template is named template.json, and it can be found here: https://github.com/AzureIaCBook/book-templates/blob/main/Chapter_03/template.json. When you deploy this template, or any of the others, be sure to change the names of the Azure resources. Most of them need to be globally unique.

3.1   *Resources*

Without a doubt, the most important part of an ARM template is the resources section. It's an array that allows you to define one or more resources. Three elements must be declared for every resource: name, type, and apiVersion. A fourth property, location, is required on most resources. There also are a few non-required elements that you can use on every resource. Some of the more commonly used ones are properties, dependsOn, condition, tags, and copy—chapter 5 covers these in detail. Besides the properties that are valid on every resource, most resources also have additional required or optional elements, which are different for each resource type.

The required fields were briefly introduced in chapter 2, but let's explore them in more detail now:

- name—Every Azure resource must have a name, and the naming rules are different for every type of resource. The name for a storage account, for example, is limited in length (3–24 characters) and can only include lowercase letters and numbers. The name for a SQL Server is permitted to be 63 characters long and may contain hyphens in addition to letters and numbers. A full list of all resources and their naming limitations is available in Microsoft's "Naming rules and restrictions for Azure resources" article (http://mng.bz/GEWR). For child resources, the format of the name is different.

- `type`—This property specifies the type of resource you want to create. The type is a combination of the resource provider's namespace and the resource type. An example of that is `Microsoft.Sql/servers`, in which `Microsoft.Sql` is the namespace and `servers` the resource type. For child resources, the type format is a little different—more on that in a bit.

- `apiVersion`—This property specifies which version of the resource type you want to use. It comes in the format of a date, such as `2019-06-01`. The version sometimes has a postfix to let you know that the version is in preview and might change. An example of that would be `2019-06-01-preview`. Because this property is required, Microsoft can change a resource type's properties without breaking your existing ARM templates. When you use the Visual Studio Code extension and have specified a recent schema version, the editor shows you the available versions.

- `location`—Using this property, you can dictate in which Azure region your resource should be deployed. Examples are `West Europe` or `East US`. You would usually place resources that interact with each other in the same region, as that gives the best performance and lowest costs. In chapter 2 you learned that resources are often deployed into a resource group. When you create a group, you also assign a location. Although the group you deploy a resource in will already have a location defined, you still need to specify that on the resource as well. It can be the same location as on the resource group, but it may be another one.

The following listing (03-01-00.json in the book's Chapter_03 GitHub folder) shows how you can combine all this information to create your first resource in the infrastructure described in the chapter introduction, the SQL Server, using a template.

Listing 3.1 A template deploying a SQL Server

```
{
    "$schema": "https://schema.management.azure.com/schemas/
        ➥ 2019-04-01/deploymentTemplate.json#",
    "contentVersion": "1.0.0.0",
    "resources": [
        {
            "type": "Microsoft.Sql/servers",
            "name": "MyFirstSQLServer",
            "apiVersion": "2019-06-01-preview",
            "location": "West Europe",
            "properties": {
                "administratorLogin": "administrator",
                "administratorLoginPassword": "mysecretpassword"
```

```
            }
        }
    ]
}
```

In the preceding listing, you can see the four mandatory fields, `type`, `name`, `api-Version`, and `location`. It also contains a non-required property named `properties`. The value of this property is of type `object`. In turn, this object has two properties that specify the `administratorLogin` and `administratorLoginPassword` for this server. In this example, the password was added in plain text. You would not do that in a real-world scenario, and you will learn how to address this later on.

3.1.1 *Child resources*

Some resources cannot exist without the context of another resource. The SQL database you're going to deploy on the SQL Server created in the previous template is such a resource: it cannot exist outside of a SQL Server. This is called a parent-child relationship between resources. Child resources are defined in one of two ways:

- Child resources are nested within the parent resource.
- Child resources are declared outside of the parent, directly in the `resources` array.

Depending on how you want to structure your templates, you can choose one approach over the other. It can be useful to define a child within the parent to group the resources and collapse them as a whole. You can't do that, however, if the parent is not defined in the same template. Beyond this limitation, which alternative you choose is a matter of personal preference. This choice will also influence how you name child resources, as is shown in the following examples. The following listing (03-01-01-child-outside-parent.json) shows an example of deploying a child resource *outside* of the parent.

> **Listing 3.2 Deploying a child outside of its parent's scope**

```
"resources": [
    {
        "type": "Microsoft.Sql/servers",
        "name": "MyFirstSQLServer",
        ...
    },
    {
        "type": "Microsoft.Sql/servers/databases",
        "name": "MyFirstSQLServer/SQLDatabase",
        ...
    }
]
```

The preceding listing shows the creation of a SQL Server and a database deployed on that server. This relationship can be seen in the `type` and `name` of the child resource, which follow this format:

```
"type": "{resource-provider-namespace}/{parent-resource-type}/
    {child-resource-type}",
"name": "{parent-resource-name}/{child-resource-name}"
```

In this example, the child's name is a combination of its own name and the name of the server, the parent, it resides on: MyFirstSQLServer/SQLDatabase. Its type is defined as Microsoft.Sql/servers/databases.

By contrast, the next listing (03-01-01-child-inside-parent.json) shows an example of how to define a child resource *within* the scope of a parent using the resources array on the parent.

Listing 3.3 Deploying a child within its parent's scope

```
"resources": [
    {
        "type": "Microsoft.Sql/servers",
        "name": "MyFirstSQLServer",
        ...
        "resources": [
            "type": "databases",
            "name": "SQLDatabase",
            ...
        ]
    }
]
```

Like listing 3.2, this listing shows how to create a SQL Server and a database deployed on that server. Since the resources property is an array, you can add more than one resource. The name and type of the child resource follow this format:

```
"type": "{child-resource-type}",
"name": "{child-resource-name}"
```

Although you get to specify databases as the child's type, the full type is Microsoft .Sql/servers/databases. You don't have to provide Microsoft.Sql/servers because it's assumed from the parent resource.

You probably noticed a few hardcoded property values in the preceding examples. In a real-world deployment, you would likely want to change these values for each environment you deploy the template to. For example, you should never use the same SQL Server password on test and production. Parameters in ARM templates allow you to get those values as input while deploying the template.

3.2 *Parameters*

Parameters are used to make a single template applicable to more than one situation. For example, suppose you have a good template that is ready for reuse between test and production environments, but there are some differences between these environments, like resource names. To capture the differences between these environments, you can use parameters and then provide values for them when you deploy your template.

Let's first discuss the various types of parameters and how you can use them in your templates. Then you will learn how to use them while deploying your templates.

3.2.1 *Parameter types*

The following example shows the simplest way to define a parameter:

```
"parameters": {
    "sqlServerName": {
        "type": "string"
    }
}
```

This snippet defines the parameter sqlServerName for the name of a SQL Server, and it has string set as its data type. You can add up to 256 parameters to a template.

When defining a parameter, you always must specify its data type. Within ARM templates, the following types are available:

- string
- int
- bool
- array
- object
- secureString
- secureObject

The following parameters section contains an example of the first three types and introduces the defaultValue property.

```
"parameters": {
    "stringParameter": {
        "type": "string",
        "defaultValue": "option 1"
    },
    "intParameter": {
        "type": "int",
        "defaultValue": 1
    },
    "boolParameter": {
        "type": "bool",
        "defaultValue": true
    }
}
```

This snippet shows you the string, int, and bool types, which are the most straightforward data types. They allow you to provide text, a number, or a true or false value. Also new in this example is the defaultValue property, which allows you to make a parameter optional and to specify a value to be used when no value is provided at the time of deployment. If you don't add a default value and don't provide a value at deploy time, you will receive an error. You will shortly see how to provide values for the parameters while deploying your template.

You can use a parameter when declaring a resource by using the `parameters()` function. It's one of the many functions you'll use while writing templates—section 3.5 of this chapter is dedicated to functions. For now, know that the `parameters()` function accepts the name of a parameter as input.

Let's put all you have learned so far into a full ARM template (03-02-00.json) as shown in the following listing.

Listing 3.4   Using parameters in a template

```
{
    "$schema": "https://schema.management.azure.com/schemas/
        ➥ 2019-04-01/deploymentTemplate.json#",
    "contentVersion": "1.0.0.0",
    "parameters": {                        ◁─── Parameters defined in
        "name": {                               the parameters section
            "type": "string"                    of a template
        },
        "sqlServerUsername": {
            "type": "string"
        },
        "sqlServerPassword": {
            "type": "securestring"
        }
    },
    "resources": [                              A parameter is used
        {                                       via the parameters()
            "type": "Microsoft.Sql/servers",    function.
            "name": "[parameters('name')]",   ◁─
            "apiVersion": "2019-06-01-preview",
            "location": "[resourceGroup().location]",
            "properties": {
                "administratorLogin": "[parameters('sqlServerUsername')]",
                "administratorLoginPassword":
                    ➥ "[parameters('sqlServerPassword')]"
            }
        }
    ]
}
```

In this example, all the hardcoded values are replaced either with a parameter or, in the case of the location, with a function call. Two parameters of type `string` were added: the name of the SQL Server and the username. The third parameter, of type `secureString`, is used for the SQL Server password. The `secureString` type is a specialized version of the `string` type. As the name hints, it is used for setting secrets like passwords or tokens. For secure data types, the Azure Resource Manager makes sure that the value is not stored and is not retrievable from tools, logs, or the Azure portal.

Within the `resources` section of this template, the SQL Server is defined and parameters are used to fill its properties. For the `location` property, the `resource-Group()` function is used. Remember that a resource group also has a location defined, and this is a way to reuse that value on your resource instead of having to declare it again. You will learn more about functions in a bit.

PARAMETERS OF TYPE ARRAY

Parameters of type `array` allow you to specify not one, but a list of values. A list of values can be useful when you want to create more than one resource of the same type. If you recall from figure 3.1, running the backend API involves two storage accounts: one to store application data, like the generated PDF files, and the other to store application logs. You could create an array parameter to fetch the names for those storage accounts.

```
"parameters": {
    "storageAccountNames": {
        "type": "array",
        "defaultValue": [
            "datastorage",
            "logstorage"
        ]
    }
}
```

This `parameters` section shows the `array` type parameter, and it has names for both storage accounts defined in the `defaultValue` property. An important thing to note here is that the type of the values in the array is not specified. In theory, you can mix different types in the array, but this is never done in practice.

You can address an array using the `[]` notation, which you might know from other languages or tools. You can also find an example in the following listing (03-02-01.json).

Listing 3.5   Using the `array` parameter type

```
{
    "$schema": "https://schema.management.azure.com/schemas/
        ➥ 2019-04-01/deploymentTemplate.json#",
    "contentVersion": "1.0.0.0",
    "parameters": {
        "storageAccountNames": {
            "type": "array",
            "defaultValue": [
                "datastorage",
                "logstorage"
            ]
        }
    },
    "resources": [
        {
            "type": "Microsoft.Storage/storageAccounts",
```

```
            "name": "[parameters('storageAccountNames')[0]]",
            "sku": {
                "name": "Standard_GRS"
            },
            "kind": "StorageV2",
            "apiVersion": "2019-04-01",
            "location": "West Europe"
        }
    ]
}
```

This snippet defines a storage account and uses the array's first element, [0], as the resource's name. In real-world scenarios, arrays are often combined with loops. Chapter 5 will discuss in detail how to loop over arrays.

PARAMETERS OF TYPE OBJECT

The object data type allows for more complex input. An array allows you to specify a list of values, but an object allows you to specify a list of key/value pairs. You can use these to pass a partial configuration as a parameter, such as for a storage account.

For the SQL database in our example, you'll need to define more properties on it than just the mandatory properties. A SQL database has a mandatory sku. The sku's name defines what type of compute and features you get, and the capacity property specifies the performance of the database. A parameter of type object allows the template user to specify these properties as a single value. The following snippet shows how you could do this.

```
"parameters": {
    "SQLDatabase": {
        "type": "object",
        "defaultValue": {
            "name": "SQLDatabase",
            "sku": {
                "name": "Basic",
                "capacity": 5
            }
        }
    }
}
```

This example shows how parameters of type object are declared, together with a defaultValue that shows an example value. It has a top-level property name and a top-level property sku. The sku property is another object that contains two properties: the name and capacity. Using parameters of type object allows for more complex inputs in templates, instead of having a separate parameter for each necessary value.

Addressing an item in the object is done using the dot operator, shown in bold in the following listing (03-02-02.json).

Listing 3.6 Using the `object` parameter type

```json
{
    "$schema": "https://schema.management.azure.com/schemas/
        ➥ 2019-04-01/deploymentTemplate.json#",
    "contentVersion": "1.0.0.0",
    "parameters": {
        "SQLDatabase": {
            "type": "object",
            "defaultValue": {
                "name": "SQLDatabase",
                "sku": {
                    "name": "Basic",
                    "capacity": 5
                }
            }
        }
    },
    "resources": [
        {
            "type": "Microsoft.Sql/servers/databases",
            "apiVersion": "2017-10-01-preview",
            "name": "[concat('MyFirstSQLServer/',
                ➥ parameters('SQLDatabase').name)]",
            "location": "West Europe",
            "sku": {
                "name": "[parameters('SQLDatabase').sku.name]",
                "capacity": "[parameters('SQLDatabase').sku.capacity]"
            },
            "properties": {
                "collation": "SQL_Latin1_General_CP1_CI_AS",
                "maxSizeBytes": 2147483648
            }
        }
    ]
}
```

This template shows the creation of a SQL database. It uses a `string` parameter for the name and the sku is an `object` parameter. In the name property for the database, you see the `concat()` function being used. Remember from section 3.1.1 on child resources that the name of a child resource, when deployed outside the scope of the parent, should include the name of the parent. In this example, that name is created by concatenating the name of the parent with that of this child. You will learn more about functions in section 3.5. The `name` in the `sku` shows how you can address a nested property in an object.

Looking closely, you can also see that the sku object's names (in the parameters value) are identical to the ones expected by the template. Knowing this, you could also write the same template as follows.

```json
"resources": [
    {
        "type": "Microsoft.Sql/servers/databases",
```

```
        "apiVersion": "2017-10-01-preview",
        "name": "[concat('MyFirstSQLServer/',
            ➡ parameters('SQLDatabase').name)]",
        "location": "West Europe",
        "sku": "[parameters('SQLDatabase').sku]",
        "properties": {
            "collation": "SQL_Latin1_General_CP1_CI_AS",
            "maxSizeBytes": 2147483648
        }
    }
]
```

Using this approach, you get to assign a parameter of type object (or a subset of that) to an object property, making the template smaller and therefore more readable and easier to maintain.

Just as there is a secureString data type to match the string type, there is also a secureObject data type to match the object type. As with the secureString type, the value of any secureObject is hidden in any logs and output.

3.2.2   *Limiting and describing parameter values*

Using the allowedValues property, you can limit the values that are valid for a parameter. For example, a SQL Server resource type can specify whether it should be reachable over its public IP address. You can specify this using the publicNetworkAccess property, which only accepts two possible values. This is a perfect example of a property with a fixed set of allowed values.

When a user tries to deploy a template and specify a value that is not in the allowedValues list, they will encounter an error. When working with tools like Visual Studio Code, they will see the allowed values to help them choose a valid value while addressing the template.

The following snippet shows how to use allowedValues.

```
"parameters": {
    "publicNetworkAccess": {
        "type": "string",
        "allowedValues": [
            "Enabled",
            "Disabled"
        ],
        "defaultValue": "Enabled"
    }
}
```

This snippet shows you a string parameter that only allows two specific values as its input, as specified in the allowedValues property: Enabled or Disabled.

Another useful property for defining parameters is the description property in the metadata object.

```
"parameters": {
    "storageSKU": {
```

```
            "type": "string",
            "metadata": {
                "description": "The type of
                ➡ replication to use for the storage account."
            }
        }
    }
}
```

As the name implies, the description property allows you to describe your parameter. The value for this property is used in tooling to help the user deploy the template.

3.2.3   *Specifying parameter values*

When you deploy your template, you'll need to specify values for each parameter that does not have a default value. There are a few ways to do that:

- Inline parameters
- Parameter files
- Fetching parameters from Key Vault

The next three subsections will discuss these options.

USING INLINE PARAMETERS

To pass inline parameters, provide the names of the parameter while using the New-AzResourceGroupDeployment command.

Imagine you have the following template to create a storage account (03-02-04.json).

Listing 3.7   An ARM template that requires a parameter

```
{
    "$schema": "https://schema.management.azure.com/schemas/
        ➡ 2019-04-01/deploymentTemplate.json#",
    "contentVersion": "1.0.0.0",
    "parameters": {
        "storageSKU": {
            "type": "string",
            "allowedValues": [
                "Standard_LRS",
                "Standard_GRS"
            ]
        }
    },
    "resources": [
        {
            "type": "Microsoft.Storage/storageAccounts",
            "apiVersion": "2021-04-01",
            "name": "MyStorageAccount",
            "kind": "StorageV2",
            "location": "West Europe",
            "sku": {
                "name": "[parameters('storageSKU')]"
            }
        }
```

```
        ]
    }
```

This template has one parameter called `storageSKU`. A deployment using PowerShell that specifies this parameter is shown in the following example. (Section 4.2.2 will go deeper into different deployment methods like PowerShell, the Azure CLI, and others.)

```
New-AzResourceGroupDeployment -Name ExampleDeployment `
    -ResourceGroupName ExampleResourceGroup `
    -TemplateFile 03-02-04.json `
    -storageSKU "Standard_LRS"
```

This example uses the `New-AzResourceGroupDeployment` PowerShell cmdlet to deploy the template. You get to specify a name and resource group for the deployment, to identify it uniquely and to specify its destination. Using the `-TemplateFile`, you specify which template to deploy. For each parameter you want to pass in, you add another parameter to the command, like `-storageSKU "Standard_LRS"` in this example.

SPECIFYING PARAMETER VALUES IN A PARAMETER FILE

Often you'll need to use parameters to specify values at runtime for different environments, like test and production. But specifying all the values every time you deploy isn't very convenient, and this is why parameter files exist. Parameter files allow you to specify and store parameters in a file, such as one for each environment.

Let's look again at the storage account template example from the previous section. You could create the following test and production parameter files (03-02-05 .parameters.test.json and 03-02-05.parameters.prod.json) to specify the parameters for each environment.

Listing 3.8 Example parameters.test.json file

```
{
    "$schema": "https://schema.management.azure.com/schemas/
        ⇒ 2015-01-01/deploymentParameters.json#",
    "contentVersion": "1.0.0.0",
    "parameters": {
        "storageSKU": {
            "value": "Standard_LRS"
        }
    }
}
```

For the test environment, using `Standard_LRS` for the SKU is good enough. Standard locally redundant storage (`Standard_LRS`) is the cheapest level of redundancy in Azure, and it ensures that all storage account data is copied three times within the same Azure region. As this is for a test environment, cost is the main driver for our choices here.

A similar file, but with a different value, is created for production as shown in the following listing.

```
{
    "$schema": "https://schema.management.azure.com/schemas/
       ➥ 2015-01-01/deploymentParameters.json#",
    "contentVersion": "1.0.0.0",
    "parameters": {
        "storageSKU": {
            "value": "Standard_GRS"
        }
    }
}
```

In the production environment, you want to be a little more resilient, so you can choose to use Standard_GRS as its SKU. With Standard geo-redundant storage (Standard_GRS), the storage account data is copied six times: three times in one region and three times in another region.

When deploying the template, you can specify which parameter file to use. If you're using PowerShell, the command would be as follows:

```
New-AzResourceGroupDeployment -Name ExampleDeployment `
  -ResourceGroupName ExampleResourceGroup `
  -TemplateFile 03-02-04.json `
  -TemplateParameterFile parameters.test.json
```

This example uses the New-AzResourceGroupDeployment PowerShell cmdlet to deploy the template. By using the -TemplateFile and -TemplateParameterFile parameters, you specify which template and parameter file to deploy.

You can also combine a parameter file and the inline parameters option in a single deployment. That would allow you to override a parameter specified in a parameters file. Take a look at the following example:

```
New-AzResourceGroupDeployment -Name ExampleDeployment `
  -ResourceGroupName ExampleResourceGroup `
  -TemplateFile 03-02-04.json `
  -TemplateParameterFile parameters.test.json `
  -storageSKU "Standard_GRS"
```

This example uses the same parameters file while deploying the storage account, but a value is also passed in for the storageSKU parameter. That takes precedence over the value in the parameters file, so the actual value in this example will be Standard_GRS instead of Standard_LRS as specified in the parameters file.

The next chapter will go into much more detail on deploying ARM templates and parameter files.

FETCHING PARAMETERS FROM A KEY VAULT

In the first example in this chapter, where a SQL Server was created, a password for the server administrator was hardcoded. You would never do that in the real world.

One way to use a parameter in that situation would be to use the `secureString` data type and set the value when deploying the template. In this chapter's scenario, however, you could also use Key Vault.

Azure Key Vault is a service that securely stores and accesses certificates, connection strings, passwords, and other secrets. Within a parameter file, you can reference secrets in that vault for use during ARM template deployment. That way, you don't have to provide secrets while deploying your templates—they are resolved from Key Vault at runtime. The following snippet shows how to do this.

```
"parameters": {
    "adminPassword": {
        "reference": {
            "keyVault": {
                "id": "/subscriptions/<subscription-id>/resourceGroups/
                    <rg-name>/providers/Microsoft.KeyVault/vaults/<vault-name>"
            },
            "secretName": "ExamplePassword"
        }
    }
}
```

Referencing a secret from Key Vault in a parameter file is done by specifying a `reference` property on the parameter, and not the `value` property you have seen before. The value for `reference` is another object that specifies the resource ID of the vault and the name of the secret in the vault using `secretName`.

> **Using functions in a parameter file**
>
> When referencing Key Vault from a parameter file, you cannot use functions like `resourceId()`. Not being able to use functions means that you must always specify the entire resource ID and cannot resolve it at runtime. That is not ideal, since it makes the template hard to reuse, and some might consider the resource ID of the Key Vault a secret itself. Specifically for a SQL Server, it would be better to use Azure Active Directory authentication, as discussed in chapter 5.

Just referencing secrets in a Key Vault and a secret in your parameter file, like the preceding one is not enough. You also need to make sure that the Azure Resource Manager can access the secret. There are two things you must set up for this to work.

First, you need to allow ARM to access the secrets while deploying. The following snippet shows how to create the Key Vault in a template that has `enabledForTemplate-Deployment` set to `true`.

```
"resources": [
    {
        "type": "Microsoft.KeyVault/vaults",
        "apiVersion": "2019-09-01",
        "name": "[parameters('keyVaultName')]",
```

```
        "location": "[resourceGroup().location]",
        "properties": {
            "sku": {
                "family": "A",
                "name": "standard"
            },
            "tenantId": "[subscription().tenantId]",
            "enabledForTemplateDeployment": true
        }
    }
]
```

In this snippet, you can find the `enabledForTemplateDeployment` property in the Key Vault `properties` object. Setting it to `true` allows you to access this vault during an ARM template deployment.

Second, the identity that is deploying the template needs to have access to the Key Vault that is referenced. This identity is your account when you are deploying from your local computer. When you're using another tool to deploy your template, the identity used with that tool needs these permissions. In chapter 8, for example, you will learn how to use Azure DevOps to deploy your templates. You will then also learn how to create and properly configure an identity for Azure DevOps.

Parameters allow you to get input from the outside world and make your templates more reusable, but you'll also need a way to store repetitive values or complex expressions. Variables are the tool for this job, so let's discuss those next.

3.3 *Variables*

Within ARM templates, variables define a value once and allow you to reuse it multiple times throughout the template. They are different from parameters in that parameter values can be set when starting a deployment, whereas variable values cannot be changed without editing the template. Parameters are for deploy-time input, whereas variables allow you to store values that you use multiple times within your template.

Just as with parameters, you define variables in a separate section of a template. The Azure Resource Manager resolves the variables and replaces each usage before the deployment starts. The value of a variable must match one of the data types we mentioned when discussing parameters. You don't have to specify the data type yourself; it is automatically inferred.

The following snippet shows the definition of a variable:

```
"variables": {
    "storageName": "myStorageAccount"
}
```

This example shows a variable of type `string` being used as the name of a storage account.

Using a variable in your templates is like using a parameter, as shown in the following listing (03-03-00.json).

```
{
    "$schema": "https://schema.management.azure.com/schemas/
        ➥ 2019-04-01/deploymentTemplate.json#",
    "contentVersion": "1.0.0.0",
    "variables": {
        "storageName": "myStorageAccount"
    },
    "resources": [
        {
            "type": "Microsoft.Storage/storageAccounts",
            "name": "[variables('storageName')]",
            "sku": {
                "name": "Standard_GRS"
            },
            "kind": "StorageV2",
            "apiVersion": "2019-04-01",
            "location": "West Europe"
        }
    ]
}
```

In this example, the storageName variable's value is used as the storage account's name by fetching it using the variables() function.

Just as with parameters, you can handle more complex scenarios using objects and arrays. In the section on parameters, you saw how to use parameter files to set specific values for a test or production environment. You can do something similar using variables as shown in the following template.

```
{
    "$schema": "https://schema.management.azure.com/schemas/
        ➥ 2019-04-01/deploymentTemplate.json#",
    "contentVersion": "1.0.0.0",
    "parameters": {
        "environmentName": {
            "type": "string",
            "allowedValues": [
                "test",
                "prod"
            ]
        }
    },
    "variables": {
        "storageSettings": {
            "test": {
                "sku": {
                    "name": "Standard_LRS"
                }
            },
            "prod": {
                "sku": {
```

```
                    "name": "Standard_GRS"
                }
            }
        }
    }
}
```

In the preceding example, a parameter is defined for the name of the environment the template is currently deploying to. Then a variable is defined to hold both the test and production settings used for creating a storage account. These can now be used in the remainder of the template by using the following expression:

```
"[variables('storageSettings')[parameters('environmentName')].sku]"
```

The variable used in the preceding expression is an array of objects. The `parameters()` function is used to point to a specific index in that array and fetch an environment setting. Since the returned value is an object, it is possible to use dot notation to get to the `sku` object (or to fetch its name using `sku.name` if you wanted to).

Now that you know how to use parameters and variables, it's time to see how you can return values from ARM template deployments using outputs.

3.4   *Outputs*

No matter what tool you use to deploy your template, you may find yourself wanting to retrieve a value from the deployment afterward. Maybe you need the name of a resource you just created or the fully qualified domain name (FQDN) to SQL Server in the next step of your deployment pipeline. The `outputs` section in the template is where you get to define such outputs. This section itself is of type `object`. The following snippet shows an example.

```
"outputs": {
    "sqlServerFQDN": {
        "type": "string",
        "value": "[reference('SqlServer').fullyQualifiedDomainName]"
    }
}
```

This example returns the FQDN for a SQL Server. The name for the returned value is specified as `sqlServerFQDN` and it's of type `string`, as specified in the `type` property. Its value is determined by using the `reference()` function, which accepts the name of a resource as input and returns its properties. In this case, the returned value is an object, and you can use dot notation to get to the needed property.

The following listing (03-04-00.json) shows a complete template that contains the same example output.

```
{
    "$schema": "https:/ /schema.management.azure.com/schemas/
        ➡ 2019-04-01/deploymentTemplate.json#",
    "contentVersion": "1.0.0.0",
    "resources": [
        {
            "type": "Microsoft.Sql/servers",
            "kind": "v12.0",
            "name": "bookexampledatabase",
            "apiVersion": "2015-05-01-preview",
            "location": "West Europe",
            "properties": {
                "administratorLogin": "bookexampledatabase",
                "administratorLoginPassword": "1234@demo22",
                "version": "12.0"
            }
        }
    ],
    "outputs": {
        "sqlServerFQDN": {
            "type": "string",
            "value":
                ➡ "[reference('bookexampledatabase').fullyQualifiedDomainName]"
        }
    }
}
```

The preceding listing deploys a SQL Server, as you have seen before. What's new here is that it also returns its FQDN as output. You can deploy this template using, for example, the Azure CLI:

```
az deployment group create \
  --name ExampleDeploymentDatabase \
  --resource-group BookExampleGroup \
  --template-file SQLServer.json \
  --query properties.outputs.sqlServerFQDN.value
```

Most names used for switches in this statement, like `--name` or `--resource-group`, are slightly different in naming but identical in usage to the ones you saw in the previous PowerShell example.

The preceding command includes the `--query` switch, which allows you to grab one specific property from the template deployment's output. It does that by executing what is called a JMESPath query. You can find more about that in Microsoft's article titled "How to query Azure CLI command output using a JMESPath query": (http://mng.bz/z4MX). In this example, the output is

```
"bookexampledatabase.database.windows.net"
```

You can always grab output from previous deployments using the `az deployment group show` command, as shown next.

```
az deployment group show \
  -n ExampleDeploymentDatabase \
  -g BookExampleGroup \
  --query properties.outputs.sqlServerFQDN.value
```

Executing the preceding snippet produces output similar to the first example. Notice that you can also use the short notation for switches like resource group and name, as in this example. For example, --name is the same as -n, and --resource-group is the same as -g. You can find all the available switches and their short notations in the Microsoft documentation for the Azure CLI (http://mng.bz/2nza). Which you use is often a personal preference. The shorter version might be easier to read at first, since the command is shorter, but it might be more confusing when you come back to the code after a while.

> **Don't use** `secureString` **or** `secureObject` **as output**
>
> While it is technically possible to output values of type `secureString` or `secure-Object`, it is not useful. The values for these types are removed from logs and deployment results, which means that the return values are always empty.

Throughout the examples so far, you have seen the use of some functions like `parameters()`, `reference()`, and `resourceGroup().location`. Now it is time to explore functions in more depth.

3.5   *Functions*

To help build templates more quickly and make them more expressive and reusable, many built-in functions are at your disposal. And even if there isn't a built-in function for your specific scenario, you can always write one of your own. The use of functions introduces logic into your templates and they are used in expressions.

3.5.1   *Expressions*

By using functions, either built-in or user-defined ones, you can create expressions to extend the default JSON language in ARM templates. Expressions start with an opening square bracket, [, end with a closing square bracket,], and can return a `string`, `int`, `bool`, `array`, or `object`. You've already seen quite a few examples in the previous code snippets, but here is another example that deploys a storage account.

```
"resources": [
    {
        "type": "Microsoft.Storage/storageAccounts",          An expression using
        "name": "[parameters('storageName')]",                the parameters()
            ...                                                function
        "location": "[resourceGroup().location]"          An expression using the
    }                                                      resourceGroup() function,
]                                                          returning an object
```

As with almost any other programming language, function calls are formatted as `functionName(arg1,arg2,arg3)`. In this example, the `parameters()` function is used with `storageName` as the argument to retrieve the value for that parameter. As you can see, string values are passed in using single quotes. In the `location` property, you can see another expression. Here the `resourceGroup()` function returns an object, and you can use dot notation to get the value of any of its properties.

Sometimes you'll find yourself wanting to assign a `null` value to a property based on a condition, and nothing otherwise. Assigning a `null` makes sure that ARM ignores the property while deploying your template. By using the `json()` function, you can assign `null` values. Consider the following example, which creates a virtual network subnet that may or may not get a routing table assigned, depending on whether it has been specified in a parameter.

Listing 3.12 Assigning `null` values inline

```
{
    "$schema": "https://schema.management.azure.com/schemas/
        ➥ 2019-04-01/deploymentTemplate.json#",
    "contentVersion": "1.0.0.0",
    "parameters": {
        "subnet": {
            "type": "object"
        }
    },
    "resources": [
        {
            "type": "Microsoft.Network/virtualNetworks/subnets",
            "location": "West Europe",
            "apiVersion": "2020-05-01",
            "name": "[parameters('subnet').name]",
            "properties": {
                "addressPrefix": "[parameters('subnet').addressPrefix]",
                "routeTable":
                    ➥ "[if(contains(parameters('subnet'), 'routeTable'),
                    ➥ json(concat('{\"id\": \"',
                    ➥ resourceId('Microsoft.Network/routeTables',
                    ➥ parameters('subnet').routeTable.name), '\"}')),
                    ➥ json('null'))]"        ◁─── Assigning the
            }                                      null value using
        }                                          json('null')
    ]
}
```

The first thing to notice in the expression on the `routeTable` property is the `contains()` function invocation on an object. This shows that you can use the `contains()` function to check whether an object has a particular property defined or not. In this example, if the `routeTable` property exists, the `json()` function is used to create the object and assign it. If it does not exist, `json('null')` is used to ignore it.

Instead of using the `json()` function to create the object in place, you could also create a variable to hold it, and then reference that, as shown in the following example (03-05-01.json).

Listing 3.13 Assigning `null` values using a variable

```
{
    "$schema": "https:/ /schema.management.azure.com/schemas/
      ➡ 2019-04-01/deploymentTemplate.json#",
    "contentVersion": "1.0.0.0",
    "parameters": {
        "subnet": {
            "type": "object"
        }
    },
    "variables": {
        "routeTable": {
            "id": "[resourceId('Microsoft.Network/routeTables',
            ➡ parameters('subnet').routeTable.name)]"
        }
    },
    "resources": [
        {
            "type": "Microsoft.Network/virtualNetworks/subnets",
            "location": "West Europe",
            "apiVersion": "2020-05-01",
            "name": "[parameters('subnet').name]",
            "properties": {
                "addressPrefix": "[parameters('subnet').addressPrefix]",
                ➡ "routeTable": "[if(contains(parameters('subnet'),          ◄─┐
                ➡ 'routeTable'), variables('routeTable'), json('null'))]"       │
            }                                                          **Assigning the null value**
        }                                                             **using json('null')**
    ]
}
```

Here you see the route table defined as a variable and used in the `routeTable` property in the `properties` object using the `variables()` function. The benefit of this is that your template is more readable, especially when the object you create in the `json()` function gets larger.

As you saw, the syntax for assigning `null` to an object is `json('null')`. You can use `json('[]')` when you need to do the same for an array type, or just use `null` on a string type.

3.5.2 Built-in functions

The list of built-in functions is quite long and is available in Microsoft's "ARM template functions" article (http://mng.bz/pOg2). This book does not cover all of them, but we'll show you the most frequently used functions. Functions are grouped into the following groups:

- Scope functions
- Logical functions
- Array functions
- Comparison functions
- Date functions
- Deployment value functions
- Numeric functions
- Object functions
- Resource functions
- String functions

The following sections explore reference and logic functions in detail. Chapter 5 describes array functions in detail when discussing loops. The other types of functions are less concerned with writing an ARM template and more with finding values for specific properties. You can look up the workings of these functions in Microsoft's documentation.

SCOPE FUNCTIONS

First up are scope functions. They allow you to get information on existing resources in Azure. Let's start with an example that deploys an Azure Key Vault (03-05-02-scope.json).

Listing 3.14 Using scope functions

```
"resources": [
    {
        "type": "Microsoft.KeyVault/vaults",
        "apiVersion": "2019-09-01",
        "name": "[parameters('keyVaultName')]",
        "location": "[resourceGroup().location]",
        "properties": {
            "sku": {
                "family": "A",
                "name": "standard"
            },
            "accessPolicies": "[parameters('accessPolicies').list]",
            "tenantId": "[subscription().tenantId]",
            "enabledForTemplateDeployment": true
        }
    }
]
```

This example uses two scope functions. First, it uses the `resourceGroup()` function to get information on the resource group that the template is deployed into. One of the returned properties is its `location`. Second, you can see the use of the `subscription()` function. That function returns information on the subscription you are deploying to, and one of its properties is the `tenantId`. That is the ID of the Azure Active Directory tenant used for authenticating requests to the Key Vault.

With the Key Vault in place, it is time to store secrets in it. Storing secrets is possible using the Azure portal, but this is a book on ARM templates, so let's practice using them instead. In the coming examples, you'll go through the following steps:

1   Create an Azure storage account.
2   Store the Management Key for that storage account in Azure Key Vault.
3   Make sure the API can read the secret from the Key Vault.

Let's start by creating the storage account itself (03-05-02-scope.json).

Listing 3.15   Creating a storage account

```
"resources": [
    {
        "type": "Microsoft.Storage/storageAccounts",
        "apiVersion": "2019-04-01",
        "name": "myStorageAccount",
        "location": "South Central US",
        "sku": {
            "name": "Standard_LRS"
        },
        "kind": "StorageV2"
    }
]
```

Before you store the key, you need to retrieve it using the `listKeys()` function:

```
listKeys(resourceId('Microsoft.Storage/storageAccounts',
    ➥ parameters('storageAccountName')), 2019-04-01').key1
```

The `listKeys()` function accepts a reference to a resource as its first input. Here the `resourceId()` function is used to get that. The identifier returned has the following format:

```
/subscriptions/{subscriptionId}/resourceGroups/{resourceGroupName}
    ➥ /providers/{resourceProviderNamespace}/{resourceType}/{resourceName}
```

The second input parameter to `listKeys` is the API version of the resource whose keys you are getting. Once the `listKeys()` function returns, you can use the `key1` or `key2` property to get one of the access keys to the storage account.

Now that you have a working snippet for fetching the storage account key, you can use the following snippet to store this key in the Key Vault (03-05-02-scope.json).

Listing 3.16   Storing a secret in a Key Vault

```
"resources": [
    {
        "type": "Microsoft.KeyVault/vaults/secrets",
        "apiVersion": "2018-02-14",
        "name": "[concat(parameters('keyVaultName'), '/',
            ➥ parameters('secretName'))]",
        "location": "[parameters('location')]",
```

```
        "properties": {
            "value": "[listKeys(resourceId('Microsoft.Storage/storageAccounts',
                ➥ parameters('storageAccountName')), '2019-04-01').key1]"
        }
    }
]
```

This snippet adds a secret with the name secretName, as defined in the template's name property. For the value of the secretName parameter, the key of the storage account is retrieved using the listKeys() function and assigned to the value property in the template's properties object.

The final step in this flow is to make sure that the API can also access the Key Vault to retrieve this secret at runtime. Your API will run on an Azure App Service. Just like the SQL database, the Azure App Service is also a child resource that always needs to run on an App Service Plan. Both are created in the following snippet (03-05-02-web-scope.json). Notice that the App Service Plan is called serverfarms in this example. That's an old name for the same thing.

Listing 3.17 Creating an App Service

```
"resources": [
    {
        "apiVersion": "2015-08-01",
        "name": "[parameters('serverFarmName')]",        ← The serverfarm is
        "type": "Microsoft.Web/serverfarms",               the parent resource.
        "location": "[resourceGroup().location]",
        "sku": {
            "name": "S1",
            "capacity": 1
        },
        "properties": {
            "name": "[parameters('serverFarmName')]"
        }
    },
    {
        "apiVersion": "2018-02-01",
        "name": "[parameters('appServiceName')]",
        "type": "Microsoft.Web/sites",
        "location": "[resourceGroup().location]",
        "dependsOn": [                                      ← The App Service
            "[resourceId('Microsoft.Web/serverfarms',         Plan is the child
                ➥ parameters('serverFarmName'))]"             resource, so
        ],                                                    you need the
        "identity": {                                         dependsOn.
            "type": "SystemAssigned"          ← The App Service gets
        },                                      an identity assigned.
        "properties": {
            "serverFarmId": "[resourceId('Microsoft.Web/serverfarms',
                ➥ providers('serverFarmName'))]"
        }
    }
]
```

The only new concept in the preceding listing is the assignment of the identity on the App Service. You could see this identity as a user and your application will run using that user. This identity can then be used from the application to authenticate with other resources easily and securely, like a Key Vault. More on the concept of identities can be found in Microsoft's "How to use managed identities for App Service and Azure Functions" article (http://mng.bz/Oo2o).

The final step is to give this identity permissions on the Key Vault. That is done by deploying the following role assignment (03-05-02-web-scope.json).

Listing 3.18   Granting App Service permissions on the Key Vault

```
"variables": {
    "keyVaultSecretReaderRoleId": "4633458b-17de-408a-b874-0445c86b69e6"
        ➥ / / RBAC Role: Key Vault Secrets User
},
"resources: [
    {
        "type": "Microsoft.KeyVault/vaults/providers/roleAssignments",
        "apiVersion": "2018-01-01-preview",
        "name": "[concat(parameters('keyVaultName'),              ⊲─┐  The name for
            ➥ '/Microsoft.Authorization/',                            roleAssignments needs
            ➥ guid(parameters('appServiceName'),                     to be globally unique.
            ➥ variables('keyVaultSecretReaderRoleId')))]",
        "dependsOn": [
            "[parameters('appServiceName')]"          roleDefinitionId
        ],                                            defines the role
        "properties": {                               to be assigned.
            "roleDefinitionId":            ⊲─────────────┘
                ➥ "[concat('/providers/Microsoft.Authorization/roledefinitions/',
                ➥ variables('keyVaultSecretReaderRoleId'))]",
            "principalId": "[reference(resourceId('Microsoft.Web/sites',    ⊲─┐
                ➥ parameters('appServiceName')), '2019-08-01',
                ➥ 'full').identity.principalId]"
        }                                                  principalId defines
    }                                                      who should get
                                                           the role.
]
```

As you can see, `roleAssignments` in the preceding listing is a child resource of the Key Vault, so the role is assigned on that scope. The role that should be applied is set using a GUID in the `roleDefinitionId` property. These GUIDs are predefined values that are the same in every Azure environment. A full list of them can be found in Microsoft's "Azure built-in roles" article (http://mng.bz/YGPK). In this example, that value is stored in a variable so you can give it a descriptive name. Finally, the `principalId` property specifies to whom the role should be assigned. Here you see that a `reference()` function is used to grab the `principalId` from the identity on the App Service that was assigned in the previous snippet.

Another resource we promised to discuss in this chapter is Application Insights. Application Insights is a service used to monitor the API. You can use it to find the

API's performance metrics, for example, or store custom metrics and report on them. Since the API in our scenario processes orders, we'll create a metric that holds each processed order's value. An Application Insights instance stores its data in a service called a Log Analytics workspace. The following snippet creates both these resources (03-05-02-app-insights-scope.json).

Listing 3.19 Creating an Application Insights instance

```
"resources": [
    {
        "name": "[variables('logAnalyticsWorkspaceName')]",
        "type": "Microsoft.OperationalInsights/workspaces",
        "apiVersion": "2020-08-01",
        "location": "[parameters('location')]",
        "properties": {
            "sku": {
                "name": "pergb2018"
            },
            "retentionInDays": 30,
            "workspaceCapping": {
                "dailyQuotaGb": -1
            }
        }
    },
    {

        "apiVersion": "2020-02-02-preview",
        "name": "[variables('applicationInsightsName')]",
        "type": "Microsoft.Insights/components",
        "kind": "web",
        "location": "[parameters('location')]",
        "dependsOn": [
            "[variables('logAnalyticsWorkspaceName')]"
        ],
        "properties": {
            "applicationId": "[variables('applicationInsightsName')]",
            "WorkspaceResourceId":
                ➥ "[resourceId('Microsoft.OperationalInsights/workspaces',
                ➥ variables('logAnalyticsWorkspaceName'))]",
            "Application_Type": "web"

        }
    }
]
```

Here you see the creation of an Application Insights resource that uses a parameter named `applicationInsightsName` for the resource's name.

To connect the API to that instance of Application Insights, you need its `InstrumentationKey`. One way to pass that to the API is to set an application setting on the Azure App Service that runs the API. The following listing shows how to do that (03-05-02-app-insights-scope.json).

Listing 3.20   Setting the `InstrumentationKey`

```
"resources": [
    {
        "name": "[concat(parameters('webappname'), '/', 'appsettings')]",
        "type": "Microsoft.Web/sites/config",
        "apiVersion": "2018-02-01",
        "location": "[resourceGroup().location]",
        "properties": {
            "APPINSIGHTS_INSTRUMENTATIONKEY": "[reference(parameters(
                ➥ 'applicationInsightsName'), '2018-05-01-preview')
                ➥ .InstrumentationKey]"
        }
    }
]
```

This snippet deploys a resource called `appsettings` within the Azure web app. Within the properties, the actual configuration—a setting called `APPINSIGHTS_INSTRUMENTATIONKEY`—is added. At runtime this setting is used by the Application Insights SDK in the API to connect to the correct Application Insights instance.

It's important here that you see that the setting gets its value by referencing the just-created Application Insights resource using the `reference()` function, in a way similar to the `resourceId()` function. In contrast with the `resourceId()` function, the `reference()` function does not specify the entire `resourceId`, but only the name of the resource that is being referenced. This shorter and more readable notation is only usable when the resource you are referencing is defined within the same template. In all other cases, you must use the `resourceId()` function. In both cases, the returned object gives you information about the Application Insights instance, and one of those properties is the `InstrumentationKey`.

LOGICAL FUNCTIONS

Other often-used functions come from the group of logical functions. Imagine that you deploy virtual machines for your internal customers, and some customers demand that you deploy those machines in an availability set, to ensure high availability. When you deploy two or more virtual machines in an availability set, Microsoft will ensure that they, for example, will never reboot the underlying hardware off of all machines at the same time.

However, you only need this availability set for the production resources. To reuse a single resource declaration that allows for both variations, you can use the following code (03-05-02-logical.json).

Listing 3.21   The `if` function

```
"variables": {
    "deployAvailabilitySet": "[and(parameters('availabilitySet'),
        ➥ equals(parameters('environment'), 'production'))]",
    "availabilitySetIdentifier": {
        "id": "[resourceId('Microsoft.Compute/availabilitySets',
            ➥ parameters('availabilitySetName'))]"
```

```
        }
    },
    "resources": [
        {
            "name": "[parameters('vmName')]",
            "type": "Microsoft.Compute/virtualMachines",
            "location": "[resourceGroup().location]",
            "apiVersion": "2017-03-30",
            "properties": {
                "availabilitySet": "[if(variables('deployAvailabilitySet'),
                    ➥ variables(availabilitySetIdentifier), json('null'))]",
                ...
            }
        }
    }
]
```

In this example, the `equals()` function is used inside another logical function, the `and()` function. The first input value to the `and()` function is a Boolean parameter to check if the use of availability sets is required for this customer. The second input value is the outcome of the `equals()` function, which checks whether you are currently deploying to your production environment.

The outcome of the `and()` function is saved in the `deployAvailabilitySet` variable. This variable is used in the template while setting the `availabilitySet` property of the virtual machine. Only when this parameter's value evaluates to `true` is the availability set defined in the variable assigned. In all other cases, the `json()` function assigns `null`.

In more extensive templates, the `if()` function is often part of a *condition*. A condition allows you to define whether a resource should be deployed at all. You will find more on that in chapter 6.

ARM templates support most of the logic functions that anyone with a programming or scripting background would expect, including `not()`, `and()`, `or()`, `equals()`, `if()`, and many more.

Most of these built-in functions are usable at any of the scopes to which you can deploy templates: the tenant, management group, subscription, and resource group. You might not be familiar with these scopes, but they will be introduced in the next chapter. For now, it's enough to know that there are different scopes in Azure, and that there is a hierarchy between them; a resource group is always defined within a subscription, a subscription within a management group, and a management group within a tenant. Although most functions can be deployed at any scope, there are exceptions, and they are well documented. As an example, take the `subscription()` function, which gives you information on the subscription you are deploying to. This function is not available when you deploy a template on the management group level, as there is no subscription involved. Subscriptions always reside within a management group and therefore at a lower level. Deploying to different scopes, including management groups, is discussed in chapter 4.

3.5.3 *User-defined functions*

Although the list of built-in functions is quite long, you may still find that you miss out on some functionality. In that case, a user-defined function can be what you need.

User-defined functions especially shine when you have complex expressions that you repeatedly reuse in a template. In the following example, you'll see a user-defined function in the functions section for capitalizing a string (03-05-03.json).

Listing 3.22 Creating a user-defined function

```
"functions": [
    {
      "namespace": "demofunction",
      "members": {
        "capitalize": {
          "parameters": [
            {
              "name": "input",
              "type": "string"
            }
          ],
          "output": {
            "type": "string",
            "value": "[concat(toUpper(first(parameters('input'))),
           ➥ toLower(skip(parameters('input'), 1)))]"
          }
        }
      }
    }
]
```

The functions section is an array where you can define more than one custom function. The first property you specify is its namespace, to make sure you don't clash with any of the built-in functions. Then, in the members array, you define one or more functions. A function definition always starts with its name, in this case, capitalize. The parameters array is used for defining input parameters, precisely the same as for a template. One limitation is that you cannot give parameters a default value. Within a user-defined function, you can only use the parameters defined in the function, not the template's parameters. The output section is where you define the actual logic of your function. You specify the output type and its value.

User-defined functions come with a few limitations. First, the functions cannot access variables, so you must use parameters to pass those values along. Functions cannot call other user-defined functions and cannot use the reference(), resourceId(), or list() functions. A workaround for these two limitations is to use those functions in the parameters while using the function (03-05-03.json) as shown in the following listing.

Listing 3.23 Using a user-defined function

```
"resources": [
    {
        "type": "Microsoft.Sql/servers",
        "name": "[demofunction.capitalize(parameters('sqlServerName'))]",
        "apiVersion": "2019-06-01-preview",
        "location": "[parameters('location')]",
        "properties": {
            "administratorLogin": "[parameters('sqlServerUsername')]",
            "administratorLoginPassword":
                "[parameters('sqlServerPassword')]"
        }
    }
]
```

The user-defined function used to create the name of the SQL Server

In the preceding example, the user-defined function is used to create a value for the SQL Server's name property. The function is used as demofunction.capitalize() and the parameter sqlServerName is used as input. So, the format to use a user-defined function is <namespace>.<functionsname>(<parameterinput>).

Summary

- Resources describe what should be deployed in Azure. They have mandatory and (often) optional properties and can either be a child or parent resource.
- Parameters in ARM templates allow for user input during deployment and thereby make a template more generic and reusable.
- Variables in ARM templates help you repeat expressions throughout a template, making a template more readable and maintainable.
- During deployment, template parameter values are provided inline, using parameter files, or they can be referenced from a Key Vault.
- Outputs are used to return values to the user deploying the ARM template so you can chain other tools after the template deployment.
- Functions in templates are used to, for example, reference resources and retrieve property values, perform logical operations, and make decisions based on input parameters.
- When needed, a custom function can be written to augment the built-in functionality.

Deploying ARM templates

4

This chapter covers

- Understanding what happens when a template is deployed
- Choosing a deployment tool
- Picking the correct template deployment scope and mode
- Understanding how authorizations, policies, and resource locks influence deployments
- Debugging template deployments

After discussing how to write ARM templates in the previous chapters, it is time for a more in-depth discussion of what happens when you deploy a template. Every deployment goes through the same series of steps after you have submitted it to Azure Resource Manager. The first part of this chapter goes through those steps one by one.

After we discuss the deployment process, we'll look at two more deployment topics: how you can use ARM to validate templates without actually deploying them, and how you can perform a dry run using a template. Such a dry run lists all the changes that would be made when deploying the template for real. Finally, we'll touch on troubleshooting templates and explain what you can do when the deployment of a template fails. Before we dive into the details of the deployment process, let's start with a quick overview.

4.1 An overview of the deployment process

All ARM deployments go through the same process for deployment. Figure 4.1 visualizes that process.

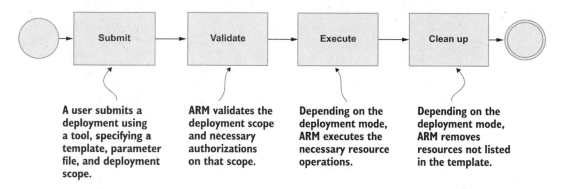

Figure 4.1 Template deployment process

First, the deployment has to be submitted to ARM. You can submit a deployment in many ways, and this chapter discusses the most common ones: the Azure CLI, Azure PowerShell, Azure SDKs, GitHub Actions, and Azure DevOps. When submitting a deployment, you specify the ARM template to deploy, provide values for parameters, and specify the *deployment scope*. The deployment scope determines where in Azure the resources declared in the template should be deployed. Section 4.2 discusses submitting a deployment in detail, including the concept of a deployment scope.

After the deployment is started, ARM performs several validations. First, the template itself is validated. Next, the deployment scope is determined, and ARM validates whether the user that started the deployment has the necessary authorizations on this scope. If the necessary authorization is not in place, the deployment stops at this point.

After the validation is completed successfully, the *execution phase* starts. In the execution phase, resources are created or updated as necessary. ARM performs as many resource operations in parallel as possible, respecting any ordering imposed by your template. During each resource operation, authorizations, policies, and locks are evaluated and applied when applicable. Section 4.3 discusses the execution phase.

When submitting the deployment, you can also specify a *deployment mode*. If the deployment mode is set to `Complete`, the deployment also goes through a *clean-up phase*. During this phase, resources in your deployment scope that are not defined in the ARM template are removed from Azure. Section 4.4 discusses this phase in detail.

Now that you have a good overview of the deployment process, let's zoom in on submitting a template for deployment.

4.2   *Submitting a deployment*

A template deployment is always started by submitting the template to ARM. But just having a template is not enough. To submit a template, you need to have four things:

- An ARM template to submit
- Optionally, a parameter file or parameter values to submit along with the template
- A deployment scope: where do you want the declared resources to be created
- An interface (a tool) to perform the submission with

Assuming you read chapter 3, you probably have at least one ARM template ready to deploy. You might also have a corresponding parameter file, but don't worry if you don't yet; later you'll learn how to specify parameter values when deploying. The following two sections discuss deployment scopes and tooling.

4.2.1   *Choosing a deployment scope*

Azure allows you to organize resources into multiple levels of groups: management groups, subscriptions, and resource groups. These groupings are important, as a template deployment always targets such a group. Figure 4.2 shows these groupings and how they relate to the Azure Active Directory (AAD).

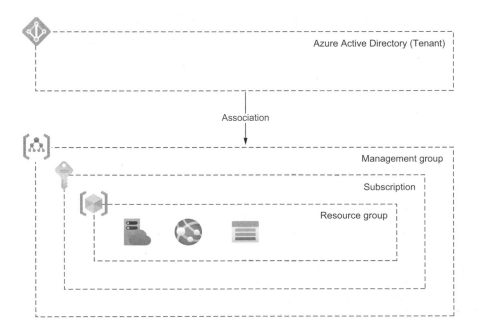

Figure 4.2   **The different types of groupings available in Azure**

When interacting with the resource manager to deploy a template, you specify one of these types of groups. That group is then called the *deployment scope*, and all resources in the template are deployed into that scope. Templates can deploy to different scopes, namely the AAD tenant, a management group, a subscription, or a resource group. Let's discuss each of these scopes in more detail, starting with the AAD tenant.

AZURE ACTIVE DIRECTORY TENANT

Azure Active Directory (AAD) is Microsoft's identity and access management service. It allows you to sign in and access resources in Microsoft 365, external SaaS applications, and Azure.

In this book, AAD will only be used in the context of management groups, subscriptions, and access to resources. AAD recognizes so-called *tenants* that represent different organizations that use Azure. Each tenant has one or more domains (such as @example.com) linked to it. All users with a username that ends in that domain belong to the tenant.

Every management group, subscription, resource group, and resource is associated with a single tenant. ARM has a trust relationship with AAD to provide the user with login and authorization functionality. When you write an ARM template that uses the tenant as the deployment scope, you can only create management groups and subscriptions.

MANAGEMENT GROUP

Management groups are the highest level of grouping within AAD. They allow you to group subscriptions into logical containers and make it easier to manage access, policies, and compliance in larger environments.

By default, there is always one root management group in every AAD tenant. This top-level management group contains all other management groups and subscriptions. It cannot be renamed or removed. The hierarchy of management groups can go as deep as six levels. When you write a template with a management group as the deployment scope, you can create subscriptions, nested management groups, Azure policies, and authorization rules.

SUBSCRIPTION

Subscriptions are the second level in the hierarchy. They are always within a management group, they can only be connected to a single Azure tenant, and they can contain multiple resource groups. Subscriptions are the billing boundary for collecting usage data and generating invoices.

You can write templates that have a subscription as the deployment scope. You can then declare authorization rules, Azure policies, and resource groups.

RESOURCE GROUP

Resource groups are the lowest type of grouping in the hierarchy and contain the resources you create, like Azure App Services, virtual machines, or SQL databases. It is recommended that you group resources that share the same lifecycle in a resource group. Resources share a lifecycle when you deploy, update, and delete them together, such as when using ARM templates.

A resource group has a location (an Azure region), and the resource group's location serves as the default location for all resources within it. Still, it can contain resources in a different Azure region. Resources can be moved between resource groups, but some limitations apply. As resource groups are only logical groupings, nothing prevents resources in different resource groups from connecting. For example, a virtual machine in one resource group can still connect to a database in another.

All the templates you have seen so far deploy resources into a resource group. The resource group is the most-used scope for deployments. Now that you know the different deployment scopes available, let's explore some of the different ways you can deploy an ARM template.

4.2.2 *Submitting a template using different tools*

Templates are submitted to ARM for deployment using a RESTful API, just as individual resources are manipulated. However, in practice, you'll almost never use this API directly but instead use a tool that encapsulates that API call. Let's look at a few of the most-used tools.

AZURE CLI

The Azure command-line interface (CLI) is a set of commands used to create and manage Azure resources. The Azure CLI is available across Azure services and is designed to get you working quickly with Azure and with an emphasis on automation.

The Azure CLI is available to install on Windows, Linux, and macOS. If you don't have the Azure CLI installed on your computer yet, you can download it from Microsoft (https://docs.microsoft.com/en-us/cli/azure/install-azure-cli). Besides running on your own system, it can be run in a Docker container or Azure Cloud Shell.

Commands for the Azure CLI always start with az. Commands executed with the Azure CLI require you to authenticate, which you can do with the az login command.

> **The Azure Cloud Shell**
> The Azure Cloud Shell is a command tool available from within the Azure portal. You open the Azure Cloud Shell by clicking the Azure Cloud Shell icon in the toolbar at the top of the Azure portal.
>
>
>
> The Azure Cloud Shell requires a storage account to operate. If you do not have one, it will create one for you when the Cloud Shell starts for the first time.

To deploy an ARM template, you use the `az deployment` command. After this command, you specify the type of deployment scope. The four keywords available are `group`, `sub`, `mg`, and `tenant`, for resource group deployments, subscription deployments, management group deployments, and tenant deployments respectively. Adding the keyword `create` completes the command. Putting this together, you deploy a template to a resource group using the `az deployment group create` command. You then need to pass in parameters to complete the command.

All deployments require a *template file* argument, which points to your ARM template file. Specifically, for resource groups, you need to specify the name of the resource group you are deploying to. All other deployment scopes require you to define a location. For example, to create a new resource group deployment, you would give the following command:

```
az login
az deployment group create
    --subscription "subscription-name-or-id"
    --resource-group "resource-group-name"
    --template-file "path-to-arm-template.json"
```

The first command opens a browser that allows you to log into Azure. The second command starts the actual deployment. It is not mandatory to specify a subscription if you have access to only one subscription. As an alternative, you can specify a default subscription using the `az account set --subscription "subscription-name-or-id"` command. To retrieve a list of all subscriptions available, you can use the `az account list` command.

Extra parameters are available for additional options, such as for setting parameters. If you have a parameter file that accompanies the template file, you can reference it using the following command:

```
az deployment group create
    --resource-group "<resource-group-name>"
    --template-file "<path-to-arm-template.json>"
    --parameters "@<path-to-parameter-file.json>"
```

In this example, the optional parameter `--subscription` is omitted, and a reference to the parameter file is added using `--parameters`. The @ symbol signifies that a file is referenced and is followed by the actual filename, like this: `--parameters @my-parameters.json`. Parameters can also be set using a JSON string. In that case, the @ symbol is omitted, and the parameters are specified using key/value pairs, like this:

```
--parameters firstParameter=example secondParameter=2
```

Finally, if you get stuck or want to explore more deployment options when creating deployments through the Azure CLI, you can use the `--help` parameter to output all available options and switches.

POWERSHELL

To deploy an ARM template using PowerShell, you first need to install the Azure PowerShell module on your local computer. There are two major versions of PowerShell: Windows PowerShell and PowerShell. PowerShell is, like the Azure CLI, cross-platform and available for Windows, Linux, and macOS. Windows PowerShell is only available for Windows. For more information about how to get started using Azure with PowerShell, see Microsoft's "Get started with Azure PowerShell" article (http://mng.bz/7yeg).

The way PowerShell commands, called *cmdlets*, work is similar to the way the Azure CLI works. In general, PowerShell cmdlets and Azure CLI commands are named and structured quite similarly.

There are multiple versions of the Azure PowerShell module available, so it is important to make sure you are working with the latest version and reading the latest documentation. Note that updating an existing environment to the latest version may introduce breaking changes. All cmdlets that are part of the newest version, called the Azure PowerShell Az module, start with an action, followed by a dash, and then `Az`, like this: `New-AzSubscriptionDeployment`.

For Azure PowerShell, the cmdlets you use are different for each type of deployment scope. For example, if you target a resource group, the PowerShell cmdlets look like this:

```
Connect-AzAccount
Set-AzContext -Subscription "xxxxxxxx-xxxx-xxxx-xxxx-xxxxxxxxxxxx"
New-AzResourceGroupDeployment
    ➥ -ResourceGroupName <resource-group-name>
    ➥ -TemplateFile <path-to-template>
```

The first cmdlet, `Connect-AzAccount`, opens a browser that allows you to log in to Azure. The second cmdlet, `Set-AzContext`, is used to select the default subscription that will be used by all other Az commands. The final cmdlet submits an ARM template for deployment.

To change the deployment scope to the subscription, you would use the following cmdlet:

```
New-AzDeployment -Location <location> -TemplateFile <path-to-template>
```

You can see that the two cmdlets are different, since the deployment scope is in the name of the command. The arguments also change, depending on the scope. Deployments that target the tenant deployment scope or the management group deployment scope have the same arguments as the cmdlets for the subscription, but the cmdlet names change to `New-AzTenantDeployment` and `New-AzManagementGroupDeployment`.

Just as when using the Azure CLI, you pass a template file and parameter using arguments:

```
New-AzResourceGroupDeployment
    ⇒  -ResourceGroupName "<resource-group-name>"
    ⇒  -TemplateFile "<path-to-arm-template.json>"
    ⇒  -TemplateParameterFile "<path-to-parameter-file.json>"
    ⇒  -firstParameter "example"
    ⇒  -secondParameter 2
```

The preceding example is similar to the deployment created in the Azure CLI section—it creates a new resource group deployment. A significant difference is that the parameter used for providing a parameter file, `TemplateParameterFile`, does not require an @ symbol and cannot be reused to provide parameter values. Instead, parameter values that you want to provide directly should be added as parameters to the cmdlet itself, like `firstParameter` and `secondParameter`.

SDKs

It is also possible to start an ARM template deployment from code. A common reason you may want to deploy from code is to provide a service that allows clients to create their own database or working environments. To make this possible, software development kits (SDKs) are available for many languages, including .NET, Java, JavaScript, Python, and many more. As there are too many languages to demonstrate, we'll use .NET as an example in this section.

In a .NET programming language like C#.NET or VB.NET, SDKs come in the form of NuGet packages. For working with Azure, you require a NuGet package called `Microsoft.Azure.Management`. Microsoft also recommends using the `Microsoft.Azure.Management.Fluent` package, which allows you to create resources in a fluent way, which is often considered more readable and easier to maintain.

> **Fluent programming**
>
> A fluent interface is an object-oriented approach to programming that uses method chaining. Its goal is to improve the readability of the code and create a domain-specific language.

Before any interaction with Azure can occur, you first need to authenticate. When using C#, authenticating would look like this:

```
var credentials = SdkContext.AzureCredentialsFactory
    .FromServicePrincipal(clientId, clientSecret, tenantId,
        AzureEnvironment.AzureGlobalCloud);

var azure = Azure
    .Configure()
    .Authenticate(credentials)
    .WithDefaultSubscription();
```

The first command starts with a reference to the static `SdkContext.AzureCredentials-Factory` property, on which the `FromServicePrincipal` method is called to create a `credentials` class for headless authentication.

NOTE Non-personal accounts, called *service principals*, use headless authentication. This form of authentication is beyond the scope of this book, but if you want to learn more, you can start with Microsoft's "Application and service principal objects in Azure Active Directory" article (http://mng.bz/mOmM).

The second command makes the actual connection to Azure, using the static `Azure` class, performing the actual authentication, and selecting the default subscription for the service principal. This result of this call is an entry point into your Azure environment, and it is captured in the variable called `azure`. It is then available for starting all sorts of operations, including template deployments:

```
azure.Deployments.Define("DeploymentName")
    .WithExistingResourceGroup("ResourceGroupName")
    .WithTemplate("<your-template-as-json-string>")
    .WithParameters(new {
        firstParameter: "example",
        secondParameter: 2
    })
    .Create();
```

In this snippet, you see how fluent syntax is used to `Define` a new deployment. The parameters that you saw in the Azure CLI and Azure PowerShell sections are used here as function calls in the fluent syntax. You have seen these options before, such as the resource group name, JSON template, and any parameters.

AUTOMATING DEPLOYMENTS

In the end, manually deploying templates is not the best way forward for most organizations. Instead, it's better to use tools to automate deployments, increasing automation and repeatability and reducing access to cloud environments using personal accounts.

One approach to automation is deploying an ARM template from a continuous integration/continuous deployment (CI/CD) pipeline. If you are already using a CI/CD pipeline for building, testing, and deploying software, it makes sense to also use pipelines for deploying your infrastructure. A more elaborate example of using Azure DevOps pipelines to do this is included in this chapter's last section.

Of course, CI/CD pipelines are not only available in Azure DevOps. Many similar software development tools allow you to implement CI/CD pipelines as well, such as these:

- GitHub Actions (Workflows)
- Octopus Deploy
- JetBrains TeamCity

As an alternative to CI/CD pipelines, you can also use Azure Deployment Manager. This is a built-in Azure tool for orchestrating complex deployments across multiple subscriptions and regions. You'll learn about this tool in chapter 12.

Now that you've learned about four approaches to submitting deployments, let's take a closer look at what happens after submission.

4.3 The execution phase

This chapter started with a flowchart that describes what happens when you submit a deployment. In this section and the following one, we'll zoom in on the last two phases: execution and clean up.

As you can see in figure 4.3, the execution phase itself executes a series of steps for every resource in the template that is being deployed. First, ARM checks if the correct role-based access control (RBAC) assignments are in place for every resource that is defined. Next, any Azure policies and resource locks on the resource are evaluated. Finally, the actual resource provisioning starts by creating a new resource or updating an existing resource.

The remainder of this section explores these steps in more detail, starting with RBAC.

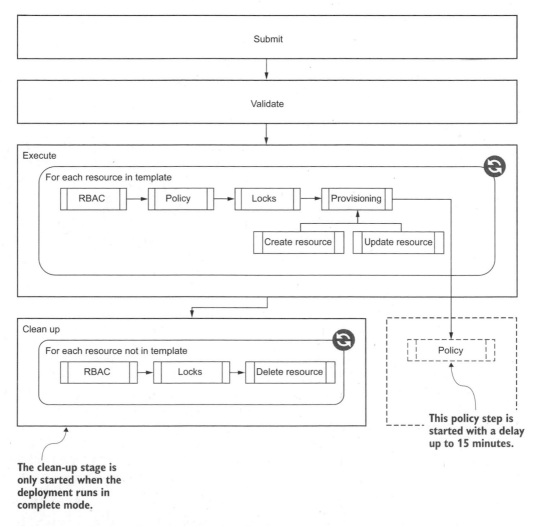

Figure 4.3 A detailed overview of the execution and clean-up phases

4.3.1   *Role-based access control*

The Azure Resource Manager is also used to assign permissions to users and validate these permissions before an action is executed. Azure RBAC gives you fine-grained control over

- Who has access?
- What resources do they have access to?
- Which level of access do they have?

In the ARM RBAC model, these three questions are answered using role assignments, which consist of three elements, relating to the three preceding questions:

- A security principal
- A scope
- A role

You can create and assign role assignments by providing values for each of these three dimensions. For example, you could assign the user Pieter Post access to the resource Rode Wagen in the role of Owner. Let's explore the different components that make up a role assignment.

SECURITY PRINCIPAL

A *security principal* in Azure is an object that represents a user, group, service principal, or managed identity. These identities are stored in the Azure Active Directory (AAD). The scope on which access is granted should belong to the same AAD as the one that contains the users.

SCOPE

By assigning a role definition on a particular scope, you limit the security principal's actions to a specific resource or resource container. For example, assigning a scope enables you to make someone a Contributor on your test subscriptions but only a Reader on production ones.

You can assign a role at four levels:

- Management group
- Subscription
- Resource group
- Resource

Since these scopes form a top-down hierarchy, any role assigned to a subscription also gives those permissions to any resource group or resource in that subscription. This means that the effective permissions on any scope are determined using an additive model. For example, when you assign an Owner role at the subscription level and a Read role on a resource group in that subscription, that security principal still has an Owner role on that resource group.

ROLE

A *role* is a collection of permissions that lists the available operations to anyone who has that role assigned. Roles can be high level, like the Contributor role on a subscription, including Read and Write access for resources of all types, or they can be specific, like the Storage Blob Data Reader, which only allows read access to Azure Blob Storage.

Which actions are part of a role is described in a *role definition*. Role definitions are Azure resources, and the following snippet shows the role definition for Storage Blob Data Reader:

```
{
    "Name": "Storage Blob Data Reader",
    "Id": "2a2b9908-6ea1-4ae2-8e65-a410df84e7d1",
    "IsCustom": false,
    "Description": "Allows read access to Azure Storage blob containers ",
    "Actions": [
        "Microsoft.Storage/storageAccounts/blobServices/containers
            /read",
        "Microsoft.Storage/storageAccounts/blobServices/
            generateUserDelegationKey/action"
    ],
    "DataActions": [
        "Microsoft.Storage/storageAccounts/blobServices/
            containers/blobs/read"
    ],
    "AssignableScopes": [ "/" ]
}
```

Every role has a mandatory `Id`, `Name`, and `Description`. Of these, only the `Id` has to be globally unique, so it is a `Guid`. The `Actions` and `DataActions` properties are lists of the actions that this role gives access to. An action always starts with a full resource type, followed by a slash and a specification of the action. The `AssignableScopes` property is a list of scopes that the role is valid for. Finally, the `IsCustom` property reflects the type of role definition. There are two types of role definitions:

- Built-in
- Custom

Built-in role definitions contain one or more permissions tied to a specific resource type. They allow you to quickly allow a particular principal to perform its responsibilities without finding the specific permissions yourself. For example, you could assign the Networking Contributor role to a user, which would allow that user to manage virtual networks but not manage any other type of resource.

Custom role definitions are used when you need to specify your own set of permissions. Let's say you want a user to be a Network Contributor and also allow them to manage VMs and storage accounts. Instead of assigning three different roles, you can create a new custom definition and only assign those permissions. Custom roles can be shared between subscriptions that are connected to the same Azure tenant.

AZURE ACTIVE DIRECTORY ROLES AND AZURE RBAC

You might also run into another type of role in Azure: Azure Active Directory roles. These roles can also be assigned to users, groups, applications, and service principals and can manage access to various Azure AD actions. For example, you could assign the User Administrator role to a user to allow them to manage users and groups.

Azure AD roles are used to manage access to Azure AD resources, whereas Azure roles are used to control access to Azure resources. We will not be using Azure Active Directory roles in the remainder of this book.

CREATING AND DEPLOYING A ROLE ASSIGNMENT USING AN ARM TEMPLATE

Role definitions and role assignments are resources in Azure, just like VMs or SQL databases. Thus, it is possible to use ARM templates to both create role definitions and assign them. Here is an example of how to create a role definition.

Listing 4.1   An ARM template for a role definition

```
{
    "$schema": "https://schema.management.azure.com/schemas/
        2018-05-01/subscriptionDeploymentTemplate.json#",
    "contentVersion": "1.0.0.0",
    "resources": [
        {
            "type": "Microsoft.Authorization/roleDefinitions",
            "apiVersion": "2018-07-01",
            "name": "ResourceGroupReader",
            "properties": {
                "roleName": "Custom Role - RG Reader",
                "description": "Sub Lvl Deployment RG reader",
                "type": "customRole",
                "isCustom": true,
                "permissions": [
                    {
                        "actions": [
                            "Microsoft.Resources/subscriptions/
                                resourceGroups/read"
                        ],
                        "notActions": []
                    }
                ],
                "assignableScopes": [ "[subscription().id]" ]
            }
        }
    ]
}
```

This template creates a custom role definition, as you can see by its `type` and `isCustom` properties. This role definition can be used to give any principal the authorizations defined in the `permissions` array. The `assignableScopes` property is set to the ID of the subscription it is deployed to, making it the only scope where this custom role definition is usable.

After creating this role, it can be assigned using the following template.

Listing 4.2 An ARM template for a role assignment

```
{
    "$schema": "https://schema.management.azure.com/schemas/
        ➥ 2019-04-01/deploymentTemplate.json#",
    "contentVersion": "1.0.0.0",
    "parameters": {
        "roleDefinitionID": {
            "type": "string"
    },
    "principalId": {
        "type": "string"
        }
    },
    "resources": [
        {
            "type": "Microsoft.Authorization/roleAssignments",
            "apiVersion": "2020-04-01-preview",
            "name": "AssignReadRoleDefinition",
            "properties": {
            "roleDefinitionId": "[resourceId('Microsoft.Authorization/
                ➥ roleDefinitions', parameters('roleDefinitionId'))]",
            "principalId": "[parameters('principalId')]",
            "scope": "[resourceGroup().id]"
        }
        }
    ]
}
```

This template assigns the role definition specified by the roleDefinitionID parameter to the principal specified by the principalId parameter. The scope is configured to be the resources group where it is deployed, as specified by the scope property.

Managing access to Azure resources is one aspect of working responsibly. Along with setting security boundaries, authorizations also help limit the impact of mistakes. By providing users with limited access to only resources they need to work with, accidental changes or deletions through user error have a limited impact.

4.3.2 *Azure Policy*

Although the nitty-gritty bits and pieces of Azure Policy are outside the scope of this book, it is a good idea to get familiar with what Azure Policy is, so you can better understand how it affects the deployment of resources. Azure Policy is a system that helps you enforce organizational standards and assess the compliance of Azure resources.

With Azure Policy, you can write Policy Definitions (also a resource type!), which describe rules you want to apply to Azure resources. After creation, a policy is assigned to any scope to make it active on that scope. That assignment is done using a Policy Assignment, which is again also a resource type.

A policy has two parts: First, a resource query specifies when the policy should apply. A possible query would be *all storage accounts in West Europe* or *all virtual machines running Windows 2019*. The second part is the *effect*, which describes what happens when a matching resource is found.

Each policy definition has only one effect. There are six types of effects available for use: append, audit, deny, modify, auditIfNotExists, and deployIfNotExists. Depending on the type of effect, the policy is evaluated either before a resource deployment or after a resource deployment.

The append, audit, deny, and modify effects are applied before a resource is created or updated. If the resource matches a policy's filter, the resource to be deployed is changed according to the specification (append or modify), the deployment is aborted (deny), or the resource is marked as incompliant (audit) for later follow-up.

The other effects are applied after a resource is deployed. These effects are useful when you want a resource always to have specific firewall settings, for example. In that case, a resource is marked as incompliant due to a missing child resource (auditIf-NotExists), or that missing child resource can automatically be deployed (deploy-IfNotExists). These effects run approximately 15 minutes after the resource provider has returned a success status code.

In figure 4.4, you can see the differences between these two groups of effects. The policy action in the execution phase refers to the append, audit, deny, and modify effects. The policy block at the bottom right refers to the auditIfNotExists and deployIfNotExists effects.

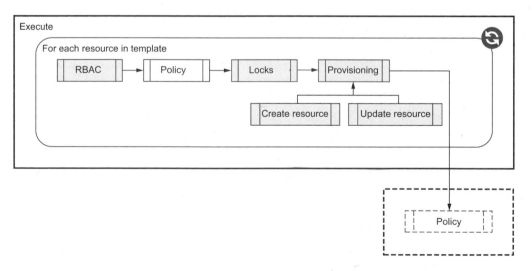

Figure 4.4   How a policy fits in the deployment process of the Azure Resource Manager

If you want to learn more about Azure Policy, you can start with Microsoft's "What is Azure Policy?" article (http://mng.bz/5QND).

4.3.3 Resource locks

Resource locks are used to prevent the accidental deletion or modification of a resource. Resource locks in themselves are also a type of resource. You can compare this to a bike lock that is "added" to a bike. Resource locks work in the same way; they are added to a resource.

There are two types of locks you can use:

- `CanNotDelete`—This type of lock ensures that users who are authorized can read and modify a resource but cannot delete it. In the Azure portal, this is shown as a delete lock.
- `ReadOnly`—This lock type ensures that authorized users can read a resource but cannot delete or modify it.

As locks are just another resource type, you can create them using an ARM template as shown in the following listing.

Listing 4.3 An ARM template to create a resource lock

```
{
    "$schema": "https://schema.management.azure.com/schemas/
        ➥ 2019-04-01/deploymentTemplate.json#",
    "contentVersion": "1.0.0.0",
    "resources": [
        {
            "type": "Microsoft.Authorization/locks",
            "apiVersion": "2016-09-01",
            "name": "rgLock",
            "properties": {
                "level": "CanNotDelete",
                "notes": "Resource Group should not be deleted."
            }
        }
    ]
}
```

By default, a lock locks the scope to which it is deployed. If you deployed this example on a resource group, it would lock that resource group and all resources using the `CanNotDelete` lock type. If you want to specify a different scope, you could use the `scope` property as follows.

Listing 4.4 An ARM template for creating a scoped resource lock

```
{
    "$schema": "https://schema.management.azure.com/schemas/
        ➥ 2019-04-01/deploymentTemplate.json#",
    "contentVersion": "1.0.0.0",
    "resources": [
        {
            "type": "Microsoft.Authorization/locks",
            "apiVersion": "2016-09-01",
            "name": "storageAccountLock",
```

```
        "scope": Microsoft.Storage/storageAccounts/storageAccountName",
        "properties": {
            "level": "CanNotDelete",
            "notes": "Storage Account should not be deleted."
        }
    }
    ]
}
```

The preceding lock would only lock the specified storage account.

Keep in mind that locking resources can have unexpected results. For example, if you put a read-only lock on a resource group containing virtual machines, you cannot reboot these machines anymore, since rebooting uses a POST request. Another example involves the limit of 800 deployments kept in the deployment history for a resource group. By default, ARM automatically starts cleaning up the deployment history so you don't hit that 800 and are blocked. But when you add a CanNotDelete lock on that resource group, ARM will no longer be able to automatically clean up your deployment history, and deployments will start failing once you reach the limit of 800 deployments.

4.3.4   *Resource provisioning*

Finally, when all the checks in the execution pipeline have passed, ARM deploys the resource as specified in the ARM template. ARM verifies whether there is already an existing resource with the same ID as the resource you are deploying before the deployment starts. If there is, ARM updates that resource to match the definition in your ARM template. If there isn't, ARM creates a new resource. This is the idempotent nature of working with ARM templates.

All these steps—checking RBAC, executing Azure policies, respecting resource locks, and provisioning the resource—are repeated for every resource defined in the template. Once these steps are completed for all resources, the clean-up phase starts.

4.4   *The clean-up phase*

After the execution phase, ARM optionally performs a clean-up phase, where resources that exist in Azure but are not specified in your template are removed.

Using the deployment mode, you decide whether this clean-up phase is executed or not. There are two deployment modes that you can choose from to decide how your infrastructure is deployed:

- Incremental
- Complete

The deployment mode is specified using an extra parameter when you submit the deployment. Using the Azure CLI, you would do this by specifying an extra parameter, like --mode Complete. Using Azure PowerShell, you would use -Mode Complete. The default value for the deployment mode is Incremental, and only when you choose a deployment mode of Complete is the clean-up phase executed.

During the clean-up phase, authorizations using RBAC and resource lock checks are performed, just as during the execution phase. If any of these checks fail, resources are not removed.

4.4.1   *Incremental deployment mode*

With `Incremental` deployments, you create or update resources as defined in your ARM template. Incremental deployments do not change resources that are not present in the ARM template. Nor will they change property values of existing resources when these properties are not specified within the template.

Suppose you are deploying an ARM template that contains a Storage Account B to a resource group that already contains another Storage Account A. In figure 4.5, you can see that Storage Account B is deployed, next to the existing Storage Account A. The result of this deployment is that you now have two different storage accounts.

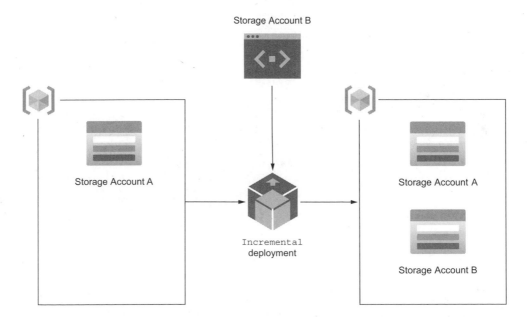

Figure 4.5   Example of an ARM template deployment using the `Incremental` deployment mode

4.4.2   *Complete deployment mode*

Using the `Complete` deployment mode, ARM changes your existing environment to precisely reflect your ARM template's content. This means that when resources exist in your cloud environment but don't exist in your ARM template, they are removed. This is done during the clean-up phase, where all these resources are cleaned up.

Figure 4.6 shows how ARM deploys the template when the deployment mode is set to `Complete`. As in the previous section, Storage Account A is present in the cloud and Storage Account B is specified in the template. After the deployment of the

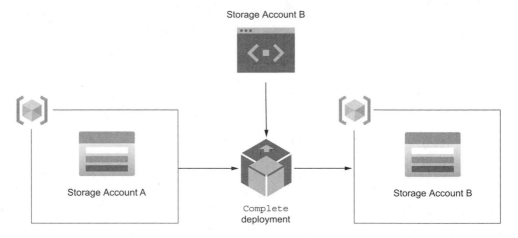

Figure 4.6   Example of an ARM template deployment using the `Complete` deployment mode

template, ARM removes Storage Account A during the clean-up phase because it was not specified in the template.

4.4.3 *Combining deployment modes*

Now let's consider these deployment modes in a real-world situation. You are the developer of a website that you host in Azure. Because your system is a worldwide success and is deployed in various Azure regions, your team decides to rename all services to keep better track of which services are deployed where. And last, but not least, you want one process to take care of all this with the least amount of downtime.

To do this, you update the code of your application to use the new names and update your templates to define the resources you need with the new name. This means that the names of the service plan and web app are changed like this:

- The `service-plan` resource is renamed to `service-plan-westeurope`.
- The `service-app` resource is renamed to `service-app-westeurope`.

To automate the creation of the new infrastructure and the removal of the old infrastructure, you decide to take a two-step approach. In figure 4.7, the same ARM template is deployed twice, the first time in `Incremental` mode, to create resources with the new names. During this deployment, the names ending in `westeurope` will be created next to the existing resources. After this creation, the new application code is deployed, which starts using the newly created infrastructure. After some time, the same template is deployed, but now in `Complete` mode. In this second deployment, the old infrastructure that is no longer needed is also removed.

> **WARNING** Please note that while the preceding approach is valid, its implications should be carefully considered in real-world scenarios. For example, using this approach with databases can potentially destroy data, as data in databases is not automatically backed up using this approach.

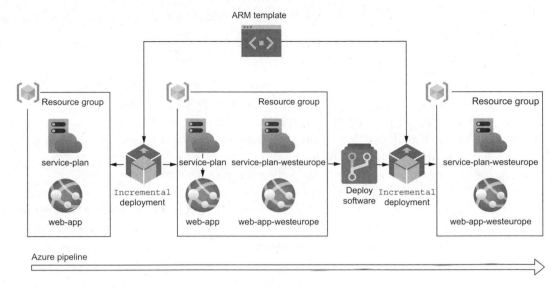

Figure 4.7   Combining incremental and complete deployment mode

Now that you have a complete understanding of what happens when you deploy an
ARM template, let's explore two approaches for validating your template and the possible deployment outcomes.

4.5   *Template validation and what-if deployments*

When working with real applications, it is important to verify whether your templates
are valid before you deploy them. Also, before making updates to existing infrastructure, you may want to verify which changes ARM will make when you deploy the template for real. For both these cases, ARM provides a solution.

4.5.1   *Validating an ARM template*

The first thing that ARM always does before it starts the actual deployment of a template is validate it. It is also possible for you to trigger this validation yourself. You can
manually trigger validation by specifying a deployment mode of `validate`:

```
az deployment group validate
    ➥ --subscription "subscription-name-or-id"
    ➥ --resource-group "resource-group-name"
    ➥ --template-file "path-to-arm-template.json"
```

The preceding example does not deploy the template but terminates after the validation phase. This way, you can validate that the template is well-formatted and valid,
that functions correctly evaluate, that there are no conflicting names, and that you
have the proper authorizations on the deployment scope.

When you are working with a CI/CD pipeline, you can use the `validate` deployment mode to check whether or not your ARM templates can deploy successfully.

Often the validation is performed as soon as possible in the pipeline to provide fast feedback to developers.

4.5.2   *What-if deployments*

What-if deployments are used for determining what would happen if you deployed an ARM template. What-if deployments are useful when you are about to make changes to a production environment and you need to verify that the correct changes will be made.

A what-if deployment goes through the complete deployment process you learned about in this chapter, but with one difference. Instead of making actual changes to your Azure environment, it outputs the changes it would make as text.

Because ARM templates can quickly become large, it can be challenging to get an overview of changes and their effect on your different environments. Performing a what-if deployment before the actual deployment gives you that little bit of extra confidence you may need to run a template.

A what-if deployment is started using the Azure CLI, like this:

```
az deployment group what-if
    --subscription "subscription-name-or-id"
    --resource-group "resource-group-name"
    --template-file "path-to-arm-template.json"
```

This is the same syntax you would use for deploying the template, but with one change. The `what-if` keyword replaces the `create` keyword. Referring back to the example in section 4.4.2, where you were performing a `Complete` deployment of Storage Account B to a resource group that already contained Storage Account A, if you were to run this as a what-if deployment, you would receive the output shown in figure 4.8.

```
C:\Users\EduardKeilholz>az deployment group what-if --mode Complete --template-file template.json --resource-group "My
-Resource-Group"
Note: The result may contain false positive predictions (noise).
You can help us improve the accuracy of the result by opening an issue here: https://aka.ms/WhatIfIssues

Resource and property changes are indicated with these symbols:
  + Create
  * Ignore

The deployment will update the following scope:

Scope: /subscriptions/16fa3d0c-8ec3-488a-bff3-b37c932cba84/resourceGroups/My-Resource-Group

  + Microsoft.Storage/storageAccounts/asufdkjashbf [2021-04-01]

      apiVersion:        "2021-04-01"
      id:                "/subscriptions/16fa3d0c-8ec3-488a-bff3-b37c932cba84/resourceGroups/My-Resource-Group/provider
s/Microsoft.Storage/storageAccounts/asufdkjashbf"
      kind:              "StorageV2"
      location:          "westeurope"
      name:              "asufdkjashbf"
      sku.name:          "Premium_LRS"
      tags.displayName:  "asufdkjashbf"
      type:              "Microsoft.Storage/storageAccounts"

  * Microsoft.Storage/storageAccounts/asdkfjhaskfhdg

Resource changes: 1 to create, 1 to ignore.
```

Figure 4.8   Executing a `what-if` deployment in PowerShell

After running the `what-if` command, you can see which changes ARM would make if the deployment were to be executed for real. In figure 4.8 you can see the two changes that we mentioned before. First, the `armtemplatebook` storage account is removed, and then the `renamedstorageaccnt` storage account is created.

Template validation and what-if deployments are great for validating your template and checking for desired outcomes, but you'll still run into deployment errors now and then. Let's take a look at how you can troubleshoot these errors.

4.6 *Troubleshooting template deployments*

The Azure Resource Manager does provide some information about errors, or problems in general, when a deployment fails. But to be honest, you need to have some experience with ARM to fully understand the error messages and know how to solve problems. Unfortunately, there is no such thing as debugging ARM templates and running through templates step by step to see which steps succeed or fail.

However, some strategies may help you get back on track when you encounter problems. One, which seems extremely obvious, but is often overlooked, is to move back to the previous working version. Once you get the old template back up and running again, you can try to move to the desired version step by step, to see where your problem is. If you run into a problem again, go back again and take an even smaller step. This way, you can locate the precise cause of the problem.

Another approach is to navigate to the Azure portal and find the failing deployment there. You can click on its details to see the error details. Sometimes this will give you the more detailed information you need to pinpoint the cause of the problem. When you browse the deployments list, you can redeploy a template by selecting it and clicking the Redeploy button. That will take you to another view in the portal, where you can edit the original template and then redeploy. This is a bit of a trial-and-error approach, but it may help you to find your issue.

The last strategy for finding the cause of your problems is to break your template into linked templates, a technique that is discussed in chapter 5. This may sound strange at first, as this feels like you will be increasing complexity. However, when you use many small, linked templates and one template that brings all these templates together, they all appear as separate deployments in the portal. You can then more easily spot where the error is located, as that specific deployment will fail. This helps in narrowing down the cause of your problem.

Summary

- Azure allows you to organize resources into different levels of groups: management groups, subscriptions, and resource groups. A template deployment always targets one of these groups.
- Management groups are the highest level and allow you to group subscriptions into logical containers, which makes it easier to manage access, policies, and compliance in larger environments.

- ARM is a built-in tool for orchestrating complex deployments across multiple subscriptions and regions.
- ARM has an option for performing a clean-up phase to remove resources that exist in Azure but are not specified in your template.
- The deployment mode allows you to decide whether the clean-up phase is executed and how your infrastructure is deployed.
- What-if deployments are used to determine what would happen if you deploy an ARM template. They are useful for verifying that the correct changes are going to be made before deploying to a production environment.

Writing advanced ARM templates

This chapter covers

- Writing an ARM template that deploys to more than one scope
- Structuring large IaC solutions into more than one template
- Dealing with dependencies and ordering resources in a deployment
- Advanced constructs like conditions, loops, and deployment scripts
- Reverse engineering existing infrastructure into an ARM template

In chapter 3 we explored the different sections of an ARM template and learned how to use all of them. In that chapter, we also worked on the infrastructure for an API that serves as the backend for a web shop that was responsible for processing the orders that come in, among other things. There was an App Service for hosting the API itself, and other components like a Key Vault, Application Insights, SQL Server and database, and storage accounts. This chapter will continue with those components and use them to go into more advanced ARM topics.

The first few sections of this chapter deal with topics that you'll run into when your templates become larger, such as how to deploy to more than one scope, how to split them up, and how to order the deployment of resources. Next up are more advanced techniques that do not necessarily relate to larger templates but are more complicated in themselves: conditions, loops, and deployment scripts. You can use these constructs to optionally deploy resources, deploy a series of similar resources, or interleave resource deployment with custom scripts. Let's first explore how to deploy to multiple scopes from a single template.

5.1 *Deploying to multiple scopes using nested templates*

When your infrastructure gets more complicated, you might run into a situation where you need to deploy resources to different scopes from within a single deployment. That's a challenge, since a template by default targets a single scope. For example, suppose you want to create a resource group and a storage account in that, within the same template. Since a resource group is deployed to the subscription but the storage account is deployed to the resource group, that requires a deployment to multiple scopes. Another example could be that your infrastructure needs a Key Vault, and you decide to deploy that into a resource group that you name shared and which is used for resources you share among applications. You then deploy a storage account for a particular application into another resource group. The account key for that storage account needs to be stored in the Key Vault, but that now lives in another resource group. Using a nested deployment allows you to make these cross-scope deployments.

As the name implies, a *nested template* is a complete template written within another template. The reason for doing this is that the nested template can target another deployment scope than the main deployment does, such as another resource group, a subscription, or a management group.

In figure 5.1 you can see a template file called template.json that contains a template like you've seen before. The greater part of that template, which we call the *main template*, is deployed to Resource Group A within Subscription A. You set the values for this resource group and subscription while starting a deployment, as you saw in chapter 4. A smaller part of this file, the nested template, is deployed into Resource Group B within Subscription B. You will shortly see how you can control the values for the resource group and subscription in a nested template. Listing 5.1 shows how you can place a nested template within a main template.

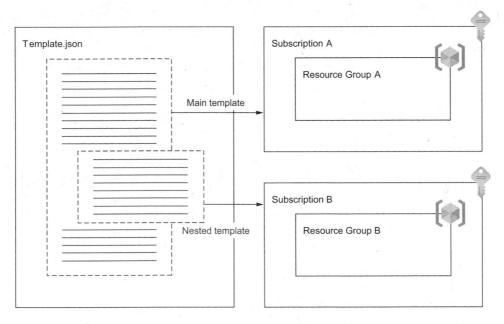

Figure 5.1 Nested templates can target a different deployment scope.

Listing 5.1 A template containing a nested template

```
{
    "$schema": "https://schema.management.azure.com/schemas/
       ➥ 2019-04-01/deploymentTemplate.json#",
    "contentVersion": "1.0.0.0",
    "parameters": {},
    "variables": {},
    "resources": [
        {
            "type": "Microsoft.Resources/deployments",
            "apiVersion": "2019-10-01",
            "name": "nestedTemplate1",
            "properties": {
                "template": {
                    <nested-template-syntax>          ◁——  At this location
                }                                           you specify a
            }                                               nested template.
        }
    ],
    "outputs": {
    }
}
```

Within the resources section in the preceding template, where you normally define resources like a storage account or SQL Server, you'll see a resource of type `Microsoft` `.Resources/deployments`. That type is being used for the nested deployments. Its most important property is the `template` property. That's where you define another complete template, including things like `schema`, `contentVersion`, `parameters`, and, of course, at least one resource.

Let's build an example that needs a nested deployment. We'll start with the following snippet, which deploys an Azure App Configuration resource.

```
{
    "type": "Microsoft.AppConfiguration/configurationStores",
    "apiVersion": "2019-11-01-preview",
    "name": "[variables('appConfigurationName')]",
    "location": "[parameters('location')]",
    "sku": {
        "name": "free"
    }
}
```

Azure App Configuration is a service that allows you to manage application settings and feature flags for one or more applications and environments in a single place. Since this is typically a resource that you share among applications and environments, like test and production, you only deploy one of these into a resource group or subscription with shared resources.

In this chapter's scenario, the API, running on the Azure App Service, will need to be able to load its settings from the Azure App Configuration service. The most secure way to access the App Configuration from the App Service is to use the App Service's managed identity. For this to work, you need to assign a reader role on the App Configuration to the App Services identity. You would typically include this role assignment in the App Service deployment, as that is where you know the identity of the App Service. The challenge here is that the App Configuration resource is shared and is therefore placed in another resource group and maybe even in another subscription. That means that you cannot deploy both the App Service and the role assignment from the same template, since that would require two different deployment scopes.

To work around this challenge, you can use a nested template to assign the required role when deploying the App Service. The following listing shows how to write a nested template within the template that deploys the App Service.

Listing 5.2   A nested template within its main template

```
{
    "$schema": "https://schema.management.azure.com/schemas/
        ➥ 2019-04-01/deploymentTemplate.json#",
    "contentVersion": "1.0.0.0",
    "parameters": {},
    "variables": {                                         RBAC role: App
        "appConfigurationReaderRoleId":                    Configuration
            ➥ "516239f1-63e1-4d78-a4de-a74fb236a071"   ◁── Data Reader
    },
```

```
"resources": [
    {
        "apiVersion": "2018-02-01",
        "name": "API",
        "type": "Microsoft.Web/sites",
        "location": "West Europe",
        "identity": {
            "type": "SystemAssigned"
        },
        "properties": {
            ...
        }
    },
    {
        "type": "Microsoft.Resources/deployments",    ◄─── The nested template resource
        "apiVersion": "2020-06-01",
        "name": "RoleAssignmentOnAppConfig",
        "resourceGroup": "<resourcegroup-appconfiguration>",
        "subscriptionId": "<subscription-appconfiguration>",    ◄──
        "dependsOn": [
            "API"
        ],                                             The subscription that
        "properties": {                                this nested template
            "mode": "Incremental",                            deploys to
            "template": {
                "$schema": "https://schema.management.azure.com/schemas/
2019-04-01/deploymentTemplate.json#",
                "contentVersion": "1.0.0.0",
                "resources": [
                    {
                        "type":
"Microsoft.AppConfiguration/configurationStores/
providers/roleAssignments",
                        "apiVersion": "2018-01-01-preview",
                        "name": "[concat('AppConfiguration',
'/Microsoft.Authorization/',
guid('API', variables('appConfigurationReaderRoleId')))]",
                        "properties": {                       roleDefinitionId
                            "roleDefinitionId":    ◄───        contains the
[concat('/providers/Microsoft.Authorization/roledefinitions/',   role you want
variables('appConfigurationReaderRoleId'))]",              to assign.
                            "principalId":    ◄──
"[reference('API', '2019-08-01', 'full').identity.principalId]"
                        }
                    }                              principalId contains a
                ]                              reference to the identity
            }                                  that's allowed access.
        }
    }
],
"outputs": {
}
}
```

The resource group that this nested template deploys to ──┐ (points to `"resourceGroup"` line)

This example deploys two resources: it first deploys the App Service that hosts the API and then deploys the role assignment using a nested template. In a nested template, you can define a different `resourceGroup` and `subscriptionId` than you are deploying the main template in, and thereby change the scope for this nested template. (You'll see an example that targets another management group shortly.) In this example, the different `resourceGroup` and `subscriptionId` are the ones that contain the App Configuration. That means that the template defined in the `template` element is deployed to that scope.

The first property within the `properties` object of the nested template is the `mode`, which is set to `incremental`. This mode refers to deployment modes you read about in section 4.4. Setting this to `incremental` might suggest that it is also possible to set it to `complete`, but that is not the case. For nested templates, the deployment mode always depends on the deployment mode of the main template. The resources defined in the nested template are automatically included in the evaluation when deploying to the same resource group. Any resource that is not defined in either the main or nested template is deleted when the main template's deployment mode is `complete`.

In this example, the nested template is used to deploy the role assignment. Deploying a role on a single resource is done by deploying a resource of type `roleAssignments` to the resource you want to assign it to. Here we deploy a role on the App Configuration resource, so the type becomes `"Microsoft.AppConfiguration/configurationStores/ providers/roleAssignments"`. The properties section has two properties: `role-DefinitionId` and `principalId`. The `roleDefinitionId` property points to the role you want to assign. That could be a built-in or custom RBAC role. This example uses the built-in App Configuration Data Reader role. The GUID used in the `appConfiguration-ReaderRoleId` variable is a static and unique role identifier that is always the same for every Azure customer, and it can be found in Microsoft's "Azure built-in roles" article (http://mng.bz/YGej). The `principalId` property points to the identity that you want to assign the role to. Here we retrieve the `principalId` of the API by using the `reference()` function and drilling into its result using `.identity.principalId`.

5.1.1 Nested templates on a management group

So far you have seen a nested template being used to deploy a resource to a different subscription or resource group. You can also use them to deploy a resource to a different management group as shown in the following listing.

Listing 5.3   A nested template on a management group

```
{
    "$schema": "https://schema.management.azure.com/schemas/
        ➥ 2019-08-01/managementGroupDeploymentTemplate.json#",
    "contentVersion": "1.0.0.0",
    "variables": {
        "rootManagementGroupName": "rootManagementGroup",
        "rootManagementGroupId":
            ➥ "[tenantResourceId('microsoft.management/managementGroups',
```

```
                    ➡ variables('rootManagementGroupName'))]",
        "testManagementGroupName": "Test",
        "testManagementGroupScope":
                    ➡ "[format('/providers/Microsoft.Management/managementGroups/{0}',
                    ➡ variables('testManagementGroupName'))]",
        "contributorRoleDefinitionId":
                    ➡ "b24988ac-6180-42a0-ab88-20f7382dd24c",
        "roleDefinitionId":
                    ➡ "[concat('/providers/Microsoft.Authorization/roledefinitions/
                    ➡ 'b24988ac-6180-42a0-ab88-20f7382dd24c',
                    ➡ variables('contributorRoleDefinitionId'))]",
        "adGroupPrincipalId": "d14b006f-f50c-4239-840c-0f0724e428f9"
    },
    "resources": [
        {
            "type": "Microsoft.Management/managementGroups",    ⬅  Creating a new
            "apiVersion": "2020-05-01",                              management
            "scope": "/",                                           group
            "name": "Test",
            "properties": {
                "details": {
                    "parent": {
                        "id": "[variables('rootManagementGroupId')]"   ⬅
                    }
                }                                                      Specifying a
            }                                                          management
        },                                                             group's parent
        {
            "type": "Microsoft.Resources/deployments",
            "apiVersion": "2019-10-01",
            "name": "ContributorRoleOnAzurePlatformEngineer",
 Setting the   "scope": "[concat('Microsoft.Management/managementGroups/',
 scope of                   ➡ variables('testManagementGroupName'))]",
 the nested    "location": "westeurope",
 template      "properties": {
                "mode": "Incremental",
                "template": {
                    "$schema":
                            ➡ "https://schema.management.azure.com/schemas/
                            ➡ 2019-04-01/deploymentTemplate.json#",
                    "contentVersion": "1.0.0.0",
                    "resources": [                      The resource type
                        {                               used to deploy a
                            "type":                     role assignment
➡ "Microsoft.Authorization/roleAssignments",   ⬅
                            "apiVersion": "2020-04-01-preview",
                            "name":
                        ➡ "[guid('/', variables('adGroupPrincipalId'),
                        ➡ variables('contributorRoleDefinitionId'))]",
                            "properties": {
                                "scope":
                  Setting           ➡ "[variables('testManagementGroupScope')]",
          the scope of the        "principalId": "[variables('adGroupPrincipalId')]",
          role assignment         "roleDefinitionId":
                                    ➡ "[variables('roleDefinitionId')]"
```

```
                         }
                     }
                 ]
             }
         }
     }
   ]
}
```

The preceding listing contains two resources. It will first create a new management group using the type `Microsoft.Management/managementGroups`. This new management group, named `Test`, will be deployed within the root management group. That is done by specifying its parent `id` in the `properties` section (`properties .details.parent.id`). The second resource deployed in this template will assign the contributor role to an AAD group on that management group. This role assignment type, namely `Microsoft.Authorization/roleAssignments`, is different than the one used in the previous example where you assigned a role on a specific resource. Since the scope is no longer present in that type, you need to specify it in the `scope` property. For that to work, however, the scope defined there must match the deployment scope. Since this template is deployed at a higher scope, the `root- Management` group, you need the nested template. In the nested template, you can set the current deployment scope by using the `scope` property to point to the new `Test` management group.

This template can be deployed at the root management group scope using the following Azure CLI command:

```
az deployment mg create \
   --location WestEurope \
   --management-group-id rootManagementGroup \
   --template-uri "azuredeploy.json"
```

Here you use the `az deployment mg create` command to deploy the template to the `rootManagementGroup` management group specified using the `--management-group-id` switch.

5.1.2   *Evaluation scope*

When deploying a nested template, you get to specify what scope to use when evaluating an expression. This scope determines how parameters, variables, and functions like `resourceGroup()` and `subscription()` are resolved. You can choose between the scope of the main template or the scope of the nested template. The `expression- EvaluationOptions` property allows you to specify which one by using either the value `inner` or `outer`, which refer to the nested and the main template respectively. The default value is `outer`.

In listing 5.2, you saw a `subscriptionId` defined in a nested template that was different from the `subscriptionId` that the template file was deployed to. Therefore, it

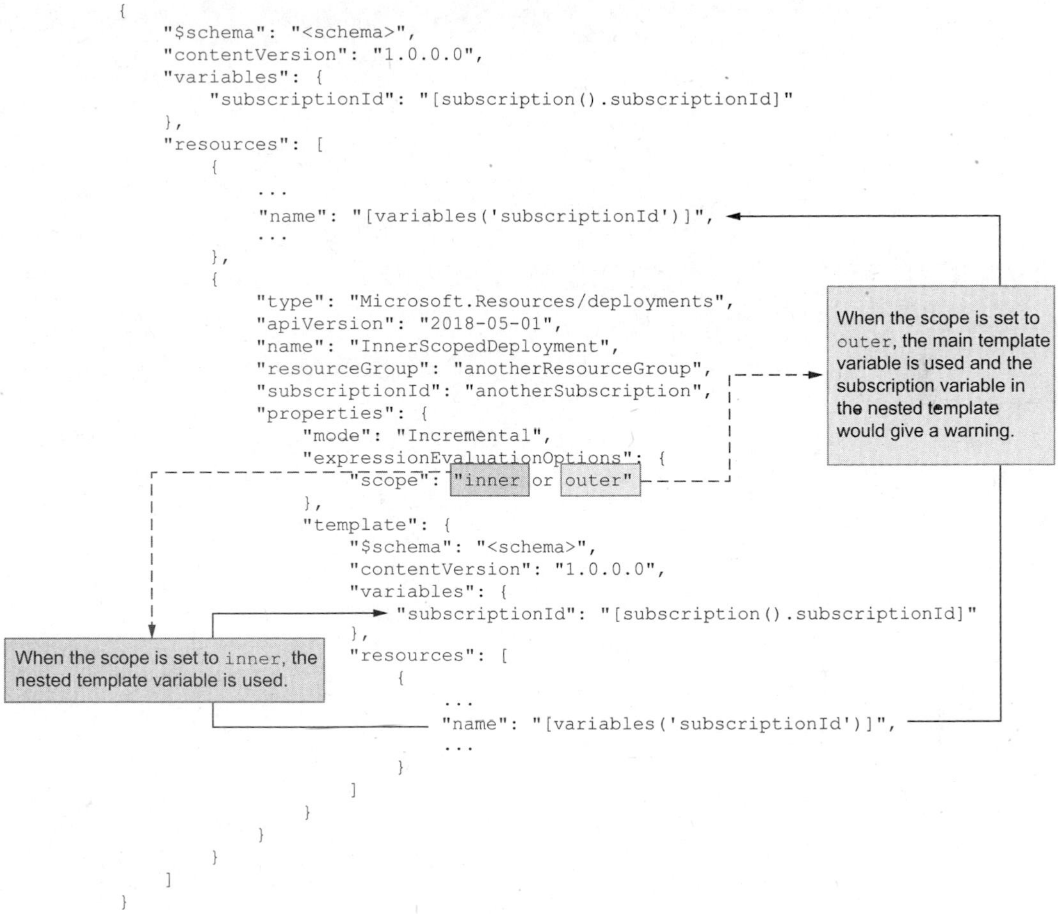

```
{
    "$schema": "<schema>",
    "contentVersion": "1.0.0.0",
    "variables": {
        "subscriptionId": "[subscription().subscriptionId]"
    },
    "resources": [
        {
            ...
            "name": "[variables('subscriptionId')]",
            ...
        },
        {
            "type": "Microsoft.Resources/deployments",
            "apiVersion": "2018-05-01",
            "name": "InnerScopedDeployment",
            "resourceGroup": "anotherResourceGroup",
            "subscriptionId": "anotherSubscription",
            "properties": {
                "mode": "Incremental",
                "expressionEvaluationOptions": {
                    "scope": "inner or outer"
                },
                "template": {
                    "$schema": "<schema>",
                    "contentVersion": "1.0.0.0",
                    "variables": {
                        "subscriptionId": "[subscription().subscriptionId]"
                    },
                    "resources": [
                        {
                            ...
                            "name": "[variables('subscriptionId')]",
                            ...
                        }
                    ]
                }
            }
        }
    ]
}
```

When the scope is set to `outer`, the main template variable is used and the subscription variable in the nested template would give a warning.

When the scope is set to `inner`, the nested template variable is used.

Figure 5.2 Function evaluation scope is determined by `expressionEvaluationOptions.scope`.

was deployed into another subscription than the main template. Suppose you're using the `subscription()` function within the nested template. When you set the scope to `outer`, that will return the subscription of the main template. When set to `inner`, it will return the subscription defined in the `subscriptionId` property in the nested template.

The example in figure 5.2 defines a variable named `subscriptionId` twice—both in the main template and in the nested template. Depending on the value of the `scope` property, the result is different.

If you specify `inner` as the scope, you can no longer reference parameters or variables defined in the main template. The consequence of this is that if your nested template requires input, you would have to specify parameters and pass values from the main template, as shown in the following listing.

Listing 5.4   A nested template that requires parameters

```
{
    "name": "templateWithParameters",
    "type": "Microsoft.Resources/deployments",
    "apiVersion": "2019-10-01",
    "properties": {
        "expressionEvaluationOptions": {
            "scope": "inner"
        },
        "mode": "Incremental",
        "parameters": {                          ◁── Specifying a value
            "vmName": {                              for the parameter
                "value": "TestVirtualMachine"        defined within
            }                                        the template
        },
        "template": {
            "$schema": "https://schema.management.azure.com/schemas/
                ➡ 2019-04-01/deploymentTemplate.json#",
            "contentVersion": "1.0.0.0",
            "parameters": {              ◁── Specifying parameters
                "vmName": {                  within the nested
                    "type": "string"         template
                }
            },
            "resources": [
                {
                    "type": "Microsoft.Compute/virtualMachines",
                    "apiVersion": "2020-06-01",
                    "name": "[parameters('vmName')]",
                    "properties": {
                        ...
                    }
                }
            ]
        }
    }
}
```

In the preceding listing, you again see a nested template, this time with the scope set to inner. To pass the VM's name in, the template now has a parameter defined: vmName. Before the nested template's definition, a value for that parameter is also specified in the main template. This is very similar to how you would specify a parameter on a normal template and then supply a variable using a parameter file.

When thinking about evaluation scopes, we recommend using inner wherever possible. An evaluation scope of inner makes sure that every nested template has a clear, defined scope and cannot accidentally reach parameters or variables from the main template.

5.1.3 Outputs

Just as with standalone templates, you can also return values from a nested template using outputs. You define them as follows:

```
{
    "type": "Microsoft.Resources/deployments",
    "apiVersion": "2019-10-01",
    "name": "nestedTemplateOutputExample",
    "properties": {
        "mode": "Incremental",
        "template": {
            ...
            "outputs": {
                "sampleName": {
                    "type": "string",
                    "value": "sampleValue"
                }
            }
        }
    }
}
```

The preceding snippet defines an output, in the `outputs` section, named `sampleName` within a nested template. You could use that output in the main template as shown in the following expression:

```
"[reference('nestedTemplateOutputExample').outputs.sampleName.value]"
```

When using nested templates to reach other deployment scopes, outputs are often the easiest way to pass generated values back to the main template.

When you start working with nested templates, you'll quickly notice that your templates become larger and larger. Now it's time to discuss how you can structure larger ARM template solutions to make them more manageable.

5.2 How to structure solutions

Small to medium solutions are best off with a single template containing all resources. It makes the solution easier to understand and maintain. For larger, more advanced solutions, you can use linked templates to break down the solution into smaller, more understandable, reusable solutions. Before diving into the details of linked templates, let's first look at two high-level approaches to structuring ARM template solutions.

5.2.1 Small to medium solutions

As said previously, small to medium solutions work best in a single file. For example, you could create one template that contains all the resources for a particular application to run. For a second application, you could then create another template. When you do so, it's good to combine resources that have the same lifecycle and that are changed together. If you also follow the advice to group resources with the same life-cycles in a resource group, you will get one ARM template per resource group. The following snippet shows an example folder structure that follows this approach.

```
+-- API
|    +-- api.json
|    +-- api.parameters.test.json
|    +-- api.parameters.prod.json
|    +-- azure-pipelines.yml
+-- Configuration
|    +-- configuration.json
|    +-- configuration.parameters.test.json
|    +-- configuration.parameters.prod.json
|    +-- azure-pipelines.yml
+-- ...
```

This example contains two root folders that relate to different application components and resource groups. Each folder represents a group of resources that is intended to be deployed independently from the others. The first one, API, contains resources to run the API. Think of the App Service plan, the App Service, and the storage accounts. The second folder, Configuration, could contain the Key Vault and App Configuration. You'll often share these resource types across multiple applications, so they have a different lifecycle. Within each folder, there is a separate template, separate parameter files, and a separate deployment pipeline (in this case, the azure-pipelines.yml files).

5.2.2   *Large solutions*

For larger solutions, it is highly recommended that you break down your templates into smaller templates. Thais allows for better readability, maintainability, and reuse of templates. One way to do this is by separating templates into *resource templates* and *composing templates*. Resource templates are the building blocks for the solution. Each of those templates creates one particular resource. There might be a resource template that creates a Key Vault, another that creates a storage account, and another that creates the App Service. Composing templates are the glue that combines the resource templates, the building blocks, into a useful infrastructure. Figure 5.3 illustrates this.

You can build up a tree structure in large solutions using composing and resource templates. It all starts with the main template, which is a special version of a composing template. The main template is the template that you reference when deploying the whole tree, and it includes all other templates, both composing templates and resource templates. Nothing prevents you from having composing templates that use other composing templates.

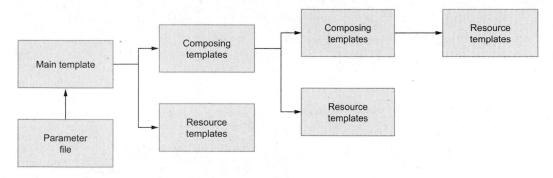

Figure 5.3 Composing templates and resource templates

Using this approach, you can build a large infrastructure while still keeping the individual templates small and readable. The folder structure for your solution could look like this:

```
+-- Composing
|   +-- API
|       +-- Main.json
|       +-- Main.parameters.test.json
|       +-- Main.parameters.prod.json
|       +-- api.json
|       +-- storage.json
|       +-- azure-pipelines.yml
|   ...
+-- Resources
|   +-- SQL
|       +-- Server.json
|       +-- Database.json
|   +-- Web
|       +-- AppService.json
|       +-- AppServicePlan.json
+-- ...
```

The preceding example contains a few resource templates in the Resources folder—those create one particular resource. For the names of the subfolders, you could use the namespace of the resource. The Composing folder contains an API folder that contains templates to deploy the infrastructure for the API. The deployment starts with the Main template, which also has two parameter files. That Main template then includes the storage.json and api.json templates, which in turn call the Resources templates. Figure 5.4 illustrates this. Now that you've seen how to structure a large solution that spans multiple files, it is time to learn how to write linked templates.

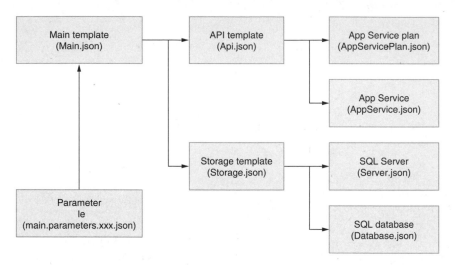

Figure 5.4   A visual representation of how the templates use one another

5.3   *Modularizing templates with linked templates*

The `linkedTemplate` resource type works much like the nested `template` you saw earlier. The difference is that instead of embedding a template within the resource, you reference another file to use as the template. Everything you learned in section 5.1 about nested templates, such as working with the evaluation scope, setting another resource group or subscription ID, parameters, or output, is identical for linked templates.

Let's look at an example:

```
{
    "type": "Microsoft.Resources/deployments",
    "apiVersion": "2019-10-01",
    "name": "linkedTemplate",
    "properties": {
        "mode": "Incremental",
        "templateLink": {
            "uri": "link/to/newStorageAccount.json",
            "contentVersion": "1.0.0.0"
        }
    }
}
```

Instead of the `template` object you saw in the nested template, a linked template has a `templateLink` object. This example uses the `uri` field in the `templateLink` object to specify the URI for another template file. If you choose to specify a `contentVersion` (optional), ARM checks if the `contentVersion` here matches the `contentVersion` specified in the linked template. If not, the deployment is aborted.

There are three ways to reference another template from a `templateLink` object:

- Using a URI
- Using a relative path
- Using a template spec

The last option, using a template spec, is discussed in chapter 10. Let's take a look at the other two options.

5.3.1 Using a URI

As you saw in the preceding example, the `uri` field allows you to call another template while deploying. The value in that field needs to be accessible over the internet using HTTP or HTTPS so that the Azure Resource Manager can use it. Therefore, you can't point to your local machine, your local network, or a private repository on GitHub or in Azure DevOps. But that does not mean that the template needs to be publicly available to everyone.

A common way of making a template available over the internet but still keeping the contents secure is by storing the template in an Azure storage account. You can then create a shared access signature (SAS) token to enable access during deployment.

```
"templateLink": {
    "uri": "[concat(variables('baseUri'),
        '/Resources/WebApp/WebApp.json')]",
    "queryString": "[parameters('containerSasToken')]",
    "contentVersion": "1.0.0.0"
}
```

The `uri` field in the preceding example is used to reference another template. It gets a value by concatenating a `baseUri`, defined in a variable for reuse, with the path to the template you want to use. That would, for example, result in the following URI:

```
https://booktemplates.blob.core.windows.net/templates/
    Resources/WebApp/WebApp.json
```

The `queryString` property is then used to add the SAS token to it. You can, for example, generate that using the Azure CLI:

```
az storage blob generate-sas \
    --account-name <storage-account> \
    --container-name <container> \
    --permissions acdrw \
    --expiry <date-time>
```

The preceding command will return a SAS token that looks similar to this one:

```
?st=2021-03-05T09%3A16%3A56Z&se=2021-03-06T09%3A16%3A56Z
    &sp=racwdl&sv=2018-03-28&sr=c
    &sig=wMp3vAaG1ThAhZ4L5wTRASFWcI6ttTH4r0z6%2FRQwfb0%3D
```

The complete URI that the linked template will use, combining the uri and query-String properties, will look like this:

```
https://booktemplates.blob.core.windows.net/templates/
    ➡ Resources/WebApp/WebApp.json?st=2021-03-05T09%3A16%3A56Z
    ➡ &se=2021-03-06T09%3A16%3A56Z&sp=racwdl
    ➡ &sv=2018-03-28&sr=c
    ➡ &sig=wMp3vAaG1ThAhZ4L5wTRASFWcI6ttTH4r0z6%2FRQwfb0%3D
```

As mentioned before, you can pass in parameters the same way as with nested templates. However, one additional method on a linked template is to use the parameters-Link property to reference a separate parameters file:

```
"templateLink": {
    "uri": "https://link/to/newStorageAccount.json",
    "contentVersion": "1.0.0.0"
},
"parametersLink": {
    "uri": "https://link/to/newStorageAccount.parameters.json",
    "contentVersion": "1.0.0.0"
}
```

The preceding example shows how to specify a parameter file as input for the linked template using the uri field in the parametersLink object. The benefit of using this approach over the separate parameters is that it becomes more manageable to group and use the values. As with the template file itself, you also need to provide the SAS token while referencing the parameter file.

LINKED TEMPLATES AND CI/CD

As you read in chapter 4, you can deploy your ARM templates using a CI/CD pipeline. That becomes a bit harder with linked templates, as they have to be accessible over the internet, so you would need to upload your templates on every change.

What you can do is copy all your templates to a new folder (container) in your storage account within the build stage in your CI/CD system. The name of the container could be the ID of the current build, for example. An example of a URL would then be something like this:

```
https://boektemplates.blob.core.windows.net/
    ➡ <BUILD-ID>/Resources/WebApp/WebApp.json
```

That would lock this specific version of the templates with this specific run of your CI/CD pipeline, since it gets its own unique name. Later on in the pipeline, during the deployment, you would point to the templates in this specific container. That ensures that you would use these versions of the templates when later running your test or production stage, even if another new pipeline run comes in between, since that would create a new container and not overwrite the existing files.

Here is a part of an example pipeline used in Azure DevOps that contains this process:

```
stages:
- stage: 'PublishTemplates'
  displayName: 'Publish Templates'
  jobs:
    - job: 'PublishTemplates'
      steps:
      - task: AzureCLI@2
        displayName: "Create container $(Build.BuildId)"
        inputs:
          azureSubscription:
              ➥ ${{ variables.azureResourceManagerConnection }}
          scriptType: 'bash'
          scriptLocation: 'inlineScript'
          inlineScript: 'az storage container create --connection-string
              ➥ "${{ variables.storageAccountConnectionString }}"
              ➥ -n $(Build.BuildId)
              ➥ --account-name ${{ variables.storageAccountName }}'
      - task: AzureCLI@2
        inputs:
          azureSubscription:
              ➥ ${{ variables.azureResourceManagerConnection }}
          scriptType: 'bash'
          scriptLocation: 'inlineScript'
          inlineScript: 'az storage blob upload-batch --account-name
              ➥ ${{ variables.storageAccountName }} -d $(Build.BuildId)
                -s $(build.artifactstagingdirectory)/templates
              ➥ --connection-string
              ➥ "${{ variables.storageAccountConnectionString }}"'
```

An Azure CLI task that creates a new container on the storage account

An Azure CLI task that uploads the templates

The template contains two tasks. The first uses the Azure CLI to create a new folder (container) within the storage account. It uses the ID of the build as its name, using `$(Build.BuildId)`. This `$(Build.BuildId)` is a predefined variable in Azure DevOps; more on that can be found in Microsoft's "Use predefined variables" article (http://mng.bz/GE4A). The second task uses the Azure CLI to upload all templates to this new container.

The next stage in the pipeline could then deploy the templates to Azure:

```
- stage: 'DeployTemplates'
  displayName: 'Deploy Templates'
  jobs:
    - job: 'DeployTemplates'
      steps:

      - task: AzureResourceManagerTemplateDeployment@3
        inputs:
          deploymentScope: 'Resource Group'
          azureResourceManagerConnection:
              ➥ ${{ variables.azureResourceManagerConnection }}
          subscriptionId: ${{ variables.subscriptionId }}
```

```
       action: 'Create Or Update Resource Group'
       resourceGroupName: 'arm-template-demo'
       location: 'West Europe'
       templateLocation: 'Linked artifact'
       csmFile: '<storageaccountUrl>/$(Build.BuildId)/
          ➥ Composing/Main.json'
       csmParametersFile: '<storageaccountUrl>/$(Build.BuildId)/
          ➥ Composing/Main.parameters.test.json'
       deploymentMode: 'Incremental'
```

The preceding snippet shows a new stage that contains one task. This task will deploy the template using the `csmFile` property pointing to the storage account. Note the use of `$(Build.BuildId)` again here to point to the same container created in the previous stage. The entire template can be found on GitHub here: http://mng .bz/z4l6.

5.3.2 *Using a relative path*

As the heading suggests, you can also address another template using a relative path instead of a full URI. You do this by specifying a relative path to the linked template:

```
{
    "type": "Microsoft.Resources/deployments",
    "apiVersion": "2020-10-01",
    "name": "childLinked",
    "properties": {
        "mode": "Incremental",
        "templateLink": {
            "relativePath": "storage/storageAccount.json",
            "queryString": "[parameters('containerSasToken')]"
        }
    }
}
```

Here, the `relativePath` property is used in the `templateLink` object. The relative path should point to a linked template, relative to the location of the template currently deploying. To make this work, the folder structure where the JSON is hosted during the deployment should look like this:

```
+-- Templates
|   +-- mainTemplate.json
|   +-- storage
|       +-- storageAccount.json
```

Remember that this relates to the storage where the files should be available over the internet during deployment. The `relativePath` option does not refer to the location on your local computer.

   In several of the examples you have seen in this book, there is a relationship between the resources. Therefore, they must be deployed in a particular order. Let's examine how you can enforce the order of deployment.

5.4   Deploying resources in order

Sometimes you'll have a pair of resources that have to deploy in a specific order. For example, the web shop presented in the scenario in chapter 3 needs an App Service to run an API. This App Service needs an App Service plan to run on, which needs to be deployed first.

Defining order in ARM templates can be done in two ways:

- *Explicitly*—Using the dependsOn element
- *Implicitly*—Using a reference to the output of another resource

5.4.1   Explicit deployment ordering

In the following listing, you'll see the creation of two resources, the App Service plan and the App Service.

Listing 5.5   Explicit ordering between resources

```
"resources": [
    {
        "name": "appServicePlan",
        "type": "Microsoft.Web/serverfarms",
        "apiVersion": "2020-06-01",
        "location": "[resourceGroup().location]",
        "sku": {
            "name": "F1",
            "capacity": 1
        }
    },
    {
        "name": "webApp",
        "type": "Microsoft.Web/sites",
        "apiVersion": "2018-11-01",
        "location": "[resourceGroup().location]",
        "dependsOn": [                        ⟵──┐ Specifying the dependency between
            "appServicePlan"                      │ resources using dependsOn
        ],
        "properties": {
            "serverFarmId": "[resourceId('Microsoft.Web/serverfarms',
        ➥       'appServicePlan')]"
        }
    }
]
```

On the second resource, the App Service, you'll find the dependsOn element. That is an array that can hold one or more references to other resources. By adding this dependsOn element, the ARM runtime can build up a dependency tree and deploy resources in the correct order. In this example, you make sure that the App Service plan is deployed first, because you specified its name in the App Service's dependsOn element.

There are three ways in which you can define the resource to wait for in the `dependsOn` element:

- `[resourceId('Microsoft.Sql/servers/', parameters('serverName'))]`—You can use the `resourceId()` function if the resource to wait for has been deployed outside of the current template, such as in a linked template or as part of another deployment.
- `[parameters('serverName')]`—You can use an expression that points to the name of another resource within the same template.
- Constant value, such as `'appServicePlan'`—You can simply specify the name of another resource deployment within the same template.

The third option is by far the most readable, but it has the downside of being static. If you change the name of the deployment, you'll need to remember to change this value as well. The second option solves that problem by reusing a parameter that specifies the name of a deployment. The first option does the same but for resources that are not defined in your current template. Since that option is less readable, you should only use it when the resource is not defined in the current template.

It's important to know that even when you define a resource as a child resource, you still need to specify its dependency. Let's look at an example in the following listing.

Listing 5.6 Mandatory dependency on a parent resource

```
"resources": [
    {
        "name": "appServicePlan",
        "type": "Microsoft.Web/serverfarms",
        "apiVersion": "2018-02-01",
        "location": "[resourceGroup().location]",
        "sku": {
            "name": "F1",
            "capacity": 1
        },
        "resources": [
            {
                "name": "webApp",
                "type": "sites",
                "apiVersion": "2018-11-01",
                "location": "[resourceGroup().location]",
                "dependsOn": [
                    "appServicePlan"
                ],
                "properties": {
                    "serverFarmId":
                        ➥ "[resourceId('Microsoft.Web/serverfarms',
                        ➥ 'appServicePlan')]"
                }
            }
        ]
```

```
        }
    ]
```

The preceding listing again deploys an App Service plan and an App Service. The App Service is defined as a child resource but still has the `dependsOn` element. If you left that out, the deployment would fail because ARM wouldn't automatically add the `dependsOn` element for you.

5.4.2   Implicit deployment ordering

Another way to enforce order while deploying a template is by using an output from a linked or nested template, as you saw in the previous section. Suppose your App Service deployment outputs the name of the App Service.

```
"outputs": {
    "webappName": {
        "type": "string",
        "value": "[variables('webappname')]"
    }
}
```

You can now use that value in another template as follows:

```
"[reference('<name-of-resource>').outputs.webappName.value]"
```

By doing that, you have implicitly specified a deployment order. The ARM runtime waits for the reference resource to be deployed, since it needs the output.

Using the explicit way of describing ordering is better in terms of understandability and the templates' readability. It also makes sure that the order is still in place when you stop using the output. So although you could use the implicit method, the general advice is not to rely on it.

Sometimes you'll want to control whether a resource in your template should be deployed or not, depending on an expression. This is what conditions allow you to do.

5.5   Conditionally deploying resources

After some hard work, the web shop you have been creating resources for throughout chapter three and this chapter becomes a huge success. The business expands into other regions, and traffic increases month after month. However, after a couple of outages, you decide that it's time to make the API more resilient. Remember, the API runs on an Azure App Service, and the way to make an App Service geo-redundant and more resilient is to deploy it into more than one region. Besides West Europe, you decide to also deploy the API into North Europe. But now that you have the app running in multiple regions, you need an Azure Traffic Manager to distribute traffic over the two deployments.

To save on costs, you decide that deploying to a second region is a bit too much for your test environment and that you don't need a Traffic Manager there. A condition allows you to dictate just that. Examine the following example.

Listing 5.7   Adding a condition on a resource

```
"resources": [
    {
        "condition": "[equals(parameters('environment'), 'production')]"     ◄────┐
        "type": "Microsoft.Network/trafficManagerProfiles",                        Using a condition
        "apiVersion": "2018-04-01",                                                 to only deploy
        "name": "[parameters('trafficManagerName')]",                            this resource to
        "location": "global",                                                      your production
        "properties": {                                                            environment
            "profileStatus": "Enabled",
            "trafficRoutingMethod": "Geographic",
            "monitorConfig": {
                "protocol": "HTTPS",
                "port": 443,
                "path": "[parameters('path')]",
                "intervalInSeconds": 10,
                "toleratedNumberOfFailures": 2,
                "timeoutInSeconds": 5,
                "expectedStatusCodeRanges":
            ➡         "[parameters('expectedStatusCodeRanges')]"
            },
            "endpoints": "[parameters('endpoints')]",
            "trafficViewEnrollmentStatus": "Disabled"
        }
    }
]
```

This example deploys the Azure Traffic Manager. The first line on the resource is the `condition` element. It accepts an expression that needs to result in a Boolean value. In this example, the condition verifies that the environment you deploy to is the production environment. Only if that condition evaluates to `true` is the Traffic Manager deployed.

Another interesting element in listing 5.7 is the `location`, which is set to `global`. A Traffic Manager is one of the few resources you don't deploy to a specific region but globally. For each user request, it determines the best endpoint to route the request to. The remainder of the configuration is specific to the Traffic Manager service and out of scope for this book.

One thing to keep in mind is that, although a condition might evaluate to `false`, the resource is still in the template and will be validated during the deployment. That means that every function you use within this resource's definition still needs to work, and inputs to those functions need to be valid. Consider the following snippet that deploys a storage account:

```
{
    "$schema": "https://schema.management.azure.com/schemas/
        ➡ 2019-08-01/managementGroupDeploymentTemplate.json#",
    "contentVersion": "1.0.0.0",
    "parameters": {
        "storageAccount": {
            "type": "object",
            "defaultValue": {
                "enabled": true,
                "name": "storageaccount",
                "sku": {
                    "name": "Standard_GRS"
                }
            }
        }
    },
    "resources": [
        {
            "condition": "[parameters('storageAccount').enabled]",
            "type": "Microsoft.Storage/storageAccounts",
            "apiVersion": "2019-04-01",
            "name": "[parameters('storageAccount').name]",
            "sku": {
                "name": "[parameters('storageAccount').sku.name]"
            },
            "kind": "StorageV2",
            "location": "West Europe"
        }
    ]
}
```

This example uses a condition to check whether the storage account should be deployed or not. Even when `enabled` is set to `false`, you would still need to provide the full object in the `storageAccount` parameter; you could not just drop the `name` and `sku` properties because references to the `name` and `sku` properties would throw errors while the template is being validated.

A workaround here could be to use the `if()` function. Instead of writing

```
"name": "[parameters('storageAccount').name]"
```

you could write

```
"name": "[if(parameters('storageAccount').enabled,
    ➡ parameters('storageAccount').name, '')]"
```

That `if()` statement checks the `enabled` property and uses the `name` property when `enabled` is set to `true`; it returns an empty string when it's set to `false`.

Another thing to note is that the name of every resource still needs to be unique. If you are using a condition to deploy one resource or the other, both resources' names need to be unique, even though only one will be deployed.

You can use `dependsOn` with a conditional resource without any issues. When the deployment condition evaluates to `false`, the resource is also deleted from all `dependsOns` by the Resource Manager.

5.5.1   *Applying conditions to output*

Conditions can also be applied to outputs. Actually, this is required when an output refers to a conditional resource. If you don't apply the condition to the output, an error will be thrown if the condition is not met, as the resource and output won't exist.

```
"outputs": {
    "resourceID": {
        "condition": "[equals(parameters('environment'), 'production')]",
        "type": "string",
        "value": "[resourceId('Microsoft.Network/trafficManagerProfiles',
            ➥ parameters('trafficManagerName'))]"
    }
}
```

This example shows how to use the `condition` element within an output. The template returns the `resourceId` of the Traffic Manager created. The `condition` element contains the same expression that's used in the resource. Therefore, the `resourceId()` function in the `value` property is only evaluated when the condition is `true`.

There are situations in which you'll want to create multiple instances of one particular resource type. You could copy the entire resource in the template, but better yet, you can use the `copy` element to implement loops.

5.6   *Using loops to create multiple resources*

In the web shop architecture, you saw two storage accounts. One is used to store the PDF files that the API generates, and the other is used to store logs. These types of data have different usage characteristics, like being publicly available or not and the level of storage redundancy they might need. You could store all the data in one storage account, but considering how the different types are used, it is better to separate the two.

To create multiple instances of the same resource type without copying and pasting the resource template, you can use the `copy` element to iterate over an array. The copy element has the following syntax:

```
"copy": {
    "name": "<name-of-loop>",
    "count": <number-of-iterations>,
    "mode": "serial" <or> "parallel",
    "batchSize": <number-to-deploy-serially>
}
```

The `name` of the copy is its unique identifier, like for any other resource. The `count` property specifies the number of resources to create. You'll often assign the length of the array you are looping over to `count`.

The mode lets you specify whether you want to create your resources in a serial or parallel way. The default here is parallel. In a parallel copy, all resources are created in parallel, and the order in which they are created is not guaranteed. But sometimes, you will need a specific order. In these cases, you can use the serial option. Serial mode deploys the resources one by one. This also helps with resources for which you cannot deploy multiple instances at the same time.

In between serial and parallel, it is also possible to have resources created in batches. For this option, choose the serial mode by setting the batchSize property to a value higher than 1 (which is the default).

Let's look at an example of how you could use the copy element to create multiple resources:

```
"variables": {
    "storageAccountNames": [
        "datastorage",
        "logstorage"
    ]
},
"resources": [
    {
        "type": "Microsoft.Storage/storageAccounts",
        "name": "[variables('storageAccountNames')[copyIndex()]]",
        "copy": {
            "name": "storagecopy",
            "count": "[length(variables('storageAccountNames'))]"
        },
        "sku": {
            "name": "Standard_GRS"
        },
        "kind": "StorageV2",
        "apiVersion": "2019-04-01",
        "location": "West Europe"
    }
]
```

The preceding example creates two storage accounts using the copy element. The names of the storage accounts are defined in an array in a variable called storage-AccountNames. Within the count property of the copy element, you can see the length() function being used, with the array as input, to determine the number of iterations.

Resources that are generated using copy need to have unique names—just like any other resources. As the resource definition is copied multiple times, the only way to do that is to generate a name through an expression. In this case, the name is read from the storageAccountNames array. You can use the copyIndex() function to get the current position in the loop and retrieve an item from a particular index in the array.

One thing to be careful of is handling empty arrays. You might use a parameter of type array, which is specified to be optional and can thus be empty. If you use that in a copy element, you will receive the following error while deploying:

```
"The template resource '[concat( 'some-prefix-', parameters( 'nameParamArray'
)[copyIndex()] )]' at line 'XX' and column 'YY' is not valid: The language
expression property array index '0' is out of bounds."
```

That happens because the resource on which you are using the copy element is still being evaluated by the runtime, even when the array is empty. The copyIndex() function returns 0, which is not a valid index on an empty array. A workaround to that issue is to use the following syntax on the name property in the previous example:

```
"name": "[if(greater(length(variables( 'storageAccountNames' )), 0),
    ➥ variables('storageAccountNames')[copyIndex()], 'emptyArray')]",
```

This snippet checks if the array's length is greater than 0 using a combination of the greater() and length() functions. If that is true, the array's value for position 0 is returned. Otherwise, a dummy value, emptyArray, is returned. As an alternative solution, you could also specify a condition on the resource to have no resources deployed at all.

In the preceding example, the copy element is used on a resource. It can also be used on the following other elements:

- Variables
- Properties
- Output

Let's address each of them in turn.

5.6.1   *Using copy on variables*

The copy element can be used within the variables element to create an array.

```
"parameters": {
    "itemCount": {
        "type": "int",
        "defaultValue": 3
    }
},
"variables": {
    "storageAccounts": {
        "copy": [
            {
                "name": "names",
                "count": "[parameters('itemCount')]",
                "input": "[concat('myStorageAccount-', copyIndex())]"
            }
        ]
    }
}
```

This `variables` element contains an object called `storageAccounts`. The `copy` element in it has a `name`, `count`, and `input` defined. Again, the `name` is the loop identifier and is used as the name for the resulting array on the `storageAccounts` object. The `count` again specifies the number of iterations. The `input` is used to specify the value for each element in the resulting array, which in this case, is a string that is a concatenation of a string and the loops index. The outcome of this `copy` element is as follows:

```
"storageAccounts": {
    "names": [
        "myStorageAccount-0",
        "myStorageAccount-1",
        "myStorageAccount-2"
    ]
}
```

The outcome is a variable with the name `storageAccounts`. That variable holds an array with three items, which results from three times the input on the `copy` element.

5.6.2 Using copy on properties

You can also use the `copy` element to create properties on a resource. Let's examine the following example, in which a virtual network with its subnets is created:

```
{
    "$schema": "https://schema.management.azure.com/schemas/
        ➡ 2019-04-01/deploymentTemplate.json#",
    "contentVersion": "1.0.0.0",
    "parameters": {
        "virtualNetworkName": {
            "type": "string"
        },
        "subnets": {
            "type": "array",
            "defaultValue": [
                {
                    "name": "firstSubnet",
                    "addressPrefix": "10.0.0.1/25"
                }
            ]
        }
    },
    "resources": [
        {
            "apiVersion": "2019-09-01",
            "name": "[parameters('virtualNetworkName')]",
            "type": "Microsoft.Network/virtualNetworks",
            "location": "West Europe",
            "properties": {
                "addressSpace": {
                    "addressPrefixes": [ "10.0.0.1/24" ]
                },
                "copy": [
```

```
                        {
                            "name": "subnets",
                            "count": "[length(parameters('subnets'))]",
                            "input": {
                                "name":
➡ "[parameters('subnets')[copyIndex('subnets')].name]",
                                "properties": {
                                    "addressPrefix":
➡ "[parameters('subnets')[copyIndex('subnets')].addressPrefix]",
                                    "privateEndpointNetworkPolicies":
                                        ➡ "Disabled"
                                }
                            }
                        }
                    ]
                }
            }
        ]
    }
}
```

The resource created here is a virtual network. That network is further divided into chunks of IP addresses, called *subnets*. You define those subnets as an array in the properties element of the virtual network. Since that is an array, you can use the copy element to fill it. Again, the copy's name becomes the resulting array's name, the count specifies the number of iterations, and the input specifies each item's format in the result.

In this example, each iteration returns an object. The end result of the copy element follows:

```
"subnets": [
    {
        "name": "firstSubnet",
        "properties": {
            "addressPrefix": "10.0.0.1/25",
            "privateEndpointNetworkPolicies": "Disabled"
        }
    },
    ...
]
```

5.6.3 *Using copy on output*

When you create multiple instances of a resource out of an array, it is sometimes necessary to return a property value from each created instance. Maybe you're creating a list of storage accounts and then you need to return a list of all primary BLOB endpoints. Since that could be a dynamic list, you can use the copy element in the outputs section to create a dynamic output in the form of an array:

```
"outputs": {
    "storageEndpoints": {
        "type": "array",
```

```
        "copy": {
            "count": "[length(parameters('storageAccountArray'))]",
            "input": "[reference(concat(copyIndex(),
                ➥ variables('baseName'))).primaryEndpoints.blob]"
        }
    }
}
```

The preceding `copy` element loops over each created storage account. In each itera-tion, the `reference()` function is used to retrieve the resource details and return the BLOB endpoint. This results in one primary BLOB endpoint for each storage account in the list.

5.6.4   *Waiting for a loop to finish, using dependsOn*

As you saw earlier, you can use the `dependsOn` element to dictate deployment order. To wait for a loop to finish, you could use the `name` of the `copy` element in the `dependsOn` element of another resource, as shown here:

```
{
    "$schema": "https://schema.management.azure.com/schemas/
        ➥ 2019-04-01/deploymentTemplate.json#",
    "contentVersion": "1.0.0.0",
    "parameters": {},
    "variables": {
        "storageAccountNames": [
            "datastorage",
            "logstorage"
        ]
    },
    "resources": [
        {
            "type": "Microsoft.Storage/storageAccounts",
            "name": "[variables('storageAccountNames')[copyIndex()]]",
            "copy": {
                "name": "storageIterator",
                "count": "[length(variables('storageAccountNames'))]"
            },
            "sku": {
                "name": "Standard_GRS"
            },
            "kind": "StorageV2",
            "apiVersion": "2019-04-01",
            "location": "West Europe"
        },
        {
            "type": "another-resource",
            "dependsOn": [ "storageIterator" ]    ◁─┐  Using dependsOn
        }                                           │  to wait for a loop
    ]                                               │  to finish
}
```

The preceding example would make the deployment of the second resource wait for a `copy` element called `StorageIterator` to finish.

Not everything in Azure is managed using ARM templates. Sometimes it is necessary to use PowerShell or the Azure CLI for automating a process. One way of doing that is to include a script in your deployment process, but another way of running that script is using a `deploymentScript` resource in an ARM template.

5.7 *Deployment scripts*

Deployment scripts are a way of executing scripts as part of an ARM deployment. This allows you to interleave script execution with resource creation, which is particularly useful for automating tasks that do not relate directly to Azure resources. For example, these are some tasks that cannot be achieved with ARM templates:

- Performing data plane operations, such as copying BLOBs or seeding databases
- Creating a self-signed certificate
- Creating an object in Azure AD
- Looking up a value from a custom system

Deployment scripts allow you to run a script within your ARM template deployment. It's a resource like all the other examples you've seen so far, and its type is `Microsoft .Resources/deploymentScripts`. Deployment scripts support Azure PowerShell and Azure CLI as scripting languages.

While deploying the templates, the deployment script launches a Linux container on Azure Container Instances, uploads your script to a storage account (1), and runs the script within the container (2, 3). Any result of the script will be pushed back and be available in your ARM template (4). Figure 5.5 illustrates this.

The fact that your script runs on Linux is important, because it sometimes limits what you can do with PowerShell. For example, you cannot do as much with PowerShell in relation to Active Directory as you could in Windows, simply because the commands do not exist in the Linux version of PowerShell Core.

Let's look at an example of how to use a deployment script resource. In chapter 3, you created a SQL Server and used various methods to provide the administrator password. Although the `secureString` type and the Key Vault reference work well, the best way to authenticate with a SQL Server is to use personal accounts stored in Active Directory instead of a shared administrator. To make that possible, you need to assign an AD identity as the administrator on the SQL Server.

Doing this involves the following steps:

1 Assign an identity to your SQL Server. This identity is used for authenticating sign-in requests with AD.
2 Assign Directory Reader permissions to the identity in the previous step.
3 Make an identity administrator on SQL. This second identity is used for connecting to the SQL server. The validity of this identity can be verified using the first identity.

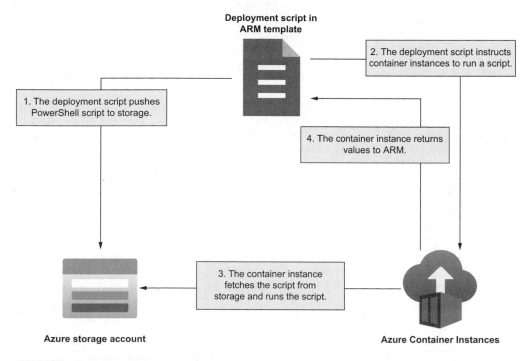

Figure 5.5   A visual representation of the deployment script process

The first step can be done using ARM templates, but the other two cannot, since they involve reading from and writing to Active Directory. Instead, a deployment script can be used to automate the task as part of an ARM deployment.

The first two steps are out of scope for this book, but step three makes for a great example of deployment scripts, so let's implement that step. The end goal here is to assign a user or group from Active Directory as the administrator on the SQL Server. That, at first, seems a simple task that can be done using the following ARM template.

Listing 5.8   A deployment script resource

```
"resources": [
    {
        "type": "Microsoft.Sql/servers/administrators",
        "name": "[concat(parameters('serverName'), '/activeDirectory')]",
        "apiVersion": "2019-06-01-preview",
        "location": "[parameters('location')]",
        "properties": {
            "administratorType": "ActiveDirectory",
            "login": "[parameters('adminLogin')]",
            "sid": "[parameters('adminObjectID')]",
            "tenantId": "[subscription().tenantId]"
        }
    }
]
```

This template deploys a resource of type `administrators` on your existing SQL Server. The `administratorType` in the `properties` object specifies that you are going to use Active Directory. The `login` and `sid` specify the user or group to use as the administrators. The hard part in this snippet is the `sid`. That is the object ID from your user or group in AD, which cannot be retrieved using an ARM template. To get the `sid`, you will have to use a scripting language like PowerShell or the Azure CLI. This makes it an ideal candidate to see how deployment scripts work. The flow is illustrated in figure 5.6.

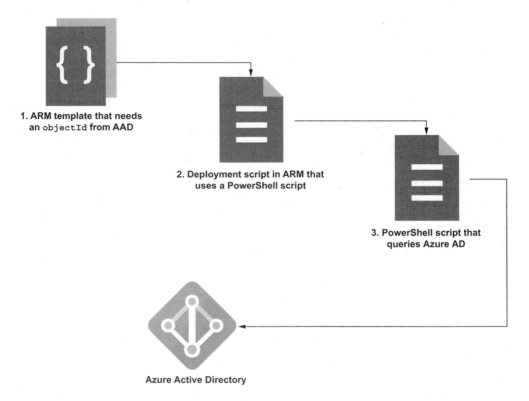

1. ARM template that needs an `objectId` from AAD

2. Deployment script in ARM that uses a PowerShell script

3. PowerShell script that queries Azure AD

Azure Active Directory

Figure 5.6   A visual representation of interacting with Azure AD using a deployment script

In figure 5.6, step 1 is where you assign the administrator to the SQL Server. As mentioned earlier, that requires you to get a value for the `sid`. Step 2 in the figure defines a deployment script resource in your ARM template. That runs a PowerShell script, step 3, that reaches out to Active Directory and returns the requested `sid` value.

Using a deployment script means creating two things: the `deploymentScripts` resource in an ARM template and a script file called from the deployment script. Let's first look at listing 5.9 for the `deploymentScript` resource (DeploymentScripts/deploymentscript.json); the PowerShell script will follow shortly.

Listing 5.9 A deployment script resource

```
"resources": [
    {
        "type": "Microsoft.Resources/deploymentScripts",
        "apiVersion": "2020-10-01",
        "name": "GetADGroupId",
        "location": "[resourceGroup().location]",
        "kind": "AzurePowerShell",
        "properties": {
            "forceUpdateTag": "[parameters('refresh')]",
            "azPowerShellVersion": "7.0",
            "primaryScriptUri": "path/to/GetGroupObjectId.ps1",
            "supportingScriptUris": [],
            "environmentVariables": [
                {
                    "name": "clientId",
                    "secureValue": "[parameters('clientId')]"
                },
                {

                    "name": "clientSecret",
                    "secureValue": "[parameters('clientSecret')]"
                }
            ],
            "arguments": "[concat('-groupName ''', parameters('groupName'),
               ''' -tenantId ', subscription().tenantId)]",
            "timeout": "PT10M",
            "cleanupPreference": "OnSuccess",
            "retentionInterval": "P1D"
        }
    }
],
"outputs": {
    "AadGroupId": {
        "value": "[reference('GetADGroupId').outputs.groupId]",
        "type": "string"
    }
}
}
```

The kind specifies what scripting language to use.

The forceUpdateTag is used to control whether to rerun the script.

Secrets are best passed in using environment variables.

The primaryScriptUri specifies the script to run on start.

Values can be passed in using arguments.

Like any resource in an ARM template, this one starts with the required properties you have seen before. The first new property is the kind, which specifies the scripting language you are using (AzurePowerShell in this case). The azPowerShellVersion property specifies the PowerShell version to use. The other option is, as mentioned before, the Azure CLI.

The remainder of the properties are defined in the properties object. First, forceUpdateTag allows you to trigger a new run of the script. When this value is different from the value during the previous deployment, the deployment script is executed. If the value remains the same, it is not. The second property, primaryScriptUri, defines the script to run, and supportingScriptUris allows you to define helper scripts. All scripts are downloaded on deployment, but only the primaryScriptUri is executed.

There is also the option to specify a script inline instead of in a separate file or files. That might work for minimal scripts, but it's not ideal for larger scripts. It becomes hard to read because the editor treats it as a string instead of a script.

There are two ways to provide input to the script: arguments or environment variables. Environments variables are a good fit when you're passing along secrets because environment variables have the secureValue option. Arguments do not have such an option and are therefore exposed in logs, which is not good for secrets. The script in this example uses a clientId and clientSecret for a service principal to log in to Active Directory. Those are secrets and are thus passed along using environment variables. The other input the script needs, the Active Directory group's name, is not a secret and is passed using an argument.

As mentioned before, the script is run within a container on Azure Container Instances. That resource is created for you when the deployment starts, but you can specify a name to use in the template. If you don't, a name is generated, which always ends with "azscripts". Next to the container instance, a storage account is created for you. That is used to store your scripts and logs. You can also assign an existing storage account if you want to.

Let's now take a look at the script itself (DeploymentScripts/script.ps1). In the example in listing 5.10, the script uses the Graph API to fetch the object ID of the group you want to use as the SQL Server administrator and return that as the groupId. Most of the script details are not important here, but in short, it does the following: it grabs secrets from the environment variables, gets an authentication token from the Graph API, and queries the API to get the object ID.

Listing 5.10 A deployment script, to be called from a deployment script resource

```
param([string] $groupName, $tenantId)

$ErrorActionPreference = 'Stop'

$clientId = $env:clientId          ◁—— Get the input secrets
$clientSecret = $env:clientSecret       using the environment
                                        variables.
$Body = @{
    'tenant' = $tenantId
    'client_id' = $clientId
    'scope' = 'https://graph.microsoft.com/.default'
    'client_secret' = $clientSecret
    'grant_type' = 'client_credentials'
}

$url = "https://login.microsoftonline.com/$tenantId/oauth2/v2.0/token"

$Params = @{
    'Uri' = $url
    'Method' = 'Post'
    'Body' = $Body
    'ContentType' = 'application/x-www-form-urlencoded'
}
```

```
$AuthResponse = Invoke-RestMethod @Params          ◁──┐  Get an authentication
                                                      │  token.
$Headers = @{
    'Authorization' = "Bearer $($AuthResponse.access_token)"
}
$groupUrl = "https://graph.microsoft.com/v1.0/groups?
➡   `$filter=displayname eq '$groupName'"
$groupResult = Invoke-RestMethod -Uri $groupUrl -Headers $Headers   ◁──┐
                                                                       │
$groupId = $groupResult.value[0].id             Invoke a request to query
                                                Active Directory for the group.

$DeploymentScriptOutputs = @{}
$DeploymentScriptOutputs['groupId'] = $groupId     ◁──┐ Set a return value in the
                                                      │ $DeploymentScriptOutputs
Write-Host "Finished!"                                  variable.
```

In the last two lines, you see how you can return a value from the script into the ARM environment. Returning outputs is done by assigning a value to a property in the DeploymentScriptOutputs object—in this case, by assigning a value to the groupId property. If you now look back at the deployment script example in listing 5.9, you'll see that you can reference script values in ARM templates in the same way as referencing outputs from nested deployments. First, you grab a reference to the resource, and second, you call the outputs property. This script's output can then be used as input to the template that deploys the administrator on the SQL Server (listing 5.8).

The script is, by default, run using the identity that runs the deployment. This means that if the script needs to perform an Azure resource action, that identity would need permissions to do that. The identity is also used to create the underlying infrastructure needed to run the script, so it needs permissions to create the storage account, container instance, and deployment script resources. You might want to separate these responsibilities and use another identity to perform these actions. The identity property on the deploymentScript resource allows you to set that, as shown in this example:

```
"resources": [
    {
        "type": "Microsoft.Resources/deploymentScripts",
        "apiVersion": "2020-10-01",
        "name": "GetADGroupId",
        "identity": {                      ◁──┐  Set an identity on a
            "type": "userAssigned",           │  deployment script.
            "userAssignedIdentities": {
                "/subscriptions/01234567-89AB-CDEF-0123-456789ABCDEF/
➡   resourceGroups/myResourceGroup/providers/
➡   Microsoft.ManagedIdentity/userAssignedIdentities/myID": {}
            }
        },
        ...
    }
]
```

The preceding snippet shows how you can set a user-defined identity on the `deployment-Script` resource.

The GitHub repository accompanying this book contains a PowerShell script that you can use to prepare your environment to run the preceding deployment script (http://mng.bz/067E). It will create a storage account and upload the script to run within the `deploymentScript`. It also creates a service principal and sets the correct permissions so it can query Azure Active Directory.

You can get details on the execution of the script in multiple places. First, logs are written to the storage account connected to the `deploymentScript`. There is a file share on the storage account that contains the execution results and the stdout file. The Azure portal can also be used to find details on the deployment. Simply navigate to the Deployment Script resource in the portal after deployment.

The overview page in figure 5.7 displays information like the provisioning state. You can also find the connected storage account and container instance. Below that, you'll find the logs. From the left menu, you can view the deployment script content, the arguments passed to the script, and the output.

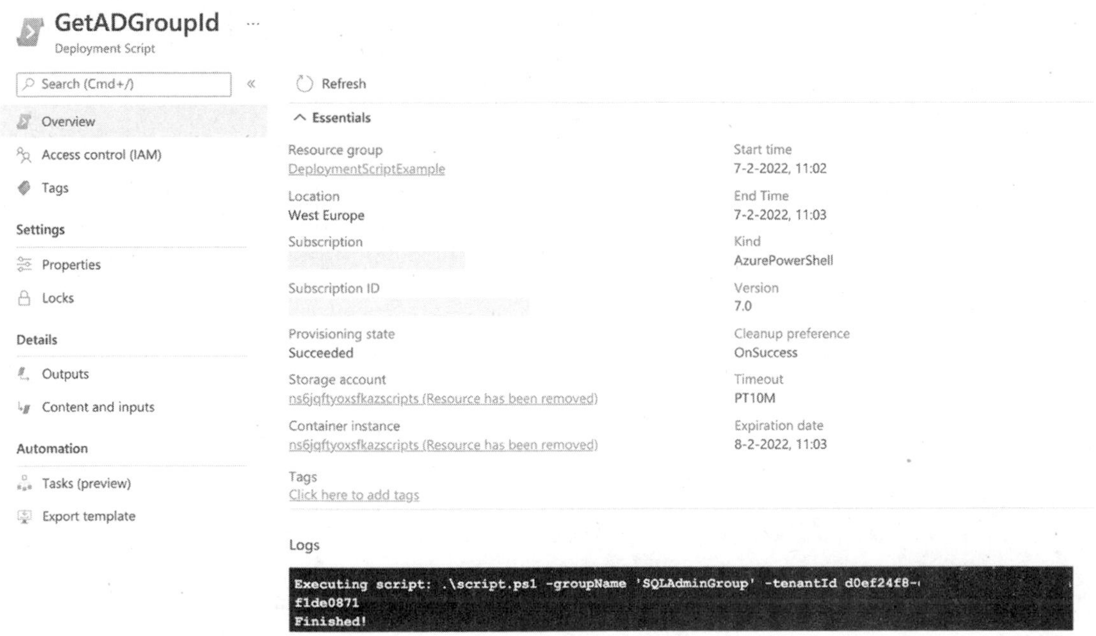

Figure 5.7   Deployment script details

In addition to the previous two options, you could also use PowerShell or the Azure CLI to get the logs. Here's an example using PowerShell:

```
Get-AzDeploymentScriptLog -Name MyDeploymentScript
    ➥ -ResourceGroupName DS-TestRg
```

The preceding command would get you the execution logs from a deployment script resource named `MyDeploymentScript`.

You can start with an empty template file when writing new ARM templates, and the extension in VS Code will help you quite a bit. However, there are a few ways to get a kickstart.

5.8   Reverse engineering a template

There are a few tools you can use to reverse engineer a template. The benefit of such an approach is that you don't have to start from scratch, but can instead copy a great deal of configuration from an existing resource. Let's explore a few options in the Azure portal.

5.8.1   Exporting templates

You'll find an option to export ARM templates for every existing resource or resource group. This option is always there, even if you did not create the resource with a template but, for example, by using the portal. The page you are looking for is found in the menu on the left when viewing any resource or resource group in the Azure portal. It is under the Automation subsection and the menu item is called Export Template. Clicking that menu item shows you a new blade with the ARM template (figure 5.8).

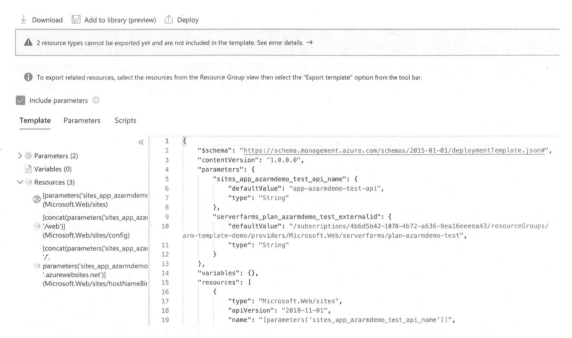

Figure 5.8   Exporting an ARM template

This feature provides you with a complete, deployable template. It contains the resources and may contain parameters if you left the checkbox for them enabled. Exporting is not yet supported for some resources, and when that happens, a warning is shown—you can see an example of this in figure 5.8.

The generated templates contain all the properties on a resource, even those that use default values, which means the templates are lengthy. You might need to trim them down a bit to keep them readable. Depending on the number of resources in a resource group, it might take a while to generate the template.

As you can see in figure 5.8, this page also contains a Deploy button. That feature allows you to deploy the template that's shown directly from the Azure portal. You could use that to quickly edit the template and check the results.

5.8.2   *Using Resource Explorer*

Another way to find a template for an existing resource is to use the Azure Resource Explorer. You can find it in the portal by selecting All Services from the menu and then searching for Resource Explorer. It will show you a tree view with two nodes, providers, and subscriptions. Within Providers, you can find information on the definitions of all Azure resource types (figure 5.9). You could use that if you need detailed

Figure 5.9   Using Resource Explorer

resource information, but the online documentation is probably easier to use. Within Subscriptions, you can find the ARM templates and all of your existing resources.

In this view, you can drill down into your resources by first clicking a specific subscription. You can then find your resources either by the provider or by the resource group that contains them. Resource Explorer won't give you a complete template, but it will give you the details of a specific resource.

5.8.3   Using the JSON view

When you navigate to an existing resource in the Azure portal, you'll see a JSON View button in the top-right corner, as in figure 5.10. Clicking that button will show the full JSON definition for the specific resource displayed. It does not provide a complete template like some of the other options—it only shows this resource and misses parameters, for example.

Figure 5.10   JSON View button on the overview page of a resource

5.8.4   For a new resource

The previous options are only useful on existing resources, but luckily there is also a way to generate a template for new resources using the Azure portal. When you create a new resource, the last step in that process shows you a Download a Template for Automation button. Figure 5.11 shows the final step in the Resource Creation wizard. This specific example shows a storage account, but the Download a Template for Automation button will be there for any resource type.

The output when you click this button is similar to exporting a template, which we discussed earlier. You again are presented with a complete template, with parameters for all the variables you specified in previous steps of the Resource Creation wizard. This option comes in handy when you want a quick start on a completely new resource.

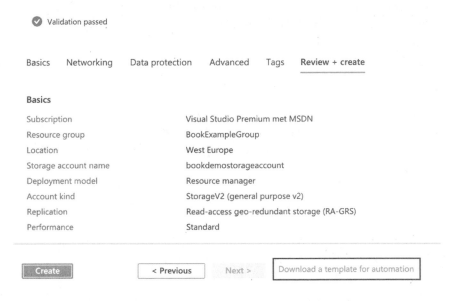

Figure 5.11   Generating a template from a Resource Creation wizard

Summary

- You can deploy to more than one deployment scope from a single ARM template by using nested deployments.
- More extensive ARM solutions can be structured by splitting them into composing and resource templates. That allows for better readability and the reuse of the templates. Medium-sized and smaller solutions can group resources by application component.
- Advanced constructs like dependsOn, conditions, and loops are used for building more complex templates that support use cases with repetition and optional resources.
- Templates can be tough to write, even using the proper tools. By exporting templates, using Resource Explorer, or downloading a template from the Resource Creation wizard, you can save yourself some time by copying template content from existing resources.

Simplifying ARM templates using the Bicep DSL

This chapter covers

- Bicep, a simpler DSL for writing ARM templates
- Transpiling Bicep files into ARM templates
- Bicep notation for resources, parameters, variables, and outputs
- Modules, an easy way to split larger templates into readable pieces

By now you are familiar with ARM templates and the process of writing and deploying them. And hopefully you are impressed with the opportunities that IaC and ARM templates, in particular, give you.

Still, you may have noticed that describing more extensive infrastructure this way is not perfect. It is generally accepted that ARM templates have several drawbacks, mainly because they are written in JSON. These are some examples:

- The JSON notation forces you to group all parameters, variables, and resources into three sections, while it might make much more sense to mix them up and order them not by type but in a way that makes sense for the human reader of the template.

- ARM templates require you to enter expression syntax (`[...]`) for invoking functions, which is a nuisance and makes templates harder to read.
- Having to conform to the JSON specification makes it impossible to introduce more powerful syntax for string interpolation and the usage of parameters and variables without using the `parameters(...)` and `variables(...)` functions.

These drawbacks have fueled much debate in the community on the usefulness of JSON as a language for IaC. This discussion's ultimate consequence has been that more and more users have moved away from ARM templates to alternatives like Terraform and Pulumi. But more recently, a new approach to dealing with the downsides of ARM templates has come up.

New languages have been developed that provide a better way of declaring Azure resources, along with tools that transpile these languages into ARM templates. A *transpiler* is a program that validates its input and transforms it into another format or language—the name is a variation on the term "compiler." One open source example of a transpiler to ARM templates is called Farmer, available at https://compositionalit .github.io/farmer. Another alternative that has recently come up is Bicep. Bicep is a single-purpose DSL for declaring Azure infrastructure. Whereas Farmer is a community project, Bicep is maintained by Microsoft.

At the time of writing, Bicep is fully supported and has been declared ready for production use by Microsoft. The version we used to write this chapter is 0.4.1124. Bicep is still under development and is prone to changes in the future. To check the latest state of the language and the tools that come with it, you can check the Bicep GitHub page (https://github.com/Azure/bicep).

This chapter discusses Bicep in detail—a new syntax for things you have already learned. While this might be a bit dry, we believe that at some point in the future, Bicep templates will replace ARM templates as the de facto language for writing IaC for Azure. Everything you have learned up to now still has value for a couple of reasons: first, Bicep is just an abstraction on top of ARM templates, and second, deploying and debugging the templates doesn't change, because Bicep is transpiled to an ARM template.

6.1 *Bicep: A transpiler*

The most straightforward way to show the benefits of Bicep over ARM templates is by exploring an example. First, look at the following definition for a storage account:

```
{
    "$schema": "https://schema.management.azure.com/schemas/
        ➥ 2019-04-01/deploymentTemplate.json#",
    "resources": [
        {
            "type": "Microsoft.Storage/storageAccounts",
            "apiVersion": "2020-08-01-preview",
            "name": "myStorageAccount",
            "location": "[resourceGroup().location]",
            "kind": "StorageV2",
```

```
        "sku": {
            "name": "Premium_LRS",
            "tier": "Premium"
        }
      }
    ]
}
```

Now compare it with the following declaration of the same storage account, this time using Bicep notation:

```
resource myStorageAccount 'Microsoft.Storage/storageAccounts
    @2020-08-01-preview' = {
    name: 'bicepstorageaccount'
    location: resourceGroup().location
    kind: 'StorageV2'
    sku: {
        name: 'Premium_LRS'
        tier: 'Premium'
    }
}
```

The name of the deployment

The actual resource name

While the notation looks quite different initially, a closer look reveals that both notations describe precisely the same resource. The most notable difference in this example is that the Bicep notation combines the type and apiVersion for a resource into a single resource declaration. The full definition for a resource declaration is

```
resource <symbolic-name> <resourceType>@<apiVersion>
```

You already know about the resourceType and apiVersion properties, but the symbolic-name is new.

The symbolic name (myStorageAccount) is *not* the name of the resource in Azure, and the resource name and the symbolic name are separate properties for a reason. First, the name of the resource in Azure that you have worked with before is still specified using the name property. The symbolic name is new with Bicep, and it's local to the template only. Symbolic names are intended for referencing the resource from within the same template and fetching its properties. You will see how to use this symbolic name later on.

> **TIP** Like for ARM templates, there is an extension for VS Code, called Bicep, to help you edit Bicep files. The extension can be installed the same way you installed the ARM templates extension. If you require instructions on how to install extensions in VS Code, please refer back to chapter 2.

There are some other differences between Bicep templates and ARM templates that you might notice:

- Bicep templates do not start with a JSON schema declaration, saving a few lines and some ceremony. There is also no wrapping array around declared resources.

- Bicep templates don't use commas to separate properties within an object. Just a newline is enough.
- Single quotes are used for opening and closing string literals.
- The `resourceGroup()` function is invoked without using expression syntax (`[...]`), which removes even more ceremony from the template. Another benefit is that you no longer have to escape double quotes in your strings.

All these syntax changes, and more, are discussed in section 6.2. But first, let's explore how to deploy a Bicep template to Azure and how to manually transpile a Bicep template into an ARM template.

6.1.1   *Deploying*

When you are working with the Azure CLI version 2.20.0 or later or Azure Power-Shell version 5.6.0 or later, you can deploy Bicep templates without manually transpiling them first. Both have been updated to transpile Bicep templates on the fly if needed. To use this new capability, you can just provide a Bicep template instead of an ARM template.

When you are working with an older version of the Azure CLI or Azure Power-Shell, or you deploy using other means, you first have to transpile the Bicep templates yourself, and then follow your existing deployment approach.

6.1.2   *Transpiling*

For transpiling a Bicep file into an ARM template, a CLI tool, also called Bicep, is provided by Microsoft. The latest version of this CLI tool is available at https://github .com/Azure/bicep/releases/latest. Builds are available for multiple operating systems and usage scenarios. After you download and install Bicep, the CLI tool should be available in your path and ready for use. As an alternative, you can install and invoke Bicep through the Azure CLI using version 2.22.0 or later. The syntax is then slightly different, as you will see when reading on.

Let's continue with the Bicep example from section 6.1. Save the example code in a file called storage-account.bicep, and run the following command:

```
bicep build storage-account.bicep
```

Or use the following command if you are using the Azure CLI:

```
az bicep build --file storage-account.bicep
```

The first parameter (`build`) to the `bicep` command is the command you need to execute for transpiling. Then you provide the `.bicep` file to be transpiled. During transpilation, not only is the Bicep template transformed into an ARM template, but the transpiler also checks the validity of the template to the fullest extent possible without connecting to your Azure environment. Checks include resource names, API versions, property names, and property types.

After running this command, you should have another file called storage-account .json that contains a resource that is the same as the first ARM template example in this chapter. This resulting ARM template can be deployed as you learned before.

If you are working with the Azure CLI version 0.22.0 or later, you can also deploy Bicep templates directly as follows:

```
az deployment group create --resource-group <resource-group-name>
    --template-file <arm-or-bicep-file>
```

When you specify a Bicep file, the file will automatically be transpiled, after which the resulting ARM template is submitted to the Azure Resource Manager.

The nice thing with a tool like Bicep is that it does not impose any constraints on your choice of template deployment tool. For example, in Azure DevOps, it is relatively straightforward to extend a pipeline with two more tasks: downloading the CLI and executing the transpilation.

> **NOTE** When using Bicep from a pipeline, do not rely on the "latest" version of Bicep. Always retrieve a specific version to guarantee repeatable results. Also, consider caching that version locally to strengthen that guarantee and limit external dependencies.

6.1.3 Decompiling

ARM templates have already been around for years, so many companies have an existing collection of those. While it is possible to only use Bicep for new templates, you might want to convert some of your existing ARM templates into Bicep templates. For example, if you have to make significant changes to an existing template, it might be better first to convert the existing ARM template to a Bicep template. Conversion takes some time, but if you go through this process once, you can then leverage the benefits of Bicep templates. Another scenario where decompiling is helpful is after exporting an ARM template from the Azure portal.

To decompile the ARM template that you generated in the previous section, use the following command:

```
bicep decompile storage-account.json
```

Or use this command with the Azure CLI:

```
az bicep decompile --file storage-account.json
```

Instead of using the `build` command, you use the `decompile` command. And instead of providing a `.bicep` file, you provide a `.json` file. This command's output is a storage-account.bicep file containing the Bicep code.

In this example, the decompile action results in precisely the same Bicep template that you started out with, but this will not always be the case. When you are decompiling more elaborate examples, differences might appear, especially around the use of variables.

In addition to better readability and the removal of ceremony like commas, Bicep also introduces other syntax differences from JSON, so let's explore those next.

6.2   *Bicep syntax differences*

Bicep notation is partially inspired by the JSON notation for ARM templates, Terraform, and other declarative and non-declarative languages. Bicep has its own notation for all the constructs you learned about in chapters 3 and 4. In the following sections, we'll revisit all these constructs and see how they work in Bicep.

6.2.1   *Parameters*

In Bicep, parameters are declared using the `param` keyword:

```
param myParameter string
```

This example declares a parameter with the name `myParameter` of type `string`. The same rules that you learned for JSON names and types apply. Bicep also supports allowed values and defaults. Here is an example using those:

```
@allowed([
    'defaultValue'
    'otherValue'
])
@secure
param myParameter string = 'defaultValue'
```

There are two things to note here: first, the use of annotations, which are keywords starting with the @ sign, and second, the inline assignment of a variable on the last line.

Annotations are used to specify one or more properties of a parameter, and they correspond to the parameter properties you know from ARM templates, like `minValue`, `maxValue`, `minLength`, `maxLength`, and `allowed`. In the preceding example, you'll see the use of `allowed` to specify acceptable values for this parameter. In this case, the annotation `@secure` is used to convert the type from `string` to `secureString`. For parameters, all annotations are optional.

Second, you can specify default values for a parameter by appending the equals sign (`=`) and a value to the parameter declaration. If no value is specified for the parameter when you deploy the template, the default value will be used.

A final difference between Bicep and ARM templates is that Bicep parameters do not have to be grouped within a root object's `parameters` property. Instead, they can be declared anywhere within the file.

> **NOTE**   At the time of writing, Bicep does not have an alternative syntax for writing parameter files. So if you want to work with parameter files, you can still write those in the ARM syntax you learned before. Since Bicep templates transpile to ARM templates, working with parameter files hasn't changed.

6.2.2 Variables

The syntax for variables is similar to that of parameters and looks like this:

```
var myVariable = {
    property: 'stringValue'
    anotherProperty: true
}
```

In this example, a variable with the name `myVariable` is declared, and a value is assigned using the equals operator. While the assignment looks similar to that of a parameter, observe that there is no type declaration. That is because the type of a variable can always be derived from its value. This is called *type inference,* and you may recognize it from programming languages. In this case, the variable is of type `object`.

6.2.3 Outputs

Declaring an output in Bicep is very similar to declaring a variable with a default value. The syntax is the same, except for the keyword, which is `output` here:

```
resource saResource 'Microsoft.Storage/storageAccounts
    ⮡ @2020-08-01-preview' = {
    name: 'myStorageAccount'
    location: resourceGroup().location
    kind: 'StorageV2'
    sku: {
        name: 'Premium_LRS'
        tier: 'Premium'
    }
}

output storageAccountId string = saResource.id
output storageAccountName string = saResource.name
```

The symbolic name is used to refer a resource, a storage account in this case.

This example declares a storage account, as you have seen many times now. The last line is new, however. It returns an `output` of type `string` with the name `storageAccountId`. For the value, the declared storage account is referenced, and its `id` property is retrieved. As you can see in this example, you no longer need the `reference(...)` function. Instead, you use the symbolic name of the declared resource. This allows the use of dot notation to access properties of any resource in the same template directly. You can create as many outputs as you want.

6.2.4 Conditions

Just as in ARM templates, Bicep templates allow for the conditional deployment of resources. To conditionally deploy a resource in Bicep, the following syntax is used:

```
param deployStorage bool = true

resource myStorageAccount 'Microsoft.Storage/storageAccounts
    ⮡ @2020-08-01-preview' = if (deployStorage == true) {
```

Start of the storage account resource declaration

```
    name: 'myStorageAccount'
    location: resourceGroup().location
    kind: 'StorageV2'
    sku: {
        name: 'Premium_LRS'
        tier: 'Premium'
    }
}
```

In the preceding example, the resources' properties come after the assignment operator and are preceded with an `if` clause. With this clause, the resource is only declared if the parentheses' condition evaluates to `true`. When transpiling to an ARM template, the `if` clause will be replaced by a `condition` property on the resource, which you saw in chapter 5.

6.2.5   *Loops*

In ARM templates, loops were hard to write and even harder to read. In chapter 5, you may well have found this the most challenging part of ARM template syntax to understand. In Bicep, loops can still be a bit tricky, but they are definitely easier to understand.

Suppose you want to create three storage accounts from within the same template, and you have declared their names within an array like this:

```
var storageAccounts = [
    'myFirstStorageAccount'
    'mySecondStorageAccount'
    'myFinalStorageAccount'
]
```

In Bicep, you can use the following syntax to create these three storage accounts in one resource declaration:

```
resource myStorageAccounts 'Microsoft.Storage/storageAccounts
    ➡ @2020-08-01-preview' = [for item in storageAccounts: {     ◁
    name: item
    location: resourceGroup().location
    kind: 'StorageV2'                                    Item is used to
    sku: {                                            retrieve the value for
        name: 'Premium_LRS',                          the current iteration.
        tier: 'Premium'
    }
}]
```

The for-item-in-list syntax is used for repeating a resource.

In this example, the second line shows the `[for item in list: { }]` syntax that is used for declaring a loop. (If you are familiar with Python comprehensions, this syntax might seem familiar, as it looks and works similarly.) For `list` you specify the name of any list, either a parameter or a variable. The name for `item` is available within the loop to reference the current item in the list, such as to retrieve its value. Please note, you can use another iterator name than `item`.

You can loop over any valid list, so you can also build a more elaborate variable structure and then use that to create storage accounts with different SKUs, like this:

```
var storageAccounts = [
    {
        name: 'myFirstStorageAccount'
        sku: {
            name: 'Premium_LRS'
            tier: 'Premium'
        }
    }
    {
        name: 'mySecondStorageAccount'
        sku: {
            name: 'Standard_LRS'
            tier: 'Standard'
        }
    }
]
```

> **BatchSize specifies how many resources are created in parallel.**

```
@batchSize(1)     ◁─┘
resource myStorageAccounts 'Microsoft.Storage/storageAccounts
    ➥ @2020-08-01-preview' = [for item in storageAccounts: {
    name: item.name
    location: resourceGroup().location
    kind: 'StorageV2'
    sku: item.sku
}]
```

In this second example, the storageAccounts variable contains a list of objects, instead of a list of strings. Each object contains both a name and an object with the SKU properties for the storage account with that name. The result is that in the loop itself, item now holds the value of each complete object in the two iterations in this loop.

Also note that this example shows a new annotation, @batchSize, which can optionally be used to specify how many resources should at most be created in parallel. Choosing a value of 1, like here, effectively instructs ARM to create resources sequentially.

Loops can also be used in outputs. For example, to return the access tier for all created storage accounts, the following syntax can be used:

```
output storageAccountAccessTiers array = [for i in range(0,
    ➥ length(storageAccounts)): myStorageAccounts[i].sku.tier]
```

Note that the use of storageAccounts within the call to the length(...) function is correct here. This is because it is not (yet) possible to iterate over a list of resources, like myStorageAccounts, directly. Here the code is "misusing" the fact that the number of items in the storageAccounts variable is the same as that in the myStorageAccounts resource list.

In this example, the for-item-in-list syntax is used again, now combined with a new function called range(...). The range(...) function generates a list of numbers, starting at the first parameter and going up to the second parameter. Combining this with the `length(...)` function is a way of generating a list of numbers—in this case, a list with two numbers: `0` and `1`. This is the list over which the loop is executed. In the output value, this number is used to access every member of the array of resources in `myStorageAccounts`, allowing for the return of its access tier.

6.2.6 *Targeting different scopes*

With Bicep it is possible to target different scopes, just as with ARM templates. Instead of specifying the correct JSON Schema, as you do with ARM templates, you can use a `targetScope` declaration at the top of the file.

To target a resource group, you can use the following syntax:

```
targetScope = 'resourceGroup'
```

As a Bicep file targets a resource group by default, this can safely be omitted. Other valid values are `subscription`, `managementGroup`, and `tenant`.

6.2.7 *Known limitations*

At the time of writing, there is not yet support for all ARM template features in Bicep. The most notable limitation is that user-defined functions are not yet supported. Similarly, it is not yet possible to declare arrays or objects on a single line instead of specifying every entry or every property, respectively, on a new line.

Now that you are familiar with the Bicep syntax, let's explore some of Bicep's benefits over vanilla ARM templates.

6.3 *Other improvements with Bicep*

In addition to addressing the downsides of the existing ARM template syntax, Bicep templates also come with other improvements.

6.3.1 *Referencing resources, parameters, and variables*

One improvement is in referencing other resources and fetching their properties. To see the difference, let's first revisit referencing a property in ARM template syntax, which you learned in chapter 3:

```
[listKeys(resourceId('Microsoft.Storage/storageAccounts',
    parameters('storageAccountName')), 2019-04-01').key1]
```

Remember how you first had to build the full `resourceId` for the function using its type and name? With Bicep, that's not necessary for resources that are declared in the sample template. Now you can use the symbolic name for the resource, which you saw earlier, and directly access any of its properties, like this:

```
listKeys(myStorageAccount.id, '2019-04-01').key1
```

Here the listKeys(...) function is called, again using two parameters. But instead of using functions, you can directly reference the resource using its symbolic name and then fetch its id property. This yields the same result as building that id manually using the resourceId(...) function. Just comparing these two code examples shows the improvement to readability.

Referencing parameters and variables works the same way as referencing a resource. If you want to refer to a parameter for setting a value, you can use it directly like this:

```
parameter storageAccountName string

resource myStorageAccount 'Microsoft.Storage/storageAccounts
   ➥ @2020-08-01-preview' = {
  name: storageAccountName
  ...
}
```

This example declares a storage account. The storage account name is not specified as a literal but references the value of the storageAccountName parameter.

One thing to note is that parameters, variables, and resources share a single namespace. Sharing a namespace means that you cannot use the same name for a parameter, variable, or resource—all names have to be unique. The single exception is outputs. Outputs can have the same name as parameters, variables, or resources. This allows you to do something like this:

```
var storageAccountName = 'myStorageAccount'

resource myStorageAccount 'Microsoft.Storage/storageAccounts
   ➥ @2020-08-01-preview' = {
  name: storageAccountName
  location: resourceGroup().location
  kind: 'StorageV2'
  sku: {
    name: 'Premium_LRS'
    tier: 'Premium'
  }
}

output storageAccountName string = storageAccountName
```

In this example, you see a typical scenario where a resource's name is generated using a variable value and is returned as an output. Reusing the same name for the variable and the output allows for better readability than using different names for the same thing.

6.3.2 *Using references in variables and outputs*

In ARM templates, it is impossible to use the reference(...) function in variables. That's because ARM calculates variable values before deploying any resource, and in that stage it cannot evaluate the reference(...) function. In a Bicep template, this problem no longer exists. To see why, take a look at the following Bicep template:

```
resource myStorageAccount 'Microsoft.Storage/storageAccounts
        ➥ @2020-08-01-preview' = {
    name: 'myStorageAccount'
    location: resourceGroup().location
    kind: 'StorageV2'
    sku: {
        name: 'Premium_LRS'
        tier: 'Premium'
    }
}

var storageAccountName = myStorageAccount.name
var accessTier = myStorageAccount.properties.accessTier

output message string = '${storageAccountName} with tier ${accessTier}'
```

In both variables in the preceding example, a storage account is referenced. Here the Bicep transpiler does something clever. Instead of simply transpiling these Bicep variables into ARM variables and using the variable value in the output, it removes the variable and inlines the complete expression that yields the parameter's result into the output. Here's an example:

```
{
  "$schema": "https://schema.management.azure.com/schemas/
        ➥ 2019-04-01/deploymentTemplate.json#",
    "variables": {
        "storageAccountName": "myStorageAccount"
    },
    "resources": [
        {
          "type": "Microsoft.Storage/storageAccounts",
          ...
        }
    ],
    "outputs": {
        "message": {
        "type": "string",
        "value": "[format('{0} was deployed with accessTier {1}', variables
            ➥ ('storageAccountName'), reference(resourceId('Microsoft
            ➥ .Storage/storageAccounts', 'myStorageAccount')).accessTier)]"
      }
    }
}
```

In the preceding example, you can see how the output's value is built up without using the `accessTier` variable. Instead, the `reference(...)` function moves into the output's value calculation, where it works.

6.3.3 Referencing existing resources

When you want to reference an existing resource on multiple occasions, you can repeatedly use the `reference(...)` function. Alternatively, you can also make that resource available in your template under a symbolic name. To do this, you can use the `existing` keyword as follows:

```
resource existingStorageAccount 'Microsoft.Storage/storageAccounts
    @2020-08-01-preview' = existing {
    name: 'preexistingstorageaccountname'
}
```

⬅ **The existing keyword indicates a pre-existing resource.**

This example does not declare a new resource at all. Instead, it builds a reference to an existing resource with the provided name. Note that if you deploy this Bicep template and the resource does not exist yet, the deployment will result in an error.

6.3.4 Dependency management

A second improvement Bicep provides is that you no longer have to declare dependencies. If you recall from chapter 5, you are required to declare all dependencies between your resources in ARM templates, even if they are already implicitly declared through a parent-child relationship. With Bicep, this is not needed anymore.

When you transpile a Bicep file to an ARM template, all implicit dependencies are automatically detected, and the correct `dependsOn` declarations are automatically generated. Implicit dependencies are parent-child relations and resources that reference each other. For example, when your app settings reference a storage account to store its key as a setting, you no longer need to declare dependencies manually.

If you want to control the deployment order of resources, and there is no implicit dependency, you can still declare your own dependencies using the `dependsOn` property. The `dependsOn` property still works precisely the same way it did in ARM templates.

6.3.5 String interpolation

Another nuisance when building larger ARM templates is the lack of built-in support for string interpolation. *String interpolation* is a technique used for building text strings out of literals, parameters, variables, and expressions. For example, take a look at the following common approach for generating names for resources based on the environment name.

```
"parameters": {
    "environmentName": {
        "type": "string",
        "allowed": [ "dev", "tst", "prd" ]
    }
},
```

```
"variables": {
    "mainStorageAccountName": "[concat('stor',
        ➥ parameters('environmentName'), 'main')]",
    "otherStorageAccountName": "[concat('stor',
        ➥ parameters('environmentName'), 'other')]",
    "somethingWebAppName": "[concat('webappp',
        ➥ parameters('environmentName'),'something')]"
},
```

While the preceding approach works quite well, it takes a few seconds to calculate the actual resource name in your mind when reading the template, and that's for this relatively simple example. Just imagine how that would work when listing tens of resources.

In Bicep templates, you no longer need to use the concat(...) function for concatenating values. Instead, you can use the ${...} syntax anywhere within a string literal, and the value between the curly braces is automatically interpreted as an expression. Here is an example:

```
@allowed([
    'dev'
    'tst'
    'prd'
])
param environmentName string

var mainStorageAccountName = 'stor${environmentName}main'
var otherStorageAccountName = 'stor${environmentName}other'
var somethingWebAppName = 'webapp${environmentName}something'
```

As you can see, the values for the three variables are now much easier to read because you no longer need to call the parameters(...) function in combination with the ${...} syntax. In this example, environmentName = 'dev', 'webapp${environment-Name}something' will evaluate to 'webappdevsomething'. As a bonus, when you are using the Bicep extension for VS Code, syntax highlighting shows where string interpolation is used, to enhance readability even more.

6.3.6   *No mandatory grouping*

One of the consequences of using JSON as the basis of ARM templates is the object notation for parameters and variables. This means all parameters and variables have to be grouped in one location in a template—usually at the start. Take a look at the following example:

```
{
    "$schema": "https://schema.management.azure.com/schemas/
        ➥ 2019-04-01/deploymentTemplate.json#",
    "contentVersion": "1.0.0.0",
    "parameters": {
        "environment": {          ◄───┤  The declaration of a
            "type": "string"               parameter
```

```
        },
      },
      "variables": {
        "webAppPlanName": "[format('myAppPlan-{0}',
            parameters('environment'))]",
        "anotherVariable": "someValue"
      },
      "resources": [                    Imagine there are tens or hundreds
                                        of lines at this location.
        {
          "type": "Microsoft.Web/serverfarms",
          "apiVersion": "2020-06-01",
          "name": "[variables('webAppPlanName')]",     The usage of
          "location": "westeurope"                      a parameter
        }
      ]
    }
```

Especially in larger templates, this made for much scrolling up and down, as parameters were all defined at the top and used much further down in the file. JSON provides no way to work around this, and you cannot declare parameter or variable keys more than once.

With the new Bicep syntax, grouping parameters at the top is no longer necessary, and you can do something like this:

```
param environment string = 'tst'       The declaration
                                        of a parameter

                                 Imagine there are tens or hundreds
                                 of lines at this location.

var webAppPlanName = 'myAppPlan-${environment}'

resource myWebApp 'Microsoft.Web/serverfarms@2020-06-01' = {
  name: webAppPlanName             The usage of
  location: 'westeurope'           a parameter
}
```

In this example, parameters are declared just before they are used. Other variables can also be declared where they are used without problems. Strictly speaking, you can even use variables before they are defined, as the declarations are eventually grouped together when the Bicep file is transpiled to an ARM template. All of this greatly enhances both the readability and understandability of the templates.

6.3.7   Comments

A final improvement of the Bicep language is the introduction of comments. While ARM templates already support comments, they have one downside: it makes the templates no longer JSON-compliant. This leads to many text editors pointing out comments as errors. Luckily, VS Code is an exception to that rule, as it understands ARM templates instead of "just" JSON.

With Bicep, this is no longer an issue. You can use comments as follows:

```
var webAppPlanName = 'myAppPlan' // A double slash starts a comment

resource myWebAppPlan 'Microsoft.Web/serverfarms@2020-06-01' = {
    name: webAppPlanName
    location: 'westeurope'
    /*
        Using slash star you can start a multi-line comment
        Star slash closes the comment
    */
}
```

In this example, there are two types of comments. A single-line comment is added using a double forward slash (//). A single-line comment does not have to start at the beginning of a line, but can start at any position on the line. A multiline comment is created by enclosing it in /* and */. You don't need to put the /* and */ on lines of their own, but it is the convention.

6.3.8   *Using the contents of other files*

In some cases, you'll need to provide a value in your Bicep template that is very long, complex, JSON, or binary. It can be hard to deal with those values in a readable way. Fortunately, from Bicep 0.4.412 onwards, a new function is available: `loadText-Content(filePath, [encoding])`. You can use this function to include the contents of any file in your Bicep.

One example where this can be beneficial is when you are executing scripts as part of a template deployment. Let's assume you have a rather lengthy PowerShell script, updateReleaseNotes.ps1, that should be invoked as part of your deployment. Instead of inlining that script into your Bicep template, you can do the following:

```
resource inlineScriptResource 'Microsoft.Resources/deploymentScripts
        ➡ @2020-10-01' = {
    name: 'inlinePowerShellScript'
    location: 'westeurope'
    kind:'AzurePowerShell'
    properties: {
        scriptContent: loadTextContent('updateReleaseNotes.ps1')   ◄─
        azPowerShellVersion: '5.0'
        retentionInterval: 'P1D'
    }
}
```

Invocation of loadTextContent to load the contents from another file

In this example, you can see how the use of `loadTextcontent(...)` helps to keep the template clean and to the point. This function also ensures that the contents of the loaded file are properly escaped. This way, both the Bicep template and the Power-Shell script can be written using their native syntax, which is a great benefit.

You can find out more about `loadTextcontent(...)` and its cousin `loadFileAs-Base64(...)`, which automatically encodes the contents using Base64, in Microsoft's "File functions for Bicep" article (http://mng.bz/v6x1).

Now that you know all about working with Bicep templates and the extra benefits they bring, let's look at another powerful new feature that allows you to split larger templates into parts: modules.

6.4 Modules

In chapter 5 you learned about linked templates as an approach to splitting larger solutions into multiple files. The downside of that approach is that the linked template has to be staged on a publicly accessible URL before it can be used. While this is possible, it is a bit of a nuisance to stage your files before you can use them as a linked template.

Bicep provides a solution to this problem. Bicep permits the use of modules that allow you to split a template into multiple files without resorting to linked templates to deploy them all together. Modules are inlined in the template when transpiling to an ARM template, giving you the benefits of both worlds:

- Multiple smaller, more readable Bicep files
- A single ARM template that you can deploy using `complete` mode, if needed

Let's start our discussion of modules by writing a module:

```
param webAppPlanName string

resource myWebAppPlan 'Microsoft.Web/serverfarms@2020-06-01' = {
    name: webAppPlanName
    location: 'westeurope'
}

output myWebAppPlanResourceId string = myWebAppPlan.id
```

If you look at this module closely, you'll see that it's nothing but a regular Bicep template. This is intentional, as every Bicep template is reusable as a module in another template. Save this snippet to a file called webAppPlan.bicep, and you can use it as a module like this:

```
module deployWebAppPlan './webAppPlan.bicep' = {
    name: 'deployWebAppPlan'
    params: {
        webAppPlanName: 'nameForTheWebAppPlan'
    }
}

var demoOutputUse = deployWebAppPlan.outputs.myWebAppPlanResourceId
```

Several new concepts are introduced here. First, the `module` keyword signals the inclusion of a module. Instead of specifying a resource type and `apiVersion`, a local file is referenced for including, using a relative path. Between the curly braces, the details for the module inclusion are defined. First, you must specify a `name` for every module. This name is used as the name for the linked deployment that the module is transpiled into. One other optional property can be specified, the `params`, for specifying the parameters declared in the module. In this case, there is only one parameter, namely `webAppPlanName`. Finally, the example shows how to retrieve outputs from the linked template deployment. If you want to include more than one module, you have to repeat this whole block, but with a different name, filename, etc.

Compiling this example to an ARM template would yield a 47-line-long ARM template. Comparing that with the 13 lines in the two preceding snippets really illustrates the added value of Bicep over ARM templates.

6.4.1 *Deploying to another scope*

When referencing a module from a template, you can also deploy the module to another scope than the main template. This is done using the `scope` property:

```
module deployWebAppPlan './webAppPlan.bicep' = {
    name: 'deployWebAppPlan'
    scope: resourceGroup('theNameOfAnotherResourceGroup')
    params: {
        webAppPlanName: 'nameForTheWebAppPlan'
    }
}

var demoOutputUse = deployWebAppPlan.outputs.myWebAppPlanResourceId
```

In the preceding example, you'll see the same module deployment as before, but with one more property: scope. The value for this property can be any of the allowed scopes: `tenant`, `management group`, `subscription`, or `resource group`. The value needs to be provided as a full resource id, like `/subscriptions/{guid}/resourceGroups/{resourceGroupName}`. The easiest way to provide a scope is using the functions `resourceGroup(...)`, `subscription(...)`, `managementGroup(...)`, and `tenant(...)`.

6.4.2 *Debugging Bicep deployments*

When you deploy a Bicep template, you are really first transpiling to an ARM template and then deploying that ARM template. The consequence is that when there is an error in your deployment, you will have to debug the ARM template, not your Bicep template.

This means, first, that you will have to deal with line-number differences. If there is a line number in your deployment error, this will correspond to a line number in the intermediate ARM template, not to a line number in your Bicep template. Unfortunately, you will have to find the corresponding location in your Bicep file yourself.

Second, the resulting ARM template will likely be hard to read. That's not just because ARM templates are more difficult to read than Bicep templates, but also because the use of modules can generate hard-to-follow, complex expressions. Also, the use of modules will result in the generation of nested templates. These two effects can make troubleshooting Bicep deployments a tough job.

But in all fairness, when you switch from ARM templates to Bicep, your chances of ending up in a debugging session are much, much lower. The Bicep extension and

Bicep transpiler will catch many errors before starting the deployment. This means that 90% of your feedback loops will be much faster, compensating for the troubles of debugging obscure, generated ARM templates.

6.5   *A larger Bicep example*

Let's now put all that you have learned together by rebuilding the infrastructure you created in chapters 3 and 5 using Bicep. Figure 6.1 illustrates this architecture to refresh your memory.

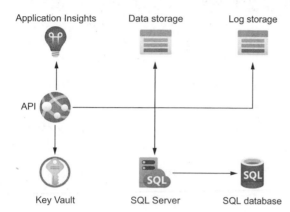

Figure 6.1   An Azure solution architecture

To recreate this architecture from scratch in Bicep, let's use the modular approach introduced in chapter 5 and create as many resource templates as we need, and a single composing template, using the following structure:

```
+-- Composing
|   +-- Main.bicep
|   +-- Main.parameters.prod.json
|   +-- Main.parameters.prod.json
|   +-- Api.bicep
|   +-- Configuration.bicep
|   +-- Storage.bicep
+-- AppConfiguration
|   +-- AppConfiguration.bicep
+-- Insights
|   +-- ApplicationInsights.bicep
+-- KeyVault
|   +-- KeyVault.bicep
+-- Sql
|   +-- SqlServer.bicep
|   +-- SqlServerDatabase.bicep
+-- Storage
|   +-- StorageAccountV2.bicep
+-- WebApp
|   +-- Serverfarm.bicep
|   +-- WebApp.bicep
```

As you already know what to build, you can use a bottom-up approach, where you first build the resource templates and later the composing templates.

6.5.1   *AppConfiguration.bicep*

The first resource template to rebuild is the template with the `AppConfiguration`. As an ARM template, this template is 30 lines and looks like this:

```
{
    "$schema": "https://schema.management.azure.com/schemas/
        ➥ 2019-04-01/deploymentTemplate.json#",
    "contentVersion": "1.0.0.0",
    "parameters": {
        "appConfigurationName": {
            "type": "string"
        },
        "skuName": {
            "type": "string",
            "defaultValue": "free"
        },
        "location": {
            "type": "string"
        }
    },
    "resources": [
        {
            "type": "Microsoft.AppConfiguration/configurationStores",
            "apiVersion": "2019-11-01-preview",
            "name": "[parameters('appConfigurationName')]",
            "location": "[parameters('location')]",
            "sku": {
                "name": "[parameters('skuName')]"
            },
            "properties": {
                "encryption": {}
            }
        }
    ]
}
```

Now we need to rewrite this as a Bicep module. First, you declare the three parameters, which are also in the ARM template:

```
param appConfigurationName string
param skuName string
param location string
```

After declaring the parameters, you can write the remainder of the template, which is a single resource:

```
resource configurationStore 'Microsoft.AppConfiguration/configurationStores
        ➥ @2019-11-01-preview' = {
    name: appConfigurationName
```

```
        location: location
        sku: {
            name: skuName
        }
        properties: {
            encryption: {}
        }
    }
```

You can again see the ease of use that Bicep brings, as 30 lines of ARM template translated into only 13 lines of Bicep in total.

6.5.2 *ApplicationInsights.bicep*

The next ARM template is ApplicationInsights.json, which looks like this:

```
{
    "$schema": "https://schema.management.azure.com/schemas/
        ➡ 2019-04-01/deploymentTemplate.json#",
    "contentVersion": "1.0.0.0",
    "parameters": {
        "applicationInsightsName": {
            "type": "string"
        },
        "logAnalyticsWorkspaceName": {
            "type": "string"
        },
        "location": {
            "type": "string"
        }
    },
    "resources": [
        {
            "apiVersion": "2020-02-02-preview",
            "name": "[parameters('applicationInsightsName')]",
            "type": "Microsoft.Insights/components",
            "kind": "web",
            "location": "[parameters('location')]",
            "dependsOn": [
                "[parameters('logAnalyticsWorkspaceName')]"
            ],
            "properties": {
                "applicationId": "[parameters('applicationInsightsName')]",
                "WorkspaceResourceId": "[resourceId('Microsoft
                    ➡ .OperationalInsights/workspaces',
                    ➡ parameters('logAnalyticsWorkspaceName'))]"
            }
        },
        {
            "name": "[parameters('logAnalyticsWorkspaceName')]",
            "type": "Microsoft.OperationalInsights/workspaces",
            "apiVersion": "2020-08-01",
            "location": "[parameters('location')]",
```

```
        "properties": {
            "sku": {
                "name": "pergb2018"
            },
            "retentionInDays": 30,
            "workspaceCapping": {
                "dailyQuotaGb": -1
            }
        }
    }
]
}
```

Again, this is quite the template—a total of 46 lines. Let's see how far that can be trimmed down by switching to Bicep. First, you can add the parameters:

```
param applicationInsightsName string
param logAnalyticsWorkspaceName string
param location string
```

Next, declare the first resource, the Application Insights component:

```
resource applicationInsightsResource 'Microsoft.Insights/components
    ➥ @2020-02-02-preview' = {
    name: applicationInsightsName
    kind: 'web'
    location: location
    dependsOn: [
        omsWorkspaceResource
    ]

    properties: {
        applicationId: applicationInsightsName
        WorkspaceResourceId: omsWorkspaceResource.id
    }
}
```

In the preceding code, you can make a small optimization. In the ARM template, the name of the Log Analytics workspace (called OMS workspace in Bicep and ARM templates for historical reasons) is used directly as the second parameter to the resourceId(...) function call. In the Bicep file, this is changed to directly reference the resource and get its id, which is much more straightforward.

Now let's add that Log Analytics workspace to make this a valid reference:

```
resource omsWorkspaceResource 'Microsoft.OperationalInsights/workspaces
    ➥ @2020-08-01' = {
    name: logAnalyticsWorkspaceName
    location: location
    properties: {
        sku: {
            name: 'PerGB2018'
        }
```

```
        retentionInDays: 30
        workspaceCapping: {
            dailyQuotaGb: -1
        }
    }
}
```

The last three Bicep snippets total 28 lines (not counting empty lines and line continuations)—not much more than half of the 46 lines of ARM template you started out with. That's not bad!

You can continue onward with the remaining six files and translate them from ARM templates into a Bicep templates. Of course, you can also experiment with bicep decompile, which you learned about in section 6.1.3. Or you can pick up the files from the book's GitHub repository at http://mng.bz/BMj0. Once all the resource templates are in place, it is time to continue with the composing templates.

6.5.3 *Configuration.bicep*

The shortest *composing* ARM template is Configuration.json, so let's transform that into Configuration.bicep together. These are the contents of the Configuration .json file:

```
{
    "$schema": "https://schema.management.azure.com/schemas/
       ➥ 2019-04-01/deploymentTemplate.json#",
    "contentVersion": "1.0.0.0",
    "parameters": {
        "keyVaultName": {
            "type": "string"
        },
        "appConfigurationName": {
            "type": "string"
        },
        "templateSettings": {
            "type": "object"
        }
    },
    "variables": {
        "templateBasePath": "[concat(parameters('templateSettings')
            ➥ .storageAccountUrl, '/',
            ➥   parameters('templateSettings').storageContainer)]"
    },
    "resources": [
        {
            "apiVersion": "2020-10-01",
            "name": "KeyVault",
            "type": "Microsoft.Resources/deployments",
            "properties": {
                "mode": "Incremental",
                "templateLink": {
```

```
                "uri": "[concat(variables('templateBasePath'),
                    ➡ '/Resources/KeyVault/KeyVault.json')]",
                "queryString": "[parameters('templateSettings')
                    ➡ .storageAccountKey]",
                "contentVersion": "1.0.0.0"
            },
            "parameters": {
                "keyVaultName": {
                    "value": "[parameters('keyVaultName')]"
                },
                "location": {
                    "value": "[parameters('templateSettings')
                        ➡ .location]"
                }
            }
        }
    },
    {
        "apiVersion": "2020-10-01",
        "name": "AppConfiguration",
        "type": "Microsoft.Resources/deployments",
        "properties": {
            "mode": "Incremental",
            "templateLink": {
                "uri": "[concat(variables('templateBasePath'),
                    ➡ '/Resources/AppConfiguration
                    ➡ /AppConfiguration.json')]",
                "queryString": "[parameters('templateSettings')
                    ➡ .storageAccountKey]",
                "contentVersion": "1.0.0.0"
            },
            "parameters": {
                "appConfigurationName": {
                    "value": "[parameters('appConfigurationName')]"
                },
                "location": {
                    "value": "[parameters('templateSettings')
                        ➡ .location]"
                }
            }
        }
    }
    ]
}
```

To convert to this Bicep, again, start with the parameters:

```
param keyVaultName string
param appConfigurationName string
param templateSettings object
```

Next, there is a `templateBasePath` variable. When converting from an ARM template to Bicep, you would normally push the variable declarations as close to the place where they are used as possible. Since both resources use the variable in this template, it makes sense to just put it directly after the `parameters` section. Still, the template's readability can be greatly improved by switching to string interpolation syntax from using the `concat()` function:

```
var templateBasePath = '${templateSettings.storageAccountUrl}/
    ➥ ${templateSettings.storageContainer}'
```

To complete the translation of the full template, the two linked deployments need to be translated next. Because linked deployments are only used here to split a larger template into smaller parts, we can abandon this approach and switch to Bicep modules. In this case, that leads to the following Bicep code:

```
module keyVaultModule '../Resources/Keyvault/KeyVault.bicep' = {
    name: 'keyVaultModule'
    params: {
        keyVaultName: keyVaultName
        location: templateSettings.location
    }
}

module appConfModule '../Resources/AppConfiguration
    ➥ /AppConfiguration.bicep' = {
    name: 'appConfigurationModule'
    params: {
        appConfigurationName: appConfigurationName
        location: templateSettings.location
    }
}
```

Once you've inserted the preceding Bicep modules, the `templateBasePath` variable and parts of the `templateSettings` parameter are obsolete. This is due to the fact that Bicep transpiles the main file and all modules into one large file, removing the need for linked files and thus these supporting variables. They can safely be removed.

The remaining composing templates, Api.json, Storage.json, and Main.json, can be translated exactly like Configuration.bicep. Again, you can practice with this yourself or copy the files from the GitHub repository.

Converting the composing templates completes the conversion from ARM templates to Bicep templates. If you want, you can now deploy the Main.bicep file using the following commands:

```
az group create --location westeurope --resource-group deploybicep
az deployment group create --resource-group deploybicep
    ➥ --templatefile Main.bicep --parameters Main.parameters.test.json
```

Before you deploy, you may have to update the value for the `env` parameter in Main .parameters.test.json to prevent collisions in Azure resource names. Also, don't forget to remove the resources once you are done to avoid incurring unnecessary costs.

Going through this exercise of converting from ARM templates to Bicep at least once is valuable, as many companies still have many ARM templates that you will probably want to convert to Bicep at some point.

Summary

- The JSON notation used for ARM templates has some drawbacks. In particular, it can become quite verbose and requires the use of expression syntax (`[...]`). Bicep is a new DSL that removes these drawbacks and also introduces other improvements, including ordering declarations in any order, performing automatic dependency management, and providing a shorthand notation for `type` and `apiVersion`.
- Bicep templates are easier to write, shorter, and more readable than ARM templates, but they have the same capabilities as ARM templates.
- You can transpile Bicep files into ARM templates, which makes them easy to integrate into existing workflows. There is also a `decompile` command that allows you to transform ARM templates into Bicep templates.
- With Bicep modules, you can quickly split templates out into multiple files and create linked deployments without writing 15 lines of ceremony. You can also use modules to deploy to multiple scopes with much more ease.
- Throughout this chapter, you have recreated the infrastructure of chapters 3 and 5, now using Bicep templates.

Complex deployments using Azure DevOps

7

This chapter covers

- The basics of Azure DevOps pipelines
- Creating and understanding service connections
- Writing and maintaining Azure DevOps pipelines
- Deploying infrastructure to the cloud using Azure DevOps pipelines

In previous chapters, you've learned a lot about the Azure Resource Manager, ARM templates, and Bicep. You've used different tools, like PowerShell and the Azure CLI, to interact with ARM. And you have used those tools to deploy templates to Azure manually. By deploying manually, however, there are no enforcements, checks, or policies in place to control the quality of the Bicep templates. Mistakes can easily be made, and this would allow developers to potentially break the production environment.

Also, working manually with the CLI means that someone needs to log in to Azure to deploy a template. That means at least one person has enough permissions on the production environment to potentially break it, and it would be best if that were not the case.

So far, you've probably stored all the templates you created while reading this book on your local system, and you've deployed them from there. If developers in a real company working on the same infrastructure were to do that, copying files back and forth, they would risk overwriting newer versions of files with older versions. It is safer to use a version control system.

Working with Azure DevOps allows you to solve these problems and eliminate the risks by automating the processes involved, while also taking control of the quality of code deployed to production.

> **Azure DevOps and Azure**
>
> This chapter is a step-by-step guide to creating multistage, multiregion pipeline-deploying infrastructure to the Azure cloud. If you want to follow along, you will need a Microsoft Azure DevOps account and a Microsoft Azure account with at least one subscription. You can create a free Azure DevOps account that is limited to a maximum of five users.

7.1 Meet Toma Toe Pizzas

In this chapter (and the next), let's suppose you work at Toma Toe Pizzas. This company delivers pizzas in several countries. The problem you're facing is that the website and ordering system run on a single web app deployed on a single service in Azure. Toma Toe is facing performance issues, mainly because the service is hosted in one Azure region, which is causing a lot of latency for visitors elsewhere on the planet. Also, the infrastructure is currently deployed manually. It's your job to solve both these problems.

Your plan is to deploy the same app in several different Azure regions and to add an Azure Traffic Manager on top of that to route traffic based on the geographical location of your users to the closest possible region. Although it's not ideal, the manual deployment process has worked so far. With the added requirement of deploying into multiple regions, however, this method is too complex and risky. The stakeholders prefer an automated process to ensure the infrastructure deployment process has a consistent outcome.

In this chapter you'll learn how to use Azure DevOps to automate the deployment of infrastructure using an Azure DevOps pipeline. This pipeline will deploy the infrastructure in three regions and configure an instance of Azure Traffic Manager as shown in figure 7.1.

Figure 7.1 shows three resource groups in three different Azure regions containing an App Service plan and an App Service. The fourth resource group contains an instance of Azure Traffic Manager redirecting your website traffic to the App Service instance closest to the visitor.

In this chapter you will craft the Bicep files required to provision the infrastructure shown in figure 7.1. You will then, from section 7.4 onwards, learn how to create an

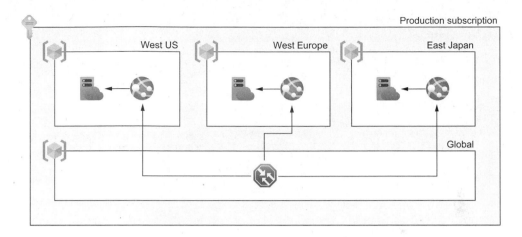

Figure 7.1 The infrastructure deployed by the Azure DevOps pipeline

Azure DevOps pipeline that will deploy the desired infrastructure in an automated fashion.

7.2 Crafting the Bicep files

Let's focus on the App Service plan and the App Service (figure 7.2). These services are, according to the infrastructure plans, deployed in three different resource groups as you saw in figure 7.1.

To provision this part of the desired infrastructure, you need an App Service plan and an App Service deployed to Azure. Let's get hands on! Navigate to a folder where you would like to create the files, and create a folder called Deployment. Inside that folder, create a new folder called Web. In this

Figure 7.2 The App Service plan and the App Service

folder, create two Bicep files: one for the App Service plan and one for the web app. The reason to name the nested folder Web is because both resources live in the Microsoft.Web namespace. You could name that folder differently, but Web describes what's inside best.

7.2.1 Describing the App Service plan

In the Web folder, create a file called serverfarms.bicep. This Bicep file will describe the App Service plan. The reason for the name serverfarms.bicep is that the name of the resource in the Azure Resource Manager is serverfarms. This is the old name of an App Service plan, but this name is still used in the Azure Resource Manager.

Because you want to deploy this App Service plan in multiple regions and in multiple stages (development, test, acceptance, production), you'll need to add parameters to allow the template to be used for these different environments and regions. In serverfarms.bicep you start by adding a few parameters as shown in the following listing (Deployment/Web/serverfarms.bicep).

Listing 7.1   Parameters in Bicep

```
param systemName string

@allowed([
    'dev'
    'test'
    'acc'
    'prod'
])
param environmentName string

@allowed([
    'we'  // West europe
    'us'  // East US (1)
    'asi' // East Japan
])
param locationAbbreviation string
```

The `systemName` parameter contains the name of your software system. In this case, `tomatoe` would be a good choice. The `environmentName` and `locationAbbreviation` parameters are there to distinguish between the different Azure regions and environments. Note that the `@allowed()` decorator allows you to define allowed values. Passing a value other than the listed values will result in an error.

Following the parameters, you describe the resource or resources you want to deploy. In this case, the App Service plan as shown in the following listing (Deployment/Web/serverfarms.bicep continued).

Listing 7.2   Adding resource to Bicep file

```
var serverFarmName =
    ➥ '${systemName}-${environmentName}-${locationAbbreviation}-plan'

resource serverFarm 'Microsoft.Web/serverfarms@2021-01-01' = {
    name: serverFarmName
    location: resourceGroup().location
    kind: 'app'
    sku: {
        name: 'B1'
        capacity: 1
    }
}

output serverFarmId string = serverFarm.id
```

In the first line, the parameter values are combined into one string, resulting in a unique name. Then the App Service plan resource is described using that name. The location of the App Service plan is set to be the same location as the resource group the App Service plan is deployed in.

In a bit, you will create the Bicep file to deploy the web app. To create that resource, you will need the ID of the App Service plan so you can link the App Service to it. You therefore declare an output on the last line of this example that returns the `id` value.

7.2.2   Describing the App Service

Next up is the Bicep file for the web app. The file will look quite similar to the App Service plan template, but it will declare an App Service instead as shown in the following listing (Deployment/Web/sites.bicep).

Listing 7.3   Deploying the web app

```
param serverFarmId string
param systemName string

@allowed([
    'dev'
    'test'
    'acc'
    'prod'
])
param environmentName string = 'prod'

@allowed([
    'we' // West europe
    'us' // East US (1)
    'asi' // East Japan
])
param locationAbbreviation string

var webAppName =
    ➥ '${systemName}-${environmentName}-${locationAbbreviation}-app'

resource webApp 'Microsoft.Web/sites@2021-01-01' = {
    name: webAppName
    location: resourceGroup().location
    kind: 'app'
    properties: {
        serverFarmId: serverFarmId
    }
}
```

There are two differences between this template and the previous one. First, this template contains one more parameter—the ID of the App Service plan. Second, this template deploys a different resource, the App Service. Because this template is fairly small and no information about the web app is needed, this template does not contain any output parameters.

7.2.3   Finalizing the template

Next you need to create the main Bicep template and call the templates you created
in the previous two sections. In the Deployment folder, create a new file called main
.bicep. This will be your main template where everything comes together as shown in
the following listing (Deployment/main.bicep).

Listing 7.4   The main template

```
targetScope = 'subscription'                    ◁——   Define the scope of the
                                                       deployment, a subscription
param systemName string = 'tomatoe'                    deployment.
param location string
param environmentName string
@allowed([
    'we' // West Europe
    'us' // East US (1)
    'asi' // East Japan
])                                                                    Describe a
param locationAbbreviation string                                  resource group.

resource resourceGroup 'Microsoft.Resources/resourceGroups@2021-04-01' = {   ◁——
    name: '${systemName}-${environmentName}-${locationAbbreviation}'
    location: location
}
                                                              Describe a module
                                                              that contains the
module appServicePlanModule 'Web/serverfarms.bicep' = {  ◁——  App Service plan
    name: 'appServicePlan'                                    resource.
    scope: resourceGroup
    params: {
        systemName: systemName
        environmentName: environmentName
        locationAbbriviation: locationAbbreviation
    }
}

module webApplicationModule 'Web/sites.bicep' = {        ◁——  Describe a module
    name: 'webApplication'                                    that contains the App
    scope: resourceGroup                                      Service resource.
    params: {
        systemName: systemName
        environmentName: environmentName
        locationAbbriviation: locationAbbreviation
        serverFarmId: appServicePlanModule.outputs.serverFarmId
    }
}
```

*Set the
scope of
the Bicep
module.*

At the top of listing 7.4, the target scope for this template is set to subscription. By
doing so, you can create a resource group inside your Bicep template and then
describe both the App Service plan and the App Service Bicep files as modules. Note
that for both modules described in the template, the scope for each module is changed
to the resource group created earlier in the template.

This main.bicep template has a few parameters without default values. To pass these values while deploying, you can create parameter files for each environment, like the two shown for production and test in listings 7.5 (Deployment/prod.parameters .json) and 7.6 (Deployment/test.parameters.json).

Listing 7.5 The production parameters file

```
{
    "$schema": "https://schema.management.azure.com/schemas/
        ➡ 2019-04-01/deploymentParameters.json#",
    "contentVersion": "1.0.0.0",
    "parameters": {
        "systemName": {
            "value": "tomatoe"
        },
        " locationAbbreviation": {
            "value": "we"
        },
        "environmentName": {
            "value": "prod"
        }

    }
}
```

Listing 7.6 The test parameters file

```
{
    "$schema": "https://schema.management.azure.com/schemas/
        ➡ 2019-04-01/deploymentParameters.json#",
    "contentVersion": "1.0.0.0",
    "parameters": {
        "systemName": {
            "value": "tomatoe"
        },
        " locationAbbreviation": {
            "value": "we"
        },
        "environmentName": {
            "value": "test"
        }

    }
}
```

These two parameter files each contain the three mandatory parameters for main.bicep.

The Bicep files are not complete yet, since the Traffic Manager is missing, but let's focus on deploying the current Bicep files in an automated fashion. In order to deploy the Bicep files using Azure DevOps, the files must be pushed to your remote source control repository.

7.3   *Storing templates in source control*

Azure Repos (repositories) is a Microsoft SaaS offering for storing source code under version control. There are two types of version control systems available in Azure DevOps, Git and TFVC (Team Foundation Version Control). Git is the most commonly used version control system today, so for the purposes of this chapter, we'll assume you're working with a Git repository.

> **NOTE**   If you don't know what TFVC is, don't bother with it. TFVC is no longer recommended, so all new projects should embrace Git.

There are several strategies for allowing multiple people to work with the same files simultaneously when working with Git repositories, and all of them involve branching. A *branch* is used to isolate work in progress from the completed work. When you are about to make a change to your infrastructure, you start by creating a branch. You then clone that branch to your local computer, where you commit one or more changes. Once you are done, you push the changes back to that branch. Once quality is secured, you can merge the changes back to the main branch.

Figure 7.3 shows one strategy for using source control, namely *trunk-based development*. A new branch is created, whose contents are initially the same as the branch it originates from. Changes are made over time and committed to that branch. Finally, the changes are pushed and merged back to the main branch.

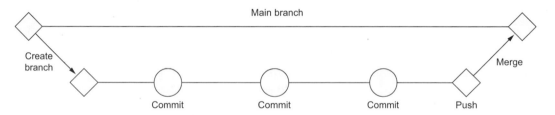

Figure 7.3   **Example of a strategy for working with source control**

By configuring branch policies on one or more of your Git branches, you can require changes to be reviewed by others, through pull requests, before those changes can be merged onto the main branch. For example, in figure 7.3 the main branch could enforce at least one person, other than the person who made the change, to approve changes between the push and the merge. This way you can enforce peer reviews for every change, prior to the merge to the main branch. How to work with Git repositories in Azure DevOps is well documented on Microsoft's "Azure Repos Git Documentation" page (http://mng.bz/QvyR).

In order to try the example in this chapter, it is a good idea to create a new project in Azure DevOps. If you are not familiar with Azure DevOps and don't know how to create a project, you can find documentation in Microsoft's "Create a project in Azure DevOps" article (http://mng.bz/XZP1). For a version control repository, choose Git (the default). Click on the Create button and wait for the process to complete. Then navigate to your project and click Repos. This will bring you to the default repository of your project. You can clone this repository on your workstation and then start working with it.

> **Details about version control systems**
>
> Although the basics of version control and code repositories in Azure DevOps are covered in the preceding section, the details are beyond the scope of this book. For detailed information about version control systems and implementing Azure DevOps solutions in general, you can read *Implementing Azure DevOps Solutions* by Henry Been and Maik van der Gaag (Packt Publishing, 2020).

Once you have cloned your repository, you can move the Bicep files you created earlier in this chapter into your Git repository. Copy the Deployment folder, including its contents, into the root of the folder that you cloned the Git repository to. Now that you have your Azure DevOps sources in order, it is time to create your pipeline.

7.4 *Automated build and release pipelines*

Modern Azure DevOps pipelines can be written in code using a language called YAML (YAML Ain't Markup Language). Azure DevOps also allows you to create build and release pipelines using building blocks that you can drag and drop into place, but this leaves your pipeline definition on the Azure DevOps server and not on your local machine as code. The advantage of writing pipelines as code is that you can leverage your version control system to control its quality. Also, by using code, your pipeline can live right next to the version of your software system it deploys, so they can evolve in the same code base.

Developers sometimes complain about the YAML syntax because it is whitespace sensitive. That means adding or leaving a single whitespace could break the script. Also, writing a pipeline from scratch can be a challenge. To make dealing with the downsides of YAML a little bit easier, you can download and install the Azure Pipelines extension for VS Code (http://mng.bz/yvyo). You can also edit pipelines online in Azure DevOps. Like the extension in VS Code, this editor provides you with feedback such as showing errors and providing IntelliSense to help you write them quicker.

Azure Pipelines is a tool that allows you to build a CI/CD pipeline. CI/CD can either stand for continuous integration/continuous *deployment* or continuous integration/continuous *delivery*. The biggest difference between the two is that continuous delivery requires a manual step to deploy to production, whereas continuous deployment does not. For Azure Pipelines, it doesn't matter—it can do both. CI/CD pipelines allow you to compile, test, and deploy your system. Having a CI/CD pipeline is essential for teams that want to work using the DevOps principles, because releasing and deploying your system in an automated fashion is one of the components in the DevOps lifecycle.

Pipelines are started by a *trigger* and typically run until the last action of the pipeline is completed, an error has occurred, or the pipeline has expired. To organize tasks to be executed in your pipeline, there are three main concepts: stages, jobs, and tasks. Figure 7.4 shows how these concepts relate to each other by illustrating a pipeline with two stages, each containing two jobs, with those jobs having a variety of tasks. The concepts of stages, jobs, and tasks are explained in the following sections.

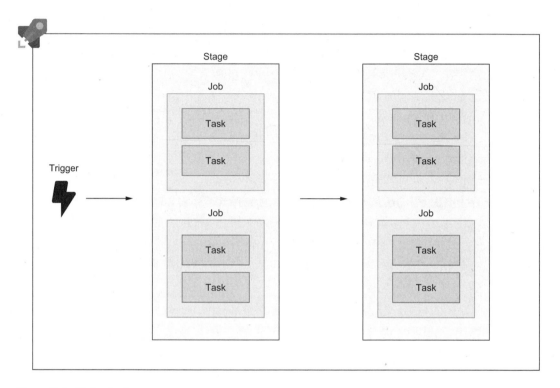

Figure 7.4   Main pipeline concepts

You can start a pipeline manually, but in most cases it's more convenient to hook the pipeline up to your source control repository. Doing this allows you to configure the pipeline to run when changes are made in your code repository. This mechanism is called a *trigger*. The next section explains triggers and points out some useful ways to configure them.

7.4.1   *Using triggers*

Azure pipelines can be triggered by several types of events. The most common triggers for pipelines listen to events on your version control system, such as a pull request being created, or one or more commits being pushed to the source control repository. There are also pipeline triggers allowing you to trigger a pipeline when another pipeline has completed. Scheduled triggers are common. These allow you to schedule your pipeline over time, such as every hour, day, or weekday.

Let's create a pipeline that first transpiles the Bicep files created in the first part of this chapter into an ARM template. It will then create a deployment, provisioning all the resources described in the Bicep files.

To make future changes and maintenance easier, you can organize your pipeline by creating a new folder in the root of your Git repository called "pipeline". This folder will contain your pipeline files. In that folder, create a new file called single-job-resource-deployment-ppl.yml. This will be your default pipeline. The following snippet will create a trigger that runs the pipeline as soon as one or more commits are pushed to the remote repository:

```
trigger:
  - main
```

In this example, you see `main` being used as the name of the branch to watch for triggers. `- main` is the default name for any new repository in Azure DevOps.

If your default branch is named differently, or if you want the pipeline to be triggered when commits are pushed to a different branch, simply change the name of the branch (`main`) to the desired branch name. You can also add more than one branch name or use wildcards to watch more than one branch for changes.

Now that your pipeline has a trigger configured, you can start adding tasks to the pipeline. These tasks are listed in the `steps` property of a job. In the following section, you will learn what tasks are and how to write them.

7.4.2   Creating tasks

Tasks are the smallest entity of an Azure pipeline. They typically do one thing. Examples of tasks that could live in your pipeline are "Restore packages," "Compile sources," "Run a PowerShell script," "Run an Azure CLI command," or "Deploy infrastructure."

Your pipeline is going to contain two tasks: one will transpile the Bicep file into an ARM template JSON file, and one will deploy that JSON file to Azure, creating all the resources described. Let's start with the task to transpile the Bicep template into ARM.

Listing 7.7   Task transpiling Bicep template to ARM template

```
- task: Bash@3
  displayName: "Transpile Bicep"
  inputs:
      targetType: 'inline'
      script: 'az bicep build --file ./deployment/main.bicep'
```

The preceding listing is an example of a task. You first specify the specific task you would like to run, which in this case is the `Bash` task. Tasks can have a version, and here you use version 3 of the task. The `displayName` property can be used to give the task a meaningful name that will be shown in the Azure DevOps UI and in the logs. This task will execute an Azure CLI command that transpiles the Bicep template into an ARM template JSON file. That is specified in the `script` property of this task.

Some tasks have a short notation that you can use. The Bash task used in this example can also be written as follows:

```
- bash: az bicep build --file ./deployment/main.bicep
  displayName: "Transpile Bicep"
```

Using this shorter notation can make your template a bit smaller and more readable.

The following task will deploy the ARM template that was created in the previous step.

Listing 7.8   Task deploying an ARM template

```
- task: AzureResourceManagerTemplateDeployment@3
  displayName: Deploy Main Template
  inputs:
      azureResourceManagerConnection: "TestEnvironment"
      deploymentScope: "Subscription"
      location: "westeurope"
      templateLocation: "Linked artifact"
      csmFile: "./deployment/main.json"
      csmParametersFile: "./deployment/test.parameters.json"
      deploymentMode: "Incremental"
```

This `AzureResourceManagerTemplateDeployment` task will deploy the ARM template for you. As you can see, this task has a few more properties to fill. Remember that the extension in VS Code will help you with that.

Now that you have created your first task, let's create a first version of your pipeline by organizing your transpile and deploy tasks in a job.

7.4.3   Grouping tasks in a job

Jobs help organize your pipeline into logical building blocks. By default, jobs will run in parallel, but you can also configure jobs to depend on one another. You will see an example of that shortly.

Jobs have a property called `steps`, and this is where you declare tasks. The tasks run in the order in which they are declared. The following listing is a pipeline that contains the trigger you created earlier, along with the transpile and deployment tasks (pipeline/single-job-resource-deployment-ppl.yml).

Listing 7.9   Pipeline deploying your Bicep template to Azure

```
trigger:
  - main

jobs:
  - job: publishbicep
    displayName: Publish bicep files as pipeline artifacts
```

```
steps:
  - bash: az bicep build --file ./deployment/main.bicep
    displayName: "Transpile Bicep"

  - task: AzureResourceManagerTemplateDeployment@3
    displayName: Deploy Main Template
    inputs:
        azureResourceManagerConnection: "TestEnvironment"   ◁──── The service
        deploymentScope: "Subscription"                           connection
        location: "westeurope"                                    used
        templateLocation: "Linked artifact"
        csmFile: "./deployment/main.json"
        csmParametersFile: "./deployment/test.parameters.json"
        deploymentMode: "Incremental"
```

This snippet contains a pipeline, triggered when changes are pushed to the main branch of your version control repository. The pipeline has a `jobs` property containing a single task. This job has a `steps` property containing two tasks, the Transpile Bicep and Deploy Main Template tasks. It is a good idea to commit and push your changes now.

The preceding example only has one job, but you can add more. The following example shows two jobs and includes the `dependsOn` property to make the jobs not run in parallel:

```
jobs:
- job: JobA
  steps:
  - script: echo hello from JobA
- job: JobB
  dependsOn: JobA
  steps:
  - script: echo hello from JobB
```

Here we have two jobs named `JobA` and `JobB`. The `dependsOn` property on `JobB` will make sure that it will only start running when `JobA` has successfully finished.

For your pipeline to work, you need a service connection. This service connection will allow you to communicate with Azure from within Azure DevOps. The following section explains more about service connections.

7.4.4 Creating service connections

A service connection is a bridge from Azure DevOps to another system. There are a lot of different types of service connections and each is designed to connect Azure DevOps with another system. In listing 7.9 you saw a service connection being used to deploy the infrastructure.

For the purposes of the pipeline you created in the previous section, you need to create an Azure Resource Manager service connection. This type of service connection allows you to communicate with the Azure Resource Manager. The service connection can be scoped to the subscription scope in Azure, as you will see in a bit.

According to Microsoft's recommendations, test and production environments are ideally separated on different Azure subscriptions. This means that, for the Toma Toe example, you need to create two service connections: one targeting a test subscription and one targeting a production subscription. If you don't have two different subscriptions, you can set your production service connection to target the same subscription as the test service connection and still follow along with all the upcoming examples.

In Azure DevOps, navigate to your project settings and click Service Connections. Next, click the New Service Connection button to create a new service connection.

Figure 7.5 shows the screen that opens when you create a new service connection. For the first service connection, select the test Azure subscription and leave the Resource Group drop-down empty. Name the service connection `TestEnvironment`. Make sure that Grant Access Permission to All Pipelines is checked. If you don't do that, you will need to allow every new pipeline to use this service connection.

New Azure service connection   ✕
Azure Resource Manager using service principal (automatic)

Scope level

◉ Subscription

◯ Management Group

◯ Machine Learning Workspace

Subscription

| Your subscription name   ⌄ |

Resource group

| ⌄ |

Details

Service connection name

| TestEnvironment |

Description (optional)

| This service connection is used to deploy cloud infrastructure to
the test environment   ● |

Security

☑ Grant access permission to all pipelines

Learn more   Back   Save
Troubleshoot

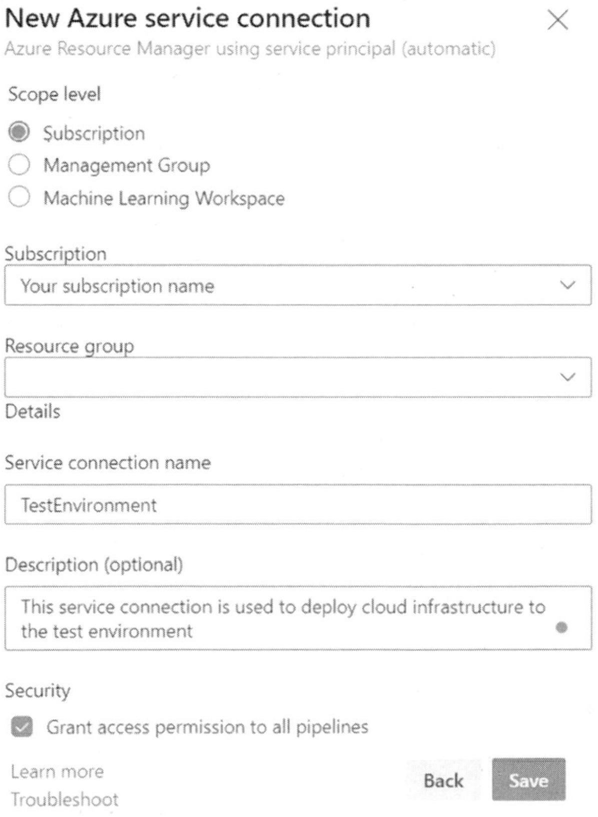

Figure 7.5   Creating a service connection in Azure DevOps

Now repeat these steps but target the production subscription and name the service connection `ProductionEnvironment`.

Permissions for creating service connections

You will need sufficient permissions to create a service connection. That's because this process will try to create a service principal in Azure, and that service principal will be given permissions on your resources in Azure. If you do not have enough permissions to create these Azure Resource Manager service connections, you can request your IT department to create two service principals and use that information to create the service connections. This would not require you to have elevated permissions in Azure.

Service connections can be decorated with barriers and toll booths if you like, in the form of *approvals* and *checks*. These approvals and checks allow you to configure requirements that must be met before the bridge is crossed. These requirements need not involve human interaction; they could involve a call to some IT system, for example. It is common to protect deployments to a production environment so that every deployment is checked and approved according to your standards.

Approvals and checks are validated just prior to when a stage starts. Azure DevOps will investigate which service connections are used and whether any approvals and checks are configured for these service connections. All approvals and checks must validate successfully for the stage to start.

To add an approval to your existing service connection, open the production service connection details. There you can find the Approvals and Checks menu, which is hidden under a button with three dots next to the Edit button, as shown in figure 7.6.

Select the Approvals and Checks option in the menu. In the view that opens, you can see that there are various options to choose from (figure 7.7).

The Approvals and Checks view shows multiple options that can be used to protect and verify a deployment. There is, for example, the Business Hours option, which lets you set the hours in which this connection can be used. Another option is to call a REST API and act on the result, or to query Azure Monitor for alerts. Click the Approvals option, and you'll be shown the dialog box in figure 7.8.

Figure 7.6   Adding an approval on a service connection

← **Approvals and checks**
ProductionEnvironment

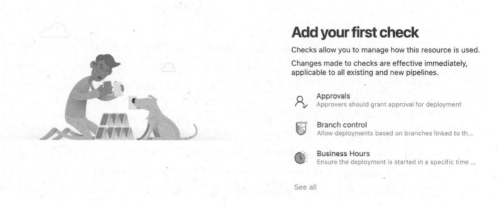

Add your first check

Checks allow you to manage how this resource is used.

Changes made to checks are effective immediately, applicable to all existing and new pipelines.

Approvals
Approvers should grant approval for deployment

Branch control
Allow deployments based on branches linked to th...

Business Hours
Ensure the deployment is started in a specific time ...

See all

Figure 7.7   The Approvals and Checks UI shows different options you can use.

Approvals   ✕

Approvers

    Eduard Keilholz ✕   Erwin Staal ✕ +

Instructions to approvers (optional)

Advanced   ∧

Minimum number of approvals required

    All   ∨

☐ Require approvers to approve in sequence
☑ Allow approvers to approve their own runs

Control options   ∧

Timeout

    30   Days   ∨

Figure 7.8   Adding an approval to a service connection

Figure 7.8 shows the configuration of an approval. In this case, both Eduard Keilholz and Erwin Staal must approve before the pipeline can proceed. If the pipeline is not approved within 30 days, the pipeline will be cancelled.

Once you have created the service connections, your pipeline can communicate with Azure. This was the last step required to make your pipeline work. Let's go to the Azure DevOps portal to configure it, so it can run your pipeline.

7.4.5   Configuring Azure DevOps to run your pipeline

Before Azure DevOps can run your pipeline, you must first make it aware of its presence. Make sure you have committed and pushed the pipeline you created in the previous section, so you can use it in Azure DevOps. Navigate to the Azure DevOps portal, and choose Pipelines in the menu. Click the New Pipeline button to create a new pipeline.

You will now get to pick the repository that contains your pipeline definition file, as shown in figure 7.9. Select Azure Repos Git. As you can see, Azure DevOps can also work with external repositories located at GitHub or Bitbucket, for example.

In the next step, select the repository you are using for this project (figure 7.10).

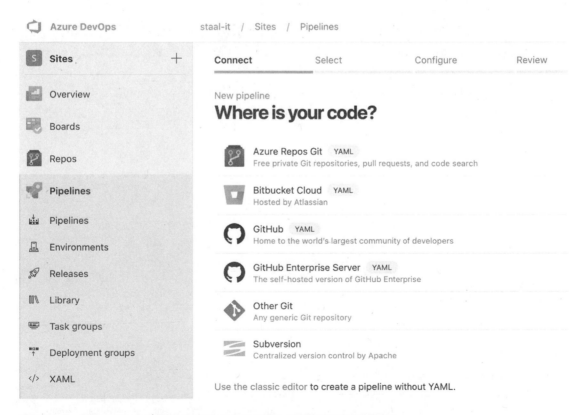

Figure 7.9   Choose your version control system while creating a new pipeline.

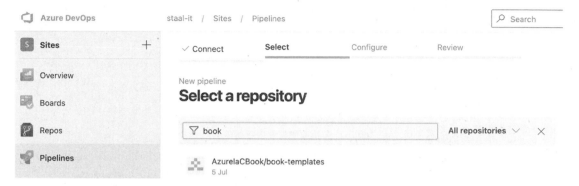

Figure 7.10   Select the repository where the pipeline file resides.

Next you need to configure your pipeline. Since your pipeline definition file is already available in source control, choose Existing Azure Pipelines YAML File. Then select the pipeline file you created earlier (pipeline/single-job-resource-deployment-ppl.yml) and click Continue.

Figure 7.11 shows the window presented when you add a new pipeline from an existing YAML file, and where you select the desired YAML file. Once you have confirmed

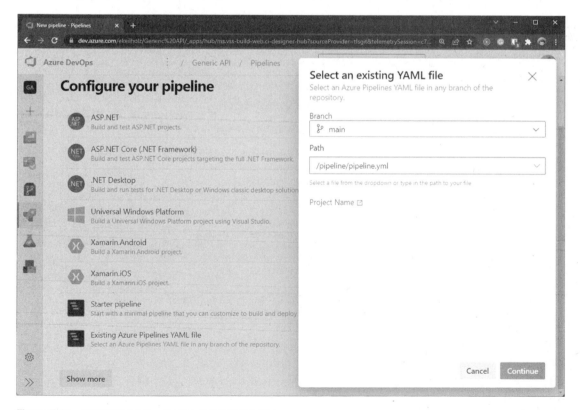

Figure 7.11   Creating a new pipeline in Azure DevOps

the creation of the pipeline by clicking the Continue button, the window closes and your pipeline details will be shown. At this point, you can click the Run button to invoke the pipeline for the very first time. Also, if you make changes to a file in your repository, and you commit and push the changes, this pipeline will be triggered.

You have now created your first pipeline, transpiling Bicep files to ARM template JSON files, and deployed them to Azure. However, this does not fully cover the requirements of the Toma Toe deployment. You haven't yet deployed to a test environment, and you may want to allow manual intervention in your pipeline, to approve deployment to a production environment, for example. The remainder of this chapter expands the pipeline so it meets the requirements of the Toma Toe website.

7.5 Adding logical phases to your pipeline

The pipeline you created earlier in this chapter works fine, but it is not the final product that will solve the Toma Toe case. The pipeline compiles and deploys the IaC template, but it does not deploy to multiple regions, nor does it create the Traffic Manager. In this section, you'll expand the pipeline so it contains the logical phases required for the Toma Toe case.

7.5.1 Identifying the logical phases

It's important to think about the logical phases your pipeline should contain. In an Azure DevOps pipeline, each such phase is called a *stage*. Pipelines can contain one or more stages, and you can configure these stages to depend on one another. Stages are major divisions in your pipeline, used to organize your jobs. Good examples of stages are "Compile this app," "Deploy to test," or "Deploy to production."

A stage can depend on a preceding stage, allowing you to take control over when a stage will run. By default, stages run sequentially. The following example will run the pipeline stages sequentially:

```
stages:
- stage: CompileApp
  jobs:
  - job:
    ...

- stage: DeployWestEu
  jobs:
  - job:
    ...
```

The previous example shows two stages: CompileApp and DeployWestEu. Because no dependency was defined, the pipeline will run these stages using the default, which is sequential.

The following snippet is the same pipeline except for the dependsOn[] property in the second stage:

```
stages:
- stage: CompileApp
  jobs:
  - job:
    ...

- stage: DeployWestEu
  dependsOn: []
  jobs:
  - job:
    ...
```

By adding `dependsOn[]`, you remove the implicit dependency on the first stage, causing your stages to run in parallel. Note that doing this for this example would actually break it. You cannot deploy an application before it has been compiled.

You can also make stages explicitly depend on one or more other stages. The following example is a fan-out and fan-in example. It will first compile the application, then deploy it into two Azure regions, and finally verify the deployment.

```
stages:
- stage: CompileApp

- stage: DeployWestEu
  dependsOn: CompileApp

- stage: DeployJapanEast
  dependsOn: CompileApp

- stage: VerifyProductionDeployment
  dependsOn:
  - DeployWestEu
  - DeployJapanEast
```

The preceding example shows a pipeline with four stages. The first stage (`Compile-App`) will run when the pipeline is triggered. The second and third stages (deploying to West Europe and Japan East) will run in parallel, but only when the `CompileApp` stage has completed successfully. Finally, the fourth stage (which verifies the production deployment) will run only when both the deployment to West Europe and the deployment to Japan East have completed successfully.

For the Toma Toe case, you can identify three stages. The first stage will contain a job that transpiles the Bicep files, the second stage will deploy the infrastructure to a test environment, and the third stage will deploy the infrastructure to a production environment.

It is important to know that stages and jobs run in different processes. They therefore often run on different underlying virtual machines. The result is that when you create a file in one stage, for example, it is not automatically available in another stage. To solve this problem, you can make use of a concept called a *pipeline artifact*.

7.5.2 Accessing artifacts from different jobs

Stages and jobs run within their own processes in the pipeline. When they are finished, any output that was created during their run will be deleted. Each run of a stage or job therefore starts with a clean slate. Whenever you want to make a file available outside of the current stage or job in the pipeline, you need to publish it as a pipeline artifact. A pipeline artifact has a name, and you can use that name in later stages or jobs to download the artifact.

In the Toma Toe case, you will require a pipeline artifact. The first stage is going to transpile Bicep files, creating an ARM template JSON file, and the remainder of the pipeline is going to deploy this JSON file in jobs organized in different stages.

Besides needing the file in other stages and jobs, there is another important benefit of using the pipeline artifact in this case. You could have called the `bicep build` command in every job and generated the JSON files again and again. However, you should not do that, because you want the pipeline to be reliable and have a consistent outcome. What could happen here is that in between the different stages or jobs, the version of Bicep could be updated, and the result of the Bicep `build` command could therefore lead to a slightly different ARM template. By reusing the ARM template that is output from your build stage in all the stages still to be executed, you ensure a consistent outcome.

Now that you know how to organize stages and make files from one stage or job available in another, let's work on the first stage. This stage will transpile the Bicep file and publish the resulting ARM template as pipeline artifact.

7.5.3 Transpiling Bicep in a pipeline stage

You can now separate the jobs for your pipeline into separate files—these files are called pipeline templates. There are two advantages of doing so. First, a separate file is reusable in your pipelines. Second, the individual pipeline files stay smaller than a pipeline template declared in a single file, making it more readable and maintainable.

Listing 7.10 shows a first pipeline template example (pipeline/templates/transpile-job.yml). This template runs the Bicep build, moves the result to a particular folder, and then creates a pipeline artifact. It is good practice to place these templates in a separate folder within your pipelines folder called "templates".

Listing 7.10 Transpile a Bicep file and publish it as a pipeline artifact

```
parameters:
  - name: artifactName
    type: string
    default: "arm-templates"

steps:
  - bash: az bicep build --file ./deployment/main.bicep
    displayName: "Transpile Main Bicep"
```

```
- task: CopyFiles@2
  displayName: "Copy JSON files to:
    ➥ $(Build.ArtifactStagingDirectory)/${{parameters.artifactName}}"
  inputs:
    SourceFolder: "deployment"
    Contents: "**/*.json"
    TargetFolder:
      ➥ "$(Build.ArtifactStagingDirectory)/${{parameters.artifactName}}"

- task: PublishPipelineArtifact@1
  displayName: "Publish Pipeline Artifact"
  inputs:
    targetPath:
      ➥ "$(Build.ArtifactStagingDirectory)/${{parameters.artifactName}}"
    artifact: "${{parameters.artifactName}}"
```

The preceding listing shows a template YAML file containing one parameter. This parameter can be used to pass in values when using the template. In this case, the parameter holds the name of the artifact it will publish, it is of type string, and it has a default value of arm-templates. If your parameter has a default value, you can also use the following short notation:

```
parameters:
- artifactName: "arm-templates"
```

The remainder of the template contains the steps property of a job with three tasks. The first task transpiles the main.bicep file into main.json. The second task copies that JSON file to an artifact staging directory used to collect files that you want to publish as pipeline artifacts. The final task publishes the artifact staging directory as a pipeline artifact.

7.5.4   *Deploying a template from a pipeline artifact*

You've created a job that transpiles the Bicep file into JSON, so now let's work on a job that deploys this JSON file (pipeline/templates/deploy-arm.yml).

Listing 7.11   Deploying infrastructure

```
parameters:
  - name: serviceConnectionName
    type: string
  - name: subscriptionId
    type: string
  - name: environmentName
    type: string
  - name: artifactName
    type: string
    default: "arm-templates"
  - name: location
    type: string
  - name: locationAbbriviation
    type: string
```

The name of the service connection that you created in section 7.4.4.

The Id of the subscription that holds the test resources.

```
steps:
  - task: DownloadPipelineArtifact@0
    displayName: "Download Artifact: ${{ parameters.artifactName }}"
    inputs:
      artifactName: "${{ parameters.artifactName }}"
      targetPath:
          ➡ $(System.ArtifactsDirectory)/${{ parameters.artifactName }}

  - task: AzureResourceManagerTemplateDeployment@3
    displayName: Deploy Main Template
    inputs:
      azureResourceManagerConnection:
          ➡ "${{ parameters.serviceConnectionName }}"
      deploymentScope: "Subscription"
      subscriptionId: "${{ parameters.subscriptionId }}"
      location: ${{ parameters.location }}
      templateLocation: "Linked artifact"
      csmFile:
          ➡ "$(System.ArtifactsDirectory)/${{parameters.artifactName}}/main.json"
      overrideParameters:
          ➡ -locationAbbreviation ${{parameters.locationAbbriviation}}
      deploymentMode: "Incremental"
```

The preceding listing contains two tasks. The first task downloads the pipeline artifacts, making the JSON files available in the current job. The second task creates a new deployment in Azure. This deployment will, as described in the Bicep templates, create a resource group and deploy the App Service plan and the web app in that resource group.

The two templates you just created don't do much on their own. You need to create one more pipeline file that will use these two templates (pipelines/multi-stage-resource-deployment-ppl.yml). Add a new pipeline file in the same folder where you placed the previous pipeline, and call this one multi-stage-resource-deployment-ppl.yml. The two templates will each be used in their own stage, so this pipeline therefore contains two stages: one that creates the ARM template using transpile-job.yml, and one that deploys that template to your test environment using deploy-arm.yml.

Listing 7.12   A multistage pipeline

```
trigger:
  - main                      ┐  This pipeline
                              │  contains multiple
                              │  stages.
stages:              ◀────────┘
  - stage: build
    displayName: Publish Bicep Files
    jobs:
      - job: publishbicep
        displayName: Publish bicep files as pipeline artifacts
        steps:
          - template: ./templates/transpile-job.yml   ◀──  Referencing another
                                                           template using the
                                                           template keyword
  - stage: deployinfratest
    dependsOn: build
    displayName: Deploy to test
```

```
jobs:
  - job: deploy_us_test
    displayName: Deploy infra to US region test
    steps:
      - template: ./templates/deploy-arm.yml
        parameters:
          serviceConnectionName: "TestEnvironment"
          subscriptionId: "<your-subscription-id>"
          environmentName: "test"
          location: "eastus"
          locationAbbreviation: "us"
```

When a template requires parameters, they are passed along.

The previous template you created, single-job-resource-deployment-ppl.yml, only used a single job and no stages. This pipeline does use stages, which is why you see the `stages` keyword used. The pipeline contains two stages, each having a single job. Instead of defining the tasks in those jobs in this file, you use the `template` keyword in the `steps` section to reference another pipeline part. The first template, transpile-job.yml, only has a single parameter, which has a default value. The second template has mandatory parameters, and values for each are passed with the template file. The result after running this template should be identical to that of single-job-resource-deployment-ppl.yml. However, this version is more readable, and you can reuse the templates, as you will see in a bit.

One aspect of the Toma Toe infrastructure has not been discussed yet, the Azure Traffic Manager. Let's dig into that.

7.6   Adding the Traffic Manager

It's now time to create the Azure Traffic Manager Bicep template, and a YAML template to deploy it. Listing 7.13 contains the Bicep module for creating the Traffic Manager (deployment/Network/trafficmanagerprofiles.bicep). Remember that the Traffic Manager is an Azure Service that can be used to route user traffic in different ways. In the Toma Toe case, you will use it to route a user to the nearest Azure App Service to optimize performance.

Listing 7.13   Creating the Azure Traffic Manager

```
param systemName string = 'tomatoe'

@allowed([
    'dev'
    'test'
    'acc'
    'prod'
])
param environmentName string

resource trafficManager
    'Microsoft.Network/trafficmanagerprofiles@2018-08-01' = {
    name: '${systemName}-${environmentName}'
    location: 'global'
```

A Traffic Manager is deployed globally.

```
            properties: {
                trafficRoutingMethod: 'Geographic'
                dnsConfig: {
                    relativeName: '${systemName}-${environmentName}'
                    ttl: 60
                }
                monitorConfig: {
                    profileMonitorStatus: 'Online'
                    protocol: 'HTTPS'
                    path: '/'
                    port: 443
                    intervalInSeconds: 30
                    toleratedNumberOfFailures: 3
                    timeoutInSeconds: 10
                }
                endpoints: [
                    {
                        name: 'eur'
                        type: 'Microsoft.Network/trafficManagerProfiles/
                    externalEndpoints'
                        properties: {
                            target:
                                '${systemName}-${environmentName}-we-
                    app.azurewebsites.net'
                            weight: 1
                            priority: 1
                            endpointLocation: 'West Europe'
                            geoMapping: [
                                'GEO-EU'
                            ]
                        }
                    }
                    {
                        name: 'asi'
                        type: 'Microsoft.Network/trafficManagerProfiles/
                    externalEndpoints'
                        properties: {
                            target:
                                '${systemName}-${environmentName}-asi-
                    app.azurewebsites.net'
                            weight: 1
                            priority: 2
                            endpointLocation: 'East Asia'
                            geoMapping: [
                                'GEO-AS'
                                'GEO-AP'
                                'GEO-ME'
                            ]
                        }
                    }
                    {
                        name: 'global'
                        type: 'Microsoft.Network/trafficManagerProfiles/
                    externalEndpoints'
                        properties: {
```

"Geographic" is used as the routing method. → `trafficRoutingMethod: 'Geographic'`

The priority is used to indicate the order of evaluation. → `priority: 1`

The geoMapping array indicates where a user should originate its request from to be directed to this endpoint. ← `'GEO-EU'`

```
            target:
          ➥     '${systemName}-${environmentName}-us-
    app.azurewebsites.net'
                weight: 1
                priority: 3
                endpointLocation: East US'
                geoMapping: [
                   'WORLD'
                ]
            }
        }
    ]
  }
}
```

You can see that one resource is created, an Azure Traffic Manager. The location is set to global, which is the only valid value for a Traffic Manager. In the endpoints array, you can see three endpoints added. The priority property allows you to define the order in which Azure should determine the correct endpoint to use. The three endpoints configured here will check if a visitor comes from Europe. If so, the visitor will be redirected to the West Europe data center. Then a similar check is performed for the Asia Pacific area. If none of these locations match the origin of the visitor (if they come from somewhere else in the world), the visitor will be redirected to the East US data center.

The next Bicep template will create the resource group for the Traffic Manager and use the module to deploy the Traffic Manager inside that resource group (deployment/trafficmgr.bicep). By adding this additional template, we keep things small and therefore more readable and reusable.

Listing 7.14   Adding a deployment file for the Traffic Manager

```
targetScope = 'subscription'

param systemName string = 'tomatoe'

@allowed([
    'dev'
    'test'
    'acc'
    'prod'
])
param environmentName string

resource resourceGroup 'Microsoft.Resources/resourceGroups@2021-04-01' = {
    name: '${systemName}-${environmentName}'
    location: deployment().location
}

module trafficManagerModule 'Network/trafficmanagerprofiles.bicep' = {
    name: 'trafficManagerModule'
    scope: resourceGroup
    params: {
        systemName: systemName
```

```
        environmentName: environmentName
    }
}
```

This template first creates the resource group in a certain Azure region—that is a mandatory property for a resource group, even if the resource inside has its location set to global like the Traffic Manager does. Once the resource group is there, the template will use the trafficmanagerprofiles.bicep module to create the Traffic Manager in that group. Now that all the Bicep files are in place, let's work on a YAML template that deploys the Traffic Manager.

7.6.1   Deploying the Traffic Manager

Before you can deploy the Traffic Manager, you first need to transpile the Bicep file just created into an ARM template. That process is identical to what you did earlier with the main.bicep template. Open the transpile-job.yml file and add the following snippet under the bash task that transpiles main.bicep, on line 7:

```
- bash: az bicep build --file ./deployment/trafficmgr.bicep
  displayName: "Transpile Traffic Manager Bicep"
```

Now that the Bicep file is transpiled and published in the pipeline artifact, you can use that to deploy it. The following listing will download the pipeline artifact and then start a new deployment (pipeline/templates/traffic-manager.yml).

Listing 7.15   Deploying the Traffic Manager

```
parameters:
  - name: serviceConnectionName
    type: string
  - name: subscriptionId
    type: string
  - name: systemName
    type: string
    default: "tomatoe"
  - name: environmentName
    type: string
  - name: artifactName
    type: string
    default: "arm-templates"
  - name: location
    type: string

steps:
  - task: DownloadPipelineArtifact@0
    displayName: "Download Artifact: ${{ parameters.artifactName }}"
    inputs:
      artifactName: "${{ parameters.artifactName }}"
      targetPath:
        ➥ $(System.ArtifactsDirectory)/${{ parameters.artifactName }}
```

```
- task: AzureResourceManagerTemplateDeployment@3
  displayName: Deploy Main Template
  inputs:
    azureResourceManagerConnection:
        ➡  "${{ parameters.serviceConnectionName }}"
    deploymentScope: "Subscription"
    subscriptionId: "${{ parameters.subscriptionId }}"
    location: ${{ parameters.location }}
    templateLocation: "Linked artifact"
    csmFile: "$(System.ArtifactsDirectory)/${{ parameters.artifactName
        ➡  }}/trafficmgr.json"
    overrideParameters: -environmentName ${{parameters.environmentName}}
    deploymentMode: "Incremental"
```

The preceding listing downloads the pipeline artifact containing the compiled Bicep files. Then it runs the deployment of the Traffic Manager. Again, this deployment will create a resource group and provision the Traffic Manager inside that group.

You have now learned how to create a pipeline, and how to combine operations in smaller files to make them more readable and reusable. If you followed along with this entire chapter, you now have a pipeline folder structure that looks like this:

```
+-- pipelines
|   +--templates
|       +--deploy-arm.yml
|       +--traffic-manager.yml
|       +--transpile-job.yml
|   +--single-job-resource-deployment-ppl.yml
|   +--multi-stage-resource-deployment-ppl.yml
```

The final section in this chapter will complete the Toma Toe case. You still need to deploy the application to multiple regions, use the Traffic Manager template, and deploy to the production environment. Let's see how that can be done!

7.7   Creating a real-world example pipeline

Now that you have learned about the basic concepts of a pipeline in Azure DevOps, let's create a fully functional multistage, multiregion pipeline that uses the templates created earlier in this chapter. The pipeline you will create looks like the schema in figure 7.12.

You can see that the full function of the pipeline is separated into three stages. One is the build stage, compiling all Bicep files. The second and third stages are deployment stages: first to test, and then to production. Using the legend, you can match the jobs in the three stages with the YAML snippets created earlier in this chapter. Let's complete the pipeline.

7.7.1   Completing the pipeline

To complete the pipeline, you'll need one additional pipeline file (pipeline/multi-region-resource-deployment-ppl.yml). This file will orchestrate the smaller pipeline

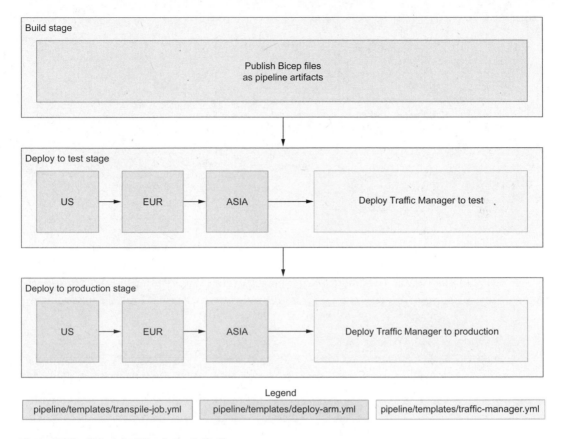

Figure 7.12   Schema of the desired pipeline

templates created earlier in this chapter as shown in listing 7.16, and extend the multi-stage-resource-deployment-ppl.yml pipeline. Create a new file in the pipeline folder called multi-region-resource-deployment-ppl.yml.

Listing 7.16   The complete pipeline

```
trigger:
  - main                    Variables are defined
                            for values that are used
                            multiple times.
variables:       ◁─
    TestSubscriptionId: "<your-subscription-id>"
    TestServiceConnectionName: "TestEnvironment"

    ProdSubscriptionId: "<your-subscription-id>"
    ProdServiceConnectionName: "ProductionEnvironment"

stages:
    - stage: build
      displayName: Publish Bicep Files
```

```
jobs:
    - job: publishbicep
      displayName: Publish bicep files as pipeline artifacts
      steps:
          - template: ./templates/transpile-job.yml

- stage: deployinfratest
  dependsOn: build
  displayName: Deploy to test

  variables:
      environmentName: "test"

  jobs:
      - job: deploy_us_test
        displayName: Deploy infra to US region test
        steps:
            - template: ./templates/deploy-arm.yml
              parameters:
                  serviceConnectionName:
                      ${{ variables.TestServiceConnectionName }}
                  subscriptionId: ${{ variables.TestSubscriptionId }}
                  location: "eastus"
                  locationAbbreviation: "us"
                  environmentName: ${{ variables.environmentName }}

      - job: deploy_eur_test
        displayName: Deploy infra to EUR region test
        dependsOn: deploy_us_test
        steps:
            - template: ./templates/deploy-arm.yml
              parameters:
                  serviceConnectionName:
                      ${{ variables.TestServiceConnectionName }}
                  subscriptionId: ${{ variables.TestSubscriptionId }}
                  location: "westeurope"
                  locationAbbreviation: "we"
                  environmentName: ${{ variables.environmentName }}

      - job: deploy_asia_test
        displayName: Deploy infra to ASIA region test
        dependsOn: deploy_eur_test
        steps:
            - template: ./templates/deploy-arm.yml
              parameters:
                  serviceConnectionName:
                      ${{ variables.TestServiceConnectionName }}
                  subscriptionId: ${{ variables.TestSubscriptionId }}
                  location: "eastasia"
                  locationAbbreviation: "asi"
                  environmentName: ${{ variables.environmentName }}

      - job: deploy_trafficmgr_test
        displayName: Deploy traffic manager test
        dependsOn: deploy_asia_test
```

This stage deploys the resources to the test environment.

The deployment to each region is not done in parallel.

```
        steps:
            - template: ./templates/traffic-manager.yml
              parameters:
                  serviceConnectionName:
                      ⇒ ${{ variables.TestServiceConnectionName }}
                  subscriptionId: ${{ variables.TestSubscriptionId }}
                  location: "westeurope"
                  environmentName: ${{ variables.environmentName }}

- stage: deployinfraprod
  dependsOn: deployinfratest
  displayName: Deploy to production
```

**This stage deploys
the resources to the
production environment.**

```
  variables:
      environmentName: "prod"

  jobs:
      - job: deploy_us_prod
        displayName: Deploy infra to US region prod
        steps:
            - template: ./templates/deploy-arm.yml
              parameters:
                  serviceConnectionName:
                      ⇒ ${{ variables.ProdServiceConnectionName }}
                  subscriptionId: ${{ variables.ProdSubscriptionId }}
                  location: "eastus"
                  locationAbbreviation: "us"
                  environmentName: ${{ variables.environmentName }}

      - job: deploy_eur_prod
        displayName: Deploy infra to EUR region prod
        dependsOn: deploy_us_prod
        steps:
            - template: ./templates/deploy-arm.yml
              parameters:
                  serviceConnectionName:
                      ⇒ ${{ variables.ProdServiceConnectionName }}
                  subscriptionId: ${{ variables.ProdSubscriptionId }}
                  location: "westeurope"
                  locationAbbreviation: "we"
                  environmentName: ${{ variables.environmentName }}

      - job: deploy_asia_prod
        displayName: Deploy infra to ASIA region prod
        dependsOn: deploy_eur_prod
        steps:
            - template: ./templates/deploy-arm.yml
              parameters:
                  serviceConnectionName:
                      ⇒ ${{ variables.ProdServiceConnectionName }}
                  subscriptionId: ${{ variables.ProdSubscriptionId }}
                  location: "eastasia"
                  locationAbbreviation: "asi"
                  environmentName: ${{ variables.environmentName }}
```

```
    - job: deploy_trafficmgr_prod
      displayName: Deploy traffic manager test
      dependsOn: deploy_asia_prod
      steps:
        - template: ./templates/traffic-manager.yml
          parameters:
            serviceConnectionName:
              ➡ ${{ variables.ProdServiceConnectionName }}
            subscriptionId: ${{ variables.ProdSubscriptionId }}
            location: "westeurope"
            environmentName: ${{ variables.environmentName }}
```

The preceding listing describes the complete pipeline. The first stage, the build stage, contains one job with a single task that executes the transpile-job.yml file that will transpile the Bicep files and publish the products (ARM template JSON files) as pipeline artifacts.

Then two quite similar stages are executed; they both use four jobs to deploy the infrastructure to either the test or production environment. The first three jobs deploy the API infrastructure in three different Azure regions, and the last job provisions the Traffic Manager that's configured to distribute the load depending on the geographical location of the website visitors. This pipeline uses the templates multiple times; for example, deploy-arm.yml is used six times.

Some of the parameters that you need to pass along aren't always different. For example, the subscriptionId parameter only has two distinct values, one for test and one for production, not six. To prevent you from having to list identical values multiple times you can use variables, which can be defined on different scopes. This pipeline uses variables on the root scope for the serviceConnectionName and subscriptionId variables but uses a variable on the stage level for the environmentName variable. Depending on the scope, the variable holds a certain value. Variables can then be used in the pipeline by using the ${{ }} notation. For the TestSubscriptionId variable, that becomes ${{ variables.TestSubscriptionId }}.

Note that a successful deployment of the preceding pipeline might not mean that everything is working. You might want to add steps to the pipeline to verify that. The next chapter will discuss testing in depth.

With this file committed and pushed to your remote Git repository, you can go back to the Azure DevOps portal and remove the previously created pipeline. Then add a new pipeline and use the pipeline/multi-region-resource-deployment-ppl.yml file. You can then run the pipeline. When you review the details of the running pipeline, you will see a representation similar to figure 7.13.

Figure 7.13 shows that the pipeline contains three stages. Each job in a stage is represented, and a status icon shows the current status of these jobs. You can click on a job to zoom in even further. This will take you to a new view showing all the details of your pipeline, including the tasks in the jobs and a log file showing you log information for each separate job.

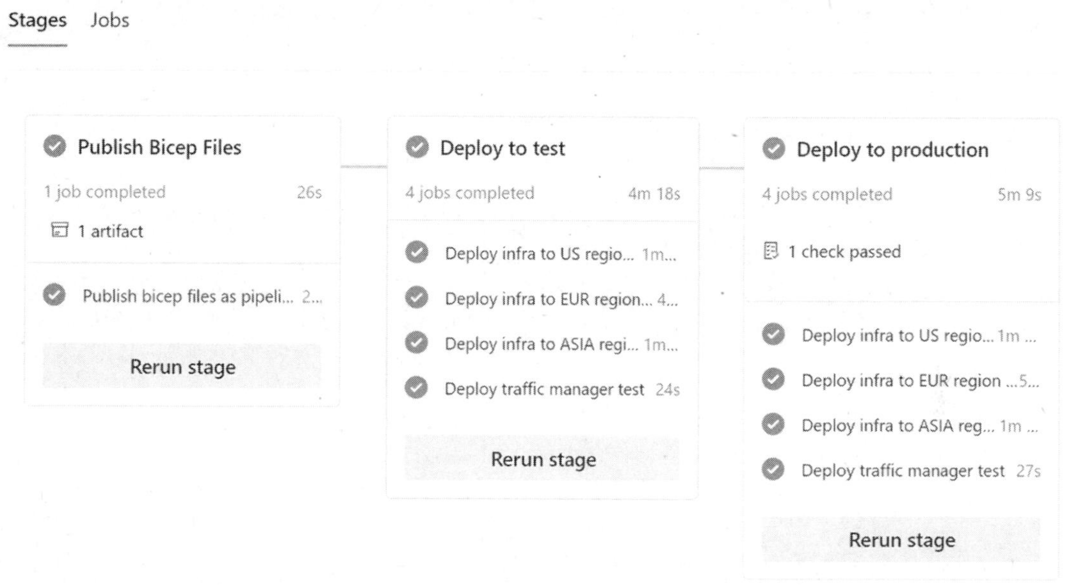

Stages   Jobs

Figure 7.13   The visual representation of your pipeline in Azure DevOps

It might be wise to now delete some of the resources you have just created. With six App Service plans, things get expensive quite quickly. Chapter 13 covers how to do that.

Summary

- Azure DevOps allows you to store your files in a Git repository. That allows you to work together with colleagues on the same code base.
- In Azure DevOps, you can create a new pipeline using the YAML syntax. Pipeline templates allow you to split pipelines into smaller, reusable parts.
- Using stages, jobs, and steps, you can organize your pipelines in readable, reusable bits.
- Service connections in Azure DevOps allow you to connect to other systems, such as Azure. On service connections you can add approvals and checks to validate deployments to production.
- Pipeline artifacts help you make outputs in one stage or pipeline available in the next. That allows you to follow the "build once, use many" principle.

Complex deployments
using GitHub Actions

This chapter covers

- Deploying the Toma Toe (chapter 7) case using GitHub Actions
- Connecting to Azure from GitHub Actions
- Handling secrets when using GitHub Actions
- Monitoring workflows while they are running

Git is currently one of the most popular source control systems around, and the GitHub platform (https://github.com), originally built around Git, is one of the most popular platforms for storing (code) projects. Throughout the years, GitHub has grown to a more mature application lifecycle management platform, including an integrated automation system called GitHub Actions.

GitHub Actions is the equivalent of an Azure DevOps pipeline that allows you to hook into events in your source control to implement CI/CD solutions in GitHub. Although both GitHub Actions and Azure Pipelines have a lot in common, there are some differences between the two. This chapter will touch upon those differences and will use the same Toma Toe use case as chapter 7. The same deployment process will be created, but this time using GitHub Actions.

There are no silver bullets in automated deployment

There are tons of systems that allow you to build and deploy software in an automated fashion. Azure DevOps and GitHub are just two of a long list of products and solutions. We chose to write examples using these two platforms because they're useful to know, but that doesn't mean other platforms (such as Octopus Deploy and TeamCity) would not do a good job.

GitHub accounts are free, and you can create one right here: https://github.com/signup. With this free account you can create an unlimited number of Git repositories, but there are some limitations. For example, the number of automation minutes is limited, as is the amount of storage.

8.1   Forking a repository

Forking is a way to copy an existing repository into a new one, while keeping references to each other. For this chapter, we created a GitHub repository that you can fork, to get you up and running quickly. Once you have logged in to GitHub, navigate to https://github.com/AzureIaCBook/github-actions-start and click the Fork button at the top right of the screen (see figure 8.1). Once it has completed, you'll have a copy of our repository that you can start with.

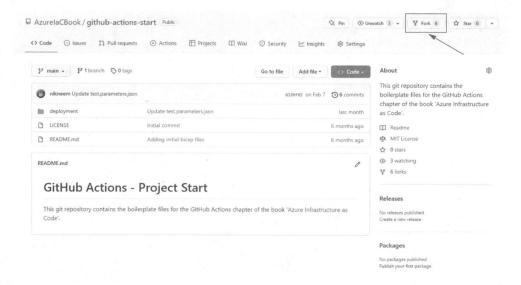

Figure 8.1   Forking a repository in GitHub

The way GitHub Actions is structured is slightly different from the way Azure DevOps is structured. Before you build the complete GitHub Actions workflow, let's look at the terminology used in GitHub Actions.

8.2   Getting to know GitHub Actions

An automation procedure in GitHub is called a *workflow*. Workflows are part of a repository and contain instructions for what the workflow must do. A workflow is triggered by an event and typically stops when an error occurs, when the workflow completes, or when the workflow is cancelled. You can look back to chapter 7 to compare the Azure DevOps pipelines described there to the GitHub Actions workflows here.

Figure 8.2 shows how GitHub Actions are structured. An *event* triggers a *workflow* containing *jobs*, resulting in *runners* executing *actions*. In the remainder of this section, these terms are explained in more detail.

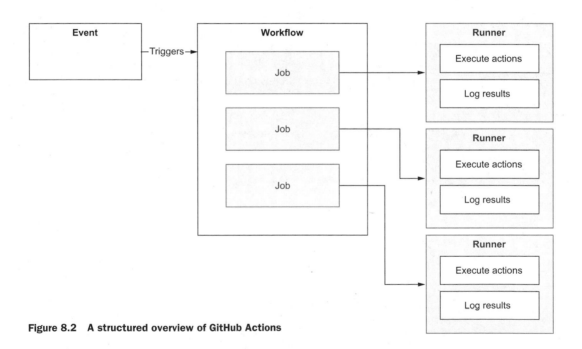

Figure 8.2   A structured overview of GitHub Actions

8.2.1   Workflow events

Workflows are triggered by an event. Like in Azure DevOps, an event can be an activity in the repository, such as pushing a commit or creating a pull request. It is also possible to trigger a workflow with a time schedule. You can even use a GitHub webhook to trigger a workflow.

8.2.2 Runners

GitHub Actions uses runners to execute sections of your workflow. Runners can be compared to agents in Azure DevOps. You can use runners hosted online by GitHub or host runners yourself. When your workflow starts, GitHub actions will reserve an idle runner and execute a job. Once the job completes (or fails), the runner will be disposed of. If your workflow has additional jobs defined, GitHub Actions will find a new idle runner, and start the new job on that new runner (as illustrated in figure 8.2). This process continues until your workflow completes or fails.

8.2.3 Jobs

GitHub has no implementation of something similar to a stage in Azure DevOps. Instead, a job is the largest possible entity in GitHub Actions that allows you to structure your workflow. Jobs run in parallel by default, but you can create dependencies between jobs to make them run sequentially.

8.2.4 Steps

A step can be referred to as an individual task. Tasks organized under the same job are executed on the same runner. This means that when steps are organized under the same job, they can share data with each other. You will learn how to share data between different jobs in section 8.3.1.

8.2.5 Actions

Actions are single commands typically structured in steps. There are tons of actions that can be used. You can find actions created by the GitHub community in GitHub Marketplace (https://github.com/marketplace?type=actions). If your desired action is not available, you can create an action yourself. There is a large GitHub community creating custom actions that you can also use.

We've touched upon the anatomy of a GitHub workflow, so now it's time to write a workflow to deploy the Toma Toe infrastructure. As you'll recall from the previous chapter, the Toma Toe infrastructure deploys a web application in three different Azure regions with an Azure Traffic Manager to route the traffic to the nearest location, based on the geographical location of the website visitor.

8.3 Building a GitHub Actions workflow

Like in Azure DevOps, a GitHub workflow is nothing more than a definition written in a YAML file, stored in your code repository. For GitHub, workflows are stored in a specific folder (.github/workflows). This means that you can create a new workflow by simply adding a YAML file to that specific folder.

As an alternative, you can create a workflow from the GitHub website. Once you're logged in, navigate to your repository and click the Actions menu item at the top of the screen. GitHub has some predefined workflows that you can choose from that may fit the needs of your code project.

There is no predefined workflow for the purpose of this chapter: transpiling a Bicep file and deploying the product (an ARM template) to the Azure cloud, so we will create a workflow file from scratch.

> ### With GitHub, you can edit files online
> GitHub has a convenient way of browsing through the files in your repository. You can even edit files in your repository using GitHub's online file editor. Although this works pretty well, the examples in this chapter assume you have cloned your repository to a local repository and will be editing the files using your favorite IDE.

You can start by creating a new file called .github/workflows/toma-toe.yml and adding the following content:

```
name: Toma Toe Workflow
on: [push]
```

The first line names your workflow, and the second line hooks into the push event on your repository. This means that your workflow will now start as soon as one or more commits are pushed to your repository.

You can commit and push these changes to your repository and then view your repository online. When you now navigate to the Actions tab of your repository, you'll see that it contains one action. The workflow will fail, however, because it doesn't contain a job. Let's address that right away.

8.3.1   Adding a job to a GitHub Actions workflow

Much like the Azure DevOps pipeline you built in chapter 7, this workflow will face the challenge of not being able to share data between jobs. This is because each job runs on a different runner. Luckily, GitHub Actions allows you to publish artifacts just like Azure DevOps pipelines can. Doing so allows you to store data from one job and use it in a subsequent job.

The first job in your workflow transpiles the two Bicep files in the repository to an ARM template and publishes these ARM template JSON files as an artifact, as shown in the following listing (.github/ workflows/toma-toe.yml).

Listing 8.1   Adding the transpile job

```
name: Toma Toe Workflow
on: [push]

jobs:
    publish-bicep:
        runs-on: ubuntu-latest
```

```
steps:
  - uses: actions/checkout@v2
  - name: Compile infrastructure
    uses: Azure/cli@1.0.4
    with:
        azcliversion: 2.23.0
        inlineScript: az bicep build --file ./deployment/main.bicep
  - name: Compile infrastructure
    uses: Azure/cli@1.0.4
    with:
        azcliversion: 2.23.0
        inlineScript: az bicep build --file ./deployment/trafficmgr.bicep
  - name: Publish Artifact
    uses: actions/upload-artifact@v2
    with:
        name: bicep-templates
        path: deployment/*.json
```

The "with" can be compared to "inputs" in Azure DevOps. It allows you to pass in parameters.

The preceding code shows the jobs declaration in the workflow. This indicates that from here on, the workflow contains jobs definitions. Jobs are defined by an identifier followed by a colon. In the preceding example, `publish-bicep` is the identifier of a new job. The `runs-on` allows you to indicate what type of operating system the runner must have and what software the runner needs to have installed. Then, in the `steps` property, four steps are defined. The first step checks out the branch the workflow runs on, to get all its contents. Then the `az bicep build` command is used to transpile the main.bicep file, followed by a similar command to transpile the trafficmgr.bicep file. Finally, the produced JSON files are published as an artifact.

When you commit and publish your changes, the workflow will immediately start again, and this time it will succeed and publish the JSON files as an artifact. If you look at the summary of your workflow, you can find these artifacts and even download them if you want to. Now let's move on to the deployment sections of GitHub Actions.

8.4   The deployment phase in GitHub Actions

In the previous section, the Bicep templates were transpiled into ARM templates and published as an artifact. In this section, we're going to fetch this artifact in later stages and deploy them to Azure.

Unlike Azure DevOps, GitHub does not have a mechanism like service connections, but a connection to Azure is mandatory to deploy infrastructure in an Azure environment. Also, although there are third-party tasks that can help you to deploy your template, a straightforward way is to use Azure CLI commands. In this section, you'll learn how to overcome the problem of connecting to Azure and deploy your template from GitHub Actions.

8.4.1   *Connecting to Azure from your GitHub workflow*

To deploy your infrastructure, you'll use the Azure CLI to allow a connection between the GitHub Actions runner and the Azure Cloud environment. Instead of using a service connection like in Azure DevOps, you can use a couple of Azure CLI commands to connect to Azure and select the correct Azure subscription. To do this, you need to generate connection information that you'll store as a secret in your GitHub repository. Note that the secrets are stored as a property of your GitHub repository and are not part of your source code. These secrets can then be used to connect to Azure and select the correct subscription.

To perform these steps, you need to install Azure CLI if it isn't installed already. You can find download and installation instructions here: https://docs.microsoft .com/cli/azure/install-azure-cli. Also, you must have access to an Azure subscription and have enough privileges (have the Owner role or the User Access Administrator role assigned) to create a service principal. This service principal will be used to connect to the Azure environment from your GitHub workflow.

8.4.2   *Generating a service principal using the Azure CLI*

To generate a service principal, open a command prompt (or the Windows Terminal) and type the following:

```
az login
az account set --subscription {subscription-id}
az ad sp create-for-rbac --name {app-name} --role contributor --scopes
    ➥ /subscriptions/{subscription-id}
```

The first command opens a browser that allows you to log in to Azure. The second command allows you to select the correct Azure subscription—you'll need to replace the placeholder with your subscription ID. The last command creates a new service principal in Azure Active Directory with the name you entered in {app-name}, and it attaches the contributor role to your service principal at the subscription level.

After the command is executed, it will output a JSON object that looks like the following:

```
{
    "appId": "guid",
    "displayName": "Name",
    "name": "http://Name",
    "password": "secret password",
    "tenant": "guid"
}
```

This JSON object must be stored as a secret in your GitHub repository. On the GitHub website, navigate to your repository and choose the Settings tab. Then, in the menu, choose Secrets, and click the New Repository Secret button to create a new secret. Give your secret a name, and paste the JSON object in the Value field of the secret. Click the Add Secret button to store the secret in your repository.

The GitHub workflow created in this chapter uses two secrets, AZURE_TEST and AZURE_PROD. One connects to a test subscription and the other connects to a production subscription. If you want to test this workflow but you only have one subscription available, you can create the two secrets and paste the same JSON value in for both.

Figure 8.3 shows the settings page of a GitHub repository. On the left you'll see the menu where Secrets is selected. In the top-right corner you'll see the button for adding secrets to your repository. At the bottom, you'll see that two secrets have been added to this repository, AZURE_TEST and AZURE_PROD, both keeping connection secrets to Azure environments.

Figure 8.3 Adding secrets to your GitHub repository

Now that the connection information is securely stored in your GitHub repository, let's adjust the GitHub workflow created earlier in this chapter so it deploys the templates.

8.5 Deploying ARM templates from GitHub Actions

The deployment of the ARM template will be executed twice, one to a test and one to a production environment. GitHub Actions allows you to write workflow definitions that you can reuse in other workflows. This deployment task is a very good subject for reuse, because it is fairly large and requires only two input parameters. Separating the deployment part of this workflow into a different workflow will make the deployment task reusable and the main workflow easier to read and maintain.

As mentioned previously, there are two input parameters: one is for the environment the deployment targets (test or production), and the other is a secret, being the connection information for the correct Azure subscription. Let's create a new workflow file and define these parameters, as shown in the following listing (.github/workflows/deployment.yml).

Listing 8.2   Adding a reusable workflow

```
name: Deployment workflow

on:                                   Normal input parameters
    workflow_call:                    are defined in the inputs
        inputs:            ◁──┘       section.
            environment:
                required: true
                type: string          Input parameters containing
        secrets:           ◁───┤      secret data are defined in the
            azure-login:             secrets section.
                required: true
```

The preceding listing shows the new workflow file. You can see that the two input parameters you require for your workflow are separated into two different sections. One is for normal input parameters, while the secrets containing sensitive data have their own section.

Let's continue working on this deployment workflow file and add the following steps to deploy the Bicep files to Azure:

1 Download the artifact. This will make the main.json, the trafficmgr.json, and the parameter files available.
2 Log in to Azure using the secrets in the GitHub repository.
3 Start the four deployments.

According to the Toma Toe case introduced in chapter 7, the same template must be deployed three times in different Azure regions. The fourth deployment will provision the Traffic Manager on top of the App Services deployed in the preceding three deployments, as shown in the following listing (.github/workflows/deployment.yml continued).

Listing 8.3   Adding the deployment to test

```
jobs:
    infrastructure-incremental-test:
        runs-on: ubuntu-latest                   Downloading
        steps:                                    the workflow
            - name: Download Artifact   ◁──┘      artifact
              uses: actions/download-artifact@v2
              with:
                  name: bicep-templates
                  path: ./infrastructure
```

**Logging
in to Azure
and selecting
the correct
subscription**

```
- name: Azure Login
  uses: azure/login@v1
  with:
      creds: ${{ secrets.azure-login }}
- name: Deploy Europe
  uses: Azure/cli@1.0.4
  with:
      azcliversion: 2.23.0
      inlineScript:
az deployment sub create --name europe --location westeurope
    --template-file ./infrastructure/main.json --parameters
    ./infrastructure/${{ inputs.environment }}.parameters.json
    --parameters locationAbbreviation=we
        - name: Deploy United States
          uses: Azure/cli@1.0.4
          with:
              azcliversion: 2.23.0
              inlineScript:
az deployment sub create --name america --location eastus
    --template-file ./infrastructure/main.json --parameters
    ./infrastructure/${{ inputs.environment }}.parameters.json
    --parameters locationAbbreviation=us
        - name: Deploy Asia
          uses: Azure/cli@1.0.4
          with:
              azcliversion: 2.23.0
              inlineScript:
az deployment sub create --name asia --location eastasia
    --template-file ./infrastructure/main.json --parameters
    ./infrastructure/${{ inputs.environment }}.parameters.json
    --parameters locationAbbreviation=asi
        - name: Traffic Manager
          uses: Azure/cli@1.0.4
          with:
              azcliversion: 2.23.0
              inlineScript: az deployment sub create --location westeurope
    --template-file ./infrastructure/trafficmgr.json
    --parameters ./infrastructure/${{ inputs.environment }}.parameters.json
```

**First deployment of
the app service in the
West Europe region**

**Deployment of the
Traffic Manager**

The preceding code defines a deployment to Azure. Note that the deployments to the Western Europe region, East US region, and Asia region are similar except for their parameters. Also, because all the deployments are using the same subscription, a `name` parameter is added to prevent creating a deployment with the same name in a different region. Not adding the name results in three deployments with the same name in different regions and will result in an error. You can see the use of the secret input parameter in the `Azure Login` action. The `environment` input parameter is used in every deployment step to determine which parameter file to pass in.

Now that the deployment steps are isolated in a separate workflow, you can call this workflow from within the toma-toe workflow, completing the GitHub Actions workflow for the Toma Toe case.

8.5.1 *Completing the deployment*

The deployment workflow in the previous section must be called twice: once to create a test environment, and once to create a production environment. To call a reusable workflow, you must know the owner, GitHub repository, path, and filename of the workflow. Also, you need to specify a version of the workflow to use. You can use the ID of a commit or a tag to identify the version of a workflow. All this information is combined into one line that specifies the workflow to call:

```
jobs:
    call-workflow-1:
        uses: {owner}/{repository}/{path-to}/workflow.yml@version
```

To complete the workflow for this chapter, you need to add two jobs for a test and production deployment. The complete template is shown in the following listing.

Listing 8.4   The complete GitHub Actions workflow

```
name: Toma Toe Workflow
on: [push]

jobs:
    publish-bicep:
        runs-on: ubuntu-latest
        steps:
            - uses: actions/checkout@v2
            - name: Compile infrastructure
              uses: Azure/cli@1.0.4
              with:
                  azcliversion: 2.23.0
                  inlineScript: az bicep build --file ./deployment/main.bicep
            - name: Compile infrastructure
              uses: Azure/cli@1.0.4
              with:
                  azcliversion: 2.23.0
                  inlineScript: az bicep build --file ./deployment/trafficmgr.bicep
            - name: Publish Artifact
              uses: actions/upload-artifact@v2
              with:
                  name: bicep-templates
                  path: deployment/*.json
    infrastructure-incremental-test:
        needs: publish-bicep
        uses: {owner}/{repository}/.github/workflows/deployment.yml@version
        with:
            environment: test
        secrets:
            azure-login: ${{ secrets.AZURE_TEST }}

    infrastructure-incremental-prod:
        needs: infrastructure-incremental-test
```

Calling the deployment workflow with parameters for the test environment

The "needs" property allows you to configure a dependency. This job depends on the publish-bicep job.

The path to this workflow must be adjusted for your environment.

Calling the deployment workflow with parameters for the production environment

```
uses: {owner}/{repository}/.github/workflows/deployment.yml@version
with:
    environment: prod
secrets:
    azure-login: ${{ secrets.AZURE_PROD }}
```

The preceding code is the complete definition of the GitHub Actions workflow that deploys the Toma Toe infrastructure to Azure. Note that the reference to the external workflow will not work as is; it must be adjusted so it contains your GitHub account name, repository name, path, and version number (or commit ID). With the needs property, jobs are configured to depend on each other. This means that the job that deploys to test will only execute when the publish-bicep job has completed successfully.

When you commit and push this workflow and navigate to your GitHub repository, you can view the workflow in the Actions tab. Figure 8.4 shows a visual representation of the last run of the workflow in Azure. The status indicates that the entire workflow ran successfully. In the middle, you'll see the three jobs: build, deploy to test, and deploy to production. At the bottom, you'll see the artifacts published by the workflow—in this case, there's only one. You can download the artifact to review its content if you need to.

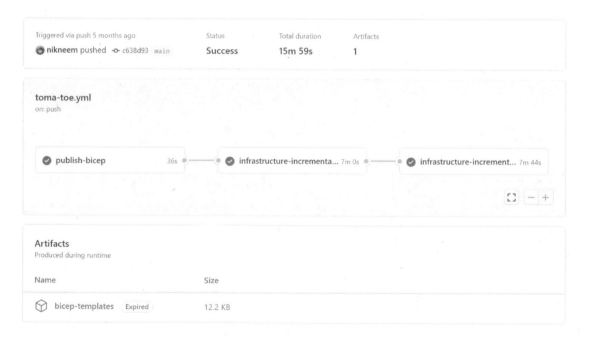

Figure 8.4   A visual representation of the workflow on GitHub

Summary

- GitHub Actions is the equivalent of Azure Pipelines. It allows you to hook into events in your source control to implement CI/CD solutions in GitHub.
- A GitHub workflow is a definition written in YAML and stored in a specific folder in your code repository.
- GitHub Actions allows you to publish artifacts so you can store data from one job and use that data in a subsequent job.
- Connecting to Azure from your GitHub workflow requires generating connection information and saving it as a secret in the GitHub repository. In this chapter, these secrets are used to connect to Azure and select the correct subscription.
- GitHub Actions workflows allow for reusability. To call a reusable workflow, you must know the owner, GitHub repository, path, and filename of the workflow.

Testing ARM templates

This chapter covers

- Writing tests to validate your code
- Choosing the best test scenario for your infrastructure
- Using different tools to test and validate your templates
- Writing custom tests using Pester and PowerShell
- Running tests in your Azure DevOps pipeline

When writing software these days, it is common to also write tests. One of the main reasons for writing tests is to verify that the code works when you write it and that the code still works after making changes later on. You write tests to build confidence that a change does not negatively impact the quality of the code and that the software is ready for deployment into production.

The same applies to testing Infrastructure as Code. When you're talking about writing software tests, you might be introduced to what is called the *test pyramid*. It describes various forms of testing and shows that each has its pros and cons. The layers within this pyramid can differ from application to application, depending on how you build yours. A simple example is shown in figure 9.1. In this pyramid, you

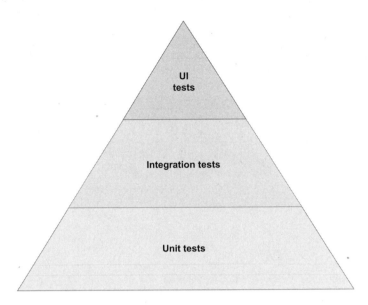

Figure 9.1   The testing pyramid for software

see three layers: unit tests, integration tests, and UI tests. You could have more layers in your scenario; for example, you might add performance testing.

In software, unit tests make up the foundation of your test suite. Unit tests test a single unit in isolation, making sure that the specific unit works as expected. What is considered to be a unit can vary, but it will most likely be a single method or, at most, a single class. Unit tests are very fast to run, and they're the easiest to write of all the test layers in the pyramid. Therefore, the number of unit tests will always, by far, outnumber any of the other test types.

The next layer in the pyramid is the integration tests. Most applications integrate with other systems, like with databases or filesystems. When you write unit tests, you leave out these systems to isolate your unit tests and ensure faster test runs. But because your application still communicates with these systems at runtime, you will need to test them working together. You will want to have as few of these integration tests as possible, since they are harder to write than unit tests. For example, you'll need to set up a database for each test run. Integration tests also tend to be more error-prone than unit tests because there are more resources and network connections involved, providing more areas where things can go wrong.

The top layer in this test pyramid is the UI tests, also known as end-to-end tests. UI tests validate whether the user interface works as expected. Tests could, for example, verify if user input triggers the right actions and if data is correctly shown to the user. The interface could be a web interface, but also a REST API or a command-line interface. In the latter case, you would talk to the API and validate, for example, the correctness of the returned JSON. These tests are often the hardest to build, as they involve the most moving parts and applications, and they take the most time to perform.

Whenever you need to create a test, you should always find the lowest layer in the pyramid that can test what you need tested. The higher you climb in the pyramid, the slower the tests become to run. They also become harder to write and are more brittle. It also becomes increasingly harder to figure out why a test failed. That's often easy to determine in a unit test, but it can take a day of work for a UI test.

Now let's apply this pyramid of tests to IaC. You could create the test pyramid in figure 9.2 for testing IaC. It involves four types of tests: static analysis and validation, unit test, integration tests, and end-to-end tests.

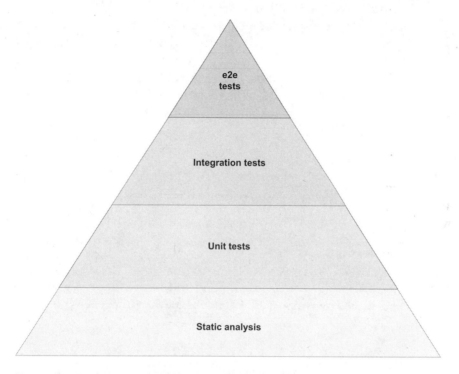

Figure 9.2   The testing pyramid for Infrastructure as Code

The following sections describe each of these layers in detail and will show you what tools are available. We'll start at the bottom of the pyramid and look at some tools that fit the lowest category—static analysis and validation.

9.1   *Static analysis and validation*

Tests that fall in this bottom layer of the test pyramid are the fastest to run. One of the main reasons for that is that they do not require your actual infrastructure to be deployed, saving much time. These tests only work on your IaC files.

Let's start by looking at another Visual Studio Code extension. It may not strictly be a static analysis tool, but it definitely will help you create templates without errors.

9.1.1   *Visual Studio Code extensions*

As mentioned earlier in the book, Visual Studio Code is a great editor for writing ARM and Bicep templates. One of the reasons for that is the availability of extensions for both file types. In chapter 2 you were introduced to the extension for ARM templates and you saw how extensions are installed. In chapter 6, you learned about the Bicep extension.

Like the ARM template extension, the Bicep extension will help you by continuously validating the template while you're writing. It will, for example, warn you when you use a particular parameter type in the wrong way. The extension also makes writing the templates easier, so you'll make fewer mistakes.

To demonstrate how this works, we'll create a simple storage account in Bicep. You will see how the extension can help you in various ways. Useful new features are being added all the time.

The `required-properties` autocompletion function is a useful feature that allows you to quickly write a working Bicep template. You start by declaring your resource and then when you type the = sign, you'll see the options shown in figure 9.3.

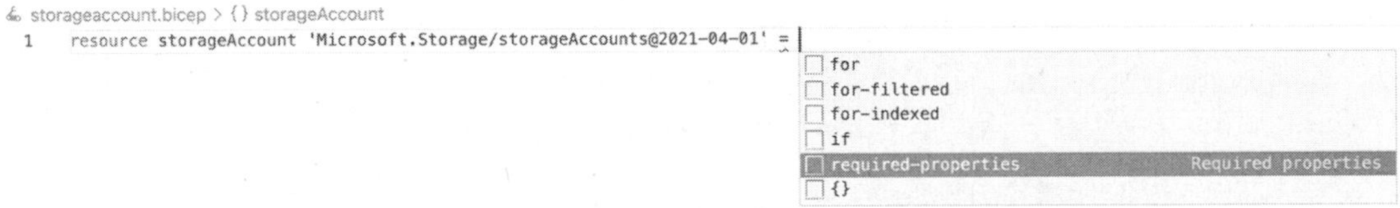

```
storageaccount.bicep > {} storageAccount
1    resource storageAccount 'Microsoft.Storage/storageAccounts@2021-04-01' =
```
```
for
for-filtered
for-indexed
if
required-properties          Required properties
{}
```

Figure 9.3   Using the `required-properties` feature

By default, the `required-properties` option will be selected. Now when you press Enter, Bicep will insert a snippet that contains all the properties you need to fill, as shown in figure 9.4.

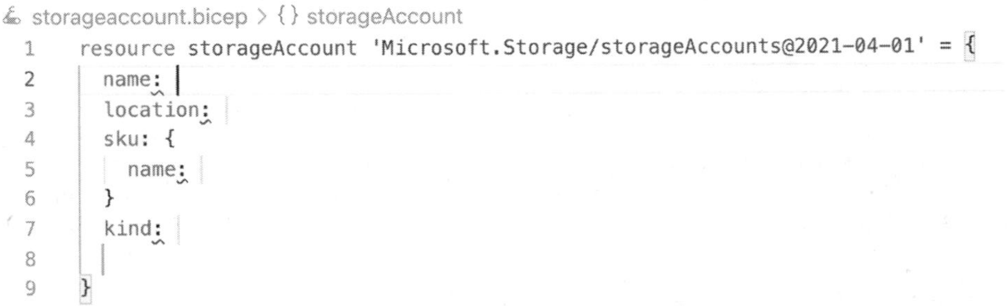

```
storageaccount.bicep > {} storageAccount
1    resource storageAccount 'Microsoft.Storage/storageAccounts@2021-04-01' = {
2      name:
3      location:
4      sku: {
5        name:
6      }
7      kind:
8
9    }
```

Figure 9.4   The `required-properties` feature in action

Now that all the required properties have been added, you can start filling them. Using this function, you are sure to never miss a required property. It saves a lot of time having to look them up in the documentation.

When you use the extension, you get what is called *IntelliSense*. It's a general term for various features that help you write code more quickly with fewer errors. One of the features is called *code completion*. When you, for example, look for specific property names, the editor will show them to you, and you don't need to look them up in the documentation, saving time and avoiding errors. Thanks to another IntelliSense feature, when you hover your cursor over an item, information on that property will be shown.

Figure 9.5 shows what you'd see if you were creating an output in Bicep to return the URL of the BLOB endpoint on a storage account. You could then use that value somewhere else in your deployment. It is easy to find the right property using auto-completion, and because you just need to press Enter or click the value, you won't make any typing errors.

```
storageaccount.bicep >  storageAccountBlobEndpoint
 1   resource storageaccount 'Microsoft.Storage/storageAccounts@2021-04-01' = {
 2     name: 'mystorage'
 3     location: 'westeurope'
 4     kind: 'StorageV2'
 5     sku: {
 6       name: 'Premium_LRS'
 7     }
 8   }
 9
10   output storageAccountBlobEndpoint string = storageaccount.properties.primaryEndpoints.
                                                    blob
                                                    dfs
                                                    file
                                                    internetEndpoints
                                                    microsoftEndpoints
                                                    queue
                                                    table
                                                    web
```

Figure 9.5 Navigating resource properties

The extension also helps by showing available properties on resources that you create. On the storage account in figure 9.6, `tags` is not a required property so it wasn't added previously. You can easily add it by creating an empty line in your template and then pressing Ctrl-spacebar. As you can see in figure 9.6, the extension will show you a list of available properties. Scroll down to the `tags` property and press Enter to insert it.

What is even more helpful is that the extension helps you find valid options for a property for the version of the resource you are creating. Let's take the `sku`'s `name` as an example. If you press the spacebar after the property, you will be shown a list with options, as you can see in figure 9.7. This makes it much easier to find and enter the proper value for the `sku`'s `name` parameter.

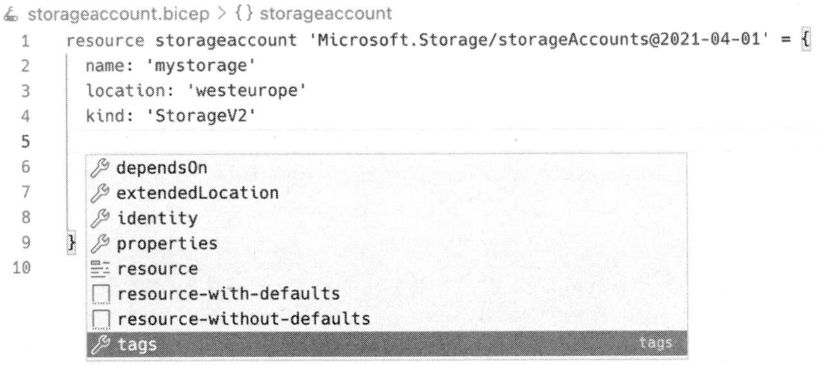

```
storageaccount.bicep > {} storageaccount
1   resource storageaccount 'Microsoft.Storage/storageAccounts@2021-04-01' = {
2     name: 'mystorage'
3     location: 'westeurope'
4     kind: 'StorageV2'
5
6          dependsOn
7          extendedLocation
8          identity
9   }      properties
10         resource
           resource-with-defaults
           resource-without-defaults
           tags                                                    tags
```

Figure 9.6   Autocompletion of properties

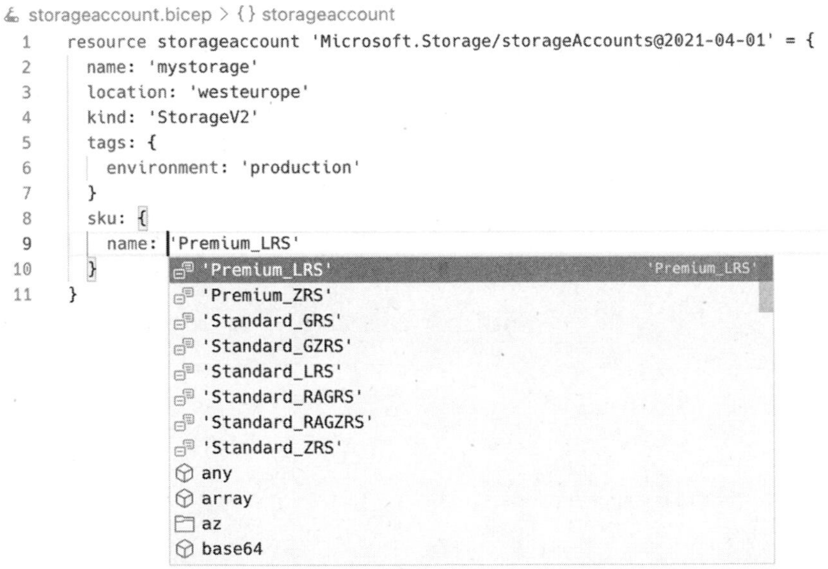

```
storageaccount.bicep > {} storageaccount
1   resource storageaccount 'Microsoft.Storage/storageAccounts@2021-04-01' = {
2     name: 'mystorage'
3     location: 'westeurope'
4     kind: 'StorageV2'
5     tags: {
6       environment: 'production'
7     }
8     sku: {
9       name: 'Premium_LRS'
10    }        'Premium_LRS'                              'Premium_LRS'
11  }          'Premium_ZRS'
               'Standard_GRS'
               'Standard_GZRS'
               'Standard_LRS'
               'Standard_RAGRS'
               'Standard_RAGZRS'
               'Standard_ZRS'
               any
               array
               az
               base64
```

Figure 9.7   Property value suggestions

On the other hand, if you do add the value manually and make a typo, the extension will help alert you with a yellow squiggly line. That's shown in figure 9.8.

Although these extensions are beneficial, you could go a step further in validating your templates before deploying them. Let's see how that can be done using either PowerShell or the Azure CLI.

```
 storageaccount.bicep > ...
 1   resource storageaccount 'Microsoft.Storage/storageAccounts@2021-04-01' = {
 2     name: 'mystorage'
 3     location: 'westeurope'
 4     kind: 'StorageV2'
 5     tags: {
 6       environment: 'production'
 7     }
 8     sku: {
 9       name: 'Premium_LRP'
10     }
11   }
12
```

Figure 9.8 Automatic property validation

9.1.2 *Validation using PowerShell or Azure CLI*

When you deploy a template to Azure using PowerShell, the Azure CLI, or Azure
DevOps, the template is validated before it is deployed. When ARM validates a tem-
plate, it checks whether the template is valid JSON and runs some other basic checks.
However, you can also run that validation without deploying.

To run the check using PowerShell, you have the following commands at your
disposal:

- `Test-AzResourceGroupDeployment`
- `Test-AzSubscriptionDeployment` (or its alias `Test-AzDeployment`)
- `Test-AzManagementGroupDeployment`
- `Test-AzTenantDeployment`

If you have ever used PowerShell to deploy a template, you might recognize these
commands. Here they start with `Test-`, but you use the `New-` equivalents during a
deployment.

When you're using the Azure CLI, you would use `az deployment group create` to
deploy a template to a resource group. To run the validation, you'd just replace `cre-
ate` with `validate`. The same applies to validating a deployment at the subscription,
management group, or tenant level.

Here is an example of an ARM template that would return an error on validation—
it's a storage account that has an incorrect name:

```
{
    "type": "Microsoft.Storage/storageAccounts",
    "apiVersion": "2019-04-01",
    "name": "ThisIsWrong",          ◁──── The name of this
    "location": "westeurope",              storage account
    "sku": {                               is wrong.
        "name": "Premium_LRS"
    },
    "kind": "StorageV2"
}
```

As you may know, the name of a storage account can only contain lowercase letters or numbers. Using capitals, as in the preceding example, therefore throws an error when you run the validation command:

```
az deployment group validate --resource-group "BookExampleGroup"
  ➥ --template-file storageaccount.json
```

The preceding example uses the Azure CLI to run the validation on a resource group deployment. The output in figure 9.9 shows why the validation failed. It nicely specifies the rules for a storage account name so you can quickly fix the problem.

```
[erwinstaal@Erwins-MacBook-Pro h3 % az deployment group validate --resource-group "BookExampleGroup" --template-fi
le storageaccount.json
{"error":{"code":"InvalidTemplateDeployment","message":"The template.deployment 'storageaccount' is not valid acc
ording to the validation procedure. The tracking id is '6be61092-401a-484d-879a-0e9e9445f5ea'. See inner errors f
or details.","details":[{"code":"PreflightValidationCheckFailed","message":"Preflight validation failed. Please r
efer to the details for the specific errors.","details":[{"code":"AccountNameInvalid","target":"ThisIsWrong","mes
sage":"ThisIsWrong is not a valid storage account name. Storage account name must be between 3 and 24 characters
in length and use numbers and lower-case letters only."}]}]}}
```

Figure 9.9 Errors after running a deployment validation

If you are using a newer version of the Azure CLI, the same approach would work for the following Bicep template:

```
resource storageAccount 'Microsoft.Storage/storageAccounts@2021-02-01' = {
    name: 'ThisIsWrong'          <-- The name of this storage account is invalid.
    kind:'StorageV2'
    sku: {
        name: 'Premium_LRS'
    }
    location: 'westeurope'
}
```

In the command, you just point to the Bicep file instead of an ARM template:

```
az deployment group validate --resource-group "BookExampleGroup"
  ➥ --template-file storageaccount.bicep
```

The Azure CLI runs a `bicep build` for you, and the output is identical.

Now that you know how to validate your templates, it is time to look at the ARM template test toolkit, which can help you enhance your static analysis of templates.

9.1.3 ARM template test toolkit

The ARM template test toolkit (ARM TTK) provides a set of default tests that check whether your templates use the recommended practices. This will help you avoid common problems in templates. When one of your templates does not comply with these recommended practices, a warning is returned. Often, a helpful suggestion is also presented to help you improve.

These are a few examples of the included tests:

- Use the correct JSON schema.
- All declared parameters must be used.
- Secure parameters can't have hardcoded defaults.
- Outputs can't include secrets.

A complete list of the included tests is available in Microsoft's "Test cases for ARM templates" article (http://mng.bz/wopB).

INSTALLING ARM TTK

ARM TTK runs on PowerShell, so make sure you have that installed on your machine. It runs on PowerShell Core, which means it works on Windows, Linux, and macOS.

To install ARM TTK, follow these steps:

1 Download the latest release of the test toolkit from https://aka.ms/arm-ttk-latest and extract it.
2 Open a PowerShell session and navigate to the folder where you just extracted the toolkit.
3 If your execution policy blocks scripts from the internet, you can unblock the script files by running the following command:

```
Get-ChildItem *.ps1, *.psd1, *.ps1xml, *.psm1 -Recurse | Unblock-File
```

Make sure you do that from the folder you extracted the toolkit to.

4 Import the module by running the following command:

```
Import-Module ./arm-ttk.psd1
```

RUNNING ARM TTK

Now that the toolkit is installed, you can run the tests. For example, you could run the tests against the template created in chapter 3. In that template you created various resources to run a web application on: an App Service, a few storage accounts, a SQL server, and more. If you haven't already downloaded those files, you can get them from the book's GitHub repository: http://mng.bz/J2QV. When you have them, navigate to the folder with those files, and run the following command:

```
Test-AzTemplate -TemplatePath ./template.json
```

This command runs all the available tests against the template, and the result should be similar to the output in figure 9.10. Tests are being added to the tool all the time, and new versions of resources in Azure might be introduced, so you might get a slightly different result when running the tests.

In figure 9.10 you can see the result for each test that was run. Most of the tests succeeded, but there were also two errors, shown in red so they stand out. Below the name of the failing tests, you'll find more information on why that particular test

```
Validating h3\template.json
  deploymentTemplate
    [+] adminUsername Should Not Be A Literal (113 ms)
    [-] apiVersions Should Be Recent (80 ms)
        Api versions must be the latest or under 2 years old (730 days) - API version 2015-08-01 of Microsoft.Web/ser
verfarms is 2109 days old
        Valid Api Versions:
        2020-06-01
        2019-08-01

    [+] artifacts parameter (5 ms)
    [+] CommandToExecute Must Use ProtectedSettings For Secrets (43 ms)
    [+] DependsOn Best Practices (35 ms)
    [+] Deployment Resources Must Not Be Debug (44 ms)
    [+] DeploymentTemplate Must Not Contain Hardcoded Uri (11 ms)
    [+] DeploymentTemplate Schema Is Correct (2 ms)
    [+] Dynamic Variable References Should Not Use Concat (2 ms)
    [+] IDs Should Be Derived From ResourceIDs (48 ms)
    [-] Location Should Not Be Hardcoded (21 ms)
        The location parameter of nested templates must not have a defaultValue property. It is "West Europe"

    [+] ManagedIdentityExtension must not be used (2 ms)
    [+] Min And Max Value Are Numbers (3 ms)
    [+] Outputs Must Not Contain Secrets (6 ms)
    [+] Parameters Must Be Referenced (62 ms)
    [+] providers apiVersions Is Not Permitted (2 ms)
    [+] ResourceIds should not contain (13 ms)
    [+] Resources Should Have Location (6 ms)
    [+] Resources Should Not Be Ambiguous (6 ms)
    [+] Secure String Parameters Cannot Have Default (2 ms)
    [+] Template Should Not Contain Blanks (4 ms)
    [+] Variables Must Be Referenced (15 ms)
    [+] Virtual Machines Should Not Be Preview (41 ms)
    [+] VM Images Should Use Latest Version (1 ms)
    [+] VM Size Should Be A Parameter (26 ms)
```

Figure 9.10   ARM TTK output for the chapter 3 template

failed. In some cases, as with the first error in this example, it also provides hints on
fixing it.

In chapter 5 you learned about more advanced ARM templates, including linked
templates. Linked templates allow you to break up a large ARM template into smaller
pieces for better readability and reuse. ARM TTK can handle such a setup, but you
need to cheat a little to make it work. Instead of specifying a specific template, you can
point the tool to a particular folder or forgo the `-TemplatePath` parameter altogether.
The tool then searches for a default template that could either be named azurede-
ploy.json or maintemplate.json. Unfortunately, you have neither in the folder for
chapter 5, since all the templates are in the Composing or Resources folder, so the
tool would throw an error if you ran it now. You can work around that by creating an
empty file called maintemplate.json in the root folder for chapter 5. Then run the following command:

```
Test-AzTemplate
```

The output will be similar to what you saw when running the tests against a single
file, but it now runs all tests against all the files by recursively going through the
folder structure. After the testing is complete, you can go through the test results for
all the files.

USING ARM TTK IN AZURE DEVOPS

Running these tests on your local computer is very useful, but it's even better to run them in a pipeline on every single change, using Azure DevOps for example. That way you are assured of high-quality templates all the time.

To run the tests, you can install the ARM TTK Extension by Sam Cogan from Visual Studio Marketplace (http://mng.bz/qYNN). Once you have installed it into your Azure DevOps environment, you can use it in a template as follows (armttk-pipeline.yml).

Listing 9.1 A YAML pipeline for running the ARM TTK tests

```
trigger:
- main

pool:
    vmImage: windows-latest        ◁──┐ Running this
                                       pipeline on
                                       Windows

steps:
- task: RunARMTTKTests@1          ◁──┐ The ARM TTK task runs the
  displayName: 'Run ARM TTK Tests'     tests using the template
  inputs:                              from chapter 3.
      templatelocation: '$(System.DefaultWorkingDirectory)\Chapter_03\'
      resultLocation: '$(System.DefaultWorkingDirectory)\Chapter_03\Publish'

- task: PublishTestResults@2          ◁──┐ The PublishTestResults
  displayName: 'Publish ARM TTK Test results'   task uploads the results
  inputs:                                        to Azure DevOps.
      testResultsFormat: 'NUnit'
      testResultsFiles: '**\*-armttk.xml'
      pathToSources: '$(System.DefaultWorkingDirectory)\Chapter_03\Publish'
      mergeTestResults: true
      failTaskOnFailedTests: true      ◁──┐ Set "condition" to "always" to
  condition: always()                       run this task when a test fails.
```

The first thing to note here is that this YAML pipeline needs to run on Windows, as the ARM TTK Extension task does not support Linux or macOS. The pipeline then contains two steps. The first one runs the tests using the task that you just installed. In this example, you can see the task run the tests against the ARM template created in chapter 3 of this book. The test outputs the test results in a format that you can push to Azure DevOps. The second task in this pipeline takes care of that. Pay attention to the last line in that task, `condition: always()`. The first task, running the tests, fails when any of the tests fail. If you don't set this condition, the second task would not be run. However, you always want to publish your test results, especially on a failure. The test results can then be viewed in Azure DevOps by going to the results of the pipeline and clicking on Tests, as shown in figure 9.11.

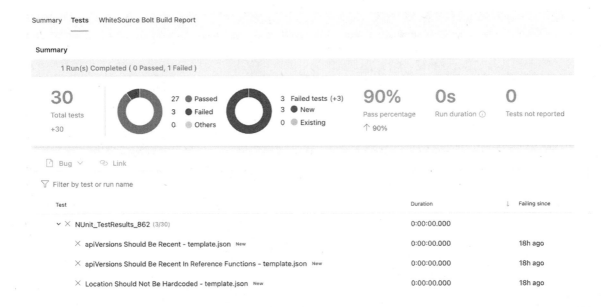

Figure 9.11   ARM TTK Extension output for the chapter 3 template

This test run had three errors, and the results clearly show which tests failed. You can click on each of the three failing tests, and more details on the failures will be displayed. As when running the ARM TTK tool using the Azure CLI, as shown earlier, you will then find more information on how to overcome the error.

You'll sometimes want to go a bit further in your testing than what the tools we've discussed so far can do for you out of the box. When that's the case, you'll have to write your own tests. Pester is a helpful tool for doing that.

9.1.4   Custom tests using Pester

Pester is a tool that allows you to write tests in PowerShell. Since PowerShell is one of the easiest ways to interact with Azure and ARM templates, Pester is ideal for this job.

Before you can write your first test, you first need to install Pester. To do that, use the following command in a PowerShell window on any platform:

```
Find-Module pester -Repository psgallery | Install-Module
```

All templates that you'll want to deploy will likely involve at least three files: the template itself, a parameter file for your test environment, and a parameter file for your production environment. The first simple test that you could write is to check if all the expected files are present. Without them, starting a deployment is useless. The following listing shows what such a test would look like using Pester (file-validation .tests.ps1).

Listing 9.2 A Pester test to run file validation tests

```
Describe "Template Validation" {          ◁─── ┐ The Describe keyword allows
    Context "Template Syntax" {                 │ you to group your tests.
                                                
        It "Has a JSON template" {        ◁───
            "azuredeploy.json" | Should -Exist   ┐ The It block is
        }                                        │ where you write
                                                 │ an actual test.
        It "Has a test parameters file" {
            "azuredeploy.parameters.test.json" | Should -Exist
        }

        It "Has a production parameters file" {
            "azuredeploy.parameters.prod.json" | Should -Exist
        }
    }
}
```

The Context keyword enables you to group your tests even further.

The `Describe` keyword on the first line allows you to group tests, and you could have one or more `Describes` per file. The next line uses the `Context` keyword. In almost all cases, `Describe` and `Context` can be used interchangeably. You'll often name the `Describe` block after the function under test and then use one or more `Contexts` to group tests based on that aspect of the function you are testing. Inside the `Context` blocks, you write the actual tests using the `It` keyword. An `It` block should contain a single test. You can use the `Should` keyword to make an assertion inside an `It` block. The first test in this example tests whether the azuredeploy.json file exists by using a `Should` combined with `-Exist`.

You can run the tests in this example in a PowerShell session by navigating to the folder where the file resides, and then running the following command:

```
Invoke-Pester -Output Detailed
```

As long as your filename ends with tests.ps1, Pester will automatically discover the tests and run them. Automatic discovery allows you to quickly run all tests in all files in a particular folder. In addition, using the `-Output` switch allows your command to display detailed results. For example, to run all tests in a single file, use the following command:

```
Invoke-Pester -Script ./file-validation.tests.ps1 -Output Detailed
```

This command should show you the output in figure 9.12. It first shows you how many tests were discovered in how many files. It then shows you the outcome of each test using your `Describe` and `Context` blocks to group the tests so you can easily find them in your files if you need to. In this example, all tests succeeded. If a test were to fail, it will be shown in red instead of green. You can also see the duration of each test. A long-running test might indicate a problem, so it's good practice to look for that.

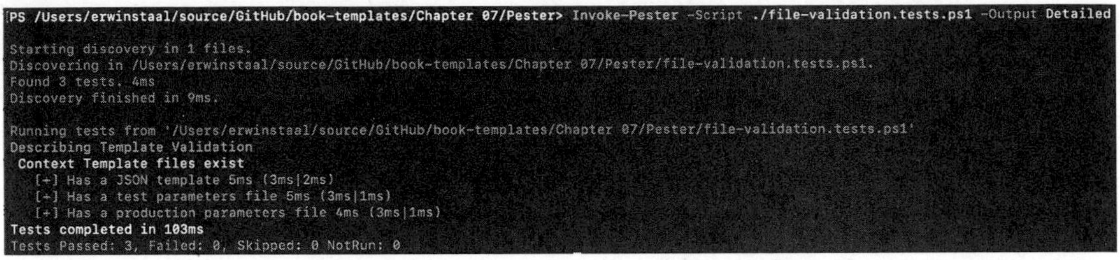

Figure 9.12   Pester test run results

Another helpful but straightforward test could be to verify the syntax of the template. Since an ARM template is valid JSON, you can use PowerShell to import the file and then create a PowerShell object from the JSON. Of course, that only works if it is valid JSON, so a missing comma or other syntax error will make the test fail. A file with such a test is shown in the following listing (syntax-validation.tests.ps1).

Listing 9.3   A Pester test to run file syntax tests

```
BeforeAll {                                              ◁————    The BeforeAll
    $templateProperties = (get-content "azuredeploy.json"         block allows
        ➦ -ErrorAction SilentlyContinue                          you to run code
        ➦ | ConvertFrom-Json -ErrorAction SilentlyContinue)      before any test
}                                                                runs.


Describe "Syntax Validation" {
    Context "The templates syntax is correct" {

        It "Converts from JSON" {
            $templateProperties | Should -Not -BeNullOrEmpty
        }

        It "should have a `$schema section" {
            $templateProperties."`$schema" | Should -Not -BeNullOrEmpty
        }

        It "should have a contentVersion section" {
            $templateProperties.contentVersion | Should -Not -BeNullOrEmpty
        }

        It "should have a parameters section" {
            $templateProperties.parameters | Should -Not -BeNullOrEmpty
        }

        It "must have a resources section" {
            $templateProperties.resources | Should -Not -BeNullOrEmpty
        }
    }
}
```

This example loads the file contents from disk and then tries to convert them into a PowerShell JSON object. It does that inside a `BeforeAll` block. As you can probably guess from that name, whatever you code in this block is executed before any test is run. After the `BeforeAll` block, this example runs a series of tests to verify whether some of the properties in an ARM template are present. It does that by again using the `Should` keyword, but this time combined with `-Not` and `-BeNullOrEmpty`.

Since these tests are written using PowerShell, you can utilize all the functionality available in PowerShell to create tests. That includes the template validation that we saw earlier, allowing you to combine custom test logic and third-party tooling easily. The following example shows how you could use the `Test-AzResourceGroupDeployment` cmdlet in a custom Pester test (template-validation.tests.ps1).

Listing 9.4   A Pester test to run template validation tests

```
# This test requires an authenticated session.
    ➡ Use Connect-AzAccount to login

BeforeAll {
    New-AzResourceGroup -Name "PesterRG" -Location "West Europe" | Out-Null
}

Describe "Content Validation" {
    Context "Template Validation" {
        It "Template azuredeploy.json passes validation" {
            $TemplateParameters = @{}
            $TemplateParameters.Add('storageAccountName', 'strpestertest')

            $output = Test-AzResourceGroupDeployment
            ➡ -ResourceGroupName "PesterRG"
            ➡ -TemplateFile "azuredeploy.json" @TemplateParameters

            $output | Should -BeNullOrEmpty
        }
    }
}

AfterAll {                              ◄─── The AfterAll keyword
    Remove-AzResourceGroup -Name "PesterRG" -Force | Out-Null    allows you to run code
}                                                                after all tests have run.
```

The preceding test first creates a new resource group that the `Test-AzResource-GroupDeployment` cmdlet needs as input, using the `BeforeAll` block. It then contains one test that creates an object in PowerShell to hold the parameters you supply when running the validation. The last line in the test verifies that the output is empty, which means there were no validation errors. Finally, an `AfterAll` block is responsible for removing the resource group. Just as a `BeforeAll` block runs before all tests, the `AfterAll` block runs after all tests are complete, even if one or more have failed. As resources in Azure might cost money even when you don't use them, the `AfterAll` block is perfect for cleaning up after tests have run and keeping costs to a minimum.

The next layer up in the test pyramid is the unit tests. Unit tests in IaC are a little different from unit tests in software. Let's dive in.

9.2   *Unit tests*

In software, unit tests are supposed to test a single unit and do that in isolation, but that makes less sense when it comes to infrastructure. While you may still want to test small pieces, you can't do that in isolation, as you always need to contact Azure. You only know whether your template is valid when you deploy your template, and not just a part of it.

In this book, we will consider a unit test to be a test that deploys a small part of the infrastructure and runs validations on that. Proper candidates for that could be one of the linked templates from chapter 5 or a Bicep module from chapter 6. The following listing shows the creation of a storage account using Bicep (Unittests/storageaccount .bicep). It uses a custom expression that you could write a test for.

Listing 9.5   A Bicep template to create a storage account

```
param name string
param location string

@allowed([
    'Premium'
    'Standard'
])
param sku string

var premiumSku = {
    name: 'Premium_LRS'
}

var standardSku = {
    name: 'Standard_LRS'
}

var skuCalculated = sku == 'Premium' ? premiumSku : standardSku     ⟵

resource storageAccount 'Microsoft.Storage/storageAccounts@2021-02-01' = {
    name: name
    location: location
    sku: skuCalculated
    kind: 'StorageV2'
}
```

A custom expression that specifies which SKU to use based on a parameter

The preceding Bicep module deploys a storage account. To do that, it allows you to supply a parameter to set the SKU as a string. That input is then used to select one of the two predefined SKU objects using two variables.

The following test verifies this behavior by deploying the template, fetching the storage account details, and running some validation on that (Unittests/unit-test.tests.ps1).

Listing 9.6   A Pester unit test

```
# This test requires an authenticated session.
   ➥ Use Connect-AzAccount to login

BeforeAll {                                  ⟵──┤ The BeforeAll block
    $resourceGroupName = 'PesterRG'                deploys the template.
    New-AzResourceGroup -Name $resourceGroupName -Location "West Europe"
        ➥ -Force | Out-Null


    $storageAccountName = 'strpestertest'
    $TemplateParameters = @{
        storageAccountName = $storageAccountName
        location = 'West Europe'
        sku = 'Premium'
    }

    New-AzResourceGroupDeployment -ResourceGroupName $resourceGroupName
        ➥ -TemplateFile "storageaccount.bicep" @TemplateParameters


    $storageAccount = Get-AzStorageAccount -Name $storageAccountName
        ➥ -ResourceGroupName $resourceGroupName

}

Describe "Deployment Validation" {
    Context "StorageAccount validation" {
                                                     This test verifies
        It "Storage account should exist" {          whether the
            $storageAccount | Should -not -be $null  expression returns
        }                                            the correct value.

        It "Storage account should have name 'Premium_LRS'" {
            $storageAccount.Sku.Name | Should -Be "Premium_LRS"   ⟵──
        }
    }
}

AfterAll {
    Remove-AzResourceGroup -Name "PesterRG" -Force | Out-Null
}
```

In the `BeforeAll` block in this test class, the template from listing 9.5 is deployed. Then the test creates a resource group to hold the test resources. Next, a PowerShell object is initialized to store the parameters passed to the `New-AzResourceGroup-Deployment` cmdlet. The last step in the `BeforeAll` block is to retrieve the created storage account to run tests against it.

The test file contains two tests. The first one verifies whether the storage account was created or not by using the `Should -not -be $null` syntax. The second test checks if the passed value to the `sku` parameter translated correctly into the SKU's tier on the storage account.

You could easily add more tests to verify other properties of the created storage account. It is, however, important to always think about what you are testing. The preceding example is a valid scenario, as it tests an admittedly simple custom expression. In contrast, it would not be helpful to verify the kind of the storage account, as its value was hardcoded in the template. If you were to write a test for that, you would effectively be testing the Azure Resource Manager, and there's no need for that, since that's something you bought and did not build yourself. The declarative nature of ARM templates and Bicep ensure that scripts are also idempotent and thus guaranteed always to give the same end state. The next level in the test pyramid is the integration tests.

9.3   Integration tests

In software, an integration test is used to verify the correctness of the relationship between two or more components. In infrastructure, you can use such tests to check how multiple parts of your infrastructure work together. Compared with unit tests, a downside of integration tests is that they need more infrastructure to be deployed, and they take more time to run.

The following example deploys two virtual networks, often abbreviated as *vnets*, with a peering between them. The peering connects the two vnets and lets traffic flow between them. You can write a test that verifies whether the state of the peering is correct after the deployment. First, though, you need to create some templates to deploy the resources (Integration-testing/vnet.bicep).

Listing 9.7   A Bicep template to create a virtual network

```
param vnetName string
param addressPrefixes array
param subnetName string
param subnetAddressPrefix string
param location string = '${resourceGroup().location}'

resource vnet 'Microsoft.Network/virtualNetworks@2020-06-01' = {     ◁──── This definition
    location: location                                                        creates a virtual
    name: vnetName                                                            network with a
    properties:{                                                              single subnet.
        addressSpace:{
            addressPrefixes:addressPrefixes
        }
        subnets:[
            {
                name:subnetName
                properties:{
                    addressPrefix: subnetAddressPrefix
                }
            }
        ]
    }
}
```

The preceding listing shows a Bicep module that deploys a single vnet. It accepts a few parameters, like the name and IP ranges for both the vnet and the first subnet.

Next, you need a template that deploys the peering between the two as shown in the following (Integration-testing/vnet-peering.bicep).

Listing 9.8 A Bicep template to create virtual network peering

```
param localVnetName string
param remoteVnetName string
param remoteVnetRg string

resource peer 'microsoft.network/virtualNetworks/
    ➥ virtualNetworkPeerings@2020-05-01' = {           ⯇─── This resource creates
    name: '${localVnetName}/peering-to-remote-vnet'          peering between two
    properties: {                                            virtual networks.
        allowVirtualNetworkAccess: true
        allowForwardedTraffic: true
        allowGatewayTransit: false
        useRemoteGateways: false
        remoteVirtualNetwork: {
            id: resourceId(remoteVnetRg, 'Microsoft.Network/virtualNetworks',
                ➥ remoteVnetName)
        }
    }
}
```

To create peering between two virtual networks, you need to deploy the preceding resource twice, as you deploy it onto one virtual network, see the name, and then point to the other. To assign the virtual network to connect to, you set the ID in the `remoteVirtualNetwork` object. Then the `resourceId()` function is used to get that identifier.

Now that you have the two modules, you can use them in the main template as follows (Integration-testing/mainDeployment.bicep).

Listing 9.9 A Bicep template to deploy networking modules

```
targetScope = 'subscription'              ⯇─── This template is
                                               deployed on the
param rg1Name string = 'rg-firstvnet'          subscription scope.
param rg1Location string = 'westeurope'
param rg2Name string = 'rg-secondvnet'
param rg2Location string = 'westeurope'
param vnet1Name string = 'vnet-first'          Two resource groups
param vnet2Name string = 'vnet-second'         are created to hold
                                               the resources.
resource rg1 'Microsoft.Resources/resourceGroups@2020-06-01' = {    ⯇───
    name: rg1Name
    location: rg1Location
}

resource rg2 'Microsoft.Resources/resourceGroups@2020-06-01' = {
    name: rg2Name
```

```
        location: rg2Location
}

module vnet1 'vnet.bicep' = {          ◁──────   Two individual
    name: 'vnet1'                                 virtual networks
    scope: resourceGroup(rg1.name)                are created.
    params: {
        vnetName: vnet1Name
        addressPrefixes: [
            '10.1.1.0/24'
        ]
        subnetName: 'd-sne${vnet1Name}-01'
        subnetAddressPrefix: '10.1.1.0/24'
    }
}

module vnet2 'vnet.bicep' = {
    name: 'vnet2'
    scope: resourceGroup(rg2.name)
    params: {
        vnetName: vnet2Name
        addressPrefixes: [
            '10.2.1.0/24'
        ]
        subnetName: 'd-sne${vnet2Name}-01'
        subnetAddressPrefix: '10.2.1.0/24'
    }
}

module peering1 'vnet-peering.bicep' = {   ◁─────   The two virtual
    name: 'peering1'                                networks are
    scope: resourceGroup(rg1.name)                  connected by
    dependsOn: [                                    deploying peering.
        vnet1
        vnet2
    ]
    params: {
        localVnetName: vnet1Name
        remoteVnetName: vnet2Name
        remoteVnetRg: rg2Name
    }
}

module peering2 'vnet-peering.bicep' = {
    name: 'peering2'
    scope: resourceGroup(rg2.name)
    dependsOn: [
        vnet2
        vnet1
    ]
    params: {
        localVnetName: vnet2Name
        remoteVnetName: vnet1Name
        remoteVnetRg: rg1Name
    }
}
```

On the first line of the preceding template, you set the `targetScope` to the level of the `subscription`. That allows you to first create the resource groups inside this template and then deploy the different modules into those resource groups. After the resource groups are created, the template continues by deploying the two virtual networks. When that is done, the peering between the two is deployed.

With the templates in place, it is time to write the test as follows (Integration-testing/integrationtesting.tests.ps1).

Listing 9.10 A Pester test to validate network peering

```
# This test requires an authenticated session.
    ➡ Use Connect-AzAccount to login

BeforeAll {
    New-AzDeployment -Location "WestEurope"
        ➡ -TemplateFile "mainDeployment.bicep"

    $vnetPeering = Get-AzVirtualNetworkPeering
        ➡ -Name "peering-to-remote-vnet"
        ➡ -VirtualNetworkName "vnet-second"
        ➡ -ResourceGroupName "rg-secondvnet"
}

Describe "Deployment Validation" {
    Context "VNet peering validation" {

        It "Vnet peering should exist" {
            $vnetPeering | Should -not -be $null
        }

        It "Peering status should be 'Connected'" {
            $vnetPeering.PeeringState | Should -Be "Connected"   ⊲─── This test validates the virtual network peering.
        }
    }
}

AfterAll {
    Remove-AzResourceGroup -Name "rg-firstvnet" -Force | Out-Null
    Remove-AzResourceGroup -Name "rg-secondvnet" -Force | Out-Null
}
```

In the `BeforeAll` block, the template is deployed. Here you see `New-AzDeployment` being used because the scope is set to `subscription` level. When the deployment finishes, one of the virtual network peerings is retrieved to use in the test. The first test then verifies whether that virtual network peering exists. The second test checks if the state of the peering is `Connected`.

You have probably noticed that running this test took a bit more time than the unit tests you looked at in the previous section. That is mainly because the deployment takes longer. In an integration test, you typically have more resources, and they depend on each other, so you can't deploy all of them in parallel. They also are a bit more expensive in terms of Azure cost, so you'll want to make sure you remove the resources automatically after each run. Now that you have seen an integration test, there is one level on the test pyramid remaining, the end-to-end test.

9.4   End-to-end tests

In software, an end-to-end test could, for example, start at the UI of your application. You could enter some data into a form, save the form, and then verify whether that was successful by retrieving the data somehow. That would test your whole application, from the UI to the API and probably to some datastore like a database. You could use a similar approach for infrastructure.

In the following example, you'll build upon the integration test infrastructure. Imagine that you have a UI application that fetches data from an API. On Azure, you could pick the Azure App Service to run both. An additional requirement is that you don't want the API to be publicly available. It should only accept connections from your UI's App Service. To implement that, you could use the App Services virtual network integration and then use a firewall to limit the traffic to the API. You could then write a test to verify whether that works after every deployment. This infrastructure is shown in figure 9.13.

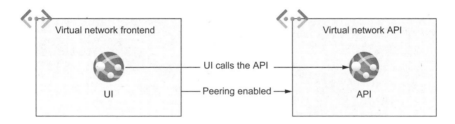

Figure 9.13   The infrastructure for the end-to-end-test scenario

While integration tests can take quite some time to run, end-to-end tests are even more time-intensive. You deploy more infrastructure and may even need to deploy an application as well. For that reason, you'll want to make sure that you only write the tests that you need: those that add business value. As these tests run on complete infrastructures that take a long time to deploy, you may decide not to remove and recreate the infrastructure on each run but let it stay between runs. That will, of course, mean that you will have to pay for those resources, even when you are not actively running tests against them.

Let's dig into the example. You first need the two Azure App Services that host your UI and API. The following Bicep module creates those resources (End-2-end-testing appservice.bicep).

Listing 9.11   A Bicep template to create an App Service

```
targetScope = 'resourceGroup'

param appName string
param subnetResourceId string
param location string = resourceGroup().location

param restrictAccess bool
param restrictAccessFromSubnetId string = ''

resource hosting 'Microsoft.Web/serverfarms@2019-08-01' = {
    name: 'hosting-${appName}'
    location: location
    sku: {
        name: 'S1'
    }
}

resource app 'Microsoft.Web/sites@2018-11-01' = {
    name: appName
    location: location
    properties: {
        serverFarmId: hosting.id
    }
}

resource netConfig 'Microsoft.Web/sites/networkConfig@2019-08-01' = {
    name: '${appName}/virtualNetwork'
    dependsOn: [
        app
    ]
    properties: {
        subnetResourceId: subnetResourceId
        swiftSupported: true
    }
}

resource config 'Microsoft.Web/sites/config@2020-12-01'
    ➥ = if (restrictAccess) {
    name: '${appName}/web'
    dependsOn: [
        app
    ]
    properties: {
        ipSecurityRestrictions: [
            {
                vnetSubnetResourceId: restrictAccessFromSubnetId
                action: 'Allow'
                priority: 100
                name: 'frontend'
            }
            {
                ipAddress: 'Any'
                action: 'Deny'
```

The definition for the Azure App Service plan

The definition for the Azure App Service

The definition for the network configuration on the Azure App Service

```
                    priority: 2147483647
                    name: 'Deny all'
                    description: 'Deny all access'
            }
        ]
    }
}
```

The preceding template is used as a module for both the UI and the API, but there are differences in how the resource should be deployed between the two, which is why there is an `if` statement. That is explained in detail shortly.

The first resource created in the template is the App Service plan. An App Service plan is a container for one or more App Services. As you see in the example, the performance of any App Service running within an App Service plan is defined on the App Service plan—all App Services share the resources. In this example, you set that performance level to `S1`.

Then you deploy an App Service. That is the resource that holds either the UI or API. It is again a relatively simple resource that needs a name and location. You also need to reference the App Service plan to run on by setting the `serverFarmId` property. You then specify two resources that configure the networking part of the UI and API. First, you deploy a resource of type `networkConfig`, which specifies in which subnet you want the App Service to run. The `subnetResourceId` property specifies that. As you'll see later on, the UI and API will both use a separate subnet in two different virtual networks.

The second resource you need to deploy to configure the networking on the App Service is the `config` resource, which allows you to configure quite a lot of things on the App Service. In this example, you use the `ipSecurityRestrictions` array to configure the network access—it allows you to define a set of rules that control incoming traffic. This template is used to create both the UI and the API, and since you only need to limit the incoming traffic on the API and not on the UI, an `if` statement acts on the `restrictAccess` Boolean. This Boolean allows you to specify whether restrictions should be in place and allows you to reuse the template. The `ipSecurity-Restrictions` array in this example contains two entries. The first one allows traffic from a specific vnet resource—the subnet in which the UI resides. The second entry dictates that all other traffic should be denied.

Next, you need to make a few modifications to the vnet definitions from the previous example (listing 9.7) to make this one work (End-2-end-testing/vnet.bicep).

Listing 9.12   A Bicep template to create a virtual network

```
targetScope = 'resourceGroup'

param vnetName string
param addressPrefixes array
param subnetName string
param subnetAddressPrefix string
param location string = '${resourceGroup().location}'
```

```
resource vnet 'Microsoft.Network/virtualNetworks@2020-06-01' = {
    location: location
    name: vnetName
    properties:{
        addressSpace:{
            addressPrefixes:addressPrefixes
        }
        subnets:[
            {
                name:subnetName
                properties:{
                    addressPrefix: subnetAddressPrefix
                    serviceEndpoints: [
                        {
                            service: 'Microsoft.Web'
                            locations:[
                                '*'
                            ]
                        }
                    ]
                    delegations: [
                        {
                            name: 'Microsoft.Web.serverFarms'
                            properties: {
                                serviceName: 'Microsoft.Web/serverFarms'
                            }
                        }
                    ]
                    privateEndpointNetworkPolicies: 'Enabled'
                    privateLinkServiceNetworkPolicies: 'Enabled'
                }
            }
        ]
    }
}

output vnetId string = vnet.id
output subnetId string = vnet.properties.subnets[0].id
```

Enabling the service endpoint for Microsoft.Web

Using delegation provides your App Service with a subnet to use.

Two settings were added to this definition. First, there is the serviceEndpoint section. A service endpoint in Azure allows you to state that traffic to a specific Azure resource should stay within the Microsoft network instead of routing over the public internet. A service endpoint is available for most Azure PaaS services. In this example, you use it to ensure that traffic from the UI to the API stays on the Microsoft backbone, which allows you to restrict the traffic, as you saw earlier. Since you are using an App Service in this example, the service property is set to Microsoft.Web. That value is different for every service that you target. In case of an Azure SQL database, for example, it would have been Microsoft.Sql.

The second added section is delegations, which you need to be able to run your App Service within your virtual network. Using a delegation, you effectively say to your App Service: "here is a subnet for you to use." Nothing else can then use that subnet, and since you are delegating this subnet to the App Service, the serviceName becomes Microsoft.Web/serverFarms.

With the two modules for the App Service (listing 9.11) and the virtual network (listing 9.12) in place, you can now write another template and use them. You can add the following configuration to the MainDeployment.bicep template (listing 9.9) used in the integration testing section (End-2-end-testing/mainDeployment.bicep).

Listing 9.13   A Bicep template using modules to create the infrastructure

```
module frontend 'appservice.bicep' = {
    name: 'frontend'
    scope: rg1
    dependsOn: [
        peering1
    ]
    params: {
        appName: 'bicepfrontend'
        subnetResourceId: vnet1.outputs.subnetId
        restrictAccess: false
    }
}
module api 'appservice.bicep' = {
    name: 'api'
    scope: rg2
    dependsOn: [
        peering2
    ]
    params: {
        appName: 'bicepapi'
        subnetResourceId: vnet2.outputs.subnetId
        restrictAccess: true
        restrictAccessFromSubnetId: vnet1.outputs.subnetId
    }
}
```

All that remains to be done is to call the appservice module twice: once for the frontend and once for the API. The difference between the two is the values you use for the parameters. You specify two different virtual networks to integrate with, and only the API network is set to restrict access to the UI's subnet.

With the infrastructure in place, it's time to deploy your application and write some tests. This is a simple UI that makes a call to the API. You can create the application by following along, or you can find it in the repository of this book (http://mng.bz/7yGV).

To create the application and deploy it, you will need to have .Net Core installed. If you don't have it already, you can download it from Microsoft: https://dotnet.microsoft.com/download.

To create the app, run dotnet new web in a terminal window. Then open Startup.cs and change it to look like the following version (End-2-end-testing/MinimalFrontend/startup.cs).

Listing 9.14   The StartUp.cs file of the sample UI application

```csharp
using System;
using System.Collections.Generic;
using System.Linq;
using System.Net.Http;
using System.Threading.Tasks;
using Microsoft.AspNetCore.Builder;
using Microsoft.AspNetCore.Hosting;
using Microsoft.AspNetCore.Http;
using Microsoft.Extensions.DependencyInjection;
using Microsoft.Extensions.Hosting;

namespace testweb
{
    public class Startup
    {
        public void ConfigureServices(IServiceCollection services)
        {
            services.AddHttpClient();
        }

        public void Configure(IApplicationBuilder app,
            IWebHostEnvironment env,
            IHttpClientFactory clientFactory)          ◄─┐  The HttpClientFactory
        {                                                │  was added using
            if (env.IsDevelopment())                     │  dependency injection.
            {
                app.UseDeveloperExceptionPage();
            }

            app.UseRouting();

            app.UseEndpoints(endpoints =>                   ┌─ A route that
            {                                               │  calls the API
                endpoints.MapGet("/", async context =>  ◄──┘  is added.
                {
                    var request = new HttpRequestMessage(HttpMethod.Get,
                        "https://bicepapi.azurewebsites.net");

                    var client = clientFactory.CreateClient();

                    var response = await client.SendAsync(request);

                    if(!response.IsSuccessStatusCode){
                        throw new Exception("Could not reach the API");
                    }

                    await context.Response.WriteAsync("API Reached!");
                });
            });
        }
    }
}
```

In the preceding listing, an `HttpClientFactory` was added to the `Configure()` function. That client is used in the `app.UseEndpoints` definition to call the API. If that API is reachable and returns an HTTP 200 status code, the UI returns a successful result. If the API is not reachable, the networking configuration was incorrect, and the UI throws an error.

The last thing left to do is to write the actual tests as follows (End-2-end-testing/end2endtesting.tests.ps1).

Listing 9.15   A Bicep test that runs the end-to-end scenario test

```
# This test requires an authenticated session;
    ➥ use Connect-AzAccount to login

BeforeAll {                                         ◄——  The BeforeAll
    New-AzDeployment -Location "WestEurope"                block sets up the
        ➥ -TemplateFile "mainDeployment.bicep"            environment.
    dotnet publish MinimalFrontend/testweb.csproj
        ➥ --configuration Release -o ./MinimalFrontend/myapp
    Compress-Archive -Path ./MinimalFrontend/myapp/*
        ➥ -DestinationPath ./MinimalFrontend/myapp.zip -Force
    Publish-AzWebApp -ResourceGroupName rg-firstvnet -Name bicepfrontend
        ➥ -ArchivePath $PSScriptRoot/MinimalFrontend/myapp.zip -Force
}


Describe "Deployment Validation" {
    Context "End 2 end test" {

        It "Frontend should be available and respond with 200" {

            $Result = try {
                Invoke-WebRequest
                    ➥ -Uri "https://bicepfrontend.azurewebsites.net/"
                    ➥ -Method GET
            }
            catch {
                $_.Exception.Response
            }

            $statusCodeInt = [int]$Result.StatusCode
            $statusCodeInt | Should -be 200          ◄——  This test verifies
        }                                                  that the UI works
        It "API should be locked and respond with 403" {   properly.

            $Result = try {
                Invoke-WebRequest
                    ➥ -Uri "https://bicepapi.azurewebsites.net/"
                    ➥ -Method GET
            }
            catch {
                $_.Exception.Response
            }
```

```
                $statusCodeInt = [int]$Result.StatusCode
                $statusCodeInt | Should -be 403
        }
    }
}

AfterAll {
    Remove-AzResourceGroup -Name "rg-firstvnet" -Force | Out-Null
    Remove-AzResourceGroup -Name "rg-secondvnet" -Force | Out-Null
}
```

> This test verifies that the API is not publicly accessible.

The `BeforeAll` block is again used to set up the environment. First, the template is deployed. After that, the simple UI application is published using `dotnet publish`. That command builds the application and generates the files you need to run the application on the Azure App Service. Next, those files are combined in an archive using the PowerShell `Compress-Archive` function. The final step in `BeforeAll` is to publish the app to Azure using the `Publish-AzWebApp` PowerShell cmdlet. You need to specify to which App Service and resource group you want to deploy the archive to.

Next come the two tests. The first one reaches out to the UI and expects an HTTP 200 status code to be returned. As stated earlier, the UI only does that when it can reach the API. It will otherwise throw an error and return the HTTP 500 error code. The second test verifies whether the API was successfully locked down. Again, you can expect an HTTP 403 error code to be returned, because of the network restriction you've put in place when calling the API directly.

The `AfterAll` section then removes the resources. You might decide to skip that step in the real world.

You have now seen that writing an end-to-end test isn't easy. It involves a lot of moving parts, it's easy to get wrong, and it takes a lot of time to run. You therefore need to be careful with writing too many of these tests. Always try first to solve your test requirements using the other test methods lower on the pyramid. Now that you have seen various ways you can use Pester to create tests, let's see how you can run them in an Azure DevOps pipeline to verify your changes automatically.

9.5 Pester in CI/CD

By running the tests in an Azure DevOps pipeline, you can easily verify your changes before deploying the template to production. This will help you get as close to guaranteeing a successful deployment as possible. To run the tests from a pipeline, you'll need to write a pipeline definition.

There are two options for running Pester tests within an Azure DevOps pipeline: use a task from the Marketplace or use a custom PowerShell script. A task from the Marketplace is the easiest option, but that won't support tests that need to connect to Azure. For example, the unit test example at the start of this chapter won't work with this approach.

That leaves the other option, which is to use a custom PowerShell script. Within the pipeline, that script will need to run using an Azure PowerShell task, which will provide you with an Azure context and connection to work with. Let's first look at the PowerShell script (RunPester.ps1).

> **Listing 9.16   A PowerShell helper script to run Pester tests in Azure DevOps**

```
param (
    [Parameter(Mandatory = $true)]
    [string]
    $ModulePath,

    [Parameter(Mandatory=$false)]
    [string]
    $ResultsPath,

    [Parameter(Mandatory=$false)]
    [string]
    $Tag = "UnitTests"
)

# Install Bicep                            <--- Install Bicep.
curl -Lo bicep https://github.com/Azure/bicep/releases/
➥ latest/download/bicep-linux-x64
chmod +x ./bicep
sudo mv ./bicep /usr/local/bin/bicep
                                                          Install Pester.
# Install Pester if needed                 <---
$pesterModule = Get-Module -Name Pester -ListAvailable
    ➥ | Where-Object {$_.Version -like '5.*'}
if (!$pesterModule) {
    try {
        Install-Module -Name Pester -Scope CurrentUser
            ➥ -Force -SkipPublisherCheck -MinimumVersion "5.0"
        $pesterModule = Get-Module -Name Pester -ListAvailable
            ➥ | Where-Object {$_.Version -like '5.*'}
    }
    catch {
        Write-Error "Failed to install the Pester module."
    }
}

Write-Host "Pester version: $($pesterModule.Version)"
$pesterModule | Import-Module

if (!(Test-Path -Path $ResultsPath)) {
    New-Item -Path $ResultsPath -ItemType Directory -Force | Out-Null
}

Write-Host "Finding tests in $ModulePath"
$tests = (Get-ChildItem -Path $ModulePath "*tests.ps1" -Recurse).FullName

$container = New-PesterContainer -Path $tests          Create a Pester
                                                       configuration
$configuration = [PesterConfiguration]@{       <---   object.
    Run         = @{
```

```
        Container = $container
    }
    Output      = @{
        Verbosity = 'Detailed'
    }
    Filter = @{
        Tag = $Tag                       Configure how
    }                                     to report test
    TestResult  = @{         ◁───        results.
        Enabled     = $true
        OutputFormat = "NUnitXml"
        OutputPath  = "$($ResultsPath)\Test-Pester.xml"
    }
}

Invoke-Pester -Configuration $configuration
```

The preceding script consists of three parts. First, it installs Bicep. Bicep is not available by default within the Azure PowerShell task, so it needs to be installed first. Second, Pester might not be installed, or an old version might be installed, so Pester is installed or upgraded. The last section of the script then runs the tests using the `Invoke-Pester` cmdlet. In contrast to previous invocations of the `Invoke-Pester` cmdlet you've seen in this chapter, here it is run by passing a configuration object. The main reason for that is that you want to collect the test results in a format that Azure DevOps will understand, so you can upload the results and make them available in the Azure DevOps UI on each run. That requires a bit of extra configuration that is only available in this more advanced configuration object and not as switches on the `Invoke-Pester` command. The preceding PowerShell script is then run within the pipeline, as shown in the following listing (pester-pipeline.yaml).

Listing 9.17 An Azure DevOps pipeline to run Pester tests

```
trigger:
- main

pool:
  vmImage: ubuntu-latest
                                        Run the PowerShell
                                        script within an
steps:                                  Azure context.
- task: AzurePowerShell@5     ◁───
  displayName: 'Run Pester Unit tests'
  inputs
    azureSubscription: <your service connection>
    ScriptType: 'FilePath'
    ScriptPath:
➡ '$(System.DefaultWorkingDirectory)/Chapter_09/Pester/RunPester.ps1'
    ScriptArguments: '-ModulePath
        ➡ "$(System.DefaultWorkingDirectory)/Chapter_09/Pester"
            ➡ -ResultsPath
                ➡ "$(System.DefaultWorkingDirectory)\Chapter_09\Pester\Publish"'
```

```
    azurePowerShellVersion: 'LatestVersion'
    workingDirectory: '$(System.DefaultWorkingDirectory)/Chapter_09/Pester'

- task: PublishTestResults@2                    ◁┐  Upload the test
    displayName: 'Publish Pester Tests'             results to Azure
    inputs:                                         DevOps.
      testResultsFormat: 'NUnit'
      testResultsFiles: '**/Test-Pester.xml'
      pathToSources:
➡ '$(System.DefaultWorkingDirectory)\Chapter_09\Pester\Publish'
      mergeTestResults: true
      failTaskOnFailedTests: true
```

This pipeline only has two steps. The first step runs the PowerShell script within an Azure context so your tests can also create and access resources in Azure. To do this, it needs a reference to a service connection with enough permissions. The second task uploads the test results that were generated in the first step to Azure DevOps. When a test does not succeed, the pipeline fails, and you can easily view the results, as shown in figure 9.14.

Figure 9.14   An Azure pipeline that ran with errors

Figure 9.14 shows two failing tests. You can click on each of them to get more details on the failure. Besides failing tests, you can also find trends on your test runs to see how things are going over time.

As you have seen in this section, it's very useful and fairly easy to run your Pester tests in Azure DevOps. That will help you feel more confident about the changes you've made and the likelihood of a successful deployment into your production environment.

Summary

- There are different types of tests: unit tests, integration tests, and end-to-end tests. Each has its own pros and cons.
- A unit test can verify the behavior of a single resource in isolation. It is the quickest test to run and therefore to be favored above integration or end-to-end tests.
- An integration test can be written to verify the correct working of two pieces of infrastructure together.
- An end-to-end test can help you verify the working of an entire set of infrastructure working together, even with an application deployed. This type of test takes a long time and is much more error prone than the other methods.
- The ARM TTK tooling can be used to evaluate templates for best practices. It can be run using an Azure DevOps pipeline to give you feedback on every change.
- Pester can be used to write custom tests. These tests can be structured using the `Describe`, `Context`, and `It` keywords. The `BeforeAll` and `AfterAll` blocks can be used to create and destroy resources before and after running tests.
- Pester tests can be run in an Azure DevOps pipeline, and the results can be viewed in the Azure DevOps portal.

Part 3

Advanced topics

The last part of the book explains how to work with IaC templates in larger organizations. We'll show you how to share templates for the purpose of governance and reusability and show you how to group deployments using the brand-new Azure deployment stacks. Next, we'll explain the concepts of Azure Policy, which allows you to govern your environment, and show you how to manage Azure Policy using IaC. Finally, we'll present some real-world case studies, explaining how IaC templates can be used for enterprise solutions.

Template specs and
Bicep registries: Building
a repository of templates

This chapter covers

- Storing ARM and Bicep templates as reusable Azure resources
- Deploying template specs using the CLI, PowerShell, or the portal
- Referencing template specs from another template
- Alternatives to using template specs

Imagine working at a large company with many teams, and all of them are running applications on Azure infrastructure. Most of these applications run on similar infrastructure, like virtual machines, Kubernetes, or App Service plans. No one will want to write the same ARM or Bicep templates over and over to create that infrastructure. And besides the repetitive work, most companies have standard approaches to this infrastructure that they will want to impose on every team. In this chapter, you'll learn how to store ARM or Bicep templates in Azure and make them available for others to reuse.

10.1   *Use case: A repository of compliant resources*

Let's say you work at Doush Bank, a bank serving millions of customers all over Europe. A bank like this has hundreds of applications maintained by hundreds of development and operations teams.

While every application is different, their architectures and the platforms that they run on are not that different in the end. Almost all of them run either on virtual machines, Azure App Service, or Azure Kubernetes Service. Doush Bank has strict guidelines on how these resources should be created and configured to comply with all the regulations that apply to banks in Europe. This poses two problems for Doush Bank that they want to solve:

- How can they use economies of scale and supply something like *default templates* to help their teams create new infrastructure more rapidly?
- How can they ensure that all infrastructure created by all the different teams stays compliant with the ever-changing guidelines?

When adopting Infrastructure as Code, a company like this will start looking for a way to reuse ARM or Bicep templates, or maybe snippets of templates, to solve problems like these.

One approach is to package and distribute templates in the same way that application libraries are distributed, using a binary management system or artifact store like Azure Artifacts or GitHub Packages. This approach is familiar to those with a development background and it's sometimes adopted due to the lack of an alternative approach.

An alternative approach first became available in 2020, and went into general availability in 2021, with the arrival of Azure template specs. A template spec is an Azure resource that is created like any other. Figure 10.1 shows the relationship between a template, a template spec, and the Azure resources defined in the template.

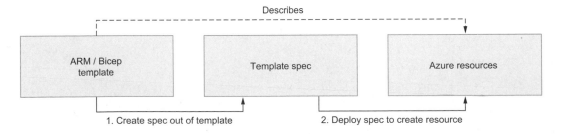

Figure 10.1   Azure template specs are reusable ARM templates.

This may sound like it's just IaC, but there is a difference here. Instead of the resources in the template being created, the template itself becomes a resource. Later, a resource deployment is done, where the resources defined in the template are created.

This chapter discusses setting up template specs in various ways, versioning them, and building a reusable components repository. Next, you'll learn how to deploy template specs in various ways, and when you should and should not consider using template specs. While template specs are the go-to option in many cases, an understanding of alternative approaches is beneficial as well, so we'll also discuss using Azure Artifacts feeds or GitHub Packages for storing templates, and the chapter will conclude with some design considerations. First, let's create a template spec.

10.2 Creating a template spec

Let's continue with the Doush Bank example and assume you are part of the team that has to create a library of preapproved building blocks that are compliant by design.

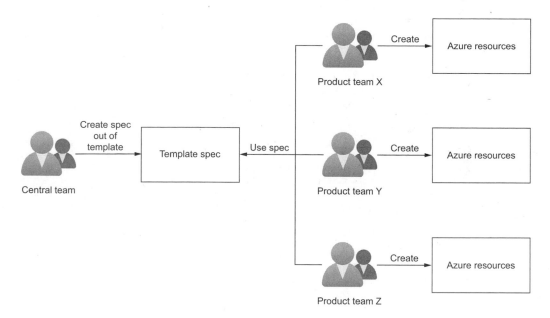

Figure 10.2   A central team creates template specs that other teams use to create Azure resources.

In figure 10.2 you see the central team and how they produce the template specs that other teams can consume. Within this team, one of the building blocks that must be created first is the compliant Windows 2019 virtual machine. This building block should contain a minimal VM configuration that contains all mandatory configuration. It might look something like the following listing (10-01.bicep).

Listing 10.1   Azure Bicep for a compliant VM

```
param virtualMachineName string
@allowed([
  'Standard_B2s'
```

```
      'Standard_D4ds_v4'
])
param virtualMachineSize string
param virtualMachineUsername string
@secure()
param virtualMachinePassword string
param virtualNetworkName string
param subnetName string
param virtualMachineIpAddress string

output compliantWindows2019VirtualMachineId =
    ➡ stringcompliantWindows2019VirtualMachine.id

resource compliantWindows2019VirtualMachine
    ➡ 'Microsoft.Compute/virtualMachines@2020-12-01'  = {
    name: virtualMachineName
    location: resourceGroup().location
    identity: {
        type: 'SystemAssigned'
    }
    properties: {
        hardwareProfile: {
            vmSize: virtualMachineSize
        }
        storageProfile: {
            imageReference: {
                publisher: 'MicrosoftWindowsServer'
                offer: 'WindowsServer'
                sku: '2019-Datacenter'
                version: 'latest'
            }
            osDisk: {
                osType: 'Windows'
                name: virtualMachineName
                createOption: 'FromImage'
                caching: 'ReadWrite'
                managedDisk: {
                    storageAccountType: 'StandardSSD_LRS'
                }
            }
        }
        osProfile: {
            computerName: virtualMachineName
            adminUsername: virtualMachineUsername
            adminPassword: virtualMachinePassword
            windowsConfiguration: {
                timeZone: 'Central Europe Standard Time'
            }
        }
        networkProfile: {
            networkInterfaces: [
                {
                    id: compliantNetworkCard.id
                }
            ]
```

This template returns the resourceId of the VM.

Start of the VM definition

```
          }
        }
      }

resource compliantNetworkCard 'Microsoft.Network/networkInterfaces         ◁──┐
  ➡ @2020-06-01' = {                                        Every VM needs at least
  name: virtualMachineName                                    one network card.
  location: resourceGroup().location
  properties: {
    ipConfigurations: [
      {
        name: 'IPConfiguration-NICE-VM1'
        properties: {
          privateIPAllocationMethod: 'Static'
          privateIPAddress: virtualMachineIpAddress
          subnet: {
            id: resourceId('Microsoft.Network/virtualNetworks/subnets',
              ➡ virtualNetworkName, subnetName)
          }
        }
      }
    ]
  }
}

resource azureAADLogin 'Microsoft.Compute/virtualMachines/extensions        ◁──┐
  ➡ @2015-06-15' = {
  name: '${virtualMachineName}/azureAADLogin'
  location: resourceGroup().location
  properties: {                                                These two
    type: 'AADLoginForWindows'                                 extensions
    publisher: 'Microsoft.Azure.ActiveDirectory'               make the VM
    typeHandlerVersion: '0.4'                                  compliant to
    autoUpgradeMinorVersion: true                              standards.
  }
}

resource AzurePolicyforWindows 'Microsoft.Compute/virtualMachines/extensions  ◁──┘
  ➡ @2015-06-15' = {
  name: '${virtualMachineName}/AzurePolicyforWindows'
  location: resourceGroup().location
  properties: {
    type: 'ConfigurationforWindows'
    publisher: 'Microsoft.GuestConfiguration'
    typeHandlerVersion: '1.1'
    autoUpgradeMinorVersion: true
  }
}
```

This building block contains the VM, the network interface it requires, and two mandatory VM extensions that have to be installed into every VM at the company. It also enforces some good practices, like keeping usernames and passwords secure and limiting usage to a limited set of precleared VM SKUs. This is the essence of template specs: in addition to permitting reuse, it allows you to define standards, configuration, or included configuration that everyone should use when working in a certain context, like a company or business unit. Note that we explicitly said "should use," as it is not possible to enforce the use of templates. To enforce standards, you should look into using Azure Policy.

Instead of deploying this VM directly, a template spec can be created out of this template with the following Azure CLI commands:

```
az group create --location westeurope --name TemplateSpecs
az ts create --resource-group TemplateSpecs --location westeurope
    ➥ --name compliantWindows2019Vm --version "1.0"
    ➥ --template-file 10-01.bicep
```

Or, if you are using an older version of the CLI that does not automatically transpile Bicep to JSON, you can use these commands:

```
az group create --location westeurope --name TemplateSpecs
az bicep build --file 10-01.bicep
az ts create --resource-group TemplateSpecs --location westeurope
    ➥ --name compliantWindows2019Vm --version "1.0"
    ➥ --template-file 10-01.json
```

It's not yet possible to deploy Azure Bicep as template specs directly, so it is necessary to manually transpile a Bicep template into an ARM template first. After transpiling, the template spec is created by invoking the `ts create` command and providing parameter values that describe where the spec should be located, the source file, spec name, and version.

If the name of a template spec is not descriptive enough, you can add a longer description using the `--description` parameter.

10.2.1 *Listing template specs*

After creating one or more template specs, you can retrieve the available specs list using `az ts list`. This command returns a JSON array containing all the available template specs.

To retrieve the details of one of listed specs, you can use the following command:

```
az ts show --resource-group TemplateSpecs --name compliantWindows2019Vm
```

This returns a JSON object detailing the template spec created before. It will look something like the following listing.

Listing 10.2   A template spec object as stored in Azure

```
{
    "description": "longer description, if needed",
    "displayName": null,
    "id": "...",
    "location": "westeurope",
```

```
    "metadata": null,
    "name": "compliantWindows2019Vm",
    "resourceGroup": "TemplateSpecs",
    "systemData": {
        "createdAt": "2021-05-30T17:35:11.805488+00:00",
        "createdBy": "henry@azurespecialist.nl",
        "createdByType": "User",
        "lastModifiedAt": "2021-05-30T17:35:12.185520+00:00",
        "lastModifiedBy": "henry@azurespecialist.nl",
        "lastModifiedByType": "User"
    },
    "tags": {},
    "type": "Microsoft.Resources/templateSpecs",
    "versions": [              Multiple versions of a template
        "1.0"                  spec can be listed here.
    ]
}
```

One of the things to note in this object is that it contains a property called `versions`.

10.2.2   Template spec versions

Inside a template spec object, there is a property called `versions` that is typed as an `array`. This hints that it is possible to store multiple versions of a template spec. You can verify this by running the following commands:

```
az ts create --resource-group TemplateSpecs --location westeurope
    --name compliantWindows2019Vm --version "2.0"
    --template-file 10-01.json

az ts show -resource-group TemplateSpecs --name compliantWindows2019Vm
```

The object that is returned this time does not only contain version 1.0 but also version 2.0. The great thing about versions is that they allow you to add new, improved template specs. Also, existing users of older versions can still trust that their versions will continue working—an important property in a supplier-consumer relationship for shared components.

Currently it is not possible to mark templates or template versions as deprecated or obsolete. It is possible, though, to remove a template spec version using the Azure CLI:

```
az ts delete --resource-group TemplateSpecs --name compliantWindows2019Vm
    --version "1.0"
```

To remove a whole template, omit the `--version` parameter.

10.2.3   Creating a template spec from multiple ARM templates

When building Bicep templates and transpiling them before deploying them as a template spec, Bicep modules are automatically included in the template. You do not have to worry about making your modules available as part of the template spec.

But if you are still working with ARM templates rather than Bicep templates, you may be wondering about linked templates. Fortunately, you can use linked templates in combinations with template specs. Assuming you have an ARM template available that contains the definitions for the VM extensions we discussed before, you can write an ARM template like the following listing (10-03.json). Here the `relativePath` property is used to reference an ARM file.

Listing 10.3   An ARM template that uses `relativePath`

```
{
    "$schema": "https://schema.management.azure.com/schemas/
      ➡ 2019-04-01/deploymentTemplate.json#",
    "contentVersion": "1.0.0.0",
    "parameters": {
        "virtualMachineName": {
            "type": "string"
        },
        ...
    },
    "resources": [
        {
            ...
        },
        {
            "type": "Microsoft.Network/networkInterfaces",
            ...
        },
        {                                              ⟵  At this point, the
            "type": "Microsoft.Resources/deployments",    deployment of a linked
            "apiVersion": "2020-10-01",                    template starts.
            "name": "[concat('vmExtensions', parameters('virtualMachineName'))]",
            "properties": {
                "mode": "Incremental",
                "templateLink": {
                    "relativePath": "10-03-vmExtensions.json"
                },
                "parameters": {
                    "virtualMachineName": {
                        "value": "[parameters('virtualMachineName')]"
                    }
                }
            }
        }
    ],
    "outputs": {
        "compliantWindows2019VirtualMachineId": {
            "type": "string",
            "value": "[resourceId('Microsoft.Compute/virtualMachines',
              ➡ parameters('virtualMachineName'))]"
        }
    }
}
```

The file can be a file on the local filesystem. ⟶ (points to "templateLink")

In the preceding listing, you can see roughly the same ARM template that you would get from transpiling the first Bicep template in this chapter (listing 10.1), except that the VM extensions have been left out. Instead, a new deployment is included that references another file on a relative path on the local filesystem, using the `relativePath` property. When you deploy this template as a template spec, that linked template is automatically discovered and included as part of the spec.

You can verify this by running the following commands, which create a third and final version of the template spec for compliant VMs and then show the details of that version:

```
az ts create --resource-group TemplateSpecs --location westeurope
    --name compliantWindows2019Vm --version "3.0"
    --template-file 10-03.json

az ts show --resource-group TemplateSpecs --name compliantWindows2019Vm
    --version "3.0"
```

Here you can see a new parameter (version) in the `ts show` command. With this parameter added, the command shows all the details of a specific version of the template spec, including the actual template and all linked templates. In this case, you would get an object that has the following shape:

```
{
    "description": null,
    "id": "...",
    "linkedTemplates": [
        {
            // The template from 10-03-vmExtensions.json
        }
    ],
    "location": "westeurope",
    "mainTemplate": {
        // The template from 10-03.json
    },
    "metadata": null,
    "name": "3.0",
    "resourceGroup": "TemplateSpecs",
    "systemData": {
        ...
    },
    "tags": {},
    "type": "Microsoft.Resources/templateSpecs/versions",
    "uiFormDefinition": null
}
```

Here you can verify that both the main template and the linked template are available as part of the template spec. For your reference, the entire file of 200 lines is included in the GitHub repository under the name 10-03-deployed-as-spec.json.

10.2.4   *Deploying a template spec using IaC is impractical*

Let's circle back to your role in the central team responsible for creating a whole series of template specs that define preapproved, compliant resources that contain a good enough default configuration for Doush Bank. One of the things your team wants to do is use DevOps practices like IaC and CI/CD for building template specs.

To do that, you might want to investigate how you can create template specs using IaC. Unfortunately, this is not as straightforward as it might seem. Under the hood, a template spec is stored as a multitude of objects. Every version is its own Azure resource, and all linked templates are stored as separate resources (called artifacts) as well.

The current recommendation is to create template specs by invoking the Azure CLI or Azure PowerShell. This advice also applies when you are creating the template specs using a CI/CD pipeline like Azure DevOps or GitHub Actions. Microsoft strongly recommends using Portal, PowerShell, or the Azure CLI for creating template specs. See Angel Perez's article "ARM Template Specs is now Public Preview!" (http://mng .bz/J2xz) for more information. Now that you have deployed a few versions of the template spec for a compliant VM with some default configuration, let's switch sides and learn how to consume a template spec.

10.3   *Deploying a template spec*

Let's now assume that you are in one of the teams required to follow the company standards, so you want to deploy the predefined compliant VM stored as a template spec. To make this possible, you must first find the complete ID of the template spec you want to deploy. You can find this ID by executing the az ts show command again, which you saw in the previous section.

```
az ts show --resource-group TemplateSpecs --name compliantWindows2019Vm
   ➥ --version "3.0"
```

This will show you the complete Azure Resource for this template spec, including its id property, which will look something like this:

```
/subscriptions/{azure-subscription-id}/resourceGroups/TemplateSpecs
   ➥ /providers/Microsoft.Resources/templateSpecs
   ➥ /compliantWindows2019Vm/versions/3.0
```

With this id in hand, you can deploy the resources declared in the template spec using the following command:

```
az group create --location westeurope --resource-group TemplatedResources
az deployment group create --resource-group TemplatedSResources
   ➥ --template-spec /subscriptions/{azure-subscription-id}
   ➥ /resourceGroups/TemplateSpecs/providers/Microsoft.Resources
   ➥ /templateSpecs/compliantWindows2019Vm/versions/3.0
```

Looking closely, you'll see that this is the same `az deployment group create` command you have used before to deploy a template, but this time another parameter set is used: instead of `--template-file`, the `--template-spec` parameter is used to point to the template spec you want to deploy. You'll also see in the example that this should include a specific version.

   If you execute this command yourself, don't forget to specify the correct parameters for putting this VM into a virtual network. These parameters were declared as part of the template spec you created in listing 10.3. If you don't have any Azure virtual networks, or you don't want to create one for this example, just pass any random value. This will fail the deployment, but you'll still see how to deploy a template spec. In the following subsection, you'll deploy a complete architecture with a virtual network and two VMs to make up for this.

   If you prefer using Azure PowerShell instead of the Azure CLI, you can accomplish the same result using these commands:

```
New-AzResourceGroupDeployment -ResourceGroupName TemplatedResources
    ➥ -TemplateSpecId /subscriptions/{azure-subscription-id}/resourceGroups
    ➥ /TemplateSpecs/providers/Microsoft.Resources/templateSpecs
    ➥ /compliantWindows2019Vm/versions/3.0
```

Finally, as you may have guessed, it is also possible to deploy template specs from the portal, as shown in figure 10.3. First, navigate to the list of all resource groups (1), optionally filter the list down if it is very long (2), and then open the resource group containing your template spec (3). Once you have found the spec, open its details by clicking the name (4).

Figure 10.3   Opening a template spec in the Azure portal

This will open a new view in the portal, with a Deploy button at the top. Clicking this button will open up a third view, as shown in figure 10.4. Once you have filled in all the values, click Review + Create to start the deployment. No matter which approach you choose—Azure CLI, Azure PowerShell, or the Azure portal—you will end up with the same result.

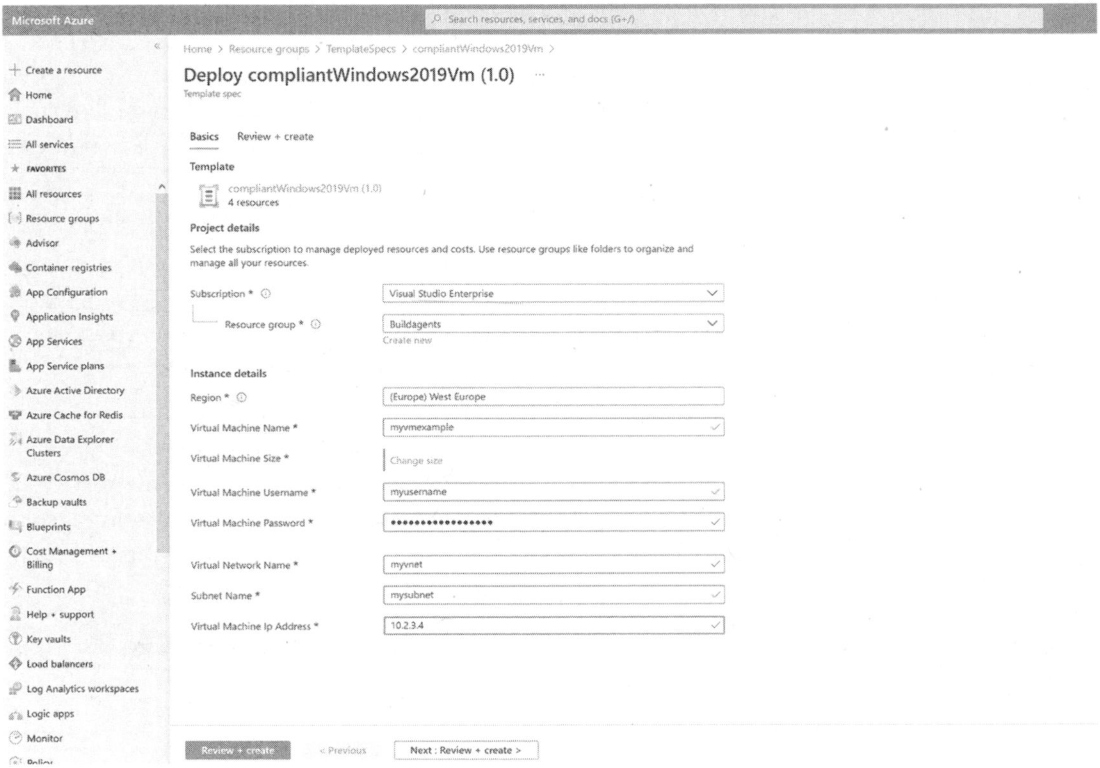

Figure 10.4   Deploying a template spec from the Azure portal

After working with template specs like this, you may find that it feels a bit ad hoc to manage infrastructure this way. Maybe it doesn't feel right to have your specs defined using IaC and to then deploy them using imperative commands, especially when you want to combine multiple specs into a single infrastructure. Don't fear, it's also possible to deploy a template spec from within an ARM or Bicep template.

10.3.1   *Deploying template specs from an ARM or Bicep template*

To complete our discussion of how template specs work, let's explore how you can reference or deploy specs from a template. To see how this can work in practice, let's take the example from the previous section and expand on it a little bit. Instead of just deploying a single VM, suppose you are tasked with deploying a more elaborate infrastructure. Something like what's shown in figure 10.5.

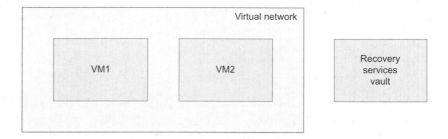

Figure 10.5   An architecture with more components

In figure 10.5, you can see an architecture that spans a virtual network with two virtual machines and one recovery services vault for backing those VMs up. The requirement for backups makes the deployment more interesting, because backups are configured using a specific resource type, the `protected item`, that requires both the ID of the virtual machine and the ID from the recovery services vault. The latter ID comes from your own deployment; the IDs of the virtual machines have to come from the template specs. In this example, you'll see how to deploy template specs and how to use the information returned by the template spec further down the line.

To help with this deployment, the central IaC team has made the spec for a compliant virtual machine available. To deploy the complete infrastructure, a Bicep template is used. In that template, the following resources have to be declared:

- The virtual network
- Two VMs, coming from the template spec
- A recovery services vault

Let's start by defining a virtual network (10-04.bicep).

Listing 10.4   Azure virtual network using Bicep

```
var virtualNetworkName = 'workloadvnet'
var subnetName = 'workloadsubnet'

resource virtualNetwork 'Microsoft.Network/virtualNetworks@2020-11-01' = {
    name: virtualNetworkName
    location: resourceGroup().location
    properties: {
        addressSpace: {
            addressPrefixes: [
                '10.0.0.0/24'
            ]
        }
```

```
        subnets: [
            {
                name: subnetName
                properties: {
                    addressPrefix: '10.0.0.0/24'
                }
            }
        ]
    }
}
```

This template contains the Bicep definition for a virtual network, using an address space containing 256 IP addresses from 10.0.0.0 to 10.0.0.255. The network contains a single subnet with the same address range called `workload` for holding both VMs.

As both VMs are created from the template spec for a compliant VM, you first need to build a variable of type `array` that contains all the parameters needed by the template spec and that differs between the two virtual machines.

```
@secure()
param vmPassword string

var virtualMachineDetails = [
    {
        ipAddress: '10.0.0.10'
        name: 'VM1'
        sku: 'Standard_B2s'
    }
    {
        ipAddress: '10.0.0.11'
        name: 'VM2'
        sku: 'Standard_D4ds_v4'
    }
]
```

This array contains two objects, each holding the variable values for one of the VMs. By now, you should be able to read and understand this Bicep code.

The following part of the template uses these objects to deploy the actual VMs, like this:

```
resource virtualMachines 'Microsoft.Resources
   ➡ /deployments@2021-01-01' = [for vm in virtualMachineDetails : {
  name: vm.name
  properties: {                                    A template spec is deployed
      mode: 'Incremental'                          as the linked template.
      templateLink: {
          id: '/subscriptions/{azure-subscription-id}/resourceGroups    ⟵
              ➡ /TemplateSpecs/providers/Microsoft.Resources/templateSpecs
              ➡ /compliantWindows2019Vm/versions/3.0'
      }
      parameters: {
          virtualNetworkName: {
```

```
                value: virtualNetworkName
            }
            subnetName: {
                value: subnetName
            }
            virtualMachineIpAddress: {
                value: vm.ipAddress
            }
            virtualMachineName: {
                value: vm.name
            }
            virtualMachineSize: {
                value: vm.sku
            }
            virtualMachineUsername: {
                value: 'bicepadmin'
            }
            virtualMachinePassword: {
                value: vmPassword
            }
        }
    }
}]
```

Combining these three snippets gives you the complete Azure Bicep file (10-04.bicep in the accompanying Git repository) for deploying a virtual network and two VMs. In this third snippet, the template spec is referenced in a way that is very similar to how it works from the Azure CLI or Azure PowerShell.

With the virtual network and VMs created, it is time to add another resource to your infrastructure, the recovery services vault:

```
var recoveryServicesVaultName = 'backupvault'

resource recoveryServicesVault 'Microsoft.RecoveryServices/vaults
    ⟹ @2021-01-01' = {
    name: recoveryServicesVaultName
    location: resourceGroup().location
    sku: {
        name: 'Standard'          Adding a property
    }                             called properties
    properties: {}    ⟵────┘      is mandatory.
}
```

The recovery services vault is a resource that requires only a `name` and `sku` to be configured. Other optional properties can be left out, but the `properties` property cannot—this is why there may be an unexpected empty object.

The vault is where the backups are stored, and it is configured using a protected item. A protected item is a resource that enables the backup of a resource. It contains references to the resource to be backed up and the backup policy that governs when backups are taken and how long they are retained.

The final snippet is complex with long expressions in it, so let's slowly prepare for that. If you are not familiar with the `protectedItems` resource for VMs, this pseudo-specification may help:

```
resource protectedItems 'Microsoft.RecoveryServices/vaults/backupFabrics
    ➡ /protectionContainers/protectedItems@2016-06-01' = {
  name: complex name
  properties: {
    protectedItemType: 'Microsoft.Compute/virtualMachines'
    policyId: resource id of the backup policy
    sourceResourceId: resource id of the protected item
  }
}
```

Besides the complex, multipart resource type, a similarly complex name is created out of five mandatory parts: the name of the services recovery vault, the containing resource group (twice), and the name of the protected virtual machine (also twice). The first entry in the `properties` array contains a fixed string for virtual machines, and the other two fields reference the backup policy to use and the resource to back up. The policy specifies how often a backup should be taken and how long backups should be retained. The resource to be protected contains the ID of a virtual machine.

If we update the previous pseudocode with the proper expressions to add it to our template, we'll get this:

For each entry in the list of details, a VM is defined.

```
resource protectedItems 'Microsoft.RecoveryServices/vaults/backupFabrics
    ➡/protectionContainers/protectedItems@2016-06-01' =
    ➡[for (vm, i) in virtualMachineDetails: {
    name: concat(recoveryServicesVaultName,
        ➡ '/Azure/iaasvmcontainer;iaasvmcontainerv2;vnetdemo;',
        ➡ virtualMachineDetails[i].name,
        ➡ '/vm;iaasvmcontainerv2;vnetdemo;', virtualMachineDetails[i].name)
    properties: {
        protectedItemType: 'Microsoft.Compute/virtualMachines'
        policyId: resourceId('Microsoft.RecoveryServices/vaults
            ➡ /backupPolicies',recoveryServicesVaultName,'DefaultPolicy')
        sourceResourceId: reference(virtualMachines[i].name).outputs    ⟵
            ➡ .compliantWindows2019VirtualMachineId.value
    }
}]
```

The sourceResourceId references the resource to back up.

The PolicyId references another resource, the backup policy.

Comparing this to the previous snippet, you can see how the different values are calculated. The first thing to note about this snippet is that it contains a `for` loop over the list of `virtualMachineDetails` created earlier. Within the loop, you can trace all the parts that make up the name, where the name of the resource group is added twice, and the virtual machine's name at position `i`.

You can also see how the different `resourceIds` are created. The backup policy ID is a fixed one, referencing the built-in policy called `DefaultPolicy`.

The final property is the resource ID of the protected item: `sourceResourceId`. This is the ID of the VM created by the template spec. This is why the spec has an output parameter—so you can pick up that output here. The `reference()` function is used to translate the name of the linked template spec deployment to a resource object. Once the object is created, the `outputs` property navigates to the value for `compliant-Windows2019VirtualMachineId`, which is the name of the output parameter.

When you're trying to understand this, remember that the complete template of this section is available on GitHub under the name 10-04.bicep, where it is much easier to read.

Adding the protected items completed this example. You have built a complete infrastructure with one virtual network, two VMs coming from a template spec, and a recovery services vault in which backups are stored for both virtual machines.

10.3.2 Upgrading to a newer version of the template spec

Once you start building deployments like the one in the previous section, you may find yourself in a bit of a pickle with versions after some time. Having different versions of the same template spec coexisting can be a two-edged sword.

Multiple versions give you, the consumer of a spec, the guarantee that older versions are still available even when the maintainer of the spec starts creating newer versions. (That's assuming they don't delete older versions unexpectedly.) Still, there is currently no mechanism for getting warnings from Azure when you aren't using the latest version of a spec. Nor is there a way to quickly check if any of your recent deployments are using outdated specs.

Consequently, you'll have to keep tabs on the maintainers of the specs you use to ensure that you do not miss service updates. And, of course, the opposite is also true: if you are the maintainer of one or more template specs, do not forget to notify your users when you release new versions, so that they can update their references as well.

As a maintainer, one thing you should be cautious about is removing older spec versions. There is, as of now, no Azure-provided way of finding out if scripts, templates, or users out there are still referencing an older version. If you delete a version, you may break the next release of a downstream team, unless you put your own process in place to prevent this.

These risks around template specs may be a reason for you to explore other options. Let's take a look at using a Bicep registry for distributing reusable ARM and Bicep templates.

10.4 An alternative: A Bicep registry

If your team and organization have fully adopted Bicep and are no longer working with ARM templates in JSON, you can consider using the Bicep registry. A Bicep registry is an Azure Container Registry (ACR) that is not used for storing Docker images, but Bicep modules instead. You can use these files when building a composing template by referencing their online location instead of a location on the filesystem.

One of the advantages of this registry is that any module you reference in the registry will be downloaded and inserted into the JSON template that results from the transpilation. This means that even if the contents of the module change, or are removed, between deployments, you can still transpile once and use that same outcome multiple times.

To work with a Bicep registry, you will first have to create a new ACR, like this:

```
az group create --resource-group BicepRegistry --location westeurope
az acr create --resource-group BicepRegistry
    ➥ --name BicepRegistryDemoUniqueName --sku Standard
```

The first line creates a new resource group for the Bicep registry, as you have seen before. The second command creates an ACR instance. The name of the instance needs to be unique, so you will have to choose your own name.

> **NOTE** If you want to learn more about Azure Container Registry, you can start with Microsoft's "Introduction to private Docker container registries in Azure" article (http://mng.bz/woRP).

Once the ACR is in place, it is time to start pushing and using modules. As you have already created a reusable module (10-01.bicep, in listing 10.1), you can reuse that and publish it as a module to your registry with the following command:

```
az bicep publish --file 10-01.bicep --target
    ➥ br:BicepRegistryDemoUniqueName.azurecr.io/bicep/modules/vm:v1
```

You start the target with `br`, which indicates that you are pushing to a Bicep registry. The path used (/bicep/modules) is not mandatory, but it is a convention used throughout the Microsoft Docs and adopted by many users. This makes it well known and can help distinguish between Bicep templates and other contents in the registry.

The part after the colon (v1) is used to identify the version of the template, and it's often called the *tag*, in the context of ACR. If you want to add a newer version when republishing the module, it is wise to increment this to v2, then v3, etc.

With this module in place, you can now write another Bicep file to use this remote module as part of the deployment (10-05.bicep).

Listing 10.5   Using a module from a Bicep registry

```
var subnetName = 'subnetName'

resource virtualNetwork 'Microsoft.Network/virtualNetworks    ◁─┐  Virtual network
    ➥ @2020-11-01' = {                                           │  declaration
  name: 'exampleVirtualNetwork'
  location: resourceGroup().location
```

```
    properties: {
        addressSpace: {
          addressPrefixes: [
              '10.0.0.0/24'
          ]
        }
        subnets: [
          {
              name: subnetName
              properties: {
                  addressPrefix: '10.0.0.0/24'
              }
          }
        ]
    }
}

module vm1Deployment 'br:BicepRegistryDemoUniqueName.azurecr.io/bicep
   ⟹ /modules/vm:v1' = {
    name: 'vm1Deployment'
    params: {
        subnetName: subnetName
        virtualMachineIpAddress: '10.0.0.1'
        virtualMachineName: 'vm1'
        virtualMachinePassword: 'dontputpasswordsinbooks'
        virtualMachineSize: 'Standard_B2s'
        virtualMachineUsername: 'bicepadmin'
        virtualNetworkName: virtualNetwork.name
    }
}
```

> **Referencing a module that is hosted in an ACR Bicep registry**

This template first creates a virtual network, which is a prerequisite for deploying a VM. Once this is in place, the module for creating a VM can be deployed by referencing it through the syntax `br:<acr-name>.azureacr.io`, followed by the path that you used before for publishing the file. As an alternative to template specs or the Bicep registry, you may also want to consider using a package manager.

10.5 Sharing templates using a package manager

You may have reasons not to host your reusable templates in template specs. Or, if you are using multiple Azure tenants, template specs will not be a viable option. Some organizations also built a repository of reusable templates before template specs were available. Whatever the reason, package repositories are an alternative to sharing templates with template specs or the Bicep registry.

Package repositories are used extensively in software development for sharing libraries between software teams. In the .NET ecosystem, the NuGet package manager is used. In the Java system, Maven is often used; JavaScript and TypeScript have NPM, and so forth. Depending on the context you are working in, one of these options is likely already being used.

The packages that are created and used by package managers are stored in package repositories, like Azure Artifacts, NuGet, MyGet, NPM, GitHub Packages, JFrog Artifactory, and many more.

> **Working with Azure Artifacts**
>
> This section contains minimal instructions for working with Azure Artifacts Feeds and is not a comprehensive discussion of all the capabilities, including securing pipelines. For more information on the use of Azure DevOps, of which Azure Artifacts is a part, the Microsoft documentation is a good place to start: http://mng.bz/7yav.

You'll learn to work with Azure Artifacts in this example, a common choice when working with Azure DevOps. Azure DevOps supports multiple package types, and in this case the *universal package* type works best.

10.5.1 Publishing an ARM template as a package

Before you can publish an ARM template to a repository, that repository needs to be created. When you're working with Azure Artifacts, a repository is called an Artifacts feed.

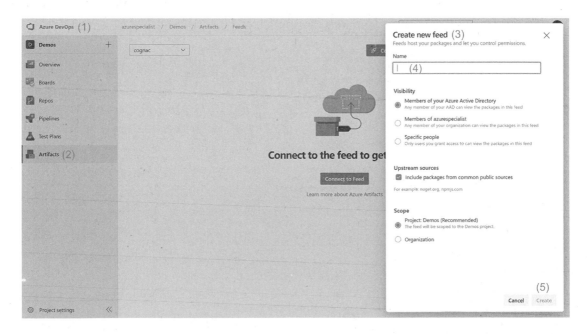

Figure 10.6   Creating an Azure Artifacts feed

To create a feed, perform the following steps (see figure 10.6):

1 Log in to your Azure DevOps account and open your working project.
2 Navigate to Artifacts in the menu on the left.
3 Click on Create Feed in the bar at the top.
4 Give the feed a name and optionally configure other options.
5 Click Create.

Once the feed is created, you can publish packages to it. Publishing packages can be done from an Azure pipeline, as you have seen before. For this example, assume there's a file called 10-06.json that contains a simple ARM template for an Azure App Service. With that template in place, you can start working on an Azure pipeline that checks this file out of source control and publishes it as a universal package (10-07.yml).

Listing 10.6 A YAML pipeline for creating and publishing a package

```
steps:
- task: CopyFiles@2                    ◁──┐  Staging the files to publish
  displayName: 'Copy template spec files to staging location'
  inputs:
      SourceFolder: '$(Build.SourcesDirectory)'
      Contents: '*.json'
      TargetFolder: '$(Build.ArtifactStagingDirectory)'

- task: UniversalPackages@0            ◁──┐  The publish
  displayName: 'Publish package'            package step
  inputs:
      command: 'publish'
      publishDirectory: '$(Build.ArtifactStagingDirectory)'   ◁──  The directory that contains the files to publish
      feedsToUsePublish: 'internal'              ◁──
      vstsFeedPublish: '<your-feed-id>'                This is an internal NuGet feed, an Azure Artifacts feed.
      vstsFeedPackagePublish: 'app-service-plan-template'
      versionOption: 'patch'         ◁──┐
                                         The versioning
                                         strategy
```

ID of the feed to publish to

The package name

In this pipeline, two steps are defined. The first step, CopyFiles, is used to copy all the files that match *.json from the templates directory to a specific location outside the sources directory from which they can be packaged. In this example, all JSON files are copied, but in larger solutions you would limit this to only the folder containing your templates. The location you copy to is called the Artifacts staging directory, and it's available using the variable Build.ArtifactStagingDirectory. Copying the files to a separate location ensures that only the desired files are packaged and not the complete contents of the sources directory.

After copying the files to the staging directory, that directory is published as a universal package. To make this possible, you have to specify the name of the package, a version increment strategy, and the ID that identifies your Artifacts feed. The feeds-ToUsePublish option is set to internal, which indicates that this is an Azure Artifacts feed and not an externally hosted NuGet feed.

The ID for the Artifacts feed is the most tricky to find. The easiest way is to store the file in source control with a dummy value, and then fill in the value when you create the pipeline, as shown in figure 10.7. First, click the Settings link (1) just before the definition of the second task. Next, in the Destination Feed drop-down list (2), select the correct feed. When you click Add (3) to update the pipeline definition, the correct ID will be inserted automatically.

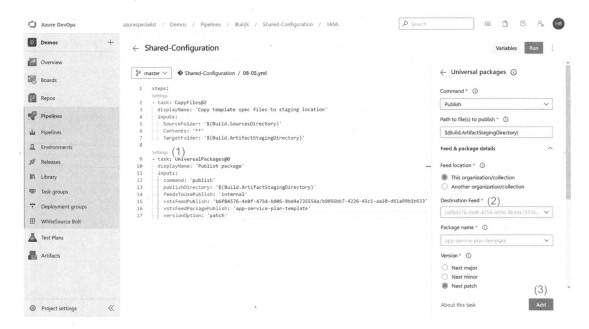

Figure 10.7   Adding the Artifact ID to a pipeline definition

After completing the settings in figure 10.7, click the Run button at the top right, and your package, containing an ARM template, will be created. You can verify this by navigating back to your Artifacts feed, where the welcome screen will have been replaced by something like figure 10.8.

Figure 10.8   An artifact has been published to the feed.

If you are wondering whether rerunning the pipeline would add a new version of the same artifact, the answer is yes. The version in the screenshot is 0.0.1, and if the pipeline were to rerun, the new version would be 0.0.2. With this package in place, let's switch gears again and see how to consume this package and use it from an Azure pipeline.

10.5.2 Deploying an ARM template that is in a package

To deploy an ARM template that is packaged and uploaded to an Azure Artifacts feed, you can also use an Azure pipeline. Such a pipeline can look like the following listing (10-07.yml).

Listing 10.7 A YAML pipeline for downloading a package

```
steps:
- task: UniversalPackages@0          Download the package
  displayName: Download ARM Template Package   from the Artifacts feed.
  inputs:
      command: download
      feedsToUse: 'internal'                    The id of the feed
      vstsFeed: '<your-feed-id>'                to download the
      vstsFeedPackage: 'app-service-plan-template'   package from
      vstsPackageVersion: '*'
      downloadDirectory: '$(Pipeline.Workspace)'   Deploy the
                                                   downloaded
- task: AzureResourceManagerTemplateDeployment@3   artifact files.
  displayName: Deploy ARM Template
  inputs:
      azureResourceManagerConnection: 'myArmServiceConnection'
      deploymentScope: 'Resource Group'
      subscriptionId: '<your-subscription-id>'
      action: 'Create Or Update Resource Group'
      resourceGroupName: 'myResourceGroup'
      location: 'West Europe'
      templateLocation: 'Linked artifact'
      csmFile: '$(Pipeline.Workspace)/10-06.json'
      overrideParameters: '-appServicePlanName myAppServicePlan'
```

If you look carefully at this pipeline definition, you'll see that the first task is the inverse of the last task in the previous pipeline. As you are downloading from the same feed you have uploaded to before, you should use the same feed ID. Instead of uploading a package, it is now downloaded. The path it is downloaded to again uses a built-in variable to reference the current execution directory of the pipeline. The second task is similar to what you have seen before: it takes the downloaded ARM template and deploys it to Azure.

Now that you have seen how to use template specs and an example of packaging templates into a package repository, you have seen two of the most common private approaches. But if you ever find yourself in a situation where you do not want to use template specs or a package manager, there is a third straightforward solution.

10.5.3 *Yet another approach*

Any discussion of approaches to sharing ARM and Bicep templates would not be complete without listing the third option, *hosting them in a public repository*. Maybe there are no reasons to keep your templates hidden. This may sound ridiculous, especially from the perspective of a business, but why would you want to keep your templates for a virtual machine, storage account, or other resource hidden? All possible configurations are available already from the documentation, and maybe there is nothing special enough to hide.

> **WARNING** This suggestion to make your templates public may not resonate with everyone, and especially with security experts. Weigh your options and make informed choices.

One particular situation where this line of thought applies is to open source projects. Just use the GitHub (or a similar platform) link to a specific commit on any file in any publicly accessible Git repository, and you are good to go. On GitHub, you can open the history of any file, navigate to a specific version, and then grab the URL to its raw version.

10.6 *Design considerations*

With all these options for reusing templates available, you might also want to consider how you want to write your reusable templates: not too big, but also not too small.

First, you'll want to avoid making templates so specific that they fit only very specific use cases, making them hard to reuse. For example, creating a reusable template containing an App Service plan, three App Services, an Application Insights account, and a Cosmos DB is probably not reusable.

You'll also want to avoid making templates that are too small and which will provide downstream users with hardly any benefit over writing templates from scratch. For example, a template with only a storage account that disables public containers is not very valuable. Your users will probably spend more time reusing that template than setting that Boolean value themselves.

Small reusable templates

There can be scenarios where minimal reusable templates do provide value. A prime example is in highly regulated environments where you're working with mandatory templates that are precertified or deemed compliant by Security, QA, or other important departments. Note that this does not mean all these templates would be small, just that some could be. While this approach is used in some companies, exploring Azure Policy as an alternative to mandatory templates can be valuable.

The sweet spot is somewhere in the middle: semi-finished products that are valuable building blocks. For example, a template with an App Service plan, a Function App

Service, and a corresponding storage account would be a common structure that could be reused by other teams.

Another thing you should think about is your versioning strategy:

- How will you inform your users of newer versions?
- How will you deprecate versions you want to remove at some point?
- When should you remove older versions, and how should you manage the downstream impact?

Besides these conceptual choices, you'll also have to choose an approach, so let's talk about that next.

10.6.1 Choosing an approach

You have learned about three tactics for sharing templates between teams or more generally between producers and consumers. But with three possible approaches, how do you select which one to use for your project?

Let's get the obvious out of the way: if there are no objections to hosting your templates at publicly accessible URLs, such as on GitHub, you should probably do that. It's the easiest, cheapest, and most straightforward approach.

If hosting at public URLs is not an option, you can choose between using template specs and a package manager. Let's explore the pros and cons of both approaches.

10.6.2 Pros and cons of template specs

Template specs are Azure's recommended and built-in approach to sharing templates. For that reason, you should probably choose template specs over using a package manager if there are no compelling reasons to do otherwise.

The first pro of template specs is that a template spec is just an Azure resource, like any other. This means that Azure RBAC applies, which means you can use the same means for governing access as you do for your other Azure resources. There's no extra hassle.

But also consider one of the downsides of Azure RBAC, which is that it does not allow you to assign a role to "everyone in my organization." This means that you'll have to set up your own "everyone" group if you want organization-wide specs.

Another pro of template specs over packages is that they allow for maximum control by the template specs writer. If the writer finds that a specific spec or version should no longer be available, they can remove it, and that's the end of it. The consequence here is that this can have downstream impacts, and if it's not communicated to consuming teams correctly, it can be frowned upon.

10.6.3 Pros and cons of using a Bicep registry

The considerations of using a Bicep registry are very similar to those surrounding template specs. The only differences are that a Bicep registry is not backwards compatible with ARM templates, which can be a con. As a pro, it enables a workflow where modules are being pulled down to your local machine or the build server, where they are transpiled along with your own IaC into a single template. When you are looking for repeatability in your deployments, creating a snapshot or immutable artifact in this way can be an important ingredient.

10.6.4 *Pros and cons of using a package manager*

What if you choose to use a package manager instead? This approach can be a big pro if a package manager is already used in your team or organization. If you reuse that package manager, you'll have solved a problem without introducing a new tool. In many organizations, that's a big pro.

Another benefit that most package managers support is creating local copies or downstream repositories. A downstream repository is another package repository that is not owned by the team that creates the reusable templates but by the team that uses the reusable templates. Whenever they want to start reusing a new template or a new version, the first step is to copy the package from the producing team's repository to their own downstream repository. This way, they ensure that all their dependencies are in their control and that packages stay available to them, as long as they do not remove the copies themselves.

Consequently, creators of reusable templates can no longer control which templates and versions their users are using. Once a template version with errors is released, they can only communicate an update, and they'll have to rely on the consuming teams to stop using the faulty version.

Depending on the package manager used, one downside can be that fine-grained access control can be more difficult or bespoke than using Azure RBAC. It is often easier to allow "everyone in the organization" to read packages from a stream.

Summary

- Template specs are written and versioned to enable others to reuse your templates.
- Template specs can be deployed directly, or by referencing them from ARM and Bicep templates.
- It is possible to build deep integrations with template specs in your ARM and Bicep templates by passing parameters and outputs back and forth.
- As an alternative to template specs, you can use the Bicep registry. It is Bicep-specific, but it enables workflows that require local transpilation of templates before deployment.
- Finally, you can use a package manager. Package managers are already in use in many organizations, which makes it unnecessary to introduce yet another tool. Package managers also help limit the downstream impact of removing template specs, as they allow consumers to create their own copies of templates.

Using deployment stacks
for grouping resources

This chapter covers

- Why you need another mechanism for grouping resources by their lifetime in Azure
- What deployment stacks are and how you can use them for grouping resources
- How deployment stacks will replace blueprints, sometime in the future

You have learned all about creating and updating Azure resources through IaC. In a template, you describe how you want your resources to be configured, and the Azure Resource Manager makes it so by creating or updating resources. Up to now, we haven't paid any attention to removing resources you do not need anymore, except for mentioning the `Complete` deployment mode in chapter 4.

In chapter 4 you learned that `Complete` deployments are a powerful but risky method for removing resources you do not need anymore. The risk lies in the fact that they remove all resources in a resource group that are not in the current deployment. If someone else deployed something to the same resource group from another context, those resources would be removed as well. In practice, this risky side of `Complete` deployments is why they are not frequently used in the real world. Some teams use them in non-production environments, but `Complete` deployments in production environments are rare. We will revisit this in more detail later in this chapter.

Because of the drawbacks of `Complete` deployments, the call for a reliable mechanism for removing resources through IaC has remained. And as we write this in the spring of 2022, a solution has been developed by the Azure Resource Manager team: *deployment stacks*. In this chapter, you'll learn why you might need another grouping mechanism for resources, in addition to resource groups and subscriptions, to remove resources in a less risky way. You will also learn how deployment stacks can be used to provision resources for others without granting control over those resources.

But first a word of warning: deployment stacks are still under heavy development by the Azure Product Group. While we wrote this chapter, the feature was still in private preview and available to only a handful of users. By the time you read this, deployment stacks might be in public preview or will enter public preview soon. Consequently, the code examples in this chapter might require some tweaking by you, as the details of deployment stacks might have changed. If you ever run into such problems, you can always find our updated code examples in the GitHub repository accompanying this book: https://github.com/AzureIaCBook/book-templates. With that out of the way, let's take a look at why you might want to start using deployment stacks.

11.1 Grouping resources by their lifetime

In Azure, your resources are organized into a multilevel hierarchy: resources are grouped into resource groups, resource groups into subscriptions, and subscriptions into management groups. This hierarchy works really well for building an extensive Azure infrastructure, where you want to delegate the responsibility for some level in the hierarchy to a business unit, department, or team. This hierarchy is often used for grouping resources by who can access them.

However, this way of grouping does not match the official Microsoft guideline for grouping resources by their lifetime. The goal should be that all resources in a resource group have the same lifecycle: they should all be created, updated, and deleted simultaneously.

These two types of groupings do not always overlap. Let's look at an example. In figure 11.1, you'll see the infrastructure for two application components that communicate over a service bus queue. To support this scenario, three resource groups are created:

- *Producer*—The compute element in this resource group has write access to the queue and is responsible for receiving work and putting messages on the queue whenever new work comes in.
- *Consumer*—The compute element in this resource group has read access to the queue and is responsible for reading the messages and completing the work described in these messages.
- *Messaging*—This resource group contains the service bus namespace, the queue, and the authorizations that identities hold on these resources.

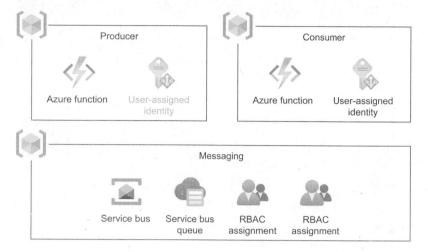

Figure 11.1   Grouping resources into resource groups

This resource group structure, shown in figure 11.1, aligns very well with the organization that works on this infrastructure: three teams, all of which are responsible for the resources in a single resource group.

However, when we look at the deployment lifecycles, another grouping can be made. For example, you might notice that there are resources in the Producer and Consumer resource groups with possibly different lifetimes, as shown in figure 11.2.

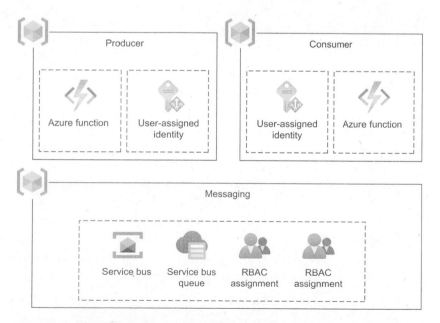

Figure 11.2   Different lifecycles, indicated by dashed lines, in the Producer and Consumer resource groups

You will recognize the following lifecycles, marked by the grey boxes:

- The user-assigned managed identities in the Producer and Consumer resource groups should have independent lifecycles because they should exist before the authorizations in the Messaging resource group can be created. However, their lifecycles should also be independent of the compute elements, as authorizations attached to the identities should remain intact when switching from Azure Functions to Azure Container Instances for hosting the compute layer.
- The service bus namespace, queue, and authorizations in the Messaging resource group have a common lifecycle.
- The actual compute elements in the Producer and Consumer resource groups share a lifecycle.

This example illustrates how a single resource group, with a sensible grouping of resources, can have resources with mixed lifetimes. This is where deployment stacks come in: they provide a custom grouping concept for organizing resources into a stack of resources with a shared lifetime.

Before we move on to explore deployment stacks in detail, let's look at why the `Complete` deployment mode you learned about in chapter 4 is not good enough for dealing with these situations.

11.1.1 *Complete deployment mode is not good enough*

The first and foremost reason why `Complete` deployments do not cover all cases is that a `Complete` deployment assumes that the scope in which resources that are no longer declared should be deleted is the same as the deployment scope. The Venn diagram in figure 11.3 illustrates this.

Here you see that `Complete` deployments do not remove existing "hidden" resources, like alert rules and RBAC assignments. Traditionally, complete deployments ignore some resource types, like role assignments and alert rules, because these resource types already existed before they were exposed as resources that could be managed through IaC. To maintain backward compatibility with how `Complete` deployments worked before these resources became available in the control pane, they are ignored during `Complete` deployments. In other words, resources that were not removed during a `Complete` deployment before will also not be removed during a `Complete` deployment in the future. Also, `Complete` deployments are limited to a single scope, so they cannot span multiple resource groups or subscriptions.

These limitations make `Complete` deployments useless for the following cases:

- When other resources in the resource group are not part of the deployment but shouldn't be removed either
- When resources in other resource groups or subscriptions are not part of the deployment scope that should be considered for removal

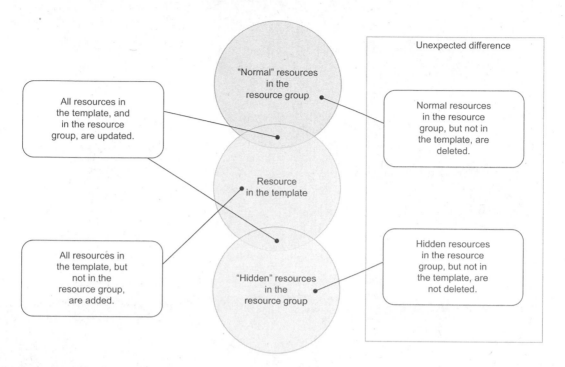

Figure 11.3 Difference between handling normal and "hidden" resources when deploying in `Complete` mode

Deployment stacks do not have these limitations. They can span multiple resource groups or subscriptions and inherently only consider resources that were part of the previous version of the stack for removal.

11.1.2 Deployment stacks to the rescue!

A deployment stack is a new type of Azure resource that acts as a custom grouping around one or more other resources. It is not a hierarchical grouping like resource groups or subscriptions but instead a group you create yourself and to which you add one or more resources using a nested template. A deployment stack can span multiple resource groups or even subscriptions, as shown in figure 11.4.

When you later update the deployment stack or the resources that are part of the stack, the stack will infer whether there are resources that were part of the stack in the previous deployment but are not in the current deployment. When that is the case, it will remove or disconnect those resources, depending on your configuration.

This might sound a bit abstract, so let's explore it using an example. In the following sections you will create, update, and remove a deployment stack to get a feeling for how it works. At first, you will create a service bus namespace with a single queue as part of a deployment stack. Later on, you will change the name of that queue in the template a few times to see how the stack handles these changes. The name of the

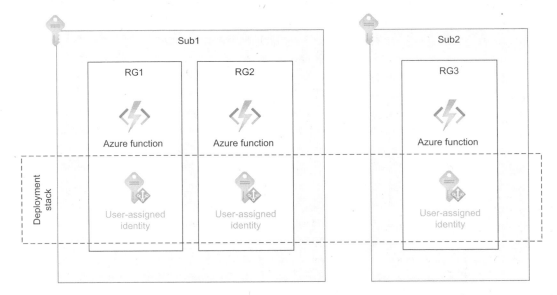

Figure 11.4   A single deployment stack can span multiple resource groups and subscriptions.

actual resource cannot be changed, so new resources will be created and old ones will be removed.

11.1.3 Creating a deployment stack

To start exploring deployment stacks, let's create a stack with a service bus namespace and a queue, as shown in the following listing.

Listing 11.1   Deploying a template stack

```
{
    "$schema": "https://schema.management.azure.com/schemas/
        ➥ 2019-04-01/deploymentTemplate.json#",
    "contentVersion": "1.0.0.0",
    "resources": [
        {
            "name": "messagingStack",
            "type": "Microsoft.Resources/deploymentStacks",
            "apiVersion": "2021-05-01-preview",
            "properties": {
                "updateBehavior": "detachResources",
                "template": {
                    "$schema": "https://schema.management.azure.com
                        ➥ /schemas/2019-04-01/deploymentTemplate.json#",
                    "contentVersion": "1.0.0.0",
                    "resources": [
                        {
                            "name": "messaging-example-stack",
                            "type": "Microsoft.ServiceBus/namespaces",
```

The new resource type for deployment stacks ⟶

The resources in a stack are described using an ARM template. ⟶

```
                "apiVersion": "2021-01-01-preview",
                "location": "[resourceGroup().location]",
                "sku": {
                    "name": "Standard"
                },
                "resources": [
                    {
                        "name": "exampleQueue",
                        "type": "queues",
                        "apiVersion": "2021-01-01-preview",
                        "dependsOn": [
                            "[resourceId('Microsoft.ServiceBus/
                                namespaces',
                                'messaging-example-stack')]"
                        ]
                    }
                ]
            }
        ]
    }
}
```

In this template you'll see a new resource type being used, `deploymentStacks`, which creates the deployment stack.

Deployment stacks have two type-specific properties: `updateBehavior` and `template`. The `updateBehavior` property is only used when you're updating a stack, so that will be discussed in the next section. The value for the `template` property is a nested template that should describe the resources that are part of the stack: in this case, a service bus namespace and a queue within that namespace.

If you deploy this template to any resource group, you will see that both the namespace and the queue are created as declared. Now, let's explore what happens when you update the stack.

11.1.4 *Updating a deployment stack*

Continuing on with the template that declares a service bus queue, let's assume the name of the queue has to be updated from `exampleQueue` to `betterExampleQueue`, due to changing requirements within the organization. If you make this change and deploy the template again, you will see that a new queue with the name `betterExample-Queue` is created, but the original `exampleQueue` queue is not removed.

This might not be what you expected, given that we introduced deployment stacks as a mechanism for automatically removing resources that are no longer part of the stack. To understand what is going on, let's take a closer look at the `updateBehavior` property. This property determines what should be done with resources that are no longer described in the stack, and it can have two values:

- detachResources—When this value is set, resources are not removed (as you have already seen) but are only detached from the stack. This behavior is very similar to the incremental nature of normal deployments.
- purgeResources—When this value is set, all resources that are no longer part of the stack are not only removed from the stack, but also removed from your Azure environment.

To test this, update your template again and set the value for updateBehavior to purgeResources and redeploy the template. What do you see? Do both queues still exist?

Again, you might be surprised that they do, but this is the correct behavior. In the second deployment you did, the first queue (exampleQueue) was removed from the stack. As a result, redeploying the same stack with updateBehavior=purgeResources did not detect the resource as missing from the stack declaration, so it did not remove the resource from Azure.

Now make a fourth and final change to your template: rename the queue for a second time and call it finalExampleQueue. If you redeploy the template one more time, you will see the expected behavior, where finalExampleQueue is created, and betterExampleQueue is removed.

To better understand what you have seen, take a look at figure 11.5. Here you see how, at first, the contents of the resource group are the same as described in the initial stack deployment. Next, the three consecutive updates are shown on the right, updating the resource group. You can see how the exampleQueue is detached from the stack at the first update, which is why it is not removed from the resource group during the third deployment.

11.1.5 *Removing a deployment stack*

When you delete a stack, the resources that were part of the stack are automatically detached: they are no longer part of the stack, but they are not removed from Azure. This is also the case in the last deployment, with updateBehavior set to purgeResources. If you want to also remove the resources, you will have to do two deployments:

1 First, deploy the stack again with updateBehavior set to purgeResources and with an empty template.
2 Once the deployment of the now empty stack is complete, you can remove the stack itself.

> NOTE   This is the behavior at the time of writing and will change in the future. The final design for deployment stacks will allow you to specify either detach or purge behavior. However, it is not yet known when this will be released.

Now that you have created, updated and deleted a deployment stack, let's take a look at another important use case that you can use deployment stacks for, namely locking resources.

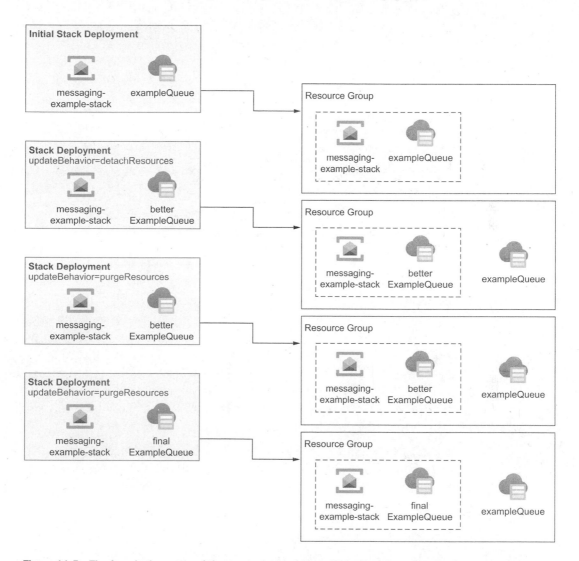

Figure 11.5   **The four deployments of the same stack and how they affect the resources in a resource group**

11.2   *Provisioning resources for others, but disallowing updates*

Imagine you are working in the central cloud team for a large organization. One of your responsibilities is providing all decentralized application teams with connectivity to the central network. In Azure you can do this using a *hub-and-spoke network*, which is an architecture where each decentralized team gets its own vnet, called a *spoke*, which is peered with a single central network, called the *hub*. It would look something like figure 11.6.

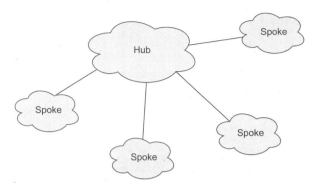

**Figure 11.6   Hub-and-spoke
network architecture**

Of course, you'll want to decide on the IP ranges for the vnets that you create for the application teams, and you'll want to deny them from changing those. But application teams should have visibility into the vnet configuration and be able to connect VMs and private endpoints to the vnet. The question is, how do you authorize others to work with a resource, yet deny them the authorization to change it?

11.2.1 Azure Blueprints: A first solution

In Azure there is an existing solution for this type of problem: Azure Blueprints. Blueprints are another syntax for IaC on Azure that you can use to describe a group of resource groups, role assignments, policy assignments, or ARM templates. A group of one or more of these resource descriptions can be combined into a single blueprint.

> **NOTE**   This discussion of Blueprints is a high-level overview on purpose. Blueprints is available in Azure today, but it has been announced that they will be replaced in the future. For that reason, we won't discuss Blueprints in depth.

Once you have written a blueprint, you can deploy it to Azure to create an initial version of the blueprint definition. Any subsequent deployment of an updated blueprint will create a new version of the blueprint.

To use a blueprint version, you assign it to a subscription. This assignment invokes the creation of all the resources described in the blueprint and the deployment of the ARM templates in the blueprint. If the blueprint specifies one or more parameters, the values for these parameters will have to be provided at the time of the assignment. Figure 11.7 shows how these concepts are related.

The first time you deploy a new blueprint into Azure, you actually create two resources: the blueprint itself, and the first blueprint version. During subsequent updates, you don't change what already exists, but only add new versions of the blueprint. This is useful if you have tens or even hundreds of blueprint assignments. An assignment is for a specific version, so you can upgrade your assignments whenever you want, instead of having an enforced update due to a change in the blueprint

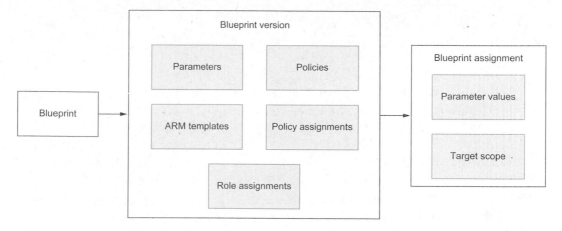

Figure 11.7   Blueprint definitions, versions, and assignments

definition. Just like a template, a blueprint can specify one or more parameters, for which values have to be provided as part of the assignment.

A common use case for blueprints is provisioning a virtual network to subscriptions, and connecting that to a central, organization-wide network. In such a situation, you would create a blueprint that creates a resource group, deploys a vnet into that resource group, and peers it to the central network.

But this solves only half of the problem: provisioning resources to a subscription. To solve the other half of the problem, blueprints offer one specific property that ARM templates and Bicep do not: a blueprint assignment can be locked. This is not a resource lock that you can apply to any resource. Instead, these locks protect all the resources that were created by the blueprint assignment from being updated or deleted, and they can only be removed by specific users.

It sounds like a wonderful solution, right? But here comes the catch: Azure Blueprints is still in preview, and it has been so for years. More recently, it has been announced that Azure Blueprints will never be formally released. Instead, deployment stacks will be enhanced with blueprint-like locking functionality so you can deploy resources to be used by others.

This will pose a challenge for you when you are in need of the functionality provided by Blueprints or deployment stacks, as you will have to choose between using a technology that you know will disappear or choosing a technology that is not fully mature yet. Which option is best will differ from context to context. If you decide you need to start using Azure Blueprints, you can read more about it in Microsoft's "What is Azure Blueprints?" article (http://mng.bz/Pn18).

Finally, it is important to know that the Product Group plans to deliver functionality for converting blueprints into deployment stacks in the future. It is not yet known whether this will be a manual or automated process.

11.3   *The future of deployment stacks*

When we were writing this chapter, deployment stacks were still in private preview. Preview means that the technology's implementation details might still change between us writing and you reading this chapter. Also, the capabilities of deployment stacks will continue to grow while the Product Group continues to work on the feature. If you want to keep getting the latest regarding deployment stacks, keep an eye on Microsoft Learn, the Azure Blog, or the GitHub repository accompanying this book.

Summary

- You can use deployment stacks for grouping resources across different resource groups and even subscriptions.
- Locking a deployment stack prevents users from updating or deleting any resource that is part of the stack, even if they have the correct authorizations on the resource.
- Azure Blueprints will be deprecated in the future, and there will be functionality for converting existing blueprints into deployment stacks.
- Deployment stacks are still under heavy development and are prone to change in the future.

Governing your subscriptions using Azure Policy

This chapter covers

- The benefits of using Azure Policy
- Using the built-in policies
- Writing, testing, and deploying custom policies
- Reviewing the current compliance status and improving it

All the examples and scenarios you have seen so far were relatively small. They covered mostly one application or were deployed to one or two subscriptions. When that is the case, it is straightforward to keep track of what resources you have running in Azure and to make sure that your solution is secure, compliant, and cost-effective. When your cloud workload gets bigger, that is much harder to do. Luckily, Azure has a built-in feature called Azure Policy that can help you govern your Azure resources, and you can use Azure Policy with Infrastructure as Code, which is then often called Policy as Code. In this chapter, you will learn how to use Azure Policy to govern Azure architectures.

Imagine you work at an enterprise organization that wants to make the move to the Azure cloud. Currently, all the teams run their applications and infrastructure in one or more on-premises data centers. What is often done in such a

275

situation is that you build something called a *landing zone* in Azure and use a hub and spoke architecture.

When explaining the concept of the Azure landing zone, it is useful to compare it to building a home. If you want to build a new home, you could choose to do everything yourself: dig the foundations, lay the bricks, and do all the plumbing. The same goes for the Azure Cloud. You could start to build the infrastructure manually, yourself, but as with a house, you might find that this is very time consuming, and you would risk making a lot of mistakes. It would be much easier to use ready-made foundations and a blueprint that shows you exactly how to do things and implement best practices. You could still customize the structure to meet your personal needs, but the building would be architecturally sound, safe, and faster to build. An Azure landing zone is exactly like that. It covers the network architecture, security, identity, and governance, allowing DevOps teams to start building right away on a perfectly laid-out foundation.

Landing zones are often implemented using a hub and spoke architecture. In this type of architecture, you have a central hub. The network in the hub acts as a central point of connectivity to on-premises resources for many spoke virtual networks, as shown in figure 12.1. You might also find other resources in the hub that are shared amongst spokes, like and Azure Firewall or Log Analytics for central log management.

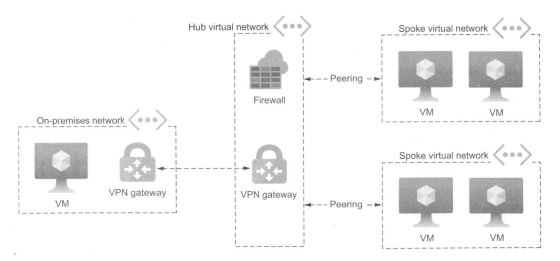

Figure 12.1   Hub and spoke architecture

In the middle of figure 12.1, you'll find the hub virtual network. It contains the resources needed to provide connectivity to the on-premises network on the left. That connection is often established using a VPN gateway or an Azure ExpressRoute. The connection in the hub network can then be used by multiple spokes, as shown on the right. Each spoke virtual network holds one workload, and the spokes allow you to isolate your workloads from those of the other teams. In spokes, you can run, for example, virtual machines (VMs), Azure web apps, and databases. More information on Azure landing zones and the hub and spoke architecture can be found in Microsoft's "What is an Azure landing zone?" article (http://mng.bz/R4AR).

The hub and all the spokes are often hosted in their own Azure subscriptions. This means that each workload gets at least two subscriptions: one for the production workload, and one for the non-production workload. When building a hub and spoke architecture, the number of subscriptions and resources that you need to manage can grow quickly. It becomes harder and harder to oversee what resources are used and how those resources are configured. For example, you might want to make sure that when a storage account is created, it is only accessible over HTTPS, or that you can never open the SSH port to the internet. You might want to prevent certain resources from being used or make sure they can only be created in certain Azure regions. You might want to ensure that every VM that is created in any spoke always has a backup policy defined. But how can you do that?

Throughout this chapter, you will learn how to use Azure Policy to govern resources and enforce standards like the examples just mentioned. But first, let's take a closer look at what policies are.

12.1 Azure Policy

Policies in Azure help you to enforce standards and assess compliance with standards in your environment. Its compliance dashboard gives you an aggregated view of the overall status of the environment. The dashboard also enables you to drill down to check the compliance status of individual resources. Policies are often used to implement use cases such as governance for resource consistency, regulatory compliance, security, cost, and management. A lot of policies for common use cases are built in, but you can also write your own. You will see examples of both throughout this chapter.

When working with policies, you will work with three resource types in Azure: policy definitions, initiatives, and assignments. Policies are defined in what is called a *policy definition*. Policies can be assigned to a scope, which you do using a *policy assignment resource*. You often, however, assign multiple policies as a group using the *initiative resource*. All these resources can be created using either an ARM template or a Bicep file.

On the left of figure 12.2, you'll see multiple policies defined. Policies are often grouped into an initiative, as shown in the middle, and that initiative is then assigned to a particular scope. The scope dictates where the policies apply. Let's dive into more detail on each of these concepts.

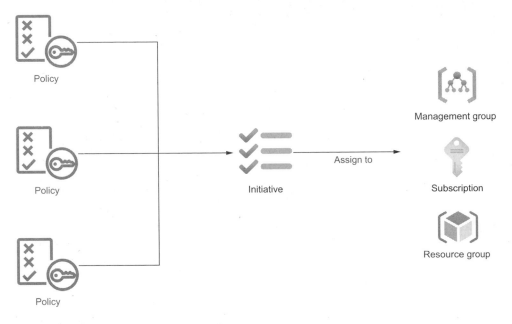

Figure 12.2   Policies, initiatives, and assignments

12.1.1   *Policy definitions*

Policy definitions contain the business rules you want to enforce. Azure Policy evaluates and compares your resources to those rules, and whenever the outcome of the evaluation does not match an expected result, a policy can trigger various effects.

Let's examine one of the built-in policies (you'll learn more about built-in policies in section 12.2) to see what a policy looks like and how it works. The following listing shows the definition for the Allowed Locations policy using Bicep (12-01.bicep).

Listing 12.1   Deny policy based on location

```
resource allowedLocations 'Microsoft.Authorization/
    ➥ policyDefinitions@2020-09-01' = {
  name: 'Allowed locations'
  properties: {
    policyType: 'BuiltIn'
    displayName: 'Allowed locations'
    description: 'This policy enables you to restrict the locations ...'
    metadata: {
        version: '1.0.0'
        category: 'General'
    }
    mode: 'Indexed'
    parameters: {
        'listOfAllowedLocations': {
            type: 'Array'
            metadata: {
```

```
                    description: 'The list of locations that can
                        ⇒ be specified when deploying resources.'
                    strongType: 'location'
                    displayName: 'Allowed locations'
                }
            }
        }
        policyRule: {          ◁────┤  The policyRule is the business
            if: {                    │  logic of the policy.
                allOf: [
                    {
                        field: 'location'
                        notIn: '[parameters(\'listOfAllowedLocations\')]'
                    }
                    {
                        field: 'location'
                        notEquals: 'global'
                    }
                    {
                        field: 'type'
                        notEquals: 'Microsoft.AzureActiveDirectory/b2cDirectories'
                    }
                ]
            }
            then: {
                effect: 'Deny'      ◁────┤  The effect that's applied
            }                            │  when the policy evaluates
        }                               │  to true
    }
}
```

This definition might look a bit overwhelming at first, introducing a lot of new terminology. For now, it's enough to learn about the basic structure. We'll walk through the details in section 12.3, where you'll learn how to create your own policies.

The business rules of the policy can be found in the `policyRule` section. That is like the query part of the definition. In this example, an `if` statement is used with multiple comparison expressions grouped in the `allOf`. All these statements are evaluated and shown in the output after evaluation, even if the first one, for example, fails.

The first comparison in the `allOf` uses a parameter. That allows you to make the policies more generic and reuse them easily. When the policy evaluates to `true`, the `effect`, as defined in the `then` section will be applied. In this example, the `Deny` effect is used. As the name implies, the deployment will be denied and therefore cancelled. There are six other effects to choose from: `Append`, `Audit`, `AuditIfNotExists`, `DeployIfNotExists`, `Disabled`, and `Modify`. You will read more about them when you learn how to write your own policy definitions in section 12.4.

The evaluation of a policy happens at different times:

- Whenever you create, update, or deleted a resource
- When a policy or initiative is assigned or updated

- During the standard compliance evaluation cycle, which happens every 24 hours
- When you trigger it manually, which you will learn how to do later

12.1.2 *Initiatives or policy sets*

Assigning individual policies is not very convenient—it means a lot of administration. You will often want to group policies together and assign them in one go. Such a group is called an *initiative*, or a *policy set*.

An initiative has a name, a description, and a list of policies. The following listing shows a simple initiative that contains the policy that was created in the previous section (12-02.bicep).

Listing 12.2   A sample initiative

```
targetScope = 'managementGroup'

param managementGroupName string

module allowedLocationsPolicyDefinition '12-01.bicep' = {
    name: 'allowedLocationsPolicyDefinition'
}

resource initiative 'Microsoft.Authorization/
    policySetDefinitions@2020-09-01' = {
  name: managementGroupName
  properties: {
    description: 'Definition set for management group
        \'${managementGroupName}\''
    policyDefinitions: [              <--- The policyDefinitions array
      {                                    contains the policies.
        policyDefinitionId:
            allowedLocationsPolicyDefinition.outputs.policyDefinitionId
      }
    ]
  }
}
```

The preceding example creates an initiative with just one policy in it, but as you can see, the policyDefinitions property is an array and can contain more. This array is filled with the resource IDs of the policy definitions you want to use. In Bicep, its quite easy to get that by using an output parameter, as shown in this example.

12.1.3 *Assignment*

Now that you have seen what a policy definition looks like and how you can group them into initiatives, you'll need to put them into action by assigning them. Assigning a policy to a scope means that the policy will be enforced on that scope, where a scope can be a resource group, subscription, or management group. When talking about an assignment, it is important to know about two types of scopes: the location of the definition, and the scope on the assignment.

DEFINITION LOCATION

A policy definition or initiative can either be deployed to a management group or to a subscription. This location sort of "maximizes" the scope to which the definition or initiative can be assigned. This means that when you deploy the policy (or initiative) definition to a subscription, you can only assign it to resources in that subscription. If you deploy it to a management group, you can assign it to any child management group or subscriptions in that management group.

Figure 12.3 shows that when you deploy a policy to the management group named Spokes, you can then assign the policy to that management group or to any of the subscriptions in it. You cannot assign it anywhere else. Not to the management group higher up in the tree, or to the Hub management group on the same level, or the Hub's children. Depending on where you want to assign the policy, you will need to deploy it appropriately in the subscription and management group hierarchy.

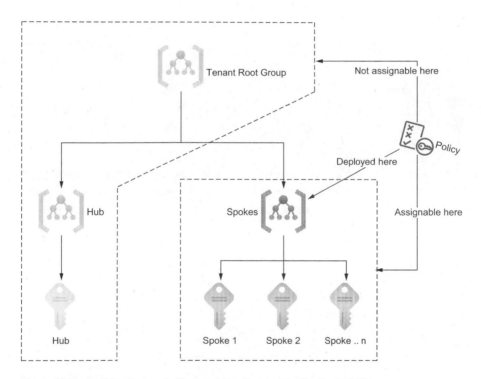

Figure 12.3   Policies have a deployment location and assignment scope.

ASSIGNMENT SCOPE

Now let's talk about the second scope that is important when using policies. When you assign a policy or an initiative to a particular scope, that assignment applies the policy on all resources on that scope and every scope below it. When you build a hub and spoke architecture like the one introduced at the beginning of the chapter, you'll often start by designing your management group and subscription layout. A very simple outcome is shown in figure 12.4.

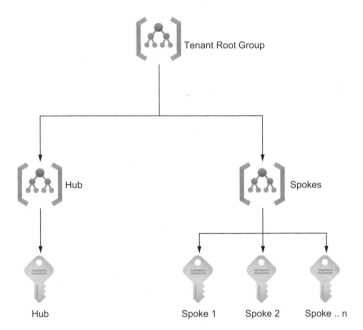

Figure 12.4   Small management group and subscription model

At the top of figure 12.4, you see the root management group that exists by default. Below that, two other management groups were created—one for the hub and one for the future spokes. In each of those management groups you'll find one or more subscriptions.

The reasons for such a hierarchy are often twofold: you can set permissions at the correct level and also assign policies at the correct level. For example, you may have policies that should apply to every resource you create, no matter the scope, such as the allowed locations policy you saw earlier. That would be an ideal candidate to assign at the Tenant Root Group management group level. Other policies or initiatives might only need to have an effect on a lower scope. You could, for example, want to assign policies that apply to all spokes but not to resources in the hub. You would assign those on the Spokes management group, as shown in figure 12.5. Assigning a policy or initiative on the Spokes management group makes it effective on all resources deployed at that scope and every subscription in it.

In Azure, a policy assignment is also modeled as a resource. To assign the initiative shown in listing 12.2, the Bicep template shown in listing 12.3 could be used (12-03.bicep).

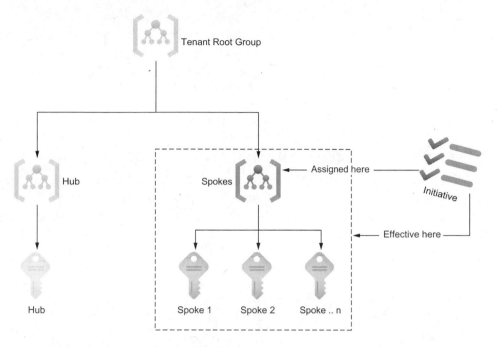

Figure 12.5   The effective scope of an assignment

Listing 12.3   A sample assignment

```
targetScope = 'managementGroup'

param managementGroupName string
param policySetName string

var managementGroupScope = '/providers/Microsoft.Management/
    ➥ managementGroups/${managementGroupName}'

resource initiativeAssignment
    ➥ 'Microsoft.Authorization/policyAssignments@2020-09-01' = {
    name: managementGroupName
    location: 'westeurope'
    properties:{
        description: 'The assignment of the policy set definition
    ➥ \'${policySetName}\' to management group \'${managementGroupName}\''
        policyDefinitionId:
    ➥ '${managementGroupScope}/providers/Microsoft.Authorization/
    ➥ policySetDefinitions/${policySetName}'
    }
}
```

> The policyDefinitionId defines the
> policy or initiative to assign.

This template has two parameters: one for the management group name to which the
initiative has been deployed (the deployment location), and another for the name of

that initiative, in the form of the `policySetName`. The resource that is deployed is of type `Microsoft.Authorization/policyAssignments`, and the scope on which you deploy it will dictate where it should have effect. In our example, you deploy this to the Spokes management group, as shown in figure 12.5, whereas the initiative itself, shown in listing 12.2, has been deployed to that same scope or to the Tenant Root Group, as shown in figure 12.3. Before you learn how to create your own policies, let's first see what Azure provides you out of the box.

12.2   *Examining the built-in policies and initiatives*

Open a browser, go to the Azure portal, and find the policy overview using the menu or by searching for "policy" in the search bar at the top. You will be taken to the Policy overview that shows your current compliance status. The compliancy status is an over-all score that shows you how well your Azure resources comply with all active policies. You will learn more about that in section 12.7. For now, navigate to the Definitions section using the button on the left, as highlighted in figure 12.6.

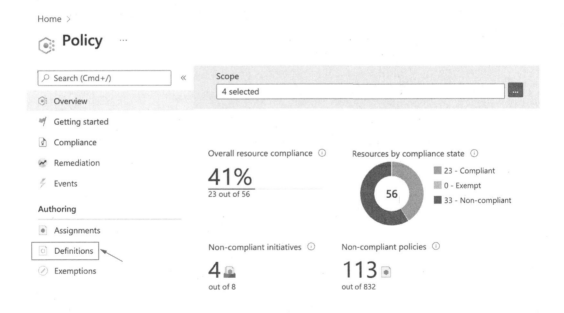

Figure 12.6   The Azure Policy dashboard with the Definitions button

You will be taken to the policy definition overview (figure 12.7). It shows a list of all the built-in and custom-created policies and initiatives. Whether an item is built-in or custom is shown in the Type column. When an item is custom, you will find its defini-tion location in the second column. That can help you to determine which assignment

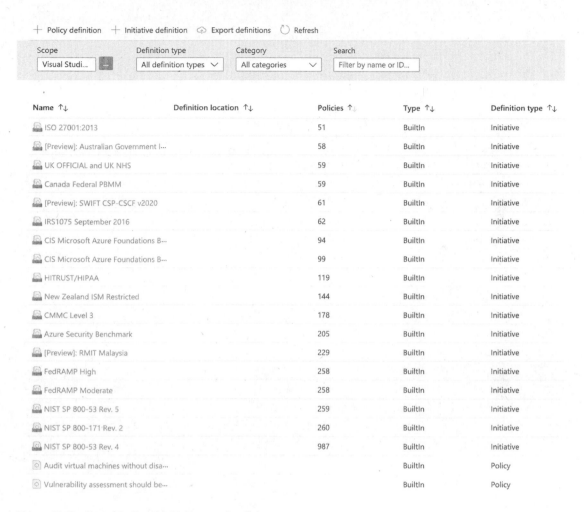

Figure 12.7 A sample list of initiatives and policies

scope you can use. The Definition Type column tells you if an item in the list is an initiative or a policy.

The list of built-in policies and initiatives is quite long, as you'll see when you scroll through it. In section 12.5 you'll see how you can use one of the built-in policies in your own custom assignments or initiatives. In the list of initiatives, you might recognize a few familiar compliance standards, like ISO 27001. Clicking on one of the initiatives will show you the list of included policies, and then clicking on one of the policies will show you its details, as in figure 12.8.

The name and description will help you figure out what the policy can do for you. Some policies can be used with different effects, which you can set when assigning the policy. The policy in figure 12.8 can be used with a `Disabled` or `AuditIfNotExists`

Figure 12.8   The details of a policy, including its definition

effect, as shown in the Available Effects property. When you want to use this policy in a custom initiative, you will need the Definition ID shown at the top right, which is the unique identifier for this policy. The policy rule of the definition is shown in JSON format. When you create your own policies, it is often helpful to find a policy that does more or less what you are looking for and then copy this JSON. You can then modify it to meet your needs.

You might want to create your own policy if you have a requirement that cannot be met by an out-of-the-box policy. The following section shows you how to do that.

12.3   Using custom policies

Although Azure Policy is already quite complete, and new policies are added frequently, you can still run into situations where you want to add one or more custom policies. Before you do, though, it's best to think about it for a moment and make sure you understand the parts involved. A custom policy is "just" another Azure resource and a policy assignment is also "just" another resource. This means that you can create resources that assign resources to govern other resources. How about that? This can be hard to grasp, and if you're struggling with this idea, it might be wise to re-read section 12.1 and study figure 12.5 a bit more.

12.3.1   Creating a custom policy

Imagine that your team is working with the hub and spoke architecture from the introduction, and they want to run a SQL Server on Azure. You want to make sure that the SQL Server is not accessible over the internet, but only via a private network. A SQL Server has a single property called `publicNetworkAccess` that you can set to either `Enabled` or `Disabled` to make it publicly available or not. Your goal is to create a policy that looks for that property and ensures it is set to `Disabled`. Otherwise, you deny the deployment.

To do this, open VS Code and create a new Bicep file called denyAnySqlServer-AccessFromInternet.bicep. Set the `targetScope` to `subscription` and add the basic policy definition structure. You can do that by using the built-in templates in VS Code. Unfortunately, there is no default for a `Deny` policy, but the `Audit` one comes close. Type `pol` and pick `res-policy-definition-audit-effect` from the list, or copy and paste the following example.

> **Listing 12.4   The policy definition structure**

```
targetScope = 'subscription'

resource policyDefinition 'Microsoft.Authorization/
    ⮕ policyDefinitions@2020-09-01' = {
  name: 'name'
  properties: {
    displayName: 'displayName'
    policyType: 'Custom'
    mode: 'All'                         ◁──  Switch between resources
    description: 'description'               that do or do not have
    metadata: {                              tags and location.
      version: '0.1.0'
      category: 'category'
    }
    parameters: {            ◁──  Using parameters
      parameterName: {            makes the definition
        type: 'String'            reusable.
        defaultValue: 'defaultValue'
        metadata: {
          displayName: 'displayName'
```

```
                    description: 'description'
                }
            }
        }
        policyRule: {                    ┌────────────────────────────┐
            if: {         ◁──────────────┤ Different logical
                allOf: [                 │ operators can be used
                    {                    │ to create the logic.
                        field: 'field'   └────────────────────────────┘
                        equals: 'conditionValue'
                    }
                    {
                        field: 'field'
                        equals: 'conditionValue'
                    }


                ]
            }
            then: {
                effect: 'Audit'
            }
        }
    }
}
```

Let's work through this basic structure of the preceding listing to understand each property. The `name` here is the name of the resource, just as in any other Bicep resource. The `displayName` is used when showing the definition in contexts such as the Azure portal. The `description` field allows you to explain the policy to your users in one or more sentences. The `policyType` allows you to indicate that the policy you are creating is a custom policy, for which the only valid value is `Custom`.

The `mode` property allows you to specify which resources to target. Some resources in Azure do not allow you to set the location, tags, or both. Setting the mode to `Indexed` makes the policy skip the evaluation of resources that do not have the location or tags properties. Setting it to `All` causes the policy to evaluate all resources.

A `metadata` object allows you to set additional information on the definition, like a version or category. The `category` is used to group policies in the portal and other interfaces.

The definition allows you to use `parameters`. They work and operate the same way as in ARM templates. You can also use the same types. Using parameters, you can make your definitions more flexible and usable in more situations. In this example, you could use a parameter for the `publicNetworkAccess` value you would like to set.

The most important part of the definition is, without a doubt, the `policyRule` section. This is where you define the business logic of the policy. The rules you define must always lead to a `true` or `false` result. The `policyRule` is the selector that determines which resources the policy applies to. Finally, you define what you want to do with a noncompliant resource by setting the `effect` in the `then` section of the `policyRule`.

A definition for your requirement on the SQL Server's public accessibility could look like the following listing (12-04.bicep).

Listing 12.5 A custom policy definition

```
targetScope = 'subscription'

resource denyAnySqlServerAccessFromInternet
    'Microsoft.Authorization/policyDefinitions@2019-09-01' = {
  name: 'denyAnySqlServerAccessFromInternet'
  properties: {
    displayName: 'Deny Any SQL Server Access from the Internet'
    policyType: 'Custom'
    mode: 'All'
    description: 'Deny Any SQL Server Access from the Internet IP address'
    metadata: {
      version: '1.0.0'
      category: 'SQL Server'
    }
    parameters: {
      effect: {                    ◁─── A parameter is
        type: 'String'                  used to set the
        allowedValues: [                effect.
          'Audit'
          'Deny'
          'Disabled'
        ]
        defaultValue: 'Deny'
      }
    }
    policyRule: {
      if: {                        allOf is an operator
        allOf: [             ◁──┘  that allows for more
          {                        than one expression.
            field: 'type'
            equals: 'Microsoft.Sql/servers'
          }
          {
            field: 'Microsoft.Sql/servers/publicNetworkAccess'
            notEquals: 'Disabled'
          }
        ]
      }
      then: {
        effect: '[parameters(\'effect\')]'
      }
    }
  }
}
```

This policy has one parameter defined that allows you to set the effect of the policy. The `allowedValues` property on that parameter shows that three effects can be used.

The policy rule defines two conditions that resources have to meet before this policy applies to them. First, the type of the source should be `Microsoft.Sql/servers`. Second, the value for `Microsoft.Sql/servers/publicNetworkAccess` should be `Disabled`. If both these conditions evaluate to `true`, hence the `allOf`, then the effect is applied.

Now that you have written your first policy, it is time to see it in action. To do that, you need to deploy the definition and then assign it to a particular scope. Use the following Azure CLI command to deploy the Bicep file that contains the definition:

```
az deployment sub create --template-file
    ➡ denyAnySqlServerAccessFromInternet.bicep -l westeurope
```

This example uses the regular syntax to deploy the definition, as it is just a standard Bicep file. You can deploy it to the current subscription, making that subscription the `definition location`, which if you remember, dictates where you can assign it. To assign this definition, you can use the following Azure CLI command:

```
az policy assignment create --name sqlPolicyAssignment -policy
    ➡ "denyAnySqlServerAccessFromInternet"
```

This command uses `policy assignment create` to assign the previously created definition and uses `sqlPolicyAssignment` as its name. When you don't specify a scope for the assignment, like in this example, the scope defaults to the deployment scope. If you have currently selected a subscription in the Azure CLI's context, that becomes the scope of the assignment. You can specify a different scope using the `--scope` parameter if you need to. Later on, you will learn how to do the assignment using Bicep. Now that the definition is deployed and assigned, it is time to test the policy.

12.3.2 *Testing a policy*

You obviously need to test the policy before you assign it to a scope in which resources are used by others. What you can do is create a separate subscription that is used to verify policies. Verifying policies can be done in multiple ways.

One option is to use the Policy extension in Visual Studio Code. For more information on how to install and configure this extension, see Microsoft's "Use Azure Policy extension for Visual Studio Code" article (http://mng.bz/2nWo). This extension will, for now, only work on Windows. After it's installed, and you start this extension, you will see that it has three sections to work with: Resources, Policies, and Evaluation. When you want to use the extension to evaluate a policy, you'll need to select an item from each of these sections.

You first select the resource against which you want to evaluate your policy. In this example, you are writing a policy for a SQL Server, so you select a SQL Server in the resources section of the extension. Navigate to it by opening the right subscription and resource group, and select it using the pin icon on the right (see figure 12.9).

In the next section, the Policies window, select the assignment in which your definition is used. In this example, that is the `sqlPolicyAssignment` assignment that you created in the previous section. You can then select the actual definition. In this example, it is the `denyAnySqlServerAccessFromInternet` policy that you deployed in the previous section. You select both using the pin icons on their right.

The three selected resources will have been added to the bottom pane of the Evaluation section of the window. Click the checkmark icon to the right of each of them to include them in your selection. Your selection should resemble figure 12.9.

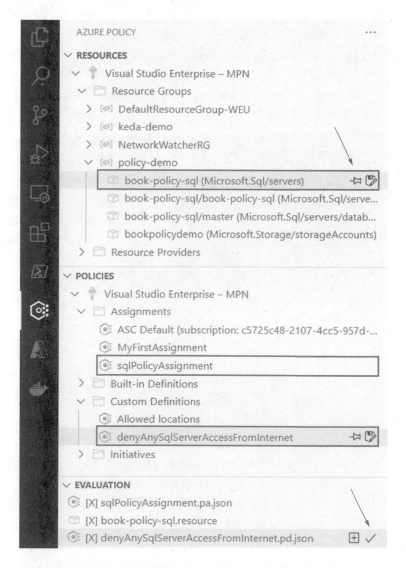

Figure 12.9   The VS Code Policy extension used to run a policy

Now that you have selected the resource, the assignment, and the definition, you can run the evaluation using the play button in the Evaluation bar. The result will open in a new pane on the right, and it will look something like the following JSON.

Listing 12.6   The policy evaluation result

```
{
    "policyEvaluations": [
        {
            "policyInfo": {
                "policyDefinitionId": "/subscriptions/
➡ c5725c48-2107-4cc5-957d-d800701b0705/providers/
➡ Microsoft.Authorization/policyDefinitions/
➡ Deny Any SQL Server Access from the Internet",
                "policyDefinitionName": "Deny Any SQL
                    ➡ Server Access from the Internet",
                "policyDefinitionDisplayName":
                    ➡ "denyAnySqlServerAccessFromInternet",
                "policyDefinitionVersion": "1.0.0",
                "policyDefinitionEffect": "Deny",
                "policyAssignmentId": "/subscriptions/
➡ c5725c48-2107-4cc5-957d-d800701b0705/providers/
➡ Microsoft.Authorization/policyAssignments/sqlPolicyAssignment",
                "policyAssignmentName": "sqlPolicyAssignment",
                "policyAssignmentScope": "/subscriptions/
                    ➡ c5725c48-2107-4cc5-957d-d800701b0705",
                "policyAssignmentParameters": {},
                "policyAssignmentEnforcementMode": "Default",
                "policyExemptionIds": []
            },
            "evaluationResult": "NonCompliant",      ⟵  The result of the
            "evaluationDetails": {                        evaluation, either
                "evaluatedExpressions": [                 Compliant or
                    {                                     NonCompliant
                        "result": "True",
                        "expressionKind": "Field",
                        "expression": "type",
                        "path": "type",
                        "expressionValue": "Microsoft.Sql/servers",
                        "targetValue": "Microsoft.Sql/servers",
                        "operator": "Equals"
                    },
                    {
                        "result": "True",
                        "expressionKind": "Field",
                        "expression":
➡ "Microsoft.Sql/servers/publicNetworkAccess",
                        "path": "properties.publicNetworkAccess",
                        "expressionValue": "******",
                        "targetValue": "Disabled",
                        "operator": "NotEquals"
                    }
                ]
            },
```

Detailed results of each expression →

```
        "effectDetails": {
            "policyEffect": "Deny",
            "existenceScope": "None"
        }
    }
],
"modifiedFields": [],
"messages": [
    "EventServiceEntry/subscriptions/
    c5725c48-2107-4cc5-957d-d800701b0705/resourceGroups/
    policy-demo/providers/Microsoft.Sql/servers/book-policy-sql",
    "DebugDuration (ms): 34, Info: RequestType: 'Validation',
ResourceType: 'Microsoft.Sql/servers', Containers: '1',
ContainersToEvaluate: '1', GotFullResourceContent: 'False',
GotTrackedContent: 'False', AltCompanionPort: 'False'",
    "Debug<null>"
]
}
```

There are two important parts to this result. The first is the `evaluationResult` property. For this example, that returns `NonCompliant` because the SQL Server was created with public access enabled. The second interesting part here is the `evaluationDetails` array that lists the results of the individual evaluation expressions. The example definition has two, so there are two results here. These results allow you to easily identify whether the `evaluationResult` is as expected and why the evaluation came to this result.

You can get a similar experience when creating a new resource through the Azure portal while the policy is effective. If you are about to create a resource that violates the policy, you will receive a validation error, as shown in figure 12.10.

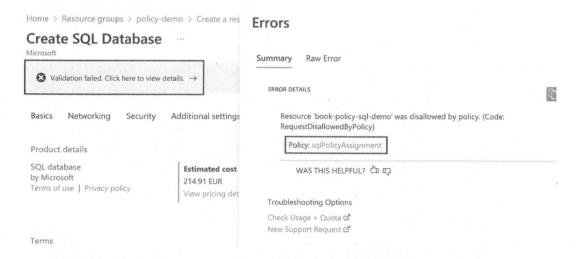

Figure 12.10   A policy error in the Azure portal while creating a resource

When you click on the validation error, you'll see which policy assignment was violated, on the right. When you click on the Raw Error link, you'll get a JSON result similar to listing 12.6.

The example in this section used the Deny effect. There are a few other effects that you can use, so let's learn more about them.

12.4   Using the different effects

Policies can use the following effects: Append, Audit, AuditIfNotExists, Deny, DeployIfNotExists, Disabled, or Modify. Remember, the effect is the thing that you want the policy to do whenever it finds a matching resource. Let's look at each of them to learn what it can do and what the syntax looks like.

12.4.1   Append effect

An often used resource in Azure is a storage account. You can imagine that in a hub and spoke architecture with a lot of spokes, there will be a lot of storage accounts. It would therefore be useful to create a policy that will add a default firewall rule. That will make the use of the storage account type more secure and compliant by default, since you limit its exposure. When you assign a policy with this rule to the Spokes management group in this chapter's scenario, you will ensure that no spoke can ever create a storage account without it.

The Append effect can be used to accomplish this goal. Append is used to add additional fields to the resource that is created or updated. It does that when the if condition in the policy rule is met. When the field you append already exists, but with a different value, the Append effect acts as a Deny effect, so the deployment will fail. The following listing shows an example of a policy with the Append effect (12-05.bicep).

Listing 12.7   A policy definition with the Append effect

```
targetScope = 'subscription'

resource appendIpToStorageFirewall 'Microsoft.Authorization/
    ➥ policyDefinitions@2020-09-01' = {
  name: 'appendIpToStorageFirewall'
  properties: {
    policyType: 'Custom'
    displayName: 'Ensure the storage account has a firewall rule'
    description: 'Add an IP address to the storage accounts firewall'
    metadata: {
      version: '1.0.0'
      category: 'Network Security'
    }
    mode: 'All'
    policyRule: {
      if: {
        field: 'type'
        equals: 'Microsoft.Storage/storageAccounts'
      }
```

```
                then: {
                    effect: 'Append'
                    details: [
                        {
    The value  ┌────▷    field: 'Microsoft.Storage/storageAccounts/
   for "field" │              ➡ networkAcls.ipRules[*]'
   is an alias.│         value: {
                            value: '40.40.40.40'
                            action: 'Allow'
                        }
                    }
                ]
            }
        }
    }
}
```

The `Append` effect has a mandatory `details` array. The preceding example contains one entry, but it can take multiple field/value pairs if you need them. This example adds a new row to the firewall ruleset of a storage account. The `ipRules` property used here is an array, and in this example, you can see the `[*]` notation being used. This means that the given value is to be added to the array. You could also use the `ipRules` property without `[*]` and provide a complete array as the value. When you do this, and the original resource already contains a non-empty array for this value, a conflict error will be thrown.

ALIASES

The value of the `field` property, `Microsoft.Storage/storageAccounts/network-Acls.ipRules[*]` in listing 12.7, is called an `alias`. You use property aliases to access specific properties for a resource type; you could see the value of the `field` property as the path to a property. Although the word *alias* might make you think that there are other ways to point to this specific property, that is not the case; you need the alias to address properties. You can find the alias for a specific property in at least two ways: use the extension in Visual Studio Code or use the Azure CLI. Using the extension, you can drill down to the resource type you want to write a policy for, as shown in figure 12.11.

In figure 12.11 you are looking for the alias on a storage account, so you drill down to it by opening the subscription, choosing Resource Providers, then Microsoft.Storage, and then selecting the storage account. A new pane with the entire resource definition in JSON will open, like the one in figure 12.12.

If you hover over the `ipRules` property, a pop-up with the aliases will show. Here you see that there are two aliases available, one with and one without `[*]`.

12.4.2 Audit effect

When your Azure landing zone with the hub and spoke architecture has been in use for a while, quite a few resources will be deployed into it. Since it is hard to come up with all the required policies when you first set up the architecture, you will want to

Figure 12.11   Using the VS Code Policy extension to find an alias

```
1   {
2     "sku": {
3       "name": "Standard_LRS",
4       "tier": "Standard"
5     },
6     "kind": "StorageV2",
7     "id": "/subscriptions/c5725c48-2107-4cc5-957d-d800701b0705/r
8     "name": "bookpolicydemo",
9     "type": "Microsoft.Storage/storageAccounts",
10    "location": "westeurope",
11    "tags": {},
12    "properties": {
13      "defaultToOAuthAuthentication": false,
14      "keyCreationTime": {
15        "key1": "2021-09-14T18:07:22.6310730Z",
16        "key2": "2021-09-14T18:07:22.6310730Z"
17      },
18      "allowCrossTenantReplication": true,
19      "privateEndpointConnections": [],
20      "minimumTlsVersion": "TLS1_2",
21      "allowBlobPublicAccess": true,
22      "a          Microsoft.Storage/storageAccounts/networkAcls.ipRules
23      "n          Microsoft.Storage/storageAccounts/networkAcls.ipRules[*]
24      "
25      "          Copy
26      "ipRules": [],
27      "defaultAction": "Allow"
28    },
```

Figure 12.12   Finding an alias while hovering over the property in the definition

create new policies after teams are onboarded onto the landing zone. It can be a good idea to create your new policies with the `Audit` effect first, and later change that to something else. This policy effect creates a warning event when evaluating a noncompliant resource, but it does not stop the resource from being created or updated. That means you can first see the policy working, and find out which already existing resources are noncompliant before blocking their deployment with another effect.

The definition of the `Audit` effect is very simple, as it does not contain any additional properties:

```
then: {
    effect: 'Audit'
}
```

Audit events are gathered and reported in dashboards, which will be discussed in section 12.7.

12.4.3   *AuditIfNotExists effect*

`AuditIfNotExists` allows you to audit a missing resource that is related to one that you are deploying. In the scenario of the hub and spoke architecture, every spoke will get its own virtual network, which will have at least one subnet. On that subnet you'll want to enforce the use of a network security group (NSG) to define what traffic is allowed in and out. You'll also want to at least audit that diagnostic settings are enabled on that NSG so you can always identify what is going on. The following policy does just that (12-06.bicep).

> **Listing 12.8   A policy definition with the `AuditIfNotExists` effect**

```
targetScope = 'subscription'

resource auditNSGwithoutLogAnalyticsEnabled 'Microsoft.Authorization/
    ➥ policyDefinitions@2020-09-01' = {
  name: 'AuditNSGwithoutLogAnalyticsEnabled'
  properties: {
    policyType: 'Custom'
    displayName: 'Log analytics should be enabled for
        ➥ Network Security Group'
    description: 'This policy requires Network Security Groups to
        ➥ have a diagnostic setting set that exports logs
        ➥ to a log analytics workspace.'
    metadata: {
      version: '1.0.0'
      category: 'Network Security'
    }
    mode: 'All'
    policyRule: {
      if: {
        field: 'type'
        equals: 'Microsoft.Network/networkSecurityGroups'
      }
```

```
              then: {
                  effect: 'AauditIfNotExists'
                  'details': {
                      'type': 'Microsoft.Insights/diagnosticSettings'
                      'existenceCondition': {
                          'allof': [
                              {
                                  'field': 'Microsoft.Insights/
                                      ➡ diagnosticSettings/metrics.enabled'
                                  'equals': 'True'
                              }
                              {
                                  'field': 'Microsoft.Insights/
                                      ➡ diagnosticSettings/logs.enabled'
                                  'equals': 'True'
                              }
                              {
                                  'field': 'Microsoft.Insights/
          diagnosticSettings/workspaceId'
                                  'exists': 'True'
                              }
                          ]
                      }
                  }
              }
          }
      }
```

Apply the effect when the statements in the existenceCondition are true.

In the `if` statement of this `policyRule`, you can see that the policy will look for type `Microsoft.Network/networkSecurityGroups`. When that is the case, the `then` will look for the related type `Microsoft.Insights/diagnosticSettings` in the `details` section and check if the `existenceCondition` on that is `true`. In this example, you want metrics or logs to be enabled, and the destination log analytics workspace should be set in the `workspaceId` property. If not, the policy will lead to an audit event. Audit events are gathered and reported in dashboards, which are discussed in section 12.7.

12.4.4 *DeployIfNotExists effect*

Like `AuditIfNotExists`, the `DeployIfNotExists` effect allows you to take action on a missing subresource, after deploying a resource. In this case, the action is not an `audit` event, but the automated deployment of another resource. This deployment is started after the related resource has been deployed successfully.

A common requirement for subscriptions, especially in the hub and spoke architecture, is to enable Microsoft Defender for specific resource types. This enhances the security and warnings on the enabled services. This gives the owner of the platform a lot of detailed insights into the security levels for all the spokes.

> **NOTE** Not too long ago, Microsoft renamed Azure Security Center to Microsoft Defender for Cloud and Azure Defender to Microsoft Defender. That's

why in some policies you'll still see references to Azure Defender or Azure
Security Center (ASC).

The following policy uses the `DeployIfNotExists` effect to enable Microsoft Defender
for storage after a new subscription has been created (12-07.bicep).

Listing 12.9   A policy definition with the `DeployIfNotExists` effect

```
targetScope = 'subscription'

resource enforceMsDefenderStoragePolicyDefinition 'Microsoft.Authorization/
 ➥ policyDefinitions@2020-09-01' = {
  name: 'msDefenderStorage_deployIfNotExists'
  properties: {
    displayName: 'Enforce Microsoft Defender for Storage'
    description: 'Enforces Microsoft Defender
       ➥ for Storage on subscriptions.'
    mode: 'All'
    policyType: 'Custom'
    policyRule: {
      if: {
        allOf: [
          {
            field: 'type'
            equals: 'Microsoft.Resources/Subscriptions'
          }
        ]
      }
      then: {
        effect: 'DeployIfNotExists'
        details: {
          type: 'Microsoft.Security/pricings'
          name: 'StorageAccounts'
          deploymentScope: 'Subscription'
          existenceScope: 'Subscription'
          roleDefinitionIds: [
            '/providers/Microsoft.Authorization/roleDefinitions/
               ➥ 8e3af657-a8ff-443c-a75c-2fe8c4bcb635'
          ]
          existenceCondition: {
            field: 'Microsoft.Security/pricings/pricingTier'
            equals: 'Standard'
          }
          deployment: {
            location: 'westeurope'
            properties: {
              mode: 'Incremental'
              template: {
                '$schema': 'https://schema.management.azure.com/
                   ➥ schemas/2015-01-01/deploymentTemplate.json#'
                contentVersion: '1.0.0.0'
                resources: [
                  {
                    type: 'Microsoft.Security/pricings'
```

Annotations:
- **deploymentScope sets where the defined template is deployed.**
- **existenceScope sets where the if section of the policy is applied.**
- **Roles needed when the template is deployed** → (points to `roleDefinitionIds`)
- **The logic for when the template should be deployed** → (points to `existenceCondition`)
- **The template that should be deployed when all evaluates to true** → (points to `template`)

```
                                    apiVersion: '2018-06-01'
                                    name: 'StorageAccounts'
                                    properties: {
                                        pricingTier: 'Standard'
                                    }
                                }
                            ]
                        }
                    }
                }
            }
        }
    }
}
```

In this `policyRule`, the `if` targets the `Microsoft.Resources/Subscriptions` type. The `details` property in the `then` contains the template that is used to deploy an additional resource when this policy is triggered. The resources to be deployed as part of the policy are specified in the `deployment` property. What you define there in the `template` property is an ARM template. In this example, that template contains one resource of type `Microsoft.Security/pricings`.

Writing that `template` section from within the Bicep file is not ideal. You don't get IntelliSense and autocompletion, for example. Instead, you can now use a new function in Bicep that allows you to load text from another file—the `template: loadText-Content()` function. You can move the contents from the `template` property in listing 12.9 into its own JSON file (securityCenterPricing.json), and then replace the original `template` entry with the following line:

```
template: loadTextContent('securityCenterPricing.json')
```

That separate file now will now be recognized as an ARM template by VS Code, making your editing experience much better. It also makes the policy much smaller and more readable (12-07-with-load-from-file.bicep).

When the `existenceCondition` evaluates to `false`, the deployment of the template is started. The `deploymentScope` accepts either `ResourceGroup` or `Subscription`, indicating a deployment at either the subscription or resource group level. Since the deployment in this example is to the subscription level, `Subscription` is set here. The `existenceScope` sets where the `if` section of the policy is applied and can be set to `ResourceGroup` or `Subscription`. Since this example needs to match the subscription type itself, this property is set to `Subscription`.

For Azure Policy to be able to deploy the template when this policy evaluates to `true`, you need to assign a managed identity to the assignment when you create it so that it can use that identity during the deployment. The `roleDefinitionIds` list in this policy specifies what roles the managed identity needs to have to be able to run the deployment in this policy. In section 12.6, when you learn how to create your own assignments using Bicep, you will also learn how to set this managed identity.

The fact that the template you specify in the policy is deployed after the initial resource has been deployed, and not during deployment, and the use of the managed identity means that you can use policies with this effect to help in edge cases other than strictly governance. In the hub and spoke architecture, for example, you'll often deploy central services like DNS and private DNS zones into the hub. Suppose that you, as a member of a spoke team, want to use and deploy a storage account into your spoke. You only want that storage account to be available over a private IP address in your own virtual network. To accomplish that, you would deploy a private link into that storage account. That, however, requires integration with the private DNS zone that was deployed centrally in the hub. You, as a spoke, do not have permissions to create your DNS record there. Using a policy could solve that problem, since you could target the private link as the resource and then create the DNS record in the template in the policy. You could then assign policy permissions to be allowed to do that. To read more on this specific scenario and implementation, read Microsoft's "Private Link and DNS integration at scale" article (http://mng.bz/1ogQ).

12.4.5   Disabled effect

The `disabled` effect allows you to pause the evaluation of a policy.

```
then: {
    effect: 'disabled'
}
```

This can be useful for testing when you parameterize the effect property in the definition, as shown in listing 12.5.

12.4.6   Modify effect

In section 12.4.1 on the `Append` effect, you read about how you could use that effect to improve the security of a storage account. Let's make that even better by using another policy to set another property on the storage account to a desired value. A storage account has a property called `allowBlobPublicAccess`. When you set that to `false`, users are required to use a form of authentication to access anything in the account—anonymous access is no longer an option.

The `Modify` effect can be used to add, update, or remove properties on a subscription, resource group, or resource. `Modify` policies are evaluated before the resource request is handed over to the resource provider. The changes that might occur because of the policy are therefore applied to the request content on the fly, when the `if` condition of the policy is met. That is different than the `DeployIfNotExists` effect, which makes its changes after the resource has been deployed by the resource provider.

Being able to modify the request and therefore the created resource is very powerful, but it's something to be wary of. The person who deploys resources to Azure might not be completely aware of all the policies that are in effect. That is especially true in the hub and spoke architecture we've been talking about in this chapter. Policies are often managed by a central team, and it might come as a surprise to someone deploying a resource that the result is different than what was defined in a template because of a policy.

The `Modify` effect might feel a bit like the `Append` effect at first, but it is much more powerful. The `Modify` effect supports three types of operations:

- `addOrReplace`—Adds the defined property or tag and its value. It even does that when the tag or property already exists with a different value. Note that this is different than the `Append` effect, which would change its effect to `deny` when trying to change a value.
- `Add`—Adds the defined property or tag and its value.
- `Remove`—Removes the defined property or tag.

With those operations, you can do the following three things:

- Add, replace, or remove tags. Remember this when you want to work with tags to set the mode of a policy to `Indexed` to exclude resources that do not have tags.
- Add or replace the managed identity on virtual machines or virtual machine scale sets.
- Add or replace values for an alias. Not all aliases can be used with the `Modify` effect—the alias needs to have a `Modifiable` attribute. You can find aliases that support this effect by using the following PowerShell command: `Get-AzPolicyAlias | Select-Object -ExpandProperty 'Aliases' | Where-Object { $_.DefaultMetadata.Attributes -eq 'Modifiable' }`.

Let's take a look at an example policy using the `Modify` effect. The following policy sets the `allowBlobPublicAccess` property on a storage account to `false` via its alias (12-08.bicep). Since that property was added in a later version of the Storage Account API, you cannot use it on older versions. Using the condition within the operation will allow you to specify that.

Listing 12.10 A policy definition with the `Modify` effect

```
targetScope = 'subscription'

resource setAllowBlobPublicAccessToFalse
    'Microsoft.Authorization/policyDefinitions@2020-09-01' = {
  name: 'setAllowBlobPublicAccessToFalse'
  properties: {
    policyType: 'Custom'
    displayName: 'Set setAllowBlobPublicAccessToFalse to
        false on a Storage Account'
    description: 'Set setAllowBlobPublicAccessToFalse to
        false on a Storage Account when the API version is
        greather than 2019-04-01'
    metadata: {
      version: '1.0.0'
      category: 'Network Security'
    }
```

```
        mode: 'All'
        policyRule: {
            if: {
                field: 'type'
                equals: 'Microsoft.Storage/storageAccounts'
            }
            then: {
                effect: 'Modify'
                details: {
                    roleDefinitionIds: [
                        '/providers/microsoft.authorization/roleDefinitions/
                           ➥ 17d1049b-9a84-46fb-8f53-869881c3d3ab'
                    ]
                    conflictEffect: 'Audit'          One or more operations
                    operations: [          ◁───────  can be defined here.
                        {
       Conditionally  ┌──▷   condition: '[greaterOrEquals(requestContext()
          run the            ➥ .apiVersion, \'2019-04-01\')]'
    operation using          operation: 'addOrReplace'
      an expression.         field: 'Microsoft.Storage/storageAccounts/
                               ➥ allowBlobPublicAccess'
                             value: false
                        }
                    ]
                }
            }
        }
    }
}
```

This example targets storage accounts, as you can see in the `if` within the `policyRule`, where the type is compared to `Microsoft.Storage/storageAccounts`.

The operations are defined in the `operations` array within the policy. Since that is an array, it allows you to alter multiple properties or tags from a single policy. Each operation has an `operation`, `field`, `value`, and `condition` property. The `operation` field may contain one of the three operations mentioned previously: `addOrReplace`, `add`, or `remove`. The `field` needs to contain an alias that points to a property on the resource. An expression can optionally be provided in the `condition` field to make the operation only do its work in specific scenarios. In this example, the property on the resource, referenced by its alias (`allowBlobPublicAccess`), will only be set when the API version of the resource deployed is greater than `2019-04-01`. This ensures you can't apply it on storage accounts that do not support the property because they are of an older version.

The `details` section defines a list with role definition IDs in the `roleDefinition-Ids` property. You have seen that one before on the `DeployIfNotExist` effect. When you use this policy in an assignment, you need to specify an identity on the assignment. The list indicates which roles the identity on the assignment needs. That identity is used when the policy needs to process the operations and during a remediation task.

12.5   *Creating your own initiative*

Now that you've seen how to write your own policies, it's time to write a custom initiative. Remember that an initiative allows you to group policies and then assign that group of policies all at once. An initiative may contain both custom and built-in policies.

The following listing creates an initiative that uses one custom policy definition (12-09.bicep).

Listing 12.11   Your own custom initiative

```
targetScope = 'subscription'

module allowedLocationsPolicyDefinition './allowedLocations.bicep' = {
    name: 'allowedLocationsPolicyDefinition'
    scope: subscription()
}

resource initiative 'Microsoft.Authorization/
    ➥ policySetDefinitions@2020-09-01' = {
    name: 'MyCustomInitiative'
    properties: {
        description: 'This policy definition set comprises the scoped
            ➥ policies for subscription \'${subscription().displayName}\''
        policyDefinitions: [
            {
                policyDefinitionId: allowedLocationsPolicyDefinition
                    ➥ .outputs.policyDefinitionId
                parameters: {
                    listOfAllowedLocations: {
                        value: [
                            'northeurope'
                            'westeurope'
                        ]
                    }
                }
            }
        ]
    }
}
```

This template first defines a module that references a custom policy. Then the actual initiative is declared, using the type `Microsoft.Authorization/policySetDefinitions`. The `policyDefinitions` array is the most interesting part. This array allows you to list one or more policy definitions. This example uses the output of the module to fetch the `policyDefinitionId`. Since this policy has a parameter, the `listOfAllowed-Locations`, you need to specify that here. The syntax for that is similar to how you would do that in an ARM template parameter file.

You can deploy this initiative using a standard Azure CLI command to deploy the Bicep file:

```
az deployment sub create --template-file policySetDefinition.bicep
    ➥ -l westeurope
```

The preceding command starts a deployment of the referenced file at the subscription level.

To add a built-in policy definition to your initiative, you need to find the definition ID. One way to do that is through the Azure portal. Go to the definitions overview, find the policy you want to use, and copy its Definition ID as shown in figure 12.13.

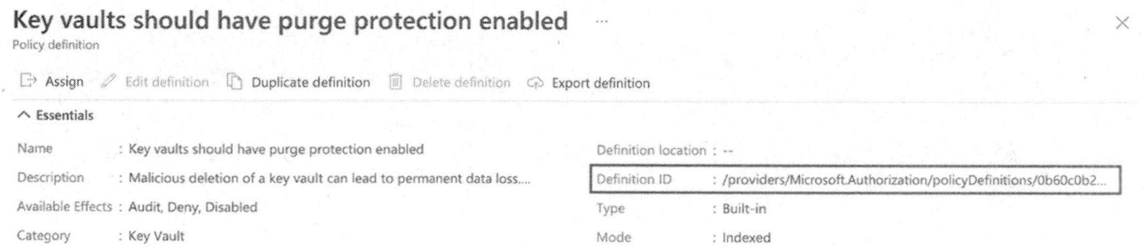

Figure 12.13   Finding the Definition ID for an existing policy

You then can add the following snippet to the `policyDefinitions` list:

```
{
  policyDefinitionId: '/providers/Microsoft.Authorization/
    policyDefinitions/0b60c0b2-2dc2-4e1c-b5c9-abbed971de53'
}
```

With the policy definition and initiative in place, let's see how you can assign them.

12.6   Assigning a policy or initiative

Policies and initiatives can't do anything until you assign them. The Bicep template for the assignment is shown in the following listing (12-10.bicep).

Listing 12.12   Your custom assignment

```
targetScope = 'subscription'

param policySetName string

resource myFirstAssignment 'Microsoft.Authorization/
    policyAssignments@2020-09-01' = {
  name: 'MyFirstAssignment'
  location: 'westeurope'
  identity:{
      type: 'SystemAssigned'
  }
  properties:{
      policyDefinitionId: '${subscription().id}/providers/Microsoft
        .Authorization/policySetDefinitions/${policySetName}'
  }
}
```

The assignment resource is of type `Microsoft.Authorization/policyAssignments`. The `policyDefinitionId` property lets you point to the policy definition or initiative you want to assign. In this example, a parameter for the name of the policy set is used. During deployment, that will be `MyCustomInitiative`, which you created in listing 12.11. Notice the use of `subscription().id` on that same line. Since the initiative is custom and was deployed to this subscription, you need to address the initiative correctly. If you look again at the small snippet at the end of the previous section, where you used a built-in policy definition, you'll see that you did not need to specify this narrow scope. That is because built-in policies and initiatives are available at any scope.

The `identity` section is used to assign a system-assigned managed identity to this assignment. Remember that the `Modify` and `DeployIfNotExists` effects can deploy or modify resources though the policy. As creating or modifying resources in Azure requires permissions, the policy system uses this identity to be allowed to make those changes in your environment. So, after you assign the policy and the identity has been created, you need to ensure that this identity gets the correct permissions to fulfill its job.

The scope of the assignment is determined by the deployment scope. That means that when you deploy this template at a subscription level, it will be effective for all resources in that subscription. The same goes for when you deploy it to a management group. It will then work for every subscription and its child resources. The following command can be used to deploy this assignment at the subscription level:

```
az deployment sub create --template-file policySetAssignment.bicep
    ➥ --parameters '{ "policySetName":
    ➥ { "value": "MyCustomInitiative" } }' -l westeurope
```

Here you again use the `az deployment sub create` command, like you have seen a few times earlier in the chapter. This time you use the `--parameters` switch to pass in the value for the `policySetName` parameter.

You can also use this command to modify an existing assignment. When you create a new subscription in Azure, as you will do a lot in a hub and spoke architecture, you might want to automatically onboard that subscription into Microsoft Defender for Cloud. Microsoft Defender for Cloud helps you keep your resources secure and follow security best practices. That is done by creating an assignment and assigning a policy initiative to your subscription as part of the onboarding. That initiative is called ASC Default and stands for Azure Security Center Default. Azure Security Center is the old name for Microsoft Defender for Cloud. You might want to change that assignment. Since every resource in Azure is addressed by its name, a policy assignment is no different. The following listing changes a property on the ASC Default assignment on a particular subscription.

Listing 12.13   An assignment updating an existing assignment

```
Param allowedContainerImagesInKubernetesClusterRegex string

resource policyAssignment 'Microsoft.Authorization/
  ➥ policyAssignments@2020-09-01' = {
  name: 'ASC Default (subscription: ${subscription().id})'
  scope: subscription()
  properties: {
    displayName: 'ASC Default (subscription: ${subscription().id})'
    policyDefinitionId: '/providers/Microsoft.Authorization/
      ➥ policySetDefinitions/${policyDefinitionId}'
    parameters: {
      'allowedContainerImagesInKubernetesClusterRegex': {
        value: allowedContainerImagesInKubernetesClusterRegex
      }
    }
  }
}
```

The name of the existing assignment can easily be found in the Azure portal or using the VS Code extension. For the assignment created by Microsoft Defender for Cloud, the name follows this syntax: `ASC Default (subscription:<subscription id>)`. So, the value in the Bicep template becomes `ASC Default (subscription: ${subscription().id})` to make it work for every subscription. The parameter section can then be used to change values on the assignment. In this example, a new value for the `allowedContainerImagesInKubernetesClusterRegex` property is set. You can find the available properties by opening the assignment in the portal, as shown in figure 12.14.

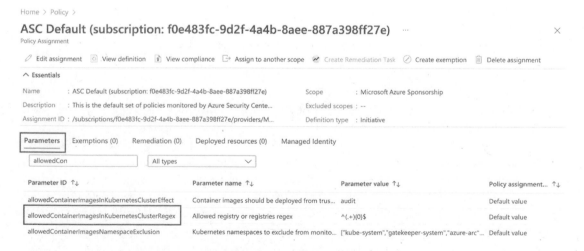

Figure 12.14   Finding the parameters on an existing assignment in the Azure portal

Figure 12.14 shows you the properties for the ASC Default assignment on a particular subscription. On that page, you'll find the parameter list. The Parameter ID is what you are looking for. Now that you have learned about policies, let's see how you can view the current compliance status and act on that.

12.7   Reviewing compliance status

In the previous section, you've been using and modifying the ASC Default assignment. Let's review its compliance status by opening a browser and navigating to the policy overview in the Azure portal (figure 12.15).

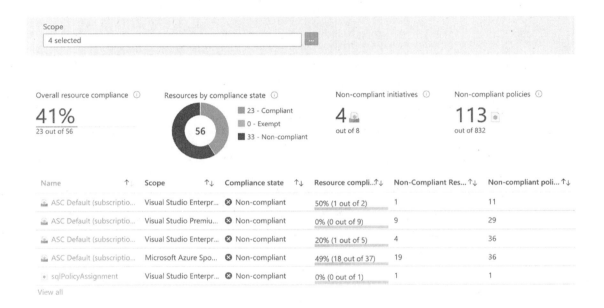

Figure 12.15   The Azure Policy dashboard, showing the compliance status

This dashboard will give you a quick insight into how compliant you are. Figure 12.15 shows an overall compliance score of 24%, which obviously isn't great. At the top of the figure, you can select the scope you want to see the compliance status for by clicking on the three dots (...) button. That allows you to scope to a particular subscription or management group. That means, for example, that every team in the hub and spoke architecture can scope to its own resources easily.

The list in the lower half of the dashboard shows you the score per initiative. Clicking on one of them will bring you to a dashboard that shows detailed information on that initiative, as shown in figure 12.16.

Home > Policy >

ASC Default (subscription: f0e483fc-9d2f-4a4b-8aee-887a398ff27e) 📌 ⋯
Initiative compliance

🔲 View definition   ✏ Edit assignment   ↱ Assign to another scope   🗑 Delete assignment   ✨ Create Remediation Task   ⊘ Create exemption

∧ Essentials

Name	: ASC Default (subscription: f0e483fc-9d2f-4a4b-8aee-887a398ff27e)	Scope	: Microsoft Azure Sponsorship
Description	: This is the default set of policies monitored by Azure Security Center. It ...	Excluded scopes	: --
Assignment ID	: /subscriptions/f0e483fc-9d2f-4a4b-8aee-887a398ff27e/providers/Micro...	Definition	: Azure Security Benchmark

Selected Scopes ⓘ

4 selected subscriptions ⌄

Compliance state ⓘ

❌ Non-compliant

Overall resource compliance ⓘ

14%
1 out of 7

Resources by compliance state ⓘ

7

■ 1 - Compliant
■ 0 - Exempt
■ 6 - Non-compliant

Non-compliant policies ⓘ

11 ◉
out of 202

Groups   Policies   Non-compliant resources   Events

Filter by group name...

Subgroup : **All subgroups**   Compliance state : **7 selected**

Name ↑↓	Compliance ↑↓	Subgroup ↑↓	Non-compliant policies ↓
⌦ Implement security for internal traffic	❌ Non-compliant	Network Security	2
⌦ Centralize security log management and analysis	❌ Non-compliant	Logging and Threat Detection	2
⌦ Connect private networks together	❌ Non-compliant	Network Security	1
⌦ Establish private network access to Azure services	❌ Non-compliant	Network Security	1
⌦ Protect applications and services from external network a...	❌ Non-compliant	Network Security	1
⌦ Use strong authentication controls for all Azure Active Di...	❌ Non-compliant	Identity Management	1
⌦ Protect and limit highly privileged users	❌ Non-compliant	Privileged Access	1
⌦ Protect sensitive data	❌ Non-compliant	Data Protection	1
⌦ Encrypt sensitive information in transit	❌ Non-compliant	Data Protection	1
⌦ Preparation - setup incident notification	❌ Non-compliant	Incident Response	1
⌦ Sustain secure configurations for Azure services	❌ Non-compliant	Posture and Vulnerability Ma...	1

Figure 12.16   A dashboard with the compliance status for a specific assignment

This view gives you detailed information on the compliance status for the individual assignment and quickly shows you all noncompliant policies. When you click on one of the noncompliant policies, you get the overview of a single noncompliant policy, as shown in figure 12.17.

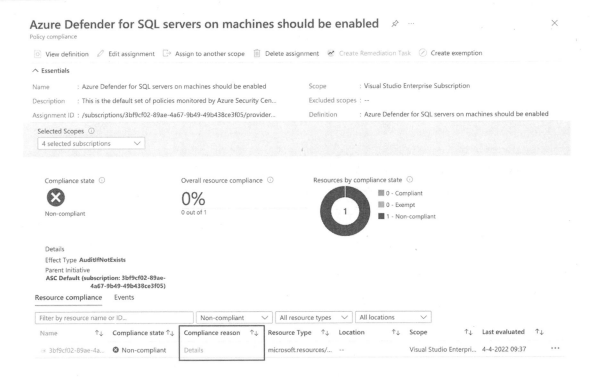

Figure 12.17   A dashboard with the compliance status for a specific policy

You get to see which resources are noncompliant, and you can drill down into the details of why a resource is noncompliant by clicking Details in the Compliance Reason column. A pane like the one in figure 12.18 will be shown. The Compliance Details pane shows you the reason for noncompliance at the bottom.

12.7.1 *Remediating noncompliant resources*

You can remediate a noncompliant resource through the policy portal, often with a single click if you have used or created a policy with the `Modify` or `DeployIfNot-Exists` effect.

Although that is a simple and quick way to fix your noncompliant resources, you might prefer to do it using IaC. That way, you change your template once and use that to make current and future resources compliant in any environment. Changes will be nicely rolled out using a deployment pipeline that has the correct permissions, and changes are tested using your regular process. Then, after at most 24 hours, the policy portal can again be checked to see whether the score improved. You can, of course, also use the VS Code Policy extension to verify whether the resource is now compliant or not by running the evaluation from there.

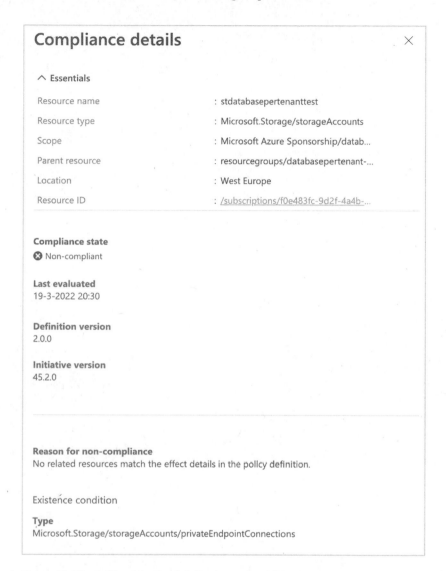

Figure 12.18   Drilling into the details of a noncompliant resource

12.7.2 Creating an exemption

You sometimes will not want, or cannot get, a resource or scope compliant with a policy for whatever reason. This mostly applies to built-in policies, like the ASC Default set that is applied to your subscription when you onboard on Microsoft Defender for Cloud. Luckily, you can create what is called an *exemption* to stop resources from being evaluated. Such an exemption can be created in Bicep as follows (12-11.bicep).

Listing 12.14   A policy exemption

```
resource privateEndpointShouldBeEnabledPolicyExemption
    ➥ 'Microsoft.Authorization/policyExemptions@2020-07-01-preview' = {
    name: 'privateEndpointShouldBeEnabledPolicyExemption'
    properties: {
        displayName: 'ASC-Private endpoint should be enabled'
        policyAssignmentId: '${subscription().id}/providers/
            ➥ Microsoft.Authorization/policyAssignments/SecurityCenterBuiltIn'
        policyDefinitionReferenceIds: [
            'privateEndpointShouldBeEnabledForMysqlServersMonitoringEffect'
            'storageAccountShouldUseAPrivateLinkConnectionMonitoringEffect'
            'privateEndpointShouldBeConfiguredForKeyVaultMonitoringEffect'
        ]
        exemptionCategory: 'Waiver'
        expiresOn: '01/01/2022 12:00'
        description: 'Using firewall rules for now.'
    }
}
```

To create an exemption, you need a resource of type `Microsoft.Authorization/ policyExemptions`. You need to tell it which assignment to target using the `policy- AssignmentId` property. The value to use can be found in the Azure portal, as shown in figure 12.19, or you can use an output when you have defined the assignment in Bicep.

Figure 12.19   Finding the Assignment ID of an existing assignment in the Azure portal

When you navigate to the assignment in the portal, one of its properties is the Assignment ID. The `policyDefinitionReferenceIds` array is filled with the reference IDs of the policies you want to create the exemption for. These, again, can be found in the Azure portal. When you click the View Definition button in figure 12.19, you will be taken to the next overview in figure 12.20.

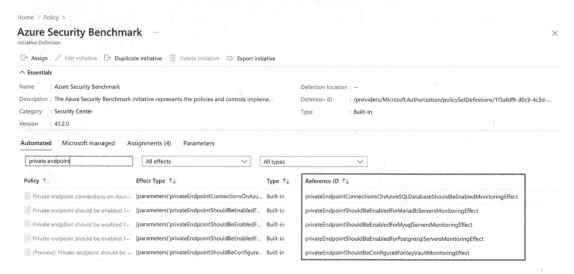

Figure 12.20   Finding the policy Reference IDs needed in an exemption

This overview shows you the policies in this definition. Here you can find the Reference IDs on the right. Use the search box to find the right one. Since `policy-DefinitionReferenceIds` is an array, you can create an exemption for one or more policies at once. The `exemptionCategory` property can hold two values: `Waiver` or `Mitigated`. You should use `Mitigated` when the policy intent is met through another method. Use `Waiver` when you temporarily accept the noncompliant resource. The `expiresOn` property can be set to make the exemption inactive after a certain date. The policies will then be effective again after this date. This is especially useful in temporary situations.

You can deploy the previous exemption with the following command:

```
az deployment sub create --template-file policyExemptions.bicep
    -l westeurope
```

When you navigate to the policy definition within the assignment on which you created the exemption, you should see the details as shown in figure 12.21. Here you see the definition for one of the policies that was included in the exemption, "Storage accounts should use private link." You can see that the compliance status is currently `Exempt`, and the bottom of the screen shows a list of resources that are covered by this policy and are now exempted.

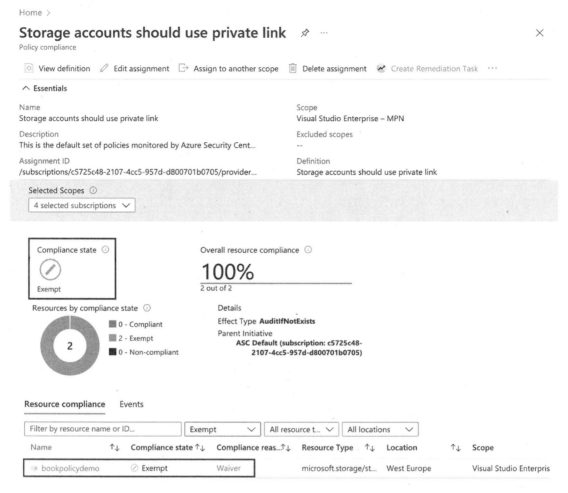

Figure 12.21   The details of a policy exemption

Summary

- Azure Policy enables you to govern your Azure environment through Policy as Code.
- A policy is defined in a policy definition that contains the business rules you want to enforce. A policy has a resource selector that specifies to which resources it applies. A policy can have any of the following effects: `Audit`, `Deny`, `Append`, `Modify`, `AuditIfNotExists`, `DeployIfNotExists`.
- An initiative can be used to group policies so that you can assign them in one go.
- Azure offers a lot of policy definitions and initiatives for you to use out of the box, helping you to implement (security) best practices.

- Using Bicep, you can create custom policies, include them in custom initiatives (with built-in policies if you want), and then assign them to a particular scope.
- Exemptions are used to (temporarily) exclude resources from being evaluated by Azure Policy.

Case studies

13

This chapter covers

- Three extensive infrastructure examples created using Azure Bicep
- A first use case that explores structuring Bicep for creating an Azure foundation, also called a landing zone or Azure platform
- A second use case that explores subscription-level deployments for preconfiguring subscriptions with minimum standards or a baseline configuration
- A third use case that builds out the infrastructure needed for a microservices architecture

With everything you've learned so far, you should be able to create all the Azure infrastructure you need, either through ARM or Bicep templates. Yet, it can be challenging to get started with larger infrastructure for the first time. To help you get started, this chapter contains three larger examples with step-by-step explanations of how the templates are structured and built.

Some parts of templates will be omitted, as they are repetitions of what you have learned already, or are very similar. The text will focus on the line of thought

316

involved in writing the templates and less on the syntax. Where parts of a template are omitted, the text will describe what you need to do to follow along, or you can look at the completed templates on GitHub (https://github.com/AzureIaCBook).

In this chapter, you will see three examples, all from different points of view. In section 13.1, you will take up the role of engineer in a central IT team that is responsible for building Azure landing zones (sometimes also called an Azure foundation, cloud foundation, or Azure platform). This team is responsible for the most abstract configuration of the Azure tenant. They own the management group structure and set up default Azure policies. A team like this is often called an *internal platform team,* and the products they bring to consuming teams are preconfigured subscriptions.

Next up, you'll take on the role of engineer in one of these teams. You'll be responsible for further tailoring the configuration of subscriptions to the standards and needs of your own department. You will concern yourself with security settings, cost management, and other resources that mostly relate to nonfunctional requirements.

In the third example, you'll take up the role of engineer in a product team. Here you will work on a larger example for an infrastructure that can be used for hosting a load-balanced, highly available microservice architecture.

All three examples will assume knowledge of the problem type at hand and how to solve that type of problem in Azure, as they will focus only on building the Bicep or ARM templates needed to execute that solution using IaC. This will not be an extensive introduction to the topics, and if you are reading this book while getting started with Azure, you may find this chapter tough to read. However, more experienced readers will benefit from these more extensive examples that show possible approaches to larger problems. Alright, let's start with building an Azure foundation.

13.1 Building an Azure foundation

In this first example, let's assume you are working in the central IT department of a medium-sized IT company. There are tens of teams working on different applications, all hosted in Azure, and you are responsible for creating the Azure subscriptions they work in. Before handing them over, you are also expected to put in some basic guardrails to ensure that the teams are using those subscriptions in accordance with the company guidelines.

13.1.1 The management group layout

As you will be creating tens or maybe even hundreds of Azure subscriptions, it makes sense to create a logical grouping of subscriptions, based on how and where they are used. There are many ways to do this, but let's say you are getting your inspiration from the cloud adoption framework (see Microsoft's "Resource organization" article: http://mng.bz/AyAe) and want to create the structure in figure 13.1.

As you might recall from earlier chapters, subscriptions can be grouped into management groups, and management groups into other management groups. The top-level

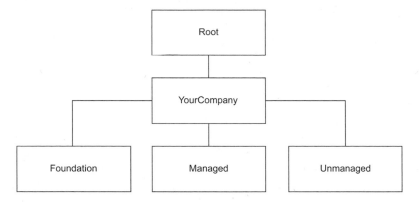

Figure 13.1   An example management group structure

management group, Root, exists by default in every Azure environment. The other groups you create, and they serve the following goals:

- *Foundation*—This management group contains all the subscriptions with foundational platform capabilities that are used by all other subscriptions.
- *Managed*—This management group contains all the subscriptions that are used by other teams for production workloads.
- *Unmanaged*—This management group contains all the subscriptions that are used by other teams for nonproduction workloads.

Finally, all these management groups are grouped into a single pseudo-root, called YourCompany. Later you will work with policies, and these cannot be created in, or assigned to, the Root management group. Hence the creation of this pseudo-root. Of course, you might make other choices, but this can be a valid approach for many situations.

Let's start working on a template to create this structure, starting with the pseudo-root. Let's refer to this template as the *company main template* from now on (13-01.bicep).

Listing 13.1   Creating a pseudo-root management group

```
targetScope = 'tenant'          ◁——┐  This template deploys to the Azure tenant,
                                    │  the top level of any Azure environment.
resource yourCompanyMG 'Microsoft.Management/managementGroups
    ➥ @2020-05-01' = {
    name: 'YourCompany'
    scope: tenant()
    properties: {
        displayName: 'Your Company'
    }
}
```

To deploy a template at the tenant scope, you can use the following command:

```
az deployment tenant create --location westeurope
  ➥ --template-file .\13-01.bicep
```

In listing 13.1, and in the code to deploy the template, you can see that this template is not targeting the resource group or subscription level but is deploying to the tenant. This is because all management groups live inside the tenant, and the hierarchy is created using a parent-child relation that you will see later. All management groups have a resource `name`, which you are advised to keep short and simple with no spaces, which in this case is `YourCompany`. You can use the `displayName` property to provide a longer, human-readable name. Let's now add another management group, as the child of the first one (13-01.bicep continued).

Listing 13.2 Adding a pseudo-root management group

```
resource FoundationMG 'Microsoft.Management/managementGroups@2020-05-01' = {
    name: 'Foundation'
    scope: tenant()
    properties: {
        displayName: 'Foundation'
        details: {                           Nesting one management
            parent: {                        group in another by
                id: yourCompanyMG.id    ◁─── referencing it as a parent
            }
        }
    }
}
```

Here you see the same structure used to create another management group, but now with another property called `parent`. This property is used to specify that this `Foundation` management group should be nested in the `YourCompany` management group.

You can now continue this template on your own, adding the remaining two management groups or get the complete template from GitHub. With the management groups in place, let's continue by assigning policies to them.

13.1.2 Assigning a policy initiative

One of the reasons many organizations use management groups is because they allow you to assign policies or policy initiatives. Assigning a policy to a management group makes it effective not only on that management group itself, but also on all the management groups below it, and on all the subscriptions within it and the management groups below it.

In the management group structure you just created, it makes sense to have only the most basic of policies on the pseudo-root, and to assign three different sets of policies to the three management groups, Foundation, Managed, and Unmanaged.

For each of those management groups, it makes sense to create a new Bicep file that you reference as a module from the previous file (13-01.bicep). Let's start by writing a template that assigns the Azure built-in ISO 27001 initiative to the `Managed` management group. This way, all the built-in policies that help you be compliant with ISO 27001 are automatically applied to all subscriptions that are used to host production workloads.

ISO 27001 (www.iso.org/isoiec-27001-information-security.html) is a widely accepted standard for information security, which should be implemented with a combination of technical and nontechnical controls. Azure provides you with a predefined set of policies with all the technical controls for adhering to this standard, namely the initiative we are assigning here (13-01-01.bicep).

Listing 13.3   Assigning a policy initiative to a management group

```
targetScope = 'managementGroup'

param managementGroupName string

var managementGroupScope = '/providers/Microsoft.Management/managementGroups/
    ${managementGroupName}'

var builtInIso27001InitiativeId = '89c6cddc-1c73-4ac1-b19c-54d1a15a42f2'

resource iso27001 'Microsoft.Authorization/policyAssignments
    @2020-09-01' = {
  name: managementGroupName
  location: 'westeurope'
  identity: {
      type: 'SystemAssigned'
  }
  properties:{
      description: 'The assignment of the ISO27001 initiative'
      policyDefinitionId: '${managementGroupScope}/providers
          /Microsoft.Authorization/policySetDefinitions
          /${builtInIso27001InitiativeId}'
  }
}
```

This template targets the `managementGroup` scope to deploy resources into the management group. Few resources can be deployed at this scope, but a policy assignment is one of them. The assignment here is just like those you saw in chapter 12. It is interesting to note that the GUID stored in the `builtInIso27001InitiativeId` variable is a constant, and it's the same for all Azure users. Instead of assigning this template directly, let's use it as a module and append the following to the template in the 13-01.bicep file.

Listing 13.4   Appending the policy assignments to the main template

```
module ManagedMGPolicyAssignments '13-01-01.bicep' = {
    name: 'ManagedMGPolicyAssignmentsDeployment'
    scope: ManagedMG
```

```
    params: {
        managementGroupName: ManagedMG.name
    }
}
```

From here on, you can build out your own policy and initiative assignments to all the management groups. You can follow the structure of using one module for all the policies or policy assignments for each management group, and including those modules in the main template. Let's now move one level down in the hierarchy and look at how you can write a template that creates a new Azure subscription as part of an example Azure foundation.

13.1.3 *Creating a management subscription*

No matter your situation, the extent to which you follow common practices or the cloud adoption framework from Microsoft, it is likely you'll need at least one subscription to implement some centralized concerns. A very common example is logging. In this section, you will create an Azure subscription, called Management, that contains a Log Analytics workspace where all the logs you want to collect can be stored.

Creating subscriptions using a Bicep or ARM template is only possible when you have an Enterprise Agreement with Microsoft or a Microsoft Customer Agreement. If you have an Enterprise or Microsoft Customer Agreement, you can look at the following Microsoft blog for instructions on creating subscriptions using templates: "Creating Subscriptions with ARM Templates" (http://mng.bz/ZA2N). Only larger organizations have such an agreement, so creating subscriptions using IaC is not available for individual learners.

If you don't have such an agreement, you can complete building your Azure foundation by manually creating a subscription called `Management` under the `Foundation` management group.

Once this is in place, you can follow these steps to create a Log Analytics resource:

1. Create a template called 13-01-02-subscription.bicep that is deployable to subscriptions and that creates a resource group with the name `Logs` in the subscription. You can manually deploy this template using the `az deployment sub` command, as you learned in chapter 2.
2. Create a template called 13-01-02-resourceGroup.bicep that creates the Log Analytics resource with the name `CentralLogStore`. You can deploy this template as a module from the 13-01-02-subscription.bicep template.

Given all that you have learned in this book, you should be able to complete these tasks on your own, or you can look up these files on GitHub. Either way, you will now have a complete management group structure, a management subscription, and a centralized log store, as illustrated in figure 13.2. In the next section, you will complete this example by creating a subscription for use by another team.

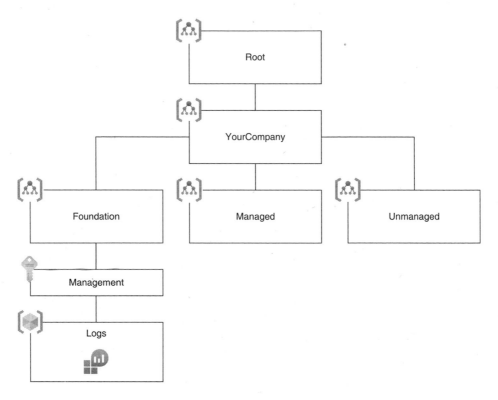

Figure 13.2   Management groups, a subscription, a resource group, and a resource

13.1.4 *Creating workload subscriptions*

An Azure foundation is only useful if you use it to provision and preconfigure subscriptions for other teams, so in this section you'll do just that. Before you can configure a subscription, you will have to create it. As this can't be done through IaC, you should manually create a subscription called ToMaToe in the Managed management group.

> **TIP**   If you cannot create new subscriptions due to licensing, authorizations, or other limits, you can also reuse a subscription you already have. Just keep in mind that in the real world you would not reuse subscriptions but generally create one or more for each consuming team.

Remember that subscriptions in this management group are destined to be handed over to the team so they can host their own applications, so you will reuse this subscription in the final section of this chapter for our third and final use case, hence the name.

But before you get to the third use case, we'll practice preconfiguring a subscription from the point of view of a centralized team. Centralized teams that manage an Azure foundation often want to preconfigure many things on subscriptions. Here you will see just one example: capturing all activity logs on an Azure subscription and storing them for a long time. Activity logs are the Azure audit logs, and they can be used to retrieve information about who made which changes. To accomplish this you are going to write—guess what? A Bicep template (13-01-03.bicep).

Listing 13.5 A template to capture activity logs in Log Analytics

```
targetScope = 'subscription'

param logAnalyticsWorkspaceId string

resource alConfig 'Microsoft.Insights/diagnosticSettings              ◁── This resource
    ➥ @2021-05-01-preview' = {                                            is used to set
  name: 'activityLogsToLogAnalytics'                                      the logging
  properties: {                                                           configuration on
    workspaceId: logAnalyticsWorkspaceId        ◁──                       the subscription.
    logs: [                                       ◁──
      {                                                        The Log Analytics
        category: 'Administrative'                             workspace to send
        enabled: true                                          the logs to
      }
      {                                                An array describing
        category: 'Security'                           which logs should be
        enabled: true                                  sent, and which not
      }
      {
        category: 'Policy'
        enabled: true
      }
      {
        category: 'Alert'
        enabled: true
      }
    ]
  }
}
```

In this template, you'll see a resource of type `Microsoft.Insights/diagnostics-Settings` that is deployed at the subscription level. These are the settings that configure a routing for subscription-level logs to be sent to one or more destinations. In this case, the logs are being sent to the Log Analytics workspace you created earlier. Finally, in the `logs` property, you define which categories of logs should be forwarded and which not. Here, only the logs in the categories `Administrative`, `Security`, `Policy`, and `Alert` are sent.

To deploy this template, you can use the following command:

```
az deployment sub create -location <location>
    ➥ --template-file 13-01-03.bicep
```

You can extend this template to further configure subscriptions as you want. For example, you can provision default resources using a deployment stack or provide access using RBAC assignments. These are just other types of Azure resources you can look up in the ARM documentation. Let's now move on to another example and take up the role of engineer in a department that receives these subscriptions and wants to tailor their configuration to their own department's needs.

13.2   *Subscription level deployments*

In this section, you will explore the options Bicep has to offer for building out an Azure subscription configuration. Let's imagine you are working as a DevOps engineer in a larger organization that has many teams working on Azure applications. Your department is responsible for about a dozen of these applications and consists of six teams. Your specific responsibility is requesting and managing the subscriptions that you receive from the central IT department and preparing them for use by the application teams in your department.

In this section you will build out an orchestrating Bicep template and a number of resource templates to do just that. As you are now working on templates that target the subscription scope, you'll need to start your template with the following:

```
targetScope = 'subscription'
```

Templates targeting the subscription scope are deployed with a slightly altered command:

```
az deployment sub create -location <location>
    --template-file <template-file>
```

With that in place, let's visit some topics that come up regularly when talking about subscription-level deployments, starting with budgets.

13.2.1   *Configuring budgets*

One of the first things that every department wants to keep tabs on is the money. By default, whenever you receive a new subscription, a default budget should be applied. To deploy a budget to a subscription, you can use the following template (13-02-01.bicep).

Listing 13.6   A subscription template for setting budgets

```
targetScope = 'subscription'                          A resource of type
                                              Microsoft.Consumption is used for
param maximumBudget int                       defining budgets and alerts on budgets.

resource defaultBudget 'Microsoft.Consumption/budgets@2021-10-01' = {
    name: 'default-budget'
    properties: {                      This is a budget that defines
        timeGrain: 'Monthly'           a monthly maximum.
        timePeriod: {
            startDate: '2021-11-01'        The date at which the
        }                                  budget becomes effective
    }
```

```
                        category: 'Cost'
 The actual    ┌─▷      amount: maximumBudget
   budget      │        notifications: {              ◁─┐   A list of one or more notification rules
               │            Actual_Over_80_Percent: {     │   that determine if and when notifications
                               enabled: true                  about the budget should be sent
                               operator: 'GreaterThanOrEqualTo'
                               threshold: 80
                               thresholdType: 'Actual'
                               contactEmails: [
                                   'henry@example.nl'
                               ]
                           }
                       }
                   }
               }
```

In this template you see an Azure budget resource being created. By themselves, budgets don't do anything, as they are not a spending limit. So, attached to this budget, a notification is set to fire whenever the forecasted spending on the subscription exceeds 80% of the budget. In a real-world situation you would add multiple notifications to a budget. For example, another notification that 90% of the allocated budget has been spent might be in order. Also, it can be beneficial to send notifications to the end user of the subscription, using lower limits. You can add this template to your orchestrating template as follows (13-02.bicep).

Listing 13.7 An orchestrating template for deploying subscription-level resources

```
targetScope = 'subscription'

module budgetDeployment '13-02-01.bicep' = {
    name: 'budgetDeployment'
    params: {
        maximumBudget: 1000
    }
}
```

13.2.2 Configuring Microsoft Defender for Cloud

Another thing you might want to preconfigure for your users is a basic Microsoft Defender for Cloud configuration. Microsoft Defender is an analysis and recommendation center that can automatically scan your resources for security misconfigurations, abuse, and other security risks.

In your organization you want to enable Microsoft Defender for Cloud by default for Key Vaults and VMs. The first because managing secrets is especially important for your teams, and the second because VMs are IaaS and leave a lot of security responsibly with your teams—you'll want to guide them with advice whenever they deploy a VM. The following template provides such a configuration (13-02-02.bicep).

Listing 13.8 Configuring Microsoft Defender for Cloud

```
targetScope = 'subscription'

var enableDefenderFor = [
    'KeyVaults'
    'VirtualMachines'
]

resource defenderPricing 'Microsoft.Security/pricings@2018-06-01' =
    [for name in enableDefenderFor: {
    name: name
    properties: {
        pricingTier: 'Standard'
    }
}]

resource MDfCContact 'Microsoft.Security/securityContacts
    @2020-01-01-preview' = {
    name: 'default'
    properties: {
        emails: 'henry@example.nl'
        alertNotifications: {
            state: 'On'
            minimalSeverity: 'High'
        }
        notificationsByRole: {
            state: 'Off'
            roles: [
            ]
        }
    }
}
```

> Enabling Microsoft Defender for Cloud is done by switching the pricing tier from basic to standard.

> The new pricing tier

> The Microsoft.Security/securityContacts resource is used to define one or more receivers for security alerts.

> The properties object describes who to alert.

> The notificationsByRole property specifies who to alert using an RBAC role name, instead of email.

This template deploys two types of resources. First, a Security Center pricing configuration is deployed. This configuration enables the Standard tier (which is paid) for Defender, enabling more advanced protection, scanning, and recommendations. This resource is deployed twice by iterating through the enableDefenderFor array, which holds the two types Defender will be enabled for.

> **NOTE** Microsoft renamed "Azure Security Center" to "Microsoft Defender for Cloud." However, when they made that change, they left the name of the resource provider and resource types unchanged, to keep backward compatibility. For this reason, you'll see both the product name (Defender for Cloud) and the technical name (Security Center) when talking about the same thing.

The second resource configures a contact to reach out to in the case of recommendations or alerts with a severity of High or Critical. You can add the deployment of this template to the template in listing 13.2, or look at the ch13-02.bicep file in the GitHub repository, after which you can redeploy the template to test your work.

13.2.3   *Creating resource groups and providing access*

Before handing the subscription over to the team that will use it, you can complete the configuration by adding one or more resource groups and providing access to specific users in the Azure Active Directory (AAD) or to AAD groups. The following listing does just that (13-02-03.bicep).

Listing 13.9   Creating a resource group and providing access to a user
---

```
targetScope = 'subscription'

var resourceGroupName = 'storageLayer'
resource storageLayerRef 'Microsoft.Resources/resourceGroups
    ➥ @2021-04-01' = {
    name: resourceGroupName
    location: 'westeurope'
}

module resourceGroupRBAC '13-02-03-roleAssignment.bicep' = {
    name: 'resourceGroupRBACDeployment'
    scope: resourceGroup(resourceGroupName)
}
```

In this listing, a `storageLayer` resource group is created. The second resource is captured in a module of its own. This is a common pattern, where you first create the container, the resource group, and next invoke the deployment of resources into that container. The only way to achieve this is by wrapping the resource in a module of its own and applying the `scope` property to the module deployment. The contents of this file, 13-02-03-roleAssignment.bicep, can be found on GitHub.

Finally, you can add the deployment of this template to the template from listing 13.2, or look at the ch13-02.bicep file in the GitHub repository. This template and the modules that it deploys are a good example of how you can preconfigure subscriptions using Bicep templates.

You can take and extend these templates with resources like policies, policy assignments, and role assignments, depending on your own interests. Using a combination of the Azure Quickstart Templates GitHub repository (https://github.com/Azure/azure-quickstart-templates) and the ARM templates reference (https://docs.microsoft.com/en-us/azure/templates), you should have all the tools you'll need to figure this out on your own. In the next section, you will switch to the perspective of a product team and use this configured subscription to deploy your application.

13.3   *Creating a highly-available microservice architecture*

For this third example, you will be transferring to another role: this time you're an engineer in a product team. Here you are working on a large web application, which is implemented using a microservices architecture. You can continue from the previous example and reuse that subscription.

There are two different frontend solutions for your system: a web user interface and a mobile app running on different platforms. To gather data, these systems communicate with a backend hosted in the cloud, using HTTPS. Since the web application and its usage is growing steadily, your company has decided to develop the backend using a microservices architecture. This case study will guide you through the architecture of this case and the Bicep template that describes it. Before we get into the details, though, let's first get an overview of the infrastructure for this case.

All resources will be provisioned in a virtual network (vnet). External (internet) traffic will be directed to an application gateway that will act as a gatekeeper to the vnet.

Figure 13.3 shows how the services will be organized. All HTTPS requests will be redirected from Azure Application Gateway to Azure API Management. API Management interprets the requested routes and directs traffic to the desired microservice. Communication between services is allowed through an Event Grid domain. This Event Grid Domain only allows traffic from a private IP by using a private endpoint.

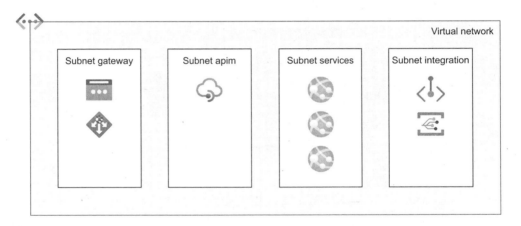

Figure 13.3   A visual representation of the virtual network with its subnets

Cost warning
If you decide to test this template, please know that this template creates resources that are potentially relatively expensive. Tear the environment down as soon as possible when you won't actually be using the resources in the infrastructure. Azure services are billed per minute, or some even per second.

To help organize the resources in this infrastructure, the template will create two resource groups, which we'll look at next.

13.3.1 Resources organized in resource groups

The template is organized using nested modules. The main template (main.bicep) is the top of the hierarchy, and it runs on the subscription scope. It creates resource groups to organize resources into logical groups. Then, for each resource group the main template calls a module that runs on the scope of that resource group to deploy the resources for that group.

Figure 13.4 shows an Azure subscription with resource groups containing the resources they will be provisioned with by the template described in this chapter. The darker resource groups in the figure are resource groups expected to be provisioned at a later stage. These resource groups will contain microservices that may be developed by your team or other teams.

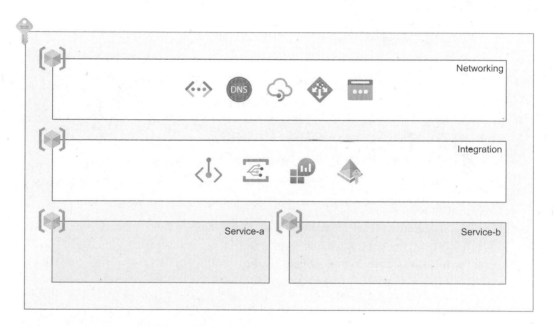

Figure 13.4 Overview of resource groups and resources

The main template will target the `subscription` scope. You have already learned how to target different scopes in a Bicep file:

```
targetScope = 'subscription'
```

The names of the two resource groups consist of the system name, its purpose, the deployment location, and the deployment environment. If your system is called "tomatoe," an example name could be `tomatoe-net-weu-prd`. The two resource groups are named `net` and `int`, for networking and integration. The system name, location, and

environment are defined as parameters. The following listing contains a fragment of
the main template (13.03/main.bicep).

Listing 13.10   Creating resource groups

```
targetScope = 'subscription'

param systemName string
param locationAbbreviation string
param environmentCode string

var resourceLocation = 'westeurope'
var resourceGroupNetworking = 'net'

resource networkingRg 'Microsoft.Resources/resourceGroups@2021-04-01' = {
    location: resourceLocation
    name: '${systemName}-${resourceGroupNetworking}-
      ➥ ${locationAbbreviation}-${environmentCode}'
    tags: {
        Kind: resourceGroupNetworking
        CostCenter: systemName
    }
}

module networkingModule 'networking.bicep' = {
    name: 'networkingModule'
    scope: networkingRg
    params: {
        ...
    }
}...
```

The preceding listing is a small fragment of the main template. It contains the parameters for the system name, location abbreviation, and environment code (development, test, acceptance, production). The actual template contains more parameters,
and most parameters have attributes to describe them or limit their values. We've
removed them here to make the example clearer. This template creates a resource
group and then deploys resources inside that resource group. This process is then
repeated for the resources required for integration.

> **Prerequisites for running this template**
>
> Because this template assumes you are going to accept web traffic to the application
> gateway, a domain name (FQDN) and SSL certificate are required. You can configure
> all these values through parameter files except for the SSL certificate.
>
> For the SSL certificate, an existing Key Vault is required with the certificate already
> in it. This Key Vault must be configured to allow access from the Azure Resource Man-
> ager. This will allow the template to control access from all services required to
> access the Key Vault.

For internal network traffic you can generate a self-signed certificate with a trusted root certificate. The following PowerShell script generates a self-signed certificate that you can use for this deployment:

```
$trustedRootCert = New-SelfSignedCertificate `
    -Type Custom `
    -CertStoreLocation "Cert:\CurrentUser\My" `
    -KeySpec Signature `
    -Subject "CN=Your Common Name" `
    -KeyExportPolicy Exportable `
    -HashAlgorithm sha256 `
    -KeyLength 4096 `
    -KeyUsageProperty Sign `
    -KeyUsage CertSign `
    -NotAfter (Get-Date).AddMonths(24)

$sslCert = New-SelfSignedCertificate `
    -Type Custom `
    -CertStoreLocation "Cert:\CurrentUser\My" `
    -KeySpec Signature `
    -Subject "CN=*.your-internal-domain.int" `
    -DnsName "*.your-internal-domain.int","your-internal-domain.int" `
    -KeyExportPolicy Exportable `
    -HashAlgorithm sha256 `
    -KeyLength 2048 `
    -Signer $trustedRootCert

Export-Certificate `
    -Type CERT `
    -Cert $trustedRootCert `
    -FilePath .\certificate-trustedroot.cer

$pfxPassword = ConvertTo-SecureString -String `
    "Passwd01" -AsPlainText -Force
Export-PfxCertificate `
    -ChainOption BuildChain `
    -Cert $sslCert `
    -FilePath .\certificate.pfx `
    -Password $pfxPassword
```

Note that you must change `your-internal-domain.int` to the actual name of your internal domain, and you may want to change the password `Passwd01` to a stronger password.

Attaching your resources to a vnet is a nice first step toward security. It provides a lot of security-related possibilities and is therefore recommended in a lot of cases. Let's see how the vnet for this case study is described.

13.3.2 *Networking with Bicep*

As mentioned previously, the Bicep templates are organized in such a fashion that all resources are declared in a Bicep file named after the resource group they are provisioned in. It is not mandatory to do so, but since this template is relatively large, it is a good idea to structure your IaC files in a way that will keep them easily maintainable, as we described in chapter 5.

The networking.bicep file will describe all resources that will end up in the networking resource group. The networking template will provision a vnet that allows for adding security measurements like a firewall and network security groups. This enables you to, for example, cut off external traffic and orchestrate traffic within the vnet.

To fit the needs of this case, a vnet will be provisioned with four subnets: gateway, apim, integration, and services. The subnets are defined as variables in Bicep—see figure 13.3 for a visual representation of this vnet (13.03/main.bicep).

```
Listing 13.11   Subnets for the vnet
```

```
var subnets = [
    {
        name: 'gateway'
        prefix: '10.0.0.0/24'
        privateEndpointNetworkPolicies: 'Enabled'
        privateLinkServiceNetworkPolicies: 'Enabled'
        delegations: []
    }
    {
        name: 'apim'
        prefix: '10.0.1.0/24'
        privateEndpointNetworkPolicies: 'Enabled'
        privateLinkServiceNetworkPolicies: 'Enabled'
        delegations: []
    }
    {
        name: 'integration'
        prefix: '10.0.2.0/24'
        privateEndpointNetworkPolicies: 'Disabled'
        privateLinkServiceNetworkPolicies: 'Enabled'
        delegations: []
    }
    {
        name: 'services'
        prefix: '10.0.3.0/24'
        privateEndpointNetworkPolicies: 'Enabled'
        privateLinkServiceNetworkPolicies: 'Enabled'
        delegations: []
    }
]
```

The gateway subnet will contain the instance of Azure Application Gateway, and the apim subnet will contain an instance of Azure API Management. The integration subnet will contain an instance of Event Grid with a private endpoint that only allows network traffic from the `services` subnet. The `services` subnet will contain all of your microservices.

To provision the vnet, a separate Bicep file is used, and it's called as a module from the main template (13.03/Network/virtualNetworks.bicep).

Listing 13.12   Describing the vnet

```
param defaultResourceName string

param addressPrefixes array
param subnets array

var resourceName = '${defaultResourceName}-vnet'

resource network 'Microsoft.Network/virtualNetworks@2021-02-01' = {
    name: resourceName
    location: resourceGroup().location
    properties: {                                        The address
        addressSpace: {                                  space of the
            addressPrefixes: addressPrefixes      ◁────  entire vnet
        }
        subnets: [for subnet in subnets: {   ◁────   Loop through the subnets
            name: subnet.name                         array to create an array
            properties: {                             of subnet objects.
                addressPrefix: subnet.prefix
                privateEndpointNetworkPolicies:
                    ➥ subnet.privateEndpointNetworkPolicies
                privateLinkServiceNetworkPolicies:
                    ➥ subnet.privateLinkServiceNetworkPolicies
                delegations: subnet.delegations
            }
        }]
    }
}
```

You can see that the subnets for this vnet are created with a loop, running through all the entries in the `subnets` array passed in as a parameter for this template. Now that the vnet is in place, let's see how you can access the deploy-time Key Vault to prepare for the deployment of API Management and Application Gateway.

13.3.3   *Using the existing keyword to set access to a Key Vault*

The template describes an instance of Application Gateway (AppGw). This AppGw will reference the certificates mentioned earlier in this chapter to allow for HTTPS traffic. You cannot download these certificates using a managed identity because the AppGw instance doesn't exist yet. This means there is no way to set permissions on the deploy-time Key Vault to allow AppGw to download the certificates.

To solve this problem, the template creates two user-assigned identities (UAIDs), which are managed identities, but created by a user instead of the system. These UAIDs are provisioned as resources and granted access to allow downloading certificates from the Key Vault. At a later stage, one of these UAIDs will be attached to API Management and the other to Application Gateway so these services can use those UAIDs for downloading the certificates. Let's see what the Bicep files that do this look like.

> **Listing 13.13   Provisioning a user assigned identity and granting access to a Key Vault**

```
resource deployTimeKeyVault 'Microsoft.KeyVault/vaults@2021-06-01-preview'
    ⮡ existing = {                                                    ◄──  The "existing" keyword
    name: deployTimeKeyVaultName                                           that indicates that the
    scope: resourceGroup(deployTimeKeyVaultResourceGroup)                  Key Vault already exists
}


module userAssignedIdentityModule
    ⮡ 'ManagedIdentity/userAssignedIdentities.bicep' = {
    name: 'userAssignedIdentityModule'
    params: {
        defaultResourceName: defaultResourceName
    }
}


module keyVaultAccessPoliciesForUaidModule
    ⮡ 'KeyVault/vaults/accessPolicies.bicep'
         ⮡   = {                                          Accessing properties
    name: 'keyVaultAccessPoliciesForUaidModule'           of this Key Vault,
    scope: resourceGroup(deployTimeKeyVaultResourceGroup)  in this case, to set
    params: {                                             permissions to
        keyVaultName: deployTimeKeyVault.name    ◄─────┘  that Key Vault
        objectId: userAssignedIdentityModule.outputs.principalId
    }
}
```

The preceding listing shows how you can use the `existing` keyword to reference a resource that should already exist by the time the deployment runs. The second block of code provisions a user assigned identity, and the third block grants *get* and *list* access to secrets and certificates on the already existing Key Vault by calling the `accessPolicies.bicep` module.

And with that, let's conclude this chapter by adding a resource that integrates into the vnet. The following listing describes an API Management (APIM) instance (13.03/ApiManagement/service.bicep). This APIM instance will integrate into the vnet with a vnet type of `Internal`. This means that the APIM instance will only be reachable for resources inside the vnet. The vnet will block external traffic to APIM. This way, you are forcing external traffic to come in on the Application Gateway, which then routes traffic to APIM. Because Application Gateway has sophisticated tools for monitoring traffic, you can filter out malicious requests at a very early stage.

Listing 13.14   Provisioning APIM with vnet integration

```
param vnetResourceId string
param subnetName string = 'apim'

resource apim 'Microsoft.ApiManagement/service@2021-04-01-preview' = {
    location: resourceGroup().location
    name: resourceName
    identity: {
        type: 'SystemAssigned, UserAssigned'
        userAssignedIdentities: {
            '${existing_identity.id}': {}
        }
    }
    sku: {
        name: apimSkuName
        capacity: 1
    }
    properties: {
        publisherName: YourCompany Inc.'
        publisherEmail: 'admin@yourcompany.com'
        virtualNetworkType: 'Internal'
        virtualNetworkConfiguration: {
            subnetResourceId: '${vnetResourceId}/subnets/${subnetName}'
        }
        ...
    }
}
```

This is where the vnet type is set to "Internal".

This is a reference to the subnet that APIM must be deployed in.

The preceding listing shows how to deploy API Management to integrate it into a vnet. We have omitted a couple of parameters and variables from the listing to keep this example readable. The module that describes the vnet outputs a full subscription resource ID that is passed in this Bicep file as the `vnetResourceId` parameter. The `subnetName` parameter (which defaults to `apim`) is used to define the subnet that API Management will be provisioned in.

And with that, you have read the final chapter of this book. Remember to clean up any resources you have created while trying things out, especially when working through this last chapter.

Thank you for reading our book! We hope you have enjoyed learning about Infrastructure as Code for Azure. Although the subject can be a bit dry and tough to master at times, you now have the tools you'll need to make your life creating and operating software products on Azure a lot easier.

If you liked this book, please let us know by posting about it on Twitter or LinkedIn. We would love to hear about your learning stories. You can reach us at @henry_been, @ed_dotnet, or @erwin_staal. And for now: happy coding!

Summary

- Templates can be nested in a hierarchical way to manage management groups, subscriptions, resource groups, and individual resources.
- Subscription-level templates can be used to preconfigure subscriptions and set minimum standards and baselines.
- You can organize your templates for a larger infrastructure, like a microservices architecture, into multiple templates that are deployed from a single orchestrating template.

index

A

AAD (Azure Active Directory) 327
  role-based access control 78
  tenant 69
actions, in GitHub 191
aliases 295
@allowed() decorator 158
allowedValues property 45, 289
Amazon Web Service (AWS)
    CloudFormation 14
and() function 63
apiVersion property 22, 37, 131
Append effect 80, 279, 294–295,
    301–302
APPINSIGHTS_
    INSTRUMENTATIONKEY
    setting 62
approvals 169
ARM (Azure Resource
    Manager) 11–14
  Bicep language 13
  control plane and data
      plane 11–12
  template deployment 66–88
    clean-up phase 82–85
    execution phase 75–82
    overview of process 67–68
    submitting 68–74
    troubleshooting
        deployments 87
    validation phase 85–86
    with Azure DevOps 155–187
    with GitHub Actions
        188–200
  templates, basics of 12–13

template sharing
  deploying templates in
      packages 259
  publishing templates as
      packages 256–259
template simplification
    129–154
  benefits of Bicep 130–134
  improvements with
      Bicep 138–145
  modules 145–147
  syntax differences 134–138
template specs
  deploying 248–253
  from multiple
      templates 245
template testing 201–233
  end-to-end tests 222–229
  integration tests 218–222
  Pester in CI/CD 229–232
  static analysis and
      validation 203–216
  unit tests 216–218
template writing 18–65
  advanced 89–128
  conditionally deploying
      resources 109–112
  creating multiple resources
      with loops 112–118
  deploying 25–27
  deploying resources in
      order 107–109
  deployment scripts 118–125
  finding examples 28
  functions 64–65
  JSON files 19–20

linked templates 102–106
monitoring
    deployments 27
nested templates 90–99
outputs 53–54
parameters 49–50
resources 38–39
reverse engineering
    templates 125–127
structuring solutions 99–101
variables 51–52
visualizing 29–31
VS Code 20–25
ARM TTK (ARM template test
    toolkit) 208–212
  installing 209
  running 209–210
  using in Azure DevOps 211–212
array parameter 114
array variable 250
ASM (Azure Service
    Management) 13–14
Audit effect 80, 279, 294–297
AuditIfNotExists effect 80, 279,
    286, 294, 297–298
automation 9
  build and release
      pipelines 163–173
  configuring DevOps to run
      pipeline 171–173
  creating service
      connections 167–171
  creating tasks 165–166
  grouping tasks in jobs
      166–167
  triggers 164–165

automation (continued)
  environment reproducibility 9
  guaranteed outcomes 9
AWS (Amazon Web Service)
  CloudFormation 14
az account list command 71
az account set –subscription 71
az bicep build command 193
az deployment command 71
az deployment group create
  command 71, 247
az deployment group show
  command 53
az deployment mg create
  command 96
az deployment sub
  command 321
az deployment sub create
  command 306
az login command 70
az ts list command 242
az ts show command 246
Azure Active Directory. See AAD
  (Azure Active Directory)
Azure Blueprints 272–273
Azure CLI 70–71
  generating service principals
    using 194–195
  template testing 207–208
Azure Cloud environment
  building foundation 317–324
    assigning policy initiative
      319–321
    creating management
      subscription 321
    creating workload
      subscriptions 322–324
    management group
      layout 317–319
  connecting from GitHub
    workflows 194
  high-available microservice
    architecture 327–335
  networking with
    Bicep 332–333
  resources organized in
    resource groups
      329–331
  use existing keyword to set
    access to key vault
      333–335
  subscription level
    deployments 324–327
  configuring budgets
    324–325

configuring Microsoft
  Defender for Cloud
    325–326
creating resource groups
  and providing
  access 327
Azure DevOps 5–6, 155–187
  automated build and release
    pipelines 163–173
  configuring Azure DevOps
    to run pipeline
      171–173
  creating service
    connections 167–171
  creating tasks 165–166
  grouping tasks in jobs
    166–167
  triggers 164–165
  creating Bicep files 157–161
    describing App Service 159
    describing App Service
      plan 157–159
    finalizing template
      160–161
  logical phases 173–178
    accessing artifacts from dif-
      ferent jobs 175
    deploying template from
      pipeline artifact
        176–178
    identifying 173–174
    transpiling Bicep in pipe-
      line stage 175–176
  real-world example pipeline
    182–187
  storing templates in source
    control 162–163
  Toma Toe Pizzas example
    156–157
  Traffic Manager 178–182
  using ARM TTK in 211–212
Azure Login action 197
Azure Policy 79–80, 275–315
  assignment 280–284
    assignment scope 281–284
    definition location 281
  built-in policies and
    initiatives 284–286
  creating initiatives 304–308
  custom policies 287–294
    creating 287–290
    testing 290–294
  different effects 294–303
    Append effect 294–295
    Audit effect 295–297

AuditIfNotExists
  effect 297–298
DeployIfNotExists
  effect 298–301
disabled effect 301
Modify effect 301–303
initiatives or policy sets 280
policy definitions 278–279
reviewing compliance
  status 308–313
creating exemptions
  311–313
remediating noncompliant
  resources 310
Azure Resource Manager. See
  ARM (Azure Resource
  Manager)
AzureResourceManagerTem-
  plateDeployment task 166
Azure Service Management
  13–14
azure variable 74

B

Bash task 165
@batchSize annotation 137
batchSize property 113
Bicep 129–154
  basics of 13
  benefits of 130–134
  creating Bicep files 157–161
    describing App Service 159
    describing App Service
      plan 157–159
    finalizing template 160–161
  decompiling 133–134
  deploying 132
  improvements 138–145
    comments 143–144
    dependency
      management 141
    no mandatory
      grouping 142–143
    referencing existing
      resources 141
    referencing resources,
      parameters, and
      variables 138–139
    string interpolation 141–142
    using contents of other
      files 144–145
    using references in variables
      and outputs 139–140
  large example 147–154

Bicep *(continued)*
modules 145–147
debugging deployments
146–147
deploying to another
scope 146
syntax differences 134–138
conditions 135–136
known limitations 138
loops 136–138
outputs 135
parameters 134
targeting different
scopes 138
variables 135
transpiling 132–133
bicep build command 175
bicep command 132
boolean data type 19
bool type 40
built-in role definitions 77

C

CanNotDelete lock 81–82
checks, approvals and 169
child resources 38–39
CI/CD (continuous integra-
tion/continuous
deployment) 74, 163
linked templates 104–106
Pester in 229–232
clean-up phase of template
deployment 82–85
combining modes 84–85
Complete deployment
mode 83–84
Incremental deployment
mode 83
code completion 205
comments, in Bicep 143–144
Complete deployment
mode 82–84, 86, 94
composing templates 100
concat(...) function 142
concat() function 44, 153
condition property 136, 303
conditions, in Bicep 135–136
configuration drift,
preventing 7–8
Configure() function 228
contains() function 55
contentVersion property 21
Context keyword 213
control plane 11–12

copy element 112–114
using on output 116–117
using on properties 115–116
using on variables 114–115
copyIndex() function 113–114
create keyword 86
csmFile parameter 106
custom role definitions 77

D

DataActions property 77
data plane 11–12
declarative approach 9–10
decompile command 133
decompiling 133–134
DefaultPolicy 253
default templates 238
defaultValue property 40, 42
delegations section 225
demofunction.capitalize()
function 65
denyAnySqlServerAccessFro-
mInternet policy 291
Deny effect 80, 279, 294
Deny policy 287
dependency management 141
dependsOn element 107–109,
117–118
dependsOn property 141, 167
deployAvailabilitySet variable 63
DeployIfNotExists effect 80,
279, 294, 298–301, 303,
306, 310
deployment mode 67
deployment property 300
deployment scope 67, 69
DeploymentScriptOutputs
object 123
deploymentScript resource 118,
120, 123–124
deployment scripts 118–125
deploymentScripts resource 120
deployment stacks for grouping
resources 263–274
future of 274
grouping resources by
lifetime 264–270
complete deployment
mode 266–267
creating deployment
stacks 268–269
removing deployment
stacks 270
solution 267–268

updating deployment
stacks 269–270
provisioning resources, but
disallowing updates
271–273
DeployWestEu stage 173
Describe keyword 213
–description parameter 242
description property 45–46
details array 295
details property 300
Disabled effect 279, 285, 294–301
disabled effect 301
displayName property 165, 319
dotnet publish command 229

E

Elasticity 4
enableDefenderFor array 326
enabledForTemplateDeploy-
ment property 50
enabled property 111
endpoints array 180
end-to-end tests 222–229
environment input
parameter 197
environmentName
parameter 158
environmentName variable 186
env parameter 153
equals() function 63
evaluationDetails array 293
evaluationResult property 293
evaluation scope 96–98
events 190
exampleQueue queue 269–270
execution phase of template
deployment 75–82
Azure Policy 79–80
resource locks 81–82
resource provisioning 82
role-based access control
76–79
AAD roles and 78
creating and deploying role
assignment using
templates 78–79
role 77
scope 76
security principal 76
existing keyword 141, 334
expiresOn property 313
explicit deployment ordering
107–109

expressionEvaluationOptions
property 96
expressions 54–56

F

feedsToUsePublish option 257
field property 295, 303
forceUpdateTag property 121
forking repositories 189–190
Foundation management
group 318, 321
FQDN (fully qualified domain
name) 52
FromServicePrincipal method 73
functions 64–65
built-in functions 56–63
logical functions 62–63
scope functions 57–62
expressions 54–56
user-defined functions 64–65

G

gateway subnet 332–333
GitHub Actions 188–200
actions 191
deploying ARM templates
195–199
deployment phase 193–195
connecting to Azure from
workflow 194
generating service principal
using Azure CLI 194–195
forking repositories 189–190
jobs 191
runners 191
steps 191
workflow events 190
workflows
adding jobs to workflows
192–193
building 191–193
Google Cloud Deployment
Manager 14–15
governing subscriptions 275–315
assignment 280–284
assignment scope 281–284
definition location 281
built-in policies and
initiatives 284–286
creating initiatives 304–308
custom policies 287–294
creating 287–290
testing 290–294

different effects 294–303
Append effect 294–295
Audit effect 295–297
AuditIfNotExists
effect 297–298
DeployIfNotExists
effect 298–301
disabled effect 301
Modify effect 301–303
initiatives or policy sets 280
policy definitions 278–279
reviewing compliance
status 308–313
creating exemptions
311–313
remediating noncompliant
resources 310
greater() function 114
groupId property 123
group keyword 71
GUIs (graphical user
interfaces) 4

H

HCL (HashiCorp Configuration
Language) 15
–help parameter 71
high-available microservice
architecture 327–335
networking with Bicep
332–333
resources organized in
resource groups 329–331
use existing keyword to set
access to key vault
333–335
hub 271
human-readable formats 10–11
auditable 11
reviewable 11
version controllable 11

I

IaC (Infrastructure as Code) 3–17
AWS CloudFormation 14
Azure Resource Manager
11–14
Azure Service
Management 13–14
Bicep language 13
control plane and data
plane 11–12
templates 12–13

benefits of 8–11
automation 9
declarative approach 9–10
human-readable format
10–11
choosing between cloud-specific and multi-cloud
solutions 16
Google Cloud Deployment
Manager 14–15
Pulumi 16
template deployment 246
Terraform 15
working with 4–8
Azure DevOps 5–6
preventing configuration
drift 7–8
id property 135, 139
if() function 63, 111
if clause 136
if condition 294
if statement 224, 279, 298
*Implementing Azure DevOps
Solutions* (Been, van der
Gaag) 163
implicit deployment
ordering 109
Incremental deployment
mode 82–84
initiative resource 277
inline parameters 46–47
InstrumentationKey
property 62
integration subnet 332–333
integration tests 218–222
IntelliSense 205
internal platform team 317
int resource group 329
int type 40
Invoke-Pester cmdlet 231
ipRules property 295
ipSecurityRestrictions array 224
IsCustom property 77
isCustom property 78
It keyword 213

J

jobs
accessing artifacts from different jobs 175
adding jobs to workflows
192–193
basics of 191
grouping tasks in jobs 166–167

jobs property 167
json() function 55–56, 63
JSON files
  installing extension in VS
    Code 20
  template writing 19–20
JSON view 127

K

key1 property 58
key2 property 58
key vault
  fetching parameters from
    48–50
  use existing keyword to set
    access to 333–335

L

length(...) function 137–138
length() function 113–114
linkedTemplate resource
  type 102
linked templates 102–106
  CI/CD 104–106
  relative paths 106
  URIs 103–106
list() function 64
listKeys(...) function 139
listKeys() function 58
loadFileAsBase64(...)
  function 144
loadTextcontent(...) function 144
loadTextContent(filePath,
  [encoding]) function 144
locationAbbreviation
  parameter 158
location property 36–37, 42, 55
logical functions 62–63
logical phases 173–178
  accessing artifacts from differ-
    ent jobs 175
  deploying template from pipe-
    line artifact 176–178
  identifying 173–174
  transpiling Bicep in pipeline
    stage 175–176
logs property 323
Logs resource group 321
loops
  creating multiple resources
    with 112–118
    using copy element on
      output 116–117

using copy element on
  properties 115–116
using copy element on
  variables 114–115
waiting for loop to
  finish 117–118
in Bicep 136–138

M

main template 90
managementGroup(...)
  function 146
management groups
  nested templates on 94–96
  submitting deployments 69
managementGroup scope 320
Management subscription 321
maxLength parameter
  property 134
maxValue parameter
  property 134
minLength parameter
  property 134
minValue parameter
  property 134
-Mode Complete parameter 82
mode property 288
Modify effect 80, 279, 294,
  301–303, 306, 310
modularizing templates
  102–106
  relative path 106
  URI 103–106
modules, Bicep 145–147
  debugging deployments
    146–147
  deploying to another
    scope 146

N

name property 22, 43–44, 59,
  65, 111, 114, 131
nested templates
  deploying to multiple
    scopes 90–99
  evaluation scope 96–98
  nested templates on
    management group
    94–96
  outputs 99
net resource group 329
not() function 63
null data type 19

O

object type 45
or() function 63
outputs 52–54
  applying conditions to 112
  deploying nested templates to
    multiple scopes 99
  in Bicep
    basics of 135
    using references in 139–140
  template writing 52–54
  using copy element on 116–117
outputs property 123, 253

P

package managers
  pros and cons of 262
  sharing templates 255–260
    deploying ARM templates
      in packages 259
    publishing ARM templates
      as packages 256–259
parameters 46–50
  in Bicep
    basics of 134
    referencing 138–139
  limiting and describing
    values 45–46
  specifying values 47–50
    fetching from key vault 48–50
    inline parameters 46–47
    specifying values in parame-
      ter file 47–48
  types 43–45
    array type 42–43
    object type 43–45
parameters() function 41, 52,
  54–55, 142
parameters array 64
–parameters switch 306
parent property 319
permissions array 78
Pester
  custom tests using 212–216
  in CI/CD 229–232
pipeline artifact 174
policies
  built-in 284–286
  custom 287–294
    creating 287–290
    testing 290–294
  definitions 278–279
policy sets 280

policy assignment resource 277
policy definition 277
PowerShell 72–73, 207–208
Pulumi 16

Q

queryString property 103–104

R

range(...) function 137
RBAC (role-based access
    control) 76–79
  AAD roles and 78
  creating and deploying role
      assignment using
      templates 78–79
  roles 77
  scope 76
  security principals 76
ReadOnly lock 81
reference() function 52, 54,
    60, 62, 64, 94, 117, 135,
    139–141, 253
relativePath property 106,
    244–245
required-properties autocomple-
    tion function 204
required-properties option 204
Resource Explorer 126–127
resourceGroup() function 42,
    55, 57, 96, 132, 146
resource groups 69–70
  creating and providing
      access 327
  deployment stacks for 263–274
  future of 274
    grouping resources by
        lifetime 264–270
    provisioning resources, but
        disallowing updates
        271–273
  resources organized in
      329–331
resource group scope 146
resource group template 12
resourceId() function 58, 62,
    64, 108, 112, 139, 150, 219
resource locks 81–82
resource provisioning 82
resources 38–39
  child resources 38–39
  conditional deployment
      109–112

applying conditions to
    output 112
  creating multiple with
      loops 112–118
    using copy element on
        output 116–117
    using copy element on
        properties 115–116
    using copy element on
        variables 114–115
    waiting for loop to
        finish 117–118
  deploying in order 107–109
    explicit deployment
        ordering 107–109
    implicit deployment
        ordering 109
  grouping, deployment stacks
      for 263–274
  in Bicep
    referencing 138–139
    referencing existing 141
  organized in resource
      groups 329–331
  reverse engineering tem-
      plates for new
      resources 127
resources array 38–39
resource templates 100
resource type 19
resourceType property 131
reverse engineering
    templates 125–127
  exporting templates 125–126
  JSON view 127
  new resources 127
  Resource Explorer 126–127
roleDefinitionId property 60,
    79, 94, 303
rootManagement group 96
runners, in GitHub 191

S

SAS (shared access signature)
    token 103
$schema object 21
scope
  choosing scope for submit-
      ting deployments 68–70
  deploying Bicep modules to
      another scope 146
  deploying nested templates to
      multiple scopes 90–99
    evaluation scope 96–98

nested templates on man-
    agement group 94–96
  outputs 99
  role-based access control 76
  scope functions 57–62
  targeting different scopes in
      Bicep 138
scope functions 57–62
–scope parameter 290
scope property 79, 81, 96–97, 327
SDKs (software development
    kits) 73–74
secretName parameter 59
secureObject type 45
secureString type 41, 45, 49, 118
secureValue environment vari-
    able option 122
serial mode 113
service connections,
    creating 167–171
shared access signature (SAS)
    token 103
software development kits
    (SDKs) 73–74
spokes 271
steps, in GitHub 191
steps property 165–167, 176,
    193
string data type 19
string interpolation 141–142
string parameter 44–45
string type 40–41, 45, 52, 135,
    176
subscription() function 57, 63,
    96–97, 146
subscriptionId parameter 186
subscriptionId property 96–97
subscription level 221
subscriptions 69
  creating management
      subscription 321
  creating workload
      subscriptions 322–324
  governing using Azure
      Policy 275–315
    assignment 280–284
    built-in policies and
        initiatives 284–286
    creating initiatives 304–308
    custom policies 287–294
    different effects 294–303
    initiatives or policy sets 280
    policy definitions 278–279
    reviewing compliance
        status 308–313

subscriptions *(continued)*
  subscription level
      deployments 324–327
    configuring budgets
      324–325
    configuring Microsoft
      Defender for
      Cloud 325–326
    creating resource groups
      and providing
      access 327
subscription scope 146, 329
subscription templates 12

T

tags 205, 254
targetScope declaration 138
tasks
  creating 165–166
  grouping in jobs 166–167
template: loadTextContent()
  function 300
templateBasePath variable
  152–153
template deployment 66–88
  clean-up phase 82–85
    combining deployment
      modes 84–85
    Complete deployment
      mode 83–84
    Incremental deployment
      mode 83
  execution phase 75–82
    Azure Policy 79–80
    resource locks 81–82
    resource provisioning 82
    role-based access
      control 76–79
  overview of process 67–68
  submitting 68–74
    choosing scope 68–70
    tools for 70–74
  troubleshooting
    deployments 87
  validation phase 85–86
  what-if deployments 86–87
template deployment, with
  Azure DevOps 155–187
  automated build and release
    pipelines 163–173
    configuring Azure DevOps
      to run pipeline 171–173
    creating service
      connections 167–171

creating tasks 165–166
grouping tasks in jobs
  166–167
triggers 164–165
creating Bicep files 157–161
describing App Service 159
describing App Service
  plan 157–159
finalizing template
  160–161
logical phases 173–178
  accessing artifacts from dif-
    ferent jobs 175
  deploying template from
    pipeline artifact
    176–178
  identifying 173–174
  transpiling Bicep in pipe-
    line stage 175–176
real-world example
  pipeline 182–187
  completing pipeline
    182–187
storing templates in source
  control 162–163
Toma Toe Pizzas
  example 156–157
Traffic Manager
  adding 178–182
  deploying 181–182
template deployment, with
  GitHub Actions 188–200
  actions 191
  deploying ARM templates
    195–199
    completing deployment
      198–199
  deployment phase 193–195
    connecting to Azure from
      workflow 194
    generating service princi-
      pal using Azure
      CLI 194–195
  forking repositories 189–190
  jobs 191
  runners 191
  steps 191
  workflow events 190
  workflows
    adding jobs to
      workflows 192–193
    building 191–193
-TemplateParameterFile
  parameter 48
-TemplatePath parameter 210

template simplification using
  Bicep 129–154
  benefits of Bicep 130–134
    decompiling 133–134
    deploying 132
    transpiling 132–133
  improvements with
    Bicep 138–145
    comments 143–144
    dependency
      management 141
    no mandatory
      grouping 142–143
    referencing existing
      resources 141
    referencing resources,
      parameters, and
      variables 138–139
    string interpolation
      141–142
    using contents of other
      files 144–145
    using references in vari-
      ables and outputs
      139–140
  large example 147–154
    AppConfiguration.bicep
      148–149
    ApplicationInsights.bicep
      149–151
    Configuration.bicep
      151–154
  modules 145–147
    debugging Bicep
      deployments 146–147
    deploying to another
      scope 146
  syntax differences 134–138
    conditions 135–136
    known limitations 138
    loops 136–138
    outputs 135
    parameters 134
    targeting different scopes
      138
    variables 135
–template-spec parameter 247
template specs
  creating 239–246
    creating from multiple
      ARM templates
      243–245
    listing template specs
      242–243
    versions 243

template specs *(continued)*
  deploying 246–253
    from ARM or Bicep
        templates 248–253
    upgrading to newer
        versions 253
    using IaC 246
  pros and cons of 261
  use case 238–239
template testing 201–233
  end-to-end tests 222–229
  integration tests 218–222
  Pester in CI/CD 229–232
  static analysis and
        validation 203–216
    ARM template test
        toolkit 208–212
    custom tests using
        Pester 212–216
    PowerShell or Azure
        CLI 207–208
    VS Code extensions 204–206
  unit tests 216–218
template writing 18–65
  deploying 25–27
  finding examples 28
  functions 64–65
    built-in functions 56–63
    expressions 54–56
    user-defined functions
        64–65
  JSON files 19–20
    installing ARM templates
        extension in VS Code 20
  monitoring deployments 27
  outputs 52–54
  parameters 46–50
    limiting and describing
        values 45–46
    specifying values 46–50
    types 43–45
  resources 38–39
  variables 50–52
  visualizing 29–31
  VS Code 20–25
    adding resources 22–24
    leveraging IntelliSense
        24–25

template writing, advanced
    89–128
  conditionally deploying
        resources 109–112
    applying conditions to
        output 112
  creating multiple resources
        with loops 112–118
    using copy on output
        116–117
    using copy on
        properties 115–116
    using copy on
        variables 114–115
    waiting for loop to
        finish 117–118
  deploying resources in
        order 107–109
    explicit deployment
        ordering 107–109
    implicit deployment
        ordering 109
  deployment scripts 118–125
  linked templates 102–106
    relative path 106
    URI 103–106
  nested templates 90–99
    evaluation scope 96–98
    nested templates on
        management group
        94–96
    outputs 99
  reverse engineering
        templates 125–127
    exporting templates
        125–126
    JSON view 127
    new resources 127
    Resource Explorer
        126–127
  structuring solutions 99–101
    large solutions 100–101
    small to medium
        solutions 99–100
tenant(...) function 146
tenantId property 57
tenant keyword 71
Tenant-level templates 12

tenants 69
tenant scope 146
Terraform 15
transpiling 132–133, 175–176
triggers 164–165
ts create command 242
ts show command 245
type inference 135
type property 22, 37, 52, 78
type resource 36

U

unit tests 216–218
updateBehavior property
    269–270

V

validate deployment mode 85
validation phase of template
    deployment 85–86
variables 50–52
  in Bicep 135
    referencing 138–139
    using references in
        139–140
  using copy element on
        114–115
variables() function 51, 56
VS Code (Visual Studio Code)
  template testing 204–206
  template writing 20–25
    adding resources 22–24
    installing extension 20
    leveraging IntelliSense
        24–25

W

what-if deployments 86–87
workflows, in GitHub
  adding jobs to workflows
        192–193
  building 191–193
  connecting to Azure
        from 194
  events 190